P9-DMY-772

The Psychology of Adolescence

The Psychology of Adolescence

second edition

ARTHUR T. JERSILD

Teachers College, Columbia University

The Macmillan Company, New York

Collier-Macmillan Limited, London

Designed by Andrew Roberts

Library of Congress catalog card number: 63–11799

The Macmillan Company, New York
Collier-Macmillan Canada, Ltd., Toronto, Ontario

Printed in the United States of America

to
CATHERINE
ALICE
and JOHN

Foreword

This second edition retains the purpose and point of view of the first, but the content has been considerably revised and new material has been added.

I have again combined a description of the objective aspects of adolescents' growth and behavior with an inquiry into the subjective meanings of what is happening in their lives. Once more a chapter on the self appears early in the text. In this I have considered both the known dimensions of the self and the role of motives and tendencies which the adolescent does not consciously perceive. The discussion of the self is meant, in part, to introduce this concept to students who may not be familiar with it; but it is designed mainly to introduce ideas that will recur in later chapters which consider ways in which the adolescent's physical, mental, emotional and social development influences and is influenced by his ideas and attitudes regarding himself.

Substantially modified portions of the book include an expanded discussion of physical growth and sexual maturation; a section on heredity, and recurring references to the interaction between genetic and environmental factors in an adolescent's development; a discussion of varying modes of thinking; a section on insight into self; new material on dreams and what might be learned from them; a considerably revised chapter on anxiety, with illustrations drawn from adolescents; a more extensive treatment of social influences, including parent-adolescent relationships, and the role of socioeconomic status; a considerable amount of added material on college-age youth; and a separate chapter on delinquency.

In various sections of the book I have called attention to the hiatus which exists between adolescents' personal preoccupations and what is offered to them, and demanded of them, in school and in the culture in which they live. My discussion in these sections is based on the view that the one who might learn most from the psychology of adolescence is the adolescent himself. This view has wide implications, for issues that adolescents must face still prevail, to a greater or lesser degree, in the lives of all of us as adults.

I am greatly indebted to many persons for help in writing this book. My greatest debt is to the research workers and authors whose findings and views I have reported. The bibliography acknowledges those whose work I have directly cited, but this list of references would have to be increased many fold if I were to give credit to everyone who has influenced the content of the book.

I am grateful to adolescents whom I have had the privilege of knowing and to those who have cooperated in the numerous research studies cited in the text. I am grateful also to my students, who often teach me more than I can teach them.

I am pleased that Phoebe Overstreet Nicholas was willing again to prepare the chapter on Vocational Development.

My wife has, as always, been patient, and she has been generous with her counsel.

Mrs. Dorothy Flapan edited the book and advised me regarding almost every detail of content and structure. I am deeply indebted to her. It is often trying, and sometimes traumatic, when someone questions the precious products of an author's pen. But it was gratifying to work with Mrs. Flapan. She did her job with a determination that was exceeded only by her friendly spirit and her uncommon good sense. If those familiar with the earlier edition find this one more trim and readable, the credit belongs to her.

I am deeply thankful to Miss Marlene Miller who helped me to locate references, aided me with her judgment, deciphered my handwriting, typed the manuscript, and took a load off my mind by assuming responsibility for managing and checking the bibliography.

Arthur T. Jersild

Contents

part one   Introduction

chapter 1
The Place of Adolescence in the Life Span:
the Transitional Years   3

chapter 2
The Adolescent Self: Known Dimensions
and Unperceived Influences   22

part two   Physical Aspects
of Development

chapter 3
The Course and Genesis of Growth   45

chapter 4
Sexual Maturation   70

chapter 5
Physical Abilities and Their Psychological Meanings   97

[ix

part three   Thought and Fantasy

chapter 6
Mental Growth   111

chapter 7
Fantasies, Daydreams, and Dreams   150

part four   Emotional Development

chapter 8
Introductory: Love, Affection, and Joy   177

chapter 9
Anger and Fear   189

chapter 10
Anxiety   207

part five   The Adolescent's
             Social World

chapter 11
Parents, Home, and Family   229

chapter 12
Adolescents and Their Peers   252

chapter 13
Heterosexual Development   272

chapter 14
Group Affinities and Cleavages   288

chapter 15
The Delinquent Adolescent   308

part six   Education and Vocation

chapter 16
The Adolescent at School   325

chapter 17
Vocational Development   351

chapter 18
Religion and Morals   373

part seven   Toward the Future

chapter 19
Personality Development and Self-Fulfillment   393

Bibliography   411
Author Index   449
Subject Index   459

part one | Introduction

Chapter 1

The Place of Adolescence in the Life Span: The Transitional Years

There is a saying: "If youth but knew, if old age but could." It has also been said that youth is so wonderful it is a shame to waste it on young people. Although these statements sound like an old person's lament over the inroads of age, they express a truth, though only the part of a truth, concerning the adolescent period of life. It is true that youth is a time of great possibility. But for many it is also a time of trial.

The writer once asked a number of adults whether they would do differently if they could live their adolescence over again. All of them said Yes. Then they were asked whether they would like to relive this period of their lives, if given a chance to do so, with the benefit of all that they had learned during and since their adolescence. All of them gave an emphatic No.

When seen from the perspective of the life span adolescence appears as the time when the surge of life reaches its highest peak. The adolescent's life is, or might be, full of opportunity to enter into new experience, to explore new relationships, to feel new resources of inner strength and ability. Adolescents have, or might have, more freedom to explore than when, as children, they were bound close to home. Older adolescents usually also have more freedom to venture than they will have at a later age when they must carry the responsibilities of a job and a family. Adolescence is also for many a time when youthful dreams of love and power have not been disturbed by the realities of life. In many ways, adolescents live in a lush season between the springtime and the summer of life. One might ask—as many do at a later time of life—Why don't they make the most of it?

Although adolescence is a time of great possibility, it is also a time when most young people must pay a price for the privilege of growing up. Their freedom to seize what life offers is curtailed both from without and from within. The outer restraints—the rules they must follow, the conditions they must conform to—are obvious, and they are strong.

The limits imposed from within are not so visible, but in many respects they are stronger. The new vistas that open before them do not clear away old habits of thinking and feeling, especially thoughts and feelings about themselves.

Even if all has gone well in their earlier development, adolescents face a promised land that is also a strange land. No matter how much help their elders try to give them, they cannot fully open the way or prepare a place. It is primarily the adolescents themselves who must find a path and build a settlement of their own before they can be at home in this strange land. They must seek to discover themselves, their reaches and limits, and their role in the adult world.

It is this striving to be and to become—to delve into the meaning of existence, as far as it can be found—that constitutes the living of a life. It is not, of course, the adolescent alone who is so occupied. But the adolescent is deeply involved in the search through which each human being, in each new generation, almost from the day of his birth, has sought to realize himself and to discover who he is, what he is, and what he might become.

Why Study the Adolescent?

We might study adolescent development because of a scholarly interest in the subject (or because it is a required course). We might also have a practical interest in studying adolescents so that we might be wiser in dealing with them. Yet another motive in studying adolescence may be a desire to learn something about oneself. Such a desire is quite understandable if the student is of adolescent age, but it is also a sound motive for an older person. There is much of the adolescent left in all of us, no matter how old we are. Anything that helps a person to face the adolescent he once was gives him a better understanding of the kind of person he now is. Indeed, any effort to understand human development is likely to be most fruitful if combined with an effort to understand oneself.

The older person who studies the adolescent has within himself a potential source of insight into issues facing the person of adolescent age —issues that once he had to face, and perhaps still faces. An older person who wishes his own adolescence had been different might gain much from a re-examination of this period of his life. Perhaps he lived under unduly rigid controls of his own making. If so, it is likely that these still govern his life. Perhaps he had ideas about himself and inner conflicts which, as he now sees it, kept him then from living life to the full. If so, it is likely that these, in similar or disguised ways, are a burden on his life today.

The Adolescent Period

The term "adolescence" is used in this book to denote a period during which the growing person makes the transition from childhood to adulthood. While it is not linked to any precise span of years, adolescence may be viewed as beginning roughly when young people begin to show signs of puberty and continuing until most of them are sexually mature, have reached their maximum growth in height, and have approximately reached their full mental growth as measured by intelligence tests. The period as covered in this book includes the years from about the age of twelve to the early twenties.

Goals of Adolescent Development

The main goals we expect the young person to achieve during the adolescent period of development are rather easy to see, but it is worthwhile to look at them briefly. Later sections of this book will discuss them in more detail. In looking at them we also get a picture of what society demands of the adolescent.

The goals of adolescent development are determined to an important degree by the young person's own growth potentials. They are determined also by demands placed upon him by the culture in which he lives. Adolescence is both a developmental and a cultural phenomenon.

The basic changes that occur spring from the adolescent's own nature. The timing and course of these changes, and the stature of mind and body the young person eventually achieves, are determined to a large degree by heredity. There is weighty evidence which indicates that predominant traits of temperament and personality may also be influenced to an important degree by heredity.

However, much of what we regard as typically "adolescent" or expect of adolescents reflects the particular culture in which we live. Moreover, the extent to which adolescents realize their potentialities and the ways in which they employ their inborn resources obviously are influenced by pressures and opportunities in the environment in which they are reared.

PHYSICAL MATURITY

One of the clearest outcomes of growth in adolescence is physical maturity. The young person reaches—or almost reaches—his full height. We say "almost" for there are some rare young people who keep getting taller after the time we usually think of as adolescence.

An even more important outcome is that the young person during adolescence becomes sexually mature in the sense of being able to beget children. In this there are large differences among individual young people: some become sexually mature rather early in their teens (or even before) while other able-bodied persons do not acquire the capacity to reproduce until their late teens or perhaps even their early twenties.

PROGRESS TOWARD
MENTAL MATURITY

Another goal of adolescent development is to achieve or almost achieve full growth of the mental capacities that are measured by the typical intelligence test. We say "almost achieve" because, as we will see later, there are persons who continue to "grow" mentally into their twenties and beyond. Some grow not only in knowledge and understanding but also in intellectual power after they have reached an age at which we usually consider adolescence to be over.

An important aspect of the adolescent's intellectual growth is an increased ability to generalize and to deal with abstractions. As youngsters approach and enter early adolescence they gain notably in their capacity to apply principles of logic, to think in terms of a theory or hypothesis.

PROGRESS TOWARD EMOTIONAL MATURITY

Another goal in adolescent development is to make some progress toward achieving emotional maturity. Again, we must speak of "progress toward," for emotional maturity is not a fixed condition that is established at any one period of life. There are two aspects of maturing emotionally that are linked psychologically with physical maturity. If all goes well, the older adolescent and young adult are capable of physical intimacy with the opposite sex. To realize the fullest personal meaning of this development it is important for them also to be ready for emotional intimacy, tenderness and the ability to give and receive affection.

Further, when young people are able physically to beget children it is important for them to assume the emotional responsibilities and to enjoy the emotional satisfactions of parents. This also calls for tenderness and the ability to feel affection. It further requires that the young persons who are heading for parenthood must be able to allow their young children to be emotionally dependent on them, just as they, during childhood, were emotionally dependent on their parents.

FINDING THE SELF

The heading of this section is borrowed from Leta S. Hollingworth's classic book on adolescence (1928). She viewed adolescence as a period when, more than at any other time of life, it is important for young people to establish convictions about their identity. They must, as far as possible, find themselves.

The self is the sum total of a person's ideas and attitudes about who and what he is. It comprises all the experiences that constitute a person's awareness of his existence. These ideas and attitudes have been evolving since earliest childhood. They show considerable stability before a person reaches adolescent years, but much happens that makes it necessary for adolescents to take a fresh look at themselves. Even though there is a hard core of continuity in their personalities, they are in a state of flux. Each must learn to live with a person who differs in many ways from the person he was before. Many go through a phase of being awkward and self-conscious. They must even become accustomed to hearing a change in the sound of their voices.

The task of "finding the self" has many other facets. Not only does an adolescent view himself as he is but he must also project himself into the future. He views himself as in a state of being and also as in a process of becoming. In planning for the future, his fantasies may clash with reality and require a revision of his dreams of what he might be.

When an adolescent is in the process of "finding himself" he faces many alternatives—at least in theory. He cannot be both a priest and a pirate, a dandy and a professor, a philosopher and a lady-killer.[1]

In the process of establishing an identity as a distinct self, many adolescents face questions about their origins and endowments. This aspect of finding the self is very difficult for orphans, adopted children, and members of minority groups against whom there is a prejudice.

One important part of the adolescent's establishment of his identity is to define and accept his sex role. As we will note in a later chapter, it seems to be more difficult for girls to accept their femininity than for boys to see themselves in a masculine role.

Another part of finding the self is to formulate, more or less clearly, a hierarchy of goals. Instead of being torn by a heterogeneous mass of inconsistent aspirations it is important for adolescents to establish their aspirations in an order of priority. Adolescents who are on the way to finding themselves have the rudiments of a philosophy of life. This philosophy is rarely formulated in the neat logic of a philosopher's book. Much of it is inarticulate. However, adolescents who have the beginnings of a philosophy of life have principles of conduct, an inner guide, as it were. They do not have to begin all over again to rethink the whole strategy of their conduct each time a new issue arises. They will be puzzled, baffled, bewildered at times and find repeatedly that "there are more things in heaven and earth, Horatio, than are dreamt of in your philosophy." But they are not unscrupulous opportunists one day and passionate idealists the next; they do not constantly waver between moral responsibility

[1] William James (1910) says, "The philosopher and lady-killer could not dwell in the same tenement of clay." In saying this he was probably speaking about himself, and he has a good point, even though he perhaps underrates the versatility of philosophers.

and irresponsibility, even though they are likely to continue to face moral conflicts.

EMANCIPATION FROM PARENTS

One of the tasks an adolescent faces in establishing an identity of his own is to outgrow dependency on his parents, to achieve what has been called emancipation from his parents. This frequently involves a struggle, mixed with rebellion. But if the adolescent satisfactorily makes this hurdle, he will be "his own man," capable of self-direction, without feeling a continuing need, as he grows older, either to depend on his parents or to defy them.

Currents in the Lives of Adolescents

FAITH

Most adolescents profess a faith formulated in terms of religious beliefs, but they also have a faith that usually is unspoken. If spoken it might be phrased in the conviction that life is worth living. This faith is usually not carefully thought out. In a sense it is imposed upon every human being: he is alive and the natural thing is to go on living. But there arc other elements.

THE SEARCH FOR MEANING

Imbedded in the striving of an adolescent who feels the throb of life is a search for meaning. From the time when adolescents as children first acquired the power to sense and to reason they sought to explore and to know the meaning of things. As they matured they asked questions about the what and why. If their questioning was not suppressed they would ask: What does it matter? What difference does it make?

As children grow older many of them become subdued in their quest for meaning. By the time they have reached adolescence, many seem convinced that it is not good to inquire too deeply into the meaning of things. The answers they get at school when they ask, for example, Why should we learn all about the French Revolution? may be quite elaborate, but they are likely to boil down to a simple, You'd better, there will be questions about it on the exam. Most adolescents become resigned to the idea that they should learn what is assigned even though it has little or no personal significance.

Yet in all adolescents, as in all human beings, a search for meaning is linked with the fact of being alive, and it goes on in many ways. The search for meaning is richly rewarded when an adolescent can find something that deeply absorbs the talents of his mind and his emotional resources. He then has a passion for life. The search for meaning takes an unfortunate turn when an adolescent finds little or nothing that is significant in what he is and does. The doors of his life open into empty rooms. There are large reaches of emptiness in the existence of those adolescents who trudge to school month after month to learn lessons that are unsuited to their talents, needs, or interests.

CHOICE

The adolescent who is moving into life is constantly faced with the necessity of making choices. Almost every person, old or young, has a conviction that he has the power to choose. The range within which he can choose may be limited. The idea of freedom may be an illusion from all logical and scientific points of view. But from the *point of view of the person himself* it is he who chooses. It is he who feels he is free to say Yes or No, to turn right or left, to plan for tomorrow or go fishing today.

Adolescents, like their elders, cannot avoid making choices and taking the consequences. Jean Paul Sartre has spoken of this in its starkest form: The freedom to choose is the only freedom man does not have the freedom to renounce. Philosophers may argue about the freedom of the will. But within himself each person feels differently: I made a choice. I might have chosen something else. Now I am stuck with it, or proud of it.

Common sense tells us that our freedom is restricted. Much of an adolescent's equipment is determined by his heredity, which he did not choose. Much of his existence is shaped by an environment he cannot control. But he still feels personally responsible for much that happens in his life. He may *think* that he is being tossed by the winds of chance, but it is hard for him to *feel* that way. As a consequence, he may feel proud, vainglorious, or ashamed. He may view his decisions with serene self-esteem. Or he may have shattering guilt.

It is on the assumption of freedom to choose that human beings with ordinary intelligence accept the notion that they can do what is right or wrong. It is because of the experience of choosing that children, from an early age, to a great or small degree, feel *responsible* for their actions. It is because of this conviction that educators and those they teach believe that they can cultivate the ability to make wise choices. It is on this same assumption that we try to learn something about them.

PURPOSES AND GOALS

Related to the search for meaning and the making of choices is the establishment of goals and purposes.

The purposes underlying an adolescent's acts may be clearly conceived or they may be only dimly recognized. He may have goals he is hardly aware of. But he does not behave in a random, helter-skelter way. The purpose a person believes he is following may not be the purpose he really is pursuing; the purpose may, to an extent, be a false purpose. However, even if the purpose he gives for his acts is not the real purpose it still, as far as he is concerned, is a purpose, and his acts, instead of being aimless, have a purpose and logic of their own.

HOPE

Much of an adolescent's life is built on hope—a clearly defined or dim but dogged assurance of what is yet to be. Hope is a precious element in the lives of all persons (it "springs eternal in the human breast"), but there are many aspects of the adolescent's career that make hope especially essential. Many of an adolescent's labors, especially at school, are geared to the future. In much of what he does he must renounce the slogan "Enjoy now, pay later" and, instead, pay now in the hope of enjoying later. Adolescents learn to write business letters when they have no business to write about. They learn medieval history against the day when they might have to teach it to others. True, according to enthusiastic adult scholars, they should learn for the joy of learning, not for some future business deal. Many youngsters do enjoy learning. Others, again, will learn almost anything to please their elders and to support a self-image of being a good student. But a large proportion of adolescents do not seem to get into the spirit of the thing.

The hopeful ones among these still go on with their labors, confident that the promissory notes they receive will be paid off in later years. Others, who are not sustained by such hopes muddle along as best they can, just manage to squeak through high school, and then live as much as possible for the passing moment. They do not desire to defer until tomorrow the things they can grasp today. Such adolescents must manage as best they can to mark time in school. Many of them cease preparing for a distant future, quit school, and get a job if one is to be had. Many marry young to persons who likewise are in a hurry. If in seizing the present moment they find something meaningful and worthwhile, they may be wiser than those who keep postponing. It is possible to defer to the future so long that the future day never arrives. But conditions are different when hope has been shattered, when adolescents have no plans for the future and also are unable to grasp what the present affords.

Trends and Stresses in Adolescent Development

The section that follows will consider some general trends in adolescent growth. It will also present viewpoints and findings regarding stresses that distinguish adolescence from other periods in the life span.

EARLIER ONSET OF ADOLESCENCE

At present adolescents mature physically earlier than their forebears. They also show certain interests and claim certain privileges at an earlier age than was true a generation or more ago.

Several American and European studies indicate that the average age at which girls reach the menarche has declined during the past hundred years, and probably is still declining. In a review of these studies, Tanner (1955, p. 92) reports that the trend in studies of various populations is "remarkably similar . . . , with the age at menarche getting earlier by $1/3$ or $1/2$ year per decade over the period 1850–1950."

Children and adolescents are taller and heavier, age by age, than they were several generations ago (Tanner, 1955). Moreover, the adolescent growth spurt comes earlier and at maturity boys and girls are taller and heavier.

Present-day adolescents show an earlier interest in the opposite sex than they did some decades ago. In one study (Hetzer, 1959), three thousand children, aged ten to fourteen, in 1957 wrote compositions on the theme, "How I am and how I would like to be." These were compared with similar compositions written in the 1920's (Busemann, 1926). In the 1957 study the body was emphasized much earlier, especially by girls. Mention of relationships with the opposite sex was found to occur three years earlier. At present American city girls have their first dates earlier than in the 1920's (W. M. Smith, 1952).

In a comparison between interests and activities reported by ninth-grade students in 1935, 1953, and 1959, Jones (1960) found that "the more recent generations of ninth-graders indicate greater maturity of heterosexual interests . . ." as well as some other notable changes. A larger proportion of the youngsters in 1953 and 1959 than in 1935 expressed interests such as: talking about having dates, talking about boy or girl friends, approving of love scenes in movies. One little sign of greater sophistication was a sharp increase in the number of boys and girls who approved the use of lipstick by girls.

An earlier interest in social relations, love, and marriage was also noted by Harris (1959), who compared problems and interests expressed by high school boys in 1957 with those expressed in another study in 1935. In recent years there has also been an increase in marriages among teen-agers (Burchinal, 1959a, 1959b, 1960).

During the past generation or two, young people have shown a more tolerant attitude toward social issues (Jones, 1960) and less condemnation of certain acts that were considered "borderland" or wrong in the twenties, such as smoking, flirting, or using slang (Pressey and Jones, 1955).

The evidence does not consistently indicate that earlier physical maturing and more precocious heterosexual interests are accompanied by accelerated maturity of the personality as a whole. The young people in Jones' study (1960) showed more serious purpose and a more tolerant attitude toward social issues. Hetzer reports, on the other hand, that while showing a considerably earlier appearance of heterosexual interests, the young people lagged behind the children of 1926 in "maturity of self-evaluation." According to Hetzer, self-perception seems to be shifted from inner-directedness to outer-directedness. There are many findings which seem to indicate that youth of college age are likely to show more sophistication in conforming to certain social norms than evidence of increased maturity in their personal convictions and values. Such evidence will be reviewed in a later section.

STRESSES AND DISLOCATIONS

Adolescents are in a transitional phase of development, but this does not make them unique. In every period of development from birth onward a person is moving from one stage to the next along life's way. There are, however, some aspects of adolescence that makes it different from other phases of growth.

The adolescent is in many ways a marginal character: too old to be treated as a child, too young to have the rights of an adult. There are several facets of this marginal existence.

Economic Unemployment

Many adolescents go through a phase where they are eager to earn their own money but find it difficult to do so. Restrictions on child labor extend into the teens, when youngsters no longer like to be viewed as children. Other impediments include compulsory school attendance, the need to get working papers and to keep them in order, special regulations against employment in certain kinds of jobs. These rules are designed to protect the young, but often the young view them as a form of discrimination. This view is strengthened when adolescents get less pay than adults for the same work. Many enterprising sixteen-year-olds working in a garage or in a store or on a farm are able to do all that the grown-up employees (and sometimes even more); yet in many places of employment they are not paid on the same scale.

Even when adolescents are not earning money they might still find a reward in being useful. This was easier in earlier generations when adolescents did essential work on the farm or in the shop or around the home. Such work often was tedious but it obviously had to be done. Often it gave them a feeling of ownership and responsibility. A farm boy or storekeeper's boy who sees that things are thriving as he goes through his daily chores is tending a farm or a store that someday may be his own. He is, besides, a useful and productive member of society.

Many present-day adolescents have difficulty in feeling they are useful. They have no cows to milk, no calves to feed. When they wash the dishes or wash the car they know they are doing something that must be done. But they are not contributing to a growing economy. They are not watching a calf grow into a fine heifer or a promising young bull. They are just doing clean-up jobs.

Legal Obligations without Legal Privileges

An adolescent is reminded of his marginal citizenship when he must accept the legal obligations of an adult without having an adult's rights. He can be drafted into the armed services. He is old enough to fight, old enough to die, but too young to vote. When earning his own keep before he is legally of age he is a man until he comes to places marked "no minors allowed."

Yet many inequalities in the treatment of adolescents are of their own making. There is a higher rate for automobile insurance for adolescent boys due to their higher accident rates. Similarly, in some communities boys in late adolescence notice that the police are notoriously more rude to them when they drive the car alone than when their fathers are along. The police often are exasperated by adolescents. But in situations such as these an adolescent with a good record will not get much comfort from the fact that he is discriminated against because the cops are angry at other adolescents.

Sexual Unemployment

A large proportion of adolescents are sexually mature and have strong sexual urges before they are able, in a legitimate way, to use their sexual capacities. A period of sexual unemployment is inevitable for a large number of young persons in a complex society. It is tied in with financial circumstances and the long period of preparation necessary for some vocations. It prevails widely even though there has been a trend toward earlier marriages in recent years. There are, of course, as Kinsey (1948) has shown, many persons who find part-time employment. But this does not remove the problem nor solve the moral issues it involves.

STORM AND STRESS

Adolescence is often described as a time of greater storm and stress (Sturm und Drang) than other periods of life. Other authorities discount this theory. There is no exact measure that will compare the stresses of an adolescent with those of a six-year-old who is beginning school or with those of an adult.

It is clear, however, that there are conspicuous signs of tension in adolescence. The delinquency rate is higher than in earlier years and higher than the crime rate in later years. There is an increase in rebellion against authority at home and at school. There is some evidence also that many adolescents are more troubled than they were previously, or will be somewhat later, about their own identity, who and what they are, their sex roles, their place in the scheme of things.

Evidence that adolescence is a time of acute stress for some (such as delinquents) does not mean that it is a stressful time for all. But it is reasonable to assume that a time which is fiery for some is at least smoky for others.

The ideas adults have concerning the carefreeness or turbulence of the adolescent period are greatly influenced by (a) the ideas they would like to regard as true and (b) the extent to which they look at or beyond the more superficial aspects of the adolescent's life. When we judge typical adolescent boys and girls (leaving out delinquents and serious trouble-makers) by their public conduct in a high school the picture is, on the whole, quite optimistic. They go about their work without much fuss. They seem to have absorbing academic or extracurricular interests. They yell themselves hoarse at football games. They look healthy and handsome, despite occasional skin blemishes and extremes of dress. Although they have their foibles, they are nice people and it is a pleasure to work with them.

Such a picture of adolescents is comfortable for adults to have in the typical school where little or no attention is given to children's emotional problems or personal concerns. It helps to justify the kind of education that is offered.

A different picture emerges when we look not only at adolescents as they appear in public but try to fathom their private, inner lives. When investigators attempt this they must first find a way to push aside the veil of secrecy that ordinarily conceals the adolescent. In a study of three hundred presumably normal high school and college girls, Frank and his associates (1953) note, "Adolescents are usually fearful of revealing their thoughts and feelings, of letting adults gain access to their reveries, their worries and aspirations. . . . While preoccupied with their personal problems and eager to find out what they should do, they will ordinarily not tell adults, even when in urgent need of help."

In an investigation in which a number of adolescents were studied over a period of years, Tryon (1944) comments that adults are quite commonly ignorant about what goes on in the process of adolescent development. According to Tryon, achieving manhood and womanhood in our society is a long, complex and often confusing task. "For the most part boys and girls work at these tasks in a stumbling, groping fashion, blindly reaching for the next step without much or any adult assistance. Many lose the way."

The picture of adolescents is especially somber in studies that have been conducted by means of projective techniques (described in Chapter 7). Frank and his associates (1953) found evidence of "more frequent and severe emotional disturbances" than they had anticipated. They also report that girls in their study had a "general fear of sex and a growing concern with their own maturing sexual capacities, not always consciously recognized."

The gloomy verdict concerning the emotional problems of adolescents that comes from studies using projective techniques must be regarded with some reservation. The validity of these techniques has not been completely established. However, when adolescents are studied in more conventional ways, through repeated private interviews, for example, by a person whom they trust, the accounts they give of themselves are far less rosy than the picture they present in public. Even the more perfunctory personality tests and adjustment inventories reveal that the typical adolescent has many problems. This is an important point to bear in mind when we try to understand adolescents. The fact that adolescents typically have problems is more significant than the question as to whether their lives are more stressful than those of older or younger persons. Actually, people have a large assortment of problems at all stages of life. Persons who are old enough to have adolescent students or children (or grandchildren) have their share along with the rest. (Studies bearing on this subject are reviewed in Chapter 10.) This should help older persons to understand adolescents. Although the particular concerns that weigh on people's minds change with age, the underlying emotional currents are much the same. A young person may worry about ever getting a job and an older person about measuring up to the job he has, but both are afraid. A father may resent the way his son uses the family car, and the son may resent the father's interference, but both are angry. So also with other emotions.

Adolescence in Retrospect

In the informal study mentioned earlier in this chapter, many persons claimed they would do differently if they could relive their adolescence, but also gave an emphatic No when asked whether they would care to go through the adolescent period again, even if they could do so with all that they had learned since. Perhaps another or a larger sampling would give another answer, but these observations suggest that an older person who has scaled the adolescent hurdle is glad to be done with it. This does not apply to adolescence alone, however. In another inquiry (unpublished) by the writer, parents were asked whether they would rear their children differently if they could have another try. Most of them said Yes. But when asked, Would you like to have a chance to try again? all of them said a fervent No.

When older people have been asked to name the happiest period of their lives far more name the years following the middle twenties than the years of childhood, late adolescence, or early adulthood. Pressey and Kuhlen (1957) review findings obtained when persons aged 65 or over designated what they regarded as the happiest time of their lives. About 50 per cent named young adulthood (age 25 to 45) as the happiest. Less than half this proportion (about 19 per cent) named the period of youth (15 to 25) and even fewer named the childhood period.

The episodes which older people view as being most satisfying center to a very large degree on happenings that are most likely to occur after a person has reached the middle twenties or so: marriage, the birth of children, home and family life, and satisfactions connected with occupation.

THE GLAMORIZED ADOLESCENT

The dreams of a relived adolescence appear in many works of fiction. In these the authors are free vicariously to glamorize the image of youth. The long arm of coincidence makes it possible for the young persons in the story to do things they could not or would not have done. The ambitious one triumphs, the idealist finds heroic things to do. The lustful boy and eager girl just happen to be together on the heath when no one is watching. Such fiction gives vicarious substance to age-long human fantasies. But fiction often distorts the facts of life.

Contending Forces

During adolescence, as in every period of life, there are forces that work against each other. There are conditions that push the young person forward and others that hold him back, especially in the early adolescent years. Adolescents have a desire to assert their own individuality and also a great need to conform. They want to be big and yet also to be protected. They harbor many conflicting motives and feelings: loyalty and an impulse to rebel; aggressive impulses and fears and guilt regarding these. There is something radical about being an adolescent, yet something conservative. The impulse to grow is strong. The impetus to venture into the new and untried is powerful, too. But while adolescents thus anticipate the new, they are also bound by the past.

CONFLICTING AND CONFUSING PRESSURES IN THE CULTURE

Adolescents face many conflicting moral and cultural pressures. They are supposed to be wholeheartedly generous, yet they see savage competition all about them. They should be ambitious but also be modest. They should stand up for their rights but also turn the other cheek.

One condition in present-day society that adds to the difficulty of adolescents is that many adults, both at home and at school, are themselves confused about issues pertaining to the discipline, teaching, and rearing of young people. Much of their confusion stems from difficulty in resolving the issue between authority and freedom. In many schools and homes there is a conflict between the ideas of being strict or lenient, autocratic or democratic. For some decades it has been emphasized that the good school is a democratic school and the good parent is a democratic parent. The view has grown that an authoritarian approach is bad.

There are findings supporting the idea that democratic procedures promote a child's development better than autocratic procedures.[2] But whatever the findings on this score may be, many adults are uncertain about what it means to be democratic or permissive. Some seem to have assumed that they should swing from one extreme to another; if their upbringing was strict, they should now be lenient; if their education was "hard," they should be "soft"; if they were closely supervised and restrained as children, their proper policy should be to allow children unlimited freedom.

Actually, of course, to allow a child (or the adolescent about whom we now are concerned) unlimited freedom in the name of being democratic is to foster chaos. No young person has within himself the wisdom,

[2] For studies and reviews of studies bearing on this issue see Baldwin *et al.* (1945), Adorno *et al.* (1950), Anderson and Anderson (1954), Landis (1954), and Watson (1957).

judgment, and ability to use unlimited freedom even if, in theory, it were possible to provide unlimited freedom.

It would be easier in many ways if all adults who deal with young persons were consistently democratic or if all were rather authoritarian and laid down the law consistently. If treated in an authoritarian way the youngsters might conform or rebel, but at least they would know what to expect of others and what others expect of them.

Some confusion in the discipline of youngsters is, of course, bound to occur, even under the most settled conditions. Circumstances of life are such that it is not humanly possible for an adult to be consistent in everything he does. But there is reason to believe that at the present time there are many adolescents who have been exposed to more than the usual amount of confusion and inconsistency. In a study directed by the writer a few years ago many parents told of their conflicts and confusion (Jersild, Woodyard, and del Solar, 1949). Some said, for example, they had been somewhat authoritarian at an earlier time, or with an older child, and now were shifting to more democratic ways. Such shifts, even if in theory they are in the right direction, are likely to involve tension both for parents and for the children. A parent or teacher who has been brought up according to one theory of child-rearing cannot easily turn about and apply another theory.[3]

Although the emphasis during the past three decades or so on more democratic ways of dealing with children has sometimes added to the burden carried by parents and teachers and thereby to the burden borne by some children, there is reason to believe that in the long run the shift toward more democratic procedures will be decidedly to the good—but in the transition there are going to be hardships.

There always has been friction between teachers and students and between the old and young. Present-day figures on delinquency and the evidences of "problem behavior" that we will discuss later in this book suggest that the friction at the present time is at least as severe now as in times past.

Some of this friction, it is true, is deceptive. When older people try to put democratic practices into effect they give young people greater freedom to show their feelings openly, including rebellion. Such freedom

[3] Some differences between the attitudes of a group of mothers and a group of grandmothers have been described by Staples and Smith (1954). Briggs and Schulz (1955) have reported findings that support the position that many families are in the process of making a transition from authoritarian to democratic attitudes. Changes in conceptions underlying family life have also been discussed by Elder (1949) and Bond (1961).

to show rebellion may make it seem that young people are wilder and less disciplined than were the youngsters of earlier generations when actually the difference is that they are more open in showing their attitudes.

THE BEARING OF CHILDHOOD ASSETS AND LIABILITIES ON ADOLESCENCE

There is a great carry-over of habits and attitudes, strengths and weaknesses from earlier years of development into adolescence. Anything that earlier in his development has helped the adolescent to be free to use and to enjoy his endowments will stand him in good stead as he faces the tasks of adolescent years. Similarly, lacks or weaknesses carried over from childhood will make the going in adolescence harder. For this reason we cannot understand the adolescent if we center our attention only upon him and upon the adolescent phase of growth. Earlier experiences that have influenced the young person's attitudes toward himself, his attitudes of self-confidence, or attitudes involving grievances or feelings of inferiority are especially important. Adolescence, in common with each phase of life, inherits what has gone before.

There are issues he must face as long as he lives. Even some of the issues that seem to have been settled—such as the choice of a vocation and even the choice of a mate—are not as completely settled as they seem to be. In the typical instance as long as he retains, as an adult, a little freedom to think and courage to inquire, he will sometimes wonder whether or not he chose correctly and, even though he may have no desire to change, why he chose as he did.

Chapter 2

The Adolescent Self: Known Dimensions and Unperceived Influences

The young person's ideas and attitudes regarding himself influence and are influenced by his response to everything that happens during adolescence. In this chapter we will consider aspects of self-appraisal which must be taken into account when, in later sections, we discuss the personal meaning of physical, mental, and social development during adolescent years. We will also discuss conditions which influence an adolescent's outlook on life in ways he himself does not perceive.

The adolescent's self is the essence of his existence as *known* to him. Here is what, for him, is the structure of his being, whether it be a palace or a prison. It is in this subjective world that he tastes the substance of his humanity, its joys and sorrows, hopes and fears, tenderness and hardness.

The self as known includes all the ideas and feelings a person has regarding the properties of his body, the qualities of his mind and his personal characteristics. It includes his beliefs, values, and convictions. It embodies the conception he has of his past, of his background, and of his future prospects. The components of the self range from neutral details of self-perception to attitudes that are charged with feeling, such as pride or shame, inferiority, self-esteem or self-reproach.

When we use the modifier *known* in describing the self we imply that a person's view of himself does not give a full accounting of what he is and how he came to be that way. It is a person's own subjective evaluation. It represents his convictions, what he knows or thinks he knows about his make-up, not what he has forgotten or is unable to perceive. It may include ideas concerning his motives which he himself will revise. It may also include views which, according to all standards except his own, are incorrect. But to him it is real. It may seem shadowy to others, but for him it is a rock as long as he maintains it.

Aspects of the Known Self

The adolescent can assess himself from several angles.

THE "ACTUAL SELF"

He has ideas and attitudes about what he "really is like." When questioned, he can (if he is candid) describe himself in detail as he thinks he is. This is what the young person regards as his actual self.

An adolescent's known self also includes his conscious attitudes of self-approval or disapproval, convictions regarding his worthiness or unworthiness. Such attitudes may range from serene self-acceptance to bitter self-rejection.

THE "IDEAL SELF"

The adolescent is also more or less aware of differences between what he is and what he wishes he might be or thinks he ought to be or is trying to become.

The sum-total of a person's view of what he wishes he were or thinks he ought to be, as distinguished from what he is, is generally called the "ideal self." The adolescent's ideal self has many facets. It includes aspirations he is vigorously striving to attain, or hopes dimly someday to realize.

Every adolescent, or adult, who calmly assesses things, sees something unfinished in himself, a weakness yet to overcome, an improvement yet to be achieved. The elements of the ideal self range from unrealistic dreams to somber ideas of improvement that will be attained.

IRRATIONAL IDEAS ABOUT SELF

A person may have a view of himself that is irrational in the light of his own later insights or in the light of all that can be known about him by others. The label *self-idealization* denotes a system of irrational ideas and attitudes regarding self. The conscious elements of this idealized image of self are, from the person's own standpoint, a reality and not just a fiction. These, accordingly, are features of what a person regards as his actual self.

Self-idealization is a form of self-deception. Such self-deception occurs when a person has irrational "fixed ideas" or "logic-tight compartments," or uses "defense mechanisms" without recognizing he is doing so, or why.

We have an example of self-idealization [1] when an adolescent who is afraid of his sexual impulses adopts an attitude of extreme prudishness, but regards his prudishness as an element of strength in his character, not as a defense built upon fear. An adolescent who is driven by a compulsion to compete has "idealized" this facet of himself when he views his competitiveness as a noble ambition, not as an expression of a need to vanquish others.

Self-idealization may take the form of regarding a weakness as a strength, as in the examples above, and also of masking admirable qualities with self-imputed weaknesses. This happens, for example, if an adolescent with good potentials disavows these with a stubborn "I'm no good" attitude. It occurs also if he repudiates his capacity for winning affection with a rigid pose of "No one could like me."

An adolescent who has self-deprecating attitudes of this sort disavows good qualities that are latent within him. When he does this there are hidden reasons behind it; we will consider these in another section. It seems incredible that a person would cripple himself in this way. Yet when we look around us we can see young people who act out disparaging views of themselves which, as seen by others, needlessly produce suffering and failure.

As we have noted, an adolescent's known self does not include forgotten aspects of his past experience which have molded his present attitudes. An example is an "irrational" fear which he cannot trace to its origins.

---

[1] An extreme example of this appears in a delusion, such as when a person is convinced that he is Napoleon. Such a delusion is abnormal, but persons who generally are regarded as normal also deceive themselves in less spectacular ways.

When walking through a field he has a mortal fear of stepping on a snake, even though there is no snake within miles. He himself may acknowledge that this fear is irrational. He is painfully aware of the fear but he cannot reconstruct, rethink, and refeel the experiences that produced it. It is as though he harbors a stranger, a foreign body, yet as long as the fear persists it is a "real" fear.

The Unknown Dimension

The fact that there are important influences in an adolescent's mental life that are not comprehended within his image of himself does not minimize the importance of the self as known. From the adolescent's point of view it is the core of his existence. But to understand him or others or ourselves, it is also essential to inquire as deeply as possible into conditions that lie, as it were, outside the self. This is one of the elementary facts of life. But it raises some thorny questions. What are these conditions and influences? And what should we call them? Just to name them has presented a problem.

Freud and his followers have managed this problem of naming to their own satisfaction better than most others. The Freudians do not directly emphasize the self as a key concept, yet the term "self" constantly slips into their writings. They have a troika, with Latin names: the *id,* the *ego,* and the *superego.* The three members of this team do not pull together very well, but somehow manage.

The *id* embodies the fundamental life urges. It consists of all the primeval passions, tendencies, and desires which a human being has in common with other creatures. In Freudian writings the id is sometimes personified as though it were a stealthy demon with a will of its own.

The *superego* embodies all the tendencies associated with the moral conscience. It also is frequently personified in Freudian writings. It frowns when the id is on the prowl, restrains the id and alerts the third member of the team, the *ego.*

The ego, as described by Freudians, comes closest to what is commonly called the self. It organizes an individual's perceptions and memories, it plans, it governs. The ego, which must mediate between the upsurge of the id and the restraints of the superego, is a very busy character. The ego is "victorious" when it succeeds "in establishing the most harmonious relations possible between the id, the superego and the forces of the outside world" (A. Freud, 1937).

In addition to this triple-headed arrangement the Freudians make a further division: the conscious and the unconscious. The id is filled with unconscious urges. Elements of the superego are unconscious. The ego has defense mechanisms which are unconscious. So there are not just three but at least five voices in the inner chorus.

The Freudians speak of the unconscious now as though it were an entity, now as though it were an attribute. There are "unconscious motives," for example, as distinguished from conscious ones, as though motives were mannikins with a consciousness or an unconsciousness of their own. In the literature one can even find references to the *unconscious* unconscious, which is somewhat complicated.

Many psychologists wince at what they regard as the looseness of this terminology. Some psychologists, on the other hand, are quite content with it, and the Freudians themselves seem to thrive on it.[2]

Whatever a psychologist's semantic preferences in this matter might be he faces one elemental truth: in addition to a person's known self—the attributes a person is consciously aware of and claims as his own—there is something else still to be accounted for. What shall we call this something else? In facing this question, writers about the self have used a number of expedients. One proposal is to speak of the "nonphenomenal" as distinguished from the "*phenomenal* self." The label "phenomenal self," in free translation, means the self that shows forth, is apparent, observable from a person's own point of view. The label "nonphenomenal," according to the proposed terminology, would cover what is not apparent to the person himself. It has also been suggested that we speak of an "unconscious self-concept."[3]

"Unconscious" is a perfectly good word, but many writers are reluctant to use it, for two reasons. One is that it refers to aspects of mind and motivation which some persons prefer to ignore. This is understand-

[2] Freudians apparently use Freudian language much more in their public pronouncements than in their private practice. In a study by the writer and his associates (Jersild, Lazar, and Brodkin, 1962) over two hundred persons participated in an evaluation of the effects of psychoanalysis. A majority described their analysis as Freudian or Freudian-oriented. In describing their experiences in therapy, however, these people very rarely used Freudian language, and all of those whom we questioned specifically about this matter said that their analysts firmly discouraged them from "intellectualizing" their condition by using Freudian vernacular (such as "my superego," "my unconscious," "my Oedipus compex").

[3] Here we would have a concept of self that the self has no concept of, which makes a pretty pickle of words.

able. The idea that a person harbors irrational notions and is swayed by motives he does not recognize is repugnant if a person fears all that it might imply.

Such an idea is also unflattering to persons who prize the intellect and like to believe that their reason reigns supreme. It is distasteful to educators at the high school and college levels if they see in it a reflection on their scholarship and an implied criticism of what they teach. Most of the teaching adolescents get at school is restricted to logical and factual aspects of the known dimensions of human experience. A teacher who believes that such instruction helps students to make maximum use of their minds is not likely to welcome the implied charge that what he teaches touches only on facets of the "conscious mind" while ignoring the "unconscious mind." This is an understandable reaction but not an adequate reason for rejecting the concept of the unconscious.

Another and better reason for hesitating to use the label *unconscious* is that it has been used loosely and it has many vague connotations. Writers often discuss *the unconscious* as though it were a separate he or she, a person within a person, a character endowed with faculties of his or her own for planning and outwitting the person in whom he or she resides.

The writer can give the position taken in this book by summarizing some points that already have been made, and adding a few statements. The adolescent's known self is, from the adolescent's standpoint, an indisputable reality. To understand him we must take account of this solid fact. It is as important in assessing him as the details we can see or measure with objective tests. His explicit rational ideas about himself rest on realistic premises of self-assessment. His irrational ideas are based on misapprehensions, but he is not aware of this. Further, the motives that determine an adolescent's conduct, ideas, and attitudes range from ones that he clearly perceives to ones he does not recognize. The process through which misapprehensions become established, and the unrecognized motives, are not embodied in the adolescent's self as he knows it. They are in the realm of the unknown, what commonly has been referred to as the unconscious.

In this book we will frequently take note of both the known and the unknown elements. We will sometimes refer to the latter as *unconscious*, but to avoid the ambiguous connotations associated with this term we will favor other labels, such as *nonconscious, unknown, unrecognized.*

Ways of Knowing the Adolescent Self

Although adolescents, as a rule, are silent about their private thoughts and feelings they disclose themselves in a variety of ways. An adult who works with them has many opportunities to get glimpses of how they regard themselves. When an adult uses these opportunities wisely, he can begin to know the adolescent as a living person rather than as just another youth or a nameless character in a textbook.

In day-to-day contacts, most of our judgments about how an adolescent regards himself are inferred from his behavior. We assume that he is rather confident in himself if he looks self-assured and that he is unsure of himself if he is a show-off. An accurate judgment about an adolescent's self-assessment from his conduct is not easy to obtain, however, especially if he is skillful in putting on a good "front" or is a retiring person. But in working with adolescents we constantly and unavoidably form judgments.

Adolescents also reveal themselves in their own words, and when we deal with them we are constantly noting and drawing inferences from what they say. The commonest self-descriptions appear in what adolescents express in ordinary conversation. A more systematic account can be obtained from what they reveal in a personal conference. Such a conference may be brief and limited to what the adolescent talks about on the spur of the moment. Or it may be an "interview in depth" conducted over a period of time, in a setting which encourages the interviewee to elaborate and rethink what he has said before and to bring in new material.

Interviews may be structured with a set of questions prepared in advance which encourage the interviewees to speak in an ordered sequence. Or they may be casual and free, allowing the interviewees to let their minds wander, to select what they wish to say in any way they please. When thus free to roam a person will bring up seemingly disconnected thoughts, feelings, and fantasies. Some of the most revealing information comes when an adolescent expresses a thought and then catches himself on the wing, so to speak, asking, "Now why did I think that? I wonder what it means?" and then by a process of "free association" goes on to explore.

Ordinarily, adolescents do not let their minds wander in this way when talking to an adult. They are likely to think the adult will regard what they say as nonsense. To perceive meaning in what adolescents confide in this way an adult must also be able to let his own mind drift along with what the adolescent says. He must listen with "the third ear."

It is possible at times to achieve a remarkable degree of communication when two persons thus allow their minds to drift. But there are strong barriers against this kind of communication. To overcome them it is necessary for the adolescent to trust the adult to whom he is going to confide. It is necessary also for both the adolescent and the adult to have the courage to risk what might happen, for when a person ventures into a process of free association he is likely to express thoughts and sentiments which he ordinarily does not disclose to others and which others ordinarily prefer not to hear.

Although this form of communication is rarely employed, we mention it here to underscore two points. First, the stream of consciousness that constitutes a person's self-awareness often is quite different from the logical order of ideas that appears in concentrated moments of thinking.[4] The reader need only to catch himself in a moment of seemingly "aimless" thought to verify this. Second, the adolescent cannot freely reveal this stream of thought and feeling if he is required to fit it into the preconceived pattern of another person's thoughts.

Direct self-description may also be obtained through written compositions on themes such as: What I like about myself, or What I don't like about myself. The meaning of such compositions will vary according to the degree adolescents are willing and able to reveal themselves. Compositions of this sort serve better as a starting point for further inquiry than as statements that can be regarded as complete.

Diaries and autobiographies offer a more extensive means of self-description. They range from brief accounts written on request to personal diaries which the young person himself has felt an urge to write.

Lengthy diaries and autobiographies frequently reveal intimate and poignant information, especially if they were kept in secret but then later entrusted to someone else. The accounts are notably revealing when adolescents have written them without intending to impress others. Some of the most revealing glimpses into the life of individual adolescents have come from diaries and autobiographies. We cannot, however, assume that those who keep such records speak for all adolescents. Those who keep diaries are a minority. They have some characteristics not found to the same degree in adolescents at large: an interest in examining their own

[4] Even the thoughts that occur to a student or professor while listening attentively to a lecture roam hither and yon, away from the ordered sequence of the lecturer's ideas.

thoughts and feelings combined with a desire to express them in words and a resolve to take time out to do so.

Among the adolescent autobiographies the writer has had the privilege to examine there were many that expressed yearnings, heartaches, and feelings of loneliness. Diarists often seem to seek solace in their own companionship. They confide, as it were, in themselves (sometimes using the word "confide," or its equivalent).[5]

SELF-DESCRIPTION INVENTORIES

Many tests have been devised to measure aspects of the known self (also frequently referred to as the "self-concept" or the "phenomenal self"). These commonly are built upon a list of adjectives or statements such as cheerfulness, generosity, irritability, attractiveness.

In one procedure, the descriptive items are listed one by one on a single form preceded by phrasing such as "I am" or "I would like to be" and followed by modifiers such as *not at all, to some degree, to a great degree*. The person marks the response to each item that best describes what he thinks he is—his "actual self." He can then also mark each item as he thinks he ought to be or desires to be (his "ideal self"). According to further instructions, he may be asked to mark each item as he thinks others would rate him or to use the items to rate other persons who are specifically named.

Another procedure is to put the items on separate cards which a person can sort into piles ranging from those that he regards as most descriptive to those he regards as least descriptive of himself. Still another procedure is to require the respondent to rank the items in an order from most to least descriptive.[6]

[5] These sentiments are often captured in the lyrics of popular songs, for example: "Me and my shadow . . . no one else to tell our troubles to."

[6] The following references illustrate or discuss approaches that have been made in the study of self-assessment or assessment of others or both. Stephenon (1935) describes what is known as the Q-sort. The subject is presented with a number of brief descriptions of personality qualities or traits, each on a separate card, and is instructed to sort these along a prearranged distribution which approximates a normal distribution. Stephenson has reviewed studies using the Q-technique (1952). Self-assessments by means of a Q-sort technique that includes a hundred statements have been reported by Rogers and Dymond (1954).

Other self-assessment instruments have been described by Berger (1952), Phillips (1951), Fey (1955), Bills, Vance and McLean (1951), Jervis (1954, 1958), and Spivack (1956).

The information obtained from such descriptions or ratings of self (and others) can be used to compare:

1. A person's claimed view of himself as he is with what he says he would like to be. It is possible to note how frequently and to what extent there is similarity or discrepancy between what he professes he is and thinks he ought to be.

2. A person's rating of himself with his rating of others. This comparison has been used to measure the relationship between self-acceptance and acceptance of others.

3. A person's rating of himself with the ratings he *thinks* others will apply to him.

4. A person's rating of himself with the ratings others actually apply to him. This shows the degree of correspondence between a person as he appears in his own eyes and how he appears in the eyes of others.

5. A person's self-rating with the ratings others think he will apply to himself.

6. A person's (a) approval of himself and (b) his approval or acceptance of others with (c) the extent to which others accept or reject him. This, if valid, gives an indication of the correspondence between self-acceptance, acceptance *of* others and acceptance *by* others.

The results obtained from inventories for self-description and evaluation of others are very interesting, especially when applied, with the consent of all concerned, to persons one knows.[7] It is fascinating to compare the qualities students attribute to themselves with the impressions one has of them and with the impressions fellow students have of them. Some students, as judged by others, are very realistic in assessing themselves, while others seem to be way off base.

Although interesting, findings from tests of this kind are useful mainly as a point of departure for further study. The information they yield cannot be accepted at face value or as a final diagnosis, for the responses are influenced by personal factors which the tests do not assess. We will discuss some limitations of these tests because in doing so we will touch upon facets of the self and of self-appraisal that are of general significance.

A person's responses to a self-assessment inventory, like his response to any opportunity for revealing himself, will be influenced by his *candor*.

[7] In several studies it has been found that self-ratings on tests such as those mentioned above show a considerable degree of consistency when scores on one rating are compared with scores obtained on the same test administered a few days or a few weeks later. ("Reliability coefficients" have ranged from the .50's to the .90's.)

He may respond with tongue in cheek, or answer all items as candidly as he can.

Responses to such inquiries will also be influenced by the person's attitudes toward the questions that are asked and the one who asks them.

Further, responses to the inquiries concerning a person's view of himself as compared with his view of others will be influenced to an undetermined degree by a desire to appear *consistent*. This can produce spurious results in the ways he rates both himself and others. For example, if I claim I am a friendly person it would be necessary, for the sake of consistency, to say that other people, likewise, tend to be friendly. To accuse *them* of being unfriendly would stamp *me* as being unfriendly.

The most serious problem in interpreting results from self-assessment instruments (or any kind of self-revelation) is that they will be influenced to an undetermined degree by a person's *insight*. No matter how frank adolescents are in revealing themselves they will differ greatly in the depths of their self-knowledge. This will differ in the degree to which they have tended to rationalize or critically examine their view of themselves. For example, a person who is vengeful and is aware of it may report that he is vengeful. Another who is equally vengeful may perceive himself as a person with a strong sense of justice, and deny any taint of vengefulness.

Major Themes in Self-Description

When young people describe themselves in their own words the characteristics they mention range from details of their physical appearance to sweeping descriptions of their personalities.

Among the characteristics adolescents name most frequently in assessing themselves are the following:

Physical: general appearance, height, weight, body build, and facial features, such as the eyes, nose, and hair.

Intellectual: such as having or not having a good ability to learn, think, reason, remember, or having or lacking curiosity.

Special talents: such as ability or lack of ability in music, dancing, the arts, and mechanics.

Interest and skill, or lack of skill, in sports and games.

Clothes and grooming, including taste in choosing clothes, hairdo, etc.

Performance in school and attitudes toward school.

Character traits and temperamental qualities, such as being easygoing or having a sense of humor.

Social attitudes and relationships, such as ability to get along with others.

The characteristics most frequently named by over a thousand adolescents in a study by the author (Jersild, 1952) fell under the headings of (a) *personality and character*, including moral qualities, inner resources, humor, poise, and emotional tendencies, and (b) *social attitudes and relationships*, including feelings about other persons. Self-descriptions under these headings were most numerous at all levels from the elementary grades through college. Students at the college level mentioned their intellectual qualities more often than those at the high school level, and this is to be expected. But even at the college level references to intellectual qualities were far less frequent than references to character and social attitudes.

The major themes adolescents emphasize cut across differences in age, sex, socioeconomic status, and intellectual ability. In describing themselves young people differ in the particular words they use and in the specific qualities they name, but they emphasize conditions people share in common much more than characteristics that set people apart. We have here what the author has called "the universal language of the self." As we move away from outer appearances and distinctions toward the inner dimensions of experience we enter a realm of fellowship such as seldom is achieved in overt conduct. The farther a person penetrates into the reaches of all that constitutes his experiences of himself the more he will identify qualities that he shares with others. The more a person realizes the nature of his own existence the more he will be capable of compassion for others.

SIGNS OF SELF-ACCEPTANCE

The adolescent who realistically accepts himself has a treasure. Within his own world, the one with meager talents who forthrightly appreciates what he has is richer than the one who is bountifully endowed but deplores himself.[8]

[8] Criteria for measuring self-acceptance and self-rejection have been described by Sheerer (1949), Spivack (1956), and in a number of other studies reviewed by Wylie (1961).

In many studies it has been assumed that a person is self-accepting to the degree that his professed "actual self" corresponds with what he claims as his "ideal self." If he says he is lazy and then claims that, for him, laziness is an ideal state, he is self-accepting on that item. On the other hand, he would receive a maximum self-rejection score on this item if he rates himself at one extreme in one response (he is lazy *all of the time*) and at the other extreme in the other (he wishes he were *never* lazy). This, however, is a superficial way of assessing self-acceptance. It suffers

The self-accepting person has a realistic appraisal of his resources combined with appreciation of his own worth; assurance about standards and convictions of his own without being a slave to the opinions of others; and realistic assessment of limitations without irrational self-reproach.

Self-accepting adolescents recognize their assets and are free to draw upon them even if they are not all that could be desired. They also recognize their shortcomings without needlessly blaming themselves. An adolescent basketball player might wish he were three inches taller. But he plays the game with the stature he has, without kicking himself for being unable to outjump the giants on the opposing team. He does not blame himself unreasonably by assuming he could be several inches taller if he had eaten the right foods, as though his height were entirely of his own making. Similarly, the self-accepting adolescent girl who is very tall will see advantages in being shorter; but she comes forth gracefully, she does not stoop as though apologizing for her height.

Among the outstanding characteristics of self-accepting adolescents are spontaneity and responsibility for self. They accept the qualities of their humanity without condemning themselves for conditions beyond their control. They do not see themselves as persons who should be above anger or fear or devoid of conflicting desires, free of human fallibility. They feel they have a right to have ideas, aspirations, and wishes of their own. They do not begrudge themselves the satisfactions of being alive.

SYMPTOMS OF SELF-REJECTION

Self-rejection includes chronic attitudes of self-disapproval and self-disparagement, self-distrust, feelings of being unworthy, not being deserving of satisfactions, reward, or success. In one of its most cruel forms, self-rejection includes severe guilt, viewing oneself as among the damned.

One sign of self-rejection is severe self-criticism, although self-criticism

---

from the underlying limitations of "self-concept" inventories that were discussed earlier in this chapter. It also rests on the dubious assumption that degree of self-acceptance can be computed by a simple process of arithmetic—so many points for each item on the test—as though items that are arithmetically equal are also psychologically equal. A person might, for example, say that he is very inartistic and wishes he were very artistic. He might also say that he is very unattractive to girls and wishes he were very attractive. He will receive the same maximum nonacceptance score on both these items, as though they counted equally, even though he does not give a second thought to his lack of artistic ability but is very much concerned about what he regards as his lack of attractiveness.

is not in itself an evidence of rejection. One mark of self-accepting persons is that they can detect and acknowledge their faults. Self-criticism is a sign of self-rejection when a person feels inferior according to a standard of appraisal that is patently incorrect, or when he deplores himself for failing to reach a standard of perfection no one could achieve.

We may suspect that adolescents are self-rejecting if they say all others are against them, view them unfairly, belittle and disapprove them. Such attitudes attributed to others may be a projection of attitudes they hold regarding themselves.[9]

Adolescents reject themselves when they automatically bow to the opinions and decisions of others, even though there is no basis for believing that the others are wiser. They show symptoms of self-rejection when they persistently judge themselves by a competitive standard as though they can feel worthy only if they surpass others.

Self-rejection also prevails when adolescents habitually strike a pose, pretending to be what they are or go out of their way to boast or to impress others. They reject themselves when they are self-destructive, plunge recklessly into one scrape after another, invite punishment or disgrace when there is nothing to gain and everything to lose.

The tragic thing about adolescents who severely reject themselves is that they often do things which cause others to confirm the low opinion they have of themselves. Deeper even than the tragedy of severe self-rejection is its pathos. The severaly self-rejecting adolescent is his own enemy. He has taken unto himself all the unkindness of his heredity and all the harshness of his environment, and then has added something more: everything is his fault and he is no good.

MASCULINITY AND FEMININITY
AS RELATED TO ATTITUDES TOWARD SELF

It appears in many respects to be more difficult for girls to formulate a clear and accepting view of their feminine identity than it is for boys to accept their masculinity.[10] In their upbringing there is more incentive for

[9] However, such a judgment about others is not necessarily a sign of self-rejection. An adolescent may correctly perceive that others are prejudiced against him and still remain convinced of his own worth (although this is not an easy thing to do). This conviction occurs, for example, when bright adolescents who ask penetrating questions in class are called "queers" by their associates but still cling to their right to raise questions.

[10] For discussions and findings dealing with this subject, see Lynn (1959), Komarovsky (1946), Wallin (1950), McKee and Sherriffs (1959).

boys to prefer to be boys than for girls to prefer to be girls. Boys have more privileges; they are less strictly supervised; they are not judged as severely as girls for misconduct; they are moving into a "man's" world.

Boys look forward to an occupation and financial independence. As girls reach and advance through adolescence, the major "occupation" many of them look forward to is marriage and motherhood; but according to convention it is the boy who chooses the girl rather than the girl who chooses the boy. It has been found that with increasing age, boys become more secure in their masculine role, while girls become less firmly identified with their feminine role. There are more girls who wish they were boys than boys who wish they were girls.

The issue of whether to be "feminine" according to prevailing stereotypes especially confronts the college girl. Unlike girls who drop out of school and settle down, more or less comfortably, as wives, the college girl faces conflicting alternatives. She faces what Komarovsky (1946) has described as the contradictory roles of being "feminine" in the traditional sense or being "modern." According to the "feminine" stereotype the girl devotes herself, more or less selflessly, to the prospect of being a wife and mother. The "modern" role, on the other hand, requires that women should regard themselves as free to assert themselves as the equals of males. Komarovsky found that many college women resolve the clash between the modern and feminine roles by pretending to be inferior when in the company of men, such as "playing dumb" when on a date, pretending ignorance of a subject, allowing the man to have the last word, and concealing academic honors which the girls had won.

In a study by Wallin (1950), which raised the same questions as Komarovsky's study, a large proportion (40 per cent or more) of college women reported that they had once or twice, several times, or very often pretended, when with men, to be inferior in artistic knowledge or taste or intellectually inferior ("played dumb" because they thought men preferred them that way) or had pretended to be athletically inferior when participating in a sport with men.

An important aspect of an adolescent's sex-role identification is to see himself as a potential mate. Full acceptance of this aspect of the sex role means that the young person sees himself actually or potentially as a person who can share not only physical but emotional intimacy with someone of the opposite sex whom he loves and trusts. But in their upbringing, many girls are taught to fear males and to distrust them (and many, as we will note later, actually have frightening or shocking experiences with males). Some girls also learn to resent males because of the privileges males receive. Such attitudes of fear, distrust, and resentment toward males represent an impairment of the girl's attitude toward herself as one who can wholeheartedly fulfill her feminine role.

THE BALANCE BETWEEN
SELF-ACCEPTANCE AND SELF-REJECTION

A number of questions arise in connection with adolescents' feelings about themselves. Does the typical adolescent tend to view himself favorably or unfavorably? How does he view adolescents as a group? Does he tend to give himself a higher or lower rating than he gives to others? Does he, in general, view himself more favorably or unfavorably than he is viewed by adults? As he moves from early through late adolescence is there a drift toward more or less self-acceptance?

Several studies have dealt with these questions. Unfortunately, the answers are inconclusive. Differing methods applied to differing populations have produced conflicting findings. Available findings indicate that the typical adolescent views himself with a blend of approval and disapproval, but the balance is more on the side of approval than disapproval (Spivack, 1956; Engel, 1959; Hess and Goldblatt, 1957). Some findings show an increase in self-acceptance with age (Spivack, 1956; Engel, 1959), while other findings show a different trend. Amatora (1957) found "a general downward trend" from age nine to age thirteen when youngsters made self-evaluations of a number of personality traits, but the trend was irregular. According to a study by Roff (1959) self-satisfaction declines through the adolescent period to the end of adolescence, when it rises slightly. From available evidence we cannot tell whether a normal sampling of adolescents, studied from year to year, would show a consistent upward or downward drift in self-approval.

Some studies show that young people tend to compare themselves more favorably with others in connection with some traits than in connection with other traits. Students who took part in a study conducted by Zazzo (1960) saw their peers as being socially more at ease, more stable, and generally more relaxed than themselves. On the other hand, Collignon (1960) found that a large proportion of youngsters, notably boys in an age range from eleven and a half to fifteen years, tended to view themselves as taller than they really were. Youngsters who attached the greatest importance to size as a feature of their total make-up tended to make the most marked errors in estimation of their own height.

Although adolescents value some traits more than others and tend to overestimate or underestimate themselves on some traits more than on others, an adolescent's self-ratings of particular traits generally regarded as desirable are likely to be more similar than dissimilar. For example, if he gives himself a favorable rating in assessing his mental characteristics, he also is likely to give himself a favorable rating when assessing his personality traits or his social relationships (Taschuk, 1957). However, ratings are more similar in some areas of self-perception than in others. In a study of ninth-graders, there was a higher degree of correspondence between self-ratings of mental and social traits than between self-ratings of mental and physical characteristics.

In a study by Brandt (1958) sixth-graders and eleventh-graders estimated how well they would do on a variety of academic and physical tasks and they estimated how well they were regarded by their peers. These estimates were then compared with their actual performance on a number of tests and their social reputation as rated by their peers. Brandt found that if a youngster is biased in one direction (such as overestimating himself) in his self-rating in one area (such as academic achievement) he tends to be biased in the same direction in other areas. "Whether an individual is accurate or inaccurate seems to depend more on his self-structure than on the specific nature of the perceived characteristic" (p. 87). Although a majority of the youngsters gave themselves higher ratings in one performance (such as spelling) than in another (such as strength of grip), one-fourth of them consistently either overrated or underrated themselves. According to Brandt this emphasizes the need for considering "major aspects of the total self-concept, rather than isolated bits of it" when we try to understand youngsters.

Available evidence also suggests that trends in self-evaluation will vary among people in different segments of the population and will be influenced by circumstances which require them to take a critical look at themselves.

An interesting study of a selected sampling of young people is reported by Sanford (1957) who obtained data regarding Vassar girls as they moved from the freshman through the senior year, and beyond. Sanford states that his research has shown that Vassar College seniors, "*on the average,* are more unstable or 'upset,' more uncertain about themselves and about life than are freshmen." The seniors reported more disturbance than the freshmen in a variety of ways, such as more depression, self-criticism, anxiety and doubt, and consciousness of conflict. A part of the picture of greater instability in seniors is "due in part to their greater ability to report the difficulties that they have" and "it is all of a piece with their better education and greater maturity." As compared with freshmen, according to Sanford, "seniors are more 'liberated.' They are more assertive, rebellious, adventurous; less passive, less submissive; they have greater breadth of consciousness, more self-insight, more familiarity with their inner life." The senior also faces the near prospect of having to leave the protection of academic life and having to "get ready to 'face the world' " and to "make crucially important decisions." She faces this prospect at a time when "She has let go the external controls she relied on as a freshman, but inner controls are still in process of formation."

These observations regarding college seniors cannot be regarded as applying to the typical young woman, or the typical college woman, as she moves from late adolescence into early adulthood.[11] However, they emphasize the differences between objective and subjective dimensions of a young person's life. From an objective point of view, the college seniors in Sanford's study had many reasons for feeling complacent about themselves: they were bright; they were about to graduate from a college that ranks high in prestige; the main hurdles of adolescence were behind them. For almost four years they had weathered rigorous academic requirements. But instead of feeling serene about these things many of them apparently were challenged to examine themselves. A person who has enough insight to question herself but has not yet found the answers is not likely to be very complacent. Her score on one of the conventional self-concept tests is likely to be less favorable than the score of one who has less insight and is not inclined to question.

ADOLESCENTS' AND ADULTS' VIEWPOINTS

Some studies indicate a discrepancy between the way in which adolescents view themselves and the way they think their elders view them. In a study by Hess and Goldblatt (1957) adolescents predicted that their elders would rate them lower than the elders actually did. The adolescents apparently believed that the average adult has a tendency to depreciate teen-agers. This study also found a discrepancy between the way in which parents think adolescents will rate themselves and the way adolescents actually did rate themselves. The findings indicate that "parents believe

[11] Elsewhere in this book we will review findings which indicate that the effects of four years in college seem to vary considerably in different colleges and do not generally lead to as much soul-searching as Sanford found in his group.

that teen-agers have unrealistically high opinions of themselves" (p. 467),
but this belief was not corroborated by the data obtained from adolescents
themselves.

Emphasis on Conformity and Social Stereotypes

Typical adolescents place great emphasis on social conformity when
assessing themselves. This is not surprising. Adolescents who are nonconformist run the risk of being outcasts. They are not alone in this for adults
likewise emphasize conformity. Even such concepts as "emotional adjustment" and "mental health" are frequently defined primarily in terms of
social conformity.[12]

To achieve the status of independent adults, it is necessary for adolescents to conform within prudent limits, but it is also necessary for them
to be nonconformists. Nonconformity linked with a healthy course of
development is a form of courage: the courage to be and to become.
When an adolescent is rebellious because that is the only way he can grow
in self-direction, he is showing courage. But an adolescent (reflecting the
attitudes of adults around him) is more likely to view such rebellion as
a fault than to feel proud about being a rebel in a good cause.

There are other facets of their worth which adolescents commonly
regard in sub-rosa fashion. The course of their sexual development is filled
with vexations, but much happens also that they properly can regard
with pride. Some of them do so in the privacy of their own thoughts.
Many girls feel a glow of pride, for example, when they have their first
menstruation (Landis, Landis, and Bolles, 1940). But few report this
glow when they tell about themselves.

A policy of keeping their self-professed weaknesses within the bounds
of respectability appears in what adolescents report about their attitudes
toward sex. When over a thousand adolescents of junior, senior, and college age told what they liked or disliked about themselves in a study by
the author (1952), not a single one directly professed any self-depreca-
tion in the area of sex. Yet we know from other sources that most adolescents have had sexual experiences of one sort or another and that at least
some of them feel guilty or uneasy about their sexual desires.[13]

There are other ways in which the accounts adolescents give of them-

[12] The tests and inventories that have been devised for self-description likewise,
to a large degree, measure claimed conventionality rather than psychological insight.

[13] Inventories that have been used in studies of the "self-concept" usually touch
upon sex obliquely, if at all. The main reason for this is not that psychologists who
devise such instruments are sexless creatures but that a self-assessment inventory
dealing frankly with sex would probably be banned.

selves echo social stereotypes. Many adolescents mention their tendency to get angry when reporting what they deplore in themselves. But rarely does an adolescent (unless closely questioned) express pride in his free-dom to feel angry and to show it when anger is justified. When describing what they regard as their faults they are far more likely to name specific manifestations than to acknowledge a more pervasive condition of weak-ness. In this respect, again, they reflect their elders.[14]

The foregoing discussion is not meant to belittle what adolescents *do* say about themselves; what they say is significant as far as it goes. It is meant rather to point to what they ordinarily *do not* report when they informally tell about themselves or when they respond to the typical self-assessment inventory. What they report is patterned on the conven-tional, censored, and rather superficial model of self-assessment which prevails among adults. No one in particular can be blamed for this. We cannot expect an adolescent to be more profound than his elders. How-ever, in the process, adolescents do themselves an injustice, both in not disclosing the nature of the predicaments of life that underlie their limita-tions and in not revealing the depths of their resources.

[14] In a study by the writer and his associates (1962) it was noted that many teachers acknowledged several symptoms of anxiety, but then denied that they were "anxious": many reported symptoms of a competitive attitude but then denied they were "competitive."

part two | Physical Aspects of Development

Chapter 3

The Course
and Genesis
of Growth

The most important single event in adolescent development occurs in the changes that take place in the young person's body. Before these changes occur the adolescent *is* a child; after they have occurred the young person can *have* a child.

Some of the physical changes are spectacular. The boy may grow as much as four inches or more in a single year (Stolz and Stolz, 1951). Some changes are dramatic. One day the girl is a child; the next day she has her first menstruation, and she is a woman. Although her first menstruation is the culmination of changes that have been going on for a long period of time, for her it is a sudden occurrence.

The timing and extent of these changes are unpredictable, from the adolescent's point of view. An authority on physical growth may be able to foretell, with considerable accuracy, how long young adolescents will continue to grow. But adolescents themselves seldom have such knowledge. And even with a great amount of knowledge much would remain unforeseeable—the profile of the new face, the pitch and timbre of the changed voice, the distribution and texture of the boy's beard, the size of his buttocks and genitals, the size and contours of the girl's breasts.

The aura of the unknown is increased by the fact that bodily changes are extremely variable when youngsters are compared with one another. One boy acquires manly characteristics while a companion remains smallish and boyish for another two years. In the meantime, the late-maturing boy may worry and wonder what is wrong with him. A girl reaches the menarche at eleven while one of her friends may not face this event until five years later.

Girls as a group outpace the boys in their physical development. The typical eighth-grade girl is physically more nearly on a par with tenth-grade boys than with the boys in her own class. Even here, however, is a further complication, for although the average girl in the early teens is biologically more mature than the average boy, the boy is more precocious in his sexual behavior.

The physical changes have important psychological repercussions as youngsters adapt themselves to their changing bodies and to the upsurge in their sexual capacities. The boy, while still so young that it seems incongruous to picture him as a father, becomes a potential mate. The girl has the figure of a woman while scarcely yet accustomed to her new clothes.

The period when physical changes are at their peak in adolescence is frequently called the awkward age. While this is not a graceful way to speak of young people, there is some truth in it. It takes time for adolescents to get used to their new equipment and to adjust to changes in their body proportions. Some adolescents go through a period when they cannot walk "naturally," and it is as though they once more have to learn the art of locomotion.

Even attributes that normally are regarded as desirable may cause embarrassment. The girl with a shapely bosom is likely for a time to be self-conscious about it. Her self-consciousness is increased when she thinks the boys are staring at her (and when she thinks this, she probably is right). A boy whose genitals have grown rapidly may be embarrassed at the thought that others are noticing them. He is especially likely to become self-conscious if he becomes tumescent at awkward moments, such as while standing before the class.

Changes in Height and Weight

Most boys and girls show a spurt in growth during adolescence. During the years immediately preceding the beginning of the growth spurt, children usually grow at a fairly even rate, and in many instances just prior to the spur may show a decline in their rate of growth. Then there is a remarkable increase in the velocity of growth, followed by a period of diminished rate, with gradually lower increments until mature height is achieved.

The age at which this growth cycle occurs varies with different children. This cycle is part of the larger constellation of physical change associated with puberty. Its time and course are more closely associated with certain other changes connected with puberty than with chronological age. In a study of 102 boys over a period of many years Stolz and Stolz (1951) found that the onset of puberal growth, as defined by them, began at ages ranging from 10.4 years to 15.75 years with an average of 12.88 years. The age at which the boys reached the end of the puberal growth period ranged from 13.10 to 17.50 years with an average of 15.33 years.

Some relationships between the rate of growth and comparative size and the onset of menstruation in girls are shown in Figure 3.1. Some of these groups of girls underwent a considerable shift in average height.

	Rank Order in Average Height from Tallest to Shortest		
Age at First Menstruation	Age 10 years	13½ years	17 years
A: before 11.5 years	B	B	E
B: 11.6 to 11.11	C	C	C
C: 12.0 to 12.5	A	E	B
D: 12.6 to 12.11	E	D	F
E: 13.0 to 13.5	D	A	D
F: 13.6 to 13.11	F	F	H
G: 14.0 to 14.5	G	G	G
H: After 14.5	H	H	A

Fig. 3.1. Comparative average height of girls, grouped according to age of first menstruation when measured at the age of 10 years, 13½ years, and 17 years (Adapted from F. K. Shuttleworth, *Sexual Maturation and the Physical Growth of Girls Age Six to Nineteen*, Monographs of the Society for Research in Child Development (1937), 11, No. 12, Fig. 11, p. 27).

A further indication of rate of growth in height as related to menarcheal age is given in Figure 3.2. Examples of patterns of growth in height are given in Figures 3.3 and 3.4.

In repeated measurements of boys from the age of six to the age of twenty Richey (1937) found that the period of most rapid growth in stature began a little before maturity (as indicated by the appearance of hair in the armpits) and continued through the puberal year.

One question that frequently concerns parents as well as growing

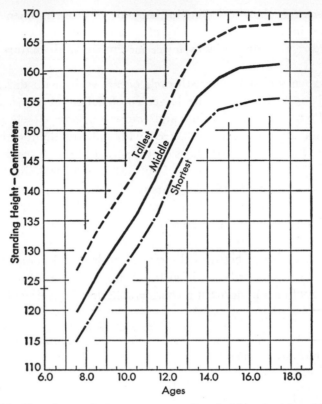

Fig. 3.2. Growth trends in average standing height of girls with the same menarcheal age, 13–0 to 13–5 (From F. K. Shuttleworth, *Sexual Maturation and the Physical Growth of Girls, Age Six to Nineteen,* Monographs of the Society for Research in Child Development (1937), 2, No. 5).

children (especially boys who are short and girls who fear they will grow too tall) is what their ultimate height is likely to be. Individual variations in the pattern of growth are so pronounced that it is hazardous to generalize from averages to individual cases, yet there are some trends that are of interest in connection with this question.

On the average, girls who are tall as preadolescent children tend to reach the menarche at an earlier age than girls who are short. They also enter the adolescent growth spurt at an earlier age. At least for a time, accordingly, such girls are tall compared with many other girls of their own age. However, ultimate stature cannot be predicted with any assurance on the basis of the height a girl happens to have reached at a particular time while the growth process is still continuing. A relatively tall girl of twelve who is sexually "mature" may be outstripped by a girl of

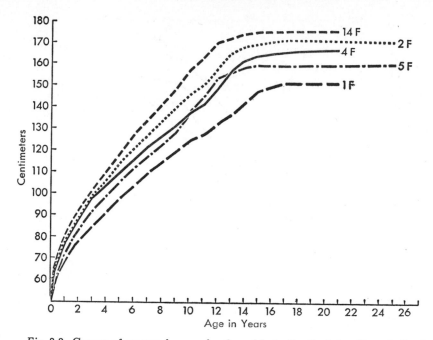

Fig. 3.3. Curves of stature by age for five girls in the Berkeley Growth Study, including the tallest female in the group (14F), the shortest, and three girls of intermediate height (From N. Bayley, "Individual Patterns of Development," *Child Development* (1956), 27, 1, p. 63).

similar age and size or even a somewhat shorter girl of similar age who is "immature" and has not yet had the full benefit of the growth spurt.

Among girls who reach the menarche at the same age, those who were tallest during earlier years are likely to continue to be taller through the adolescent years and at maturity.

There is a high correspondence between the comparative height of boys at the beginning and at the end of the puberal growth cycle. Stolz and Stolz (1951) found a correlation of .819 between the height of boys at the onset and at the end of the puberal period. This is a very impressive correlation; yet it also means that many shifts would occur if the boys were arranged in the order of their height, from the tallest to the shortest at the beginning of the period, and rearranged again in order of height at the end. The fact that boys nonetheless show a very marked tendency to remain tall or short appears from other data in the Stolz study. For example, there were thirteen boys (in one group of eighty-three) who were shorter at the end of the puberal growth cycle than some of the boys in the group were at the beginning.

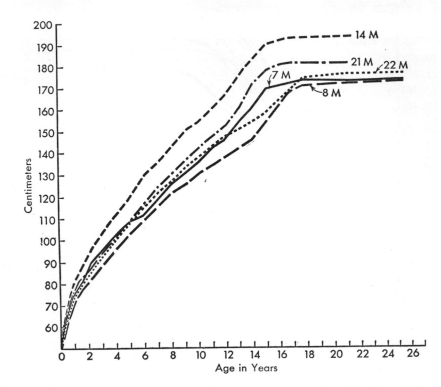

Fig. 3.4. Curves of stature by age for five boys in the Berkeley Growth Study, including the tallest male in the group (14M), the shortest, and three boys of intermediate height (From N. Bayley, "Individual Patterns of Development," *Child Development* (1956), 27, 1, p. 62).

SEX DIFFERENCES
IN HEIGHT AND WEIGHT

During the early years of life boys surpass girls in height and, as a matter of common observation, the average adult male is several inches taller than the average female. However, there is a period in adolescence during which girls are slightly taller than boys of similar age and family background. The average girl for a time also is heavier than the average boy, but then the growth curves cross each other and boys continue to make large gains after the curve for girls has begun to taper off.

Changes in Bodily Proportions

Different parts of the body grow at different rates, and achieve their maximum size at different times. At the time of birth, for example, a child's head length constitutes a far longer proportion of his total body length than at maturity. At birth his legs are comparatively shorter than they will be at maturity. The trunk is relatively longer at birth than are the thighs and the legs. Similarly, the trunk is relatively longer than are the arms. Differing growth rates such as the foregoing illustrate two principles that can be observed in the child's development almost from the time of conception, namely that growth tends to proceed in a *cephalo-caudal* direction (from the head toward the tail) and in a *proximodistal* direction (from the main stem to the extremities).

RELATION OF BODY BUILD
TO RATE OF SEXUAL MATURATION

Early-maturing boys tend to have broad hips and narrow shoulders, while late-maturing boys tend to be characteristically slender-hipped and (comparatively) long-legged (Bayley, 1943). Late-maturing girls tend to have broad shoulders. In other words, the boy who matures earlier veers somewhat toward the body build of girls (who, as a group, mature earlier than boys), while the late-maturing girl veers somewhat toward the masculine build (broad shoulders). Bayley points out that this does not mean, however, that the early-maturing boy is more feminine or the late-maturing girl more masculine in the total trend and direction of their development.

Skeletal Growth

There are interesting relationships between the development of the skeleton and other physical developments at the onset of puberty. As a child matures, bone structures that at first were soft and cartilaginous become more "osseous," more "bony," dense, hard and brittle. X-ray pictures have been used to study this process of ossification, or hard-bone formation. Among areas that have been singled out for study are the wrist, hand, foot, elbow, knee, hip, and shoulder (see *e.g.,* Flory, 1936a, and Todd, 1937).

Examinations of bone development provide ratings of what is called "skeletal age." The typical six-year-old has a "skeletal age" of six. Children of the same chronological age, however, differ considerably in skeletal age. One six-year-old may have bone structure that is characteristic of a seven-year-old. His chronological age is six, but his skeletal age is seven. Another six-year-old's bone development may not have gone beyond what is normal at age five. His skeletal age is five.

Skeletal age is closely related to growth in size. According to Bayley: "At a given skeletal age we may say that a child has achieved a given proportion of his eventual adult body dimensions. Consequently, mature size can be predicted with fair accuracy if a child's present size and skeletal age are known" (Bayley, 1943, p. 45).

Skeletal age likewise gives a better prediction than chronological age of the onset of puberty in girls, as indicated by first menstruation (Todd, 1930).

Girls are more advanced than boys in skeletal development at birth, and they continue more advanced during childhood. When they enter elementary school, they are about one year ahead of boys. At the time they enter high school they are about two years ahead of the boys (Flory, 1936).

There is a relationship between skeletal maturity and a variety of other factors, such as strength, motor ability, and body build (Bayley, 1941; Bayley and Jones, 1941).

Fatty Tissues and Fat Deposits

For a time during adolescence boys and girls differ considerably in the development of adipose (fat-bearing) tissue. A study by Reynolds (1951) offers interesting information on this subject. Reynolds obtained repeated x-ray measurements of the thickness of fat layers in various areas of the bodies of boys and girls during a twelve-year period beginning when the children were six-and-a-half years old. During a period prior to and including the middle teens (12.5 to 15.5 years) boys showed a drop while girls showed a continuing gain in cumulative volume of fat in six areas of the body. In the period from 15.5 to 17.5 years, boys showed a gain and girls a loss in these same areas. But girls maintained a considerably higher ratio of fat into the late teens (using averages at 6.5 years as a standard of 100, the total breadth of fat layers in six areas of the body rose to 136 in boys and 162 in girls at the age of 17.5 years).[1]

The differences between boys and girls when at their peak are especially marked in some areas of the body, including the region where the upper thigh has its largest girth and the chest at the nipple level. Beyond the middle teens the differences become less marked, although the average mature girl has a larger proportion of fat than the average mature boy.

Girls show this "rounding of the figure" more than boys, but many boys for a time have increased deposits of fat in various areas of their bodies. In some boys not only is there a transient swelling of the breasts but there may be a slight secretion (Greulich et al., 1938). Enlarged breasts, if noticeable, may be embarrassing to boys. They become acutely embarrassing if they are so large that they bob up and down when a boy walks or runs. Wattenberg (1955) gives a poignant example of a boy with this difficulty; the boy was jeered by his schoolmates and was so mortified that he had himself excused from physical education classes.

A large proportion of boys have, for a time, what Stolz and Stolz (1951) have called "male-inappropriate" fat deposits in the breasts, thighs, and lower part of the trunk. They estimate that at least 50 per cent of boys for a time show an increase in girdle-fat. Temporary fat deposits in the genital area which make a boy's penis seem shorter than it actually is are likely to add to a boy's feeling of inadequacy about his manliness.

The amount and distribution of fat in an adolescent's body is complicated from both a physical and a psychological point of view. An obvious cause of being fat is eating too much fat-producing food. But there is not a one-to-one relationship between food intake and fatness. Some people "eat like a horse" and stay slim, others get fat. Moreover, a person cannot control where he will bulge the most just by eating more or less food. Some people get fat all over. Some "lay on fat" in the midriff, others in the thighs. Some have an "underslung" build and others an "overslung" build. Some are rather slim, but have fat legs.

Differences in contours appear among persons whether they eat much or little. They are probably due to genetic factors. Because of this, an adolescent who tries to control his or her weight faces a complicated

[1] The correlations between total fat breadth and total weight were as follows at 11.5 and 15.5 years:

Age Level	Boys	Girls
11.5 years	.74	.71
15.5 years	.69	.91

problem. When a girl who has fat thighs but is slim elsewhere goes on a diet, she may impair rather than improve her general appearance, for while she is reducing her thigh girth her face may have a thin and drawn look.

There is a further complication, for the size of a particular part of the body which seems "fat" may be due not to fat but to the size of other tissues. This is brought out in the study by Reynolds (1950). The bodily contours are determined to varying degrees by fat, muscle, and bone and the shape of the skeleton; and adolescents vary in the proportions of total body-weight consisting of fat, muscle, and bone. Due to differences in bone structure, a girl who looks very "hippy" may actually have a thinner layer of fat than other girls who have a narrower bone structure and look slimmer. As a result of varying proportions of muscle, fat, and bone tissue, standard height-weight tables may be very misleading when applied to a given individual. "There are fat 'under-weight' children and lean 'over-weight' children" (Garn, 1960, p. 31).

PSYCHOLOGICAL IMPLICATIONS OF OBESITY

Obesity has many psychological as well as biochemical facets. In our culture, and in many other cultures, slimness is admired and obesity is deplored. The idea that a roly-poly person is jovial and serene is probably more a fiction and pretense than a fact. One writer has expressed this view by saying, "Imprisoned in every fat man a thin one is wildly signaling to be let out." The same would perhaps be even more true for a fat woman or a fat girl.

Obesity is often viewed as something funny; but from the obese person's own point of view, it is likely to be far more pathetic than funny. Rightly or wrongly, the fat person is likely to blame himself for being the way he is—he eats too much; he should control his diet. Then when he keeps on devouring food and remains as fat as ever, he is likely to have feelings of guilt and self-contempt.[2] There is nothing funny about that.

The remedy does not seem to be simply to prescribe a rigid diet or reducing pills. His propensity for overeating may have profound psychological roots which no simple prescription will remove. Overeating has

---

[2] According to Garn (1960, p. 27), there are six chances out of ten that the fat adolescent "will eat a broad path directly into fat adulthood."

many psychological meanings. Some people apparently overeat to allay anxiety. For some girls obesity is a kind of protection. While deploring their unattractiveness they also may use this unattractiveness as a means of shielding themselves from "men and sex and the responsibilities of adult womanhood which they dread even more than the disgrace of being fat" (Bruch, 1947, p. 376). Some apparently overeat as a way of grasping all they can get. Some seem to be resigned to the idea that the only gratification life can offer them is the pleasure of eating.

When these influences prevail, a young person is not simply facing the transient problem of a temporary increase in fat deposits during adolescence, but a more basic personality problem. A condition of obesity which is linked with self-contempt is rooted in compulsions that perpetuate the self-contempt. Instead of being the butt of jests and jokes, such a person needs sympathy and help.[3]

Heredity and Adolescence

The course and outcomes of an adolescent's development are determined by an interaction between his genetic endowment and the nurture and experiences provided by his environment. When he began life as a single cell he possessed biochemical substances, known as genes, which are the basis of heredity. These genes play a crucial role in determining the nature and course of his development. Interaction between a person's genetic endowment and the environment begins the moment he is conceived. His potential nature requires nurture from the beginning, even in the womb.

Although heredity has a vital bearing on each person's life, it has been far more often ignored than emphasized in studies of adolescents. One reason perhaps is that investigators regard a person's genetic endowment as something belonging to the past about which not much can be done. Another reason is that the influences of genetic and environmental factors are so intertwined, notably in the psychological sphere, that it is difficult to disentangle them. The fact that it is difficult to trace the influence of heredity helps to explain but obviously does not justify the widespread policy of ignoring genetic factors.

[3] The plight of the excessively fat person from a psychological point of view has been discussed in a revealing way by Bruch (1940, 1947). Bruch describes life situations and emotional experiences that provoke an increased desire for food, leading to obesity. She notes that unfortunate experiences may lead genetically predisposed persons to face their problems by overeating (1940).

GENOTYPES AND PHENOTYPES

In addition to all that shows forth in their appearance and conduct adolescents have latent genetic potentialities. Some of these may become apparent at a later time. Some never become apparent but can be transmitted to their children. The term *phenotype* denotes all that shows, all that is manifest, in an individual's make-up. The term *genotype* denotes the person's total genetic endowment, both manifest and latent.

In early adolescence a boy's phenotype has no whiskers. But in due time he grows whiskers. These are part of his genetic endowment. Until his beard shows, his phenotype is whiskerless, but his genotype is whiskered.

A person's phenotype represents the outcome, in his particular case, of the action of his genes, their interaction with each other, and their interaction with his environment. Some aspects of the phenotype are unchanging, others are fluid, modifiable, and compounded by many forces. At a given time a person's phenotype may include long legs because he inherited genes that produced long legs, a body that is thin because he is not eating enough, and a sour disposition due to the fact that he has just failed to get something he wants. His genotype is usually more stable, permanent and unchangeable.

The genetic factors which can produce a discrepancy between an adolescent's phenotype and genotype are complex and intricate. To describe them would fill a whole book, but we will touch briefly on some of them.[4]

The genes that generate hereditary characteristics may be *dominant* or *recessive*. Dominant genes usually prevail over the recessive ones, but the recessive ones are not lost. Their effects may appear in a later combination. Among the genes that determine eye color, for example, the brown determiners are usually dominant over those that might produce blue. Accordingly, when his father has a pure strain of brown and his mother a pure strain of blue, the child will have brown eyes. But this child will have the genes for blue eyes in his germ plasm. If now this person mates with another of similar hereditary background several combinations are possible in *their* offspring. The child might inherit brown elements from both parents. Then the resulting phenotype is brown and so is the geno-

---

[4] Some readers no doubt are familiar with this material. Others may wish to go more deeply into it. Recommended references are Ausubel (1958), Boyd (1953), Kallman (1953), and Montagu (1959).

type. Or he might inherit brown from one parent and blue from the other; the resulting phenotype is brown, but the genotype contains both brown and blue. Or he might inherit elements of blue from both parents; and then the phenotype and genotype are both blue.

In connection with many other traits, there likewise may be an exact or a close correspondence, or a discrepancy between the genotype and the phenotype.

The concordance or discrepancy between phenotype and genotype is influenced by many other factors. Many characteristics are determined by multiple genes. In the case of height, for example, the ramifications are quite complicated, for an individual's total height is influenced by sets of genes which determine the length of his legs, thighs, trunk, neck, and head. Through various chance combinations of these genes it is possible for parents and their children, and for brothers or sisters, to have exactly the same height or to differ considerably.

The element of chance is diminished somewhat by the fact that height is influenced to some degree by "selective breeding." A child with a tall mother is more likely than not to have a father who also is tall, since tall women generally prefer mates who are as tall as themselves. Likewise, a child with a short father is likely also to have a short mother, for men in our culture generally prefer to mate with women who are not taller than they. Such selective mating during several generations would tend to produce "pure" strains of tallness and shortness and a close correspondence between phenotypes and genotypes. But other conditions that produce diversity are at work, including the fact that persons of all statures are not completely averse to choosing mates who are shorter or taller than themselves.

A diversity between the genotype and the phenotype can be serious if a person has a phenotype that is "normal" and healthy but a genotype which includes hereditary weaknesses.

Genes differ not only in dominance and recessiveness, and in their interaction with one another, but also in their degree of dominance and recessiveness. There are some genes, or sets of genes, that almost invariably dominate and others that do not.

Among the special conditions which genes produce with varying degrees of dominance and recessiveness are certain allergies, certain blood types and blood deficiencies, many conditions connected with the hair (such as pattern of baldness), susceptibility to certain forms of mental illness, predisposition to rheumatic fever.

INTERACTIONS BETWEEN GENETIC
AND ENVIRONMENTAL FACTORS
PRIOR TO ADOLESCENCE

Many lines of evidence support the dictum that "the child is the father of the man." When we ask how this fatherhood comes about, we face the fact that each adolescent's personality emerges from interaction between his heredity and his environment. In this interaction there is a three-fold influence: first, the environment can enhance or impair development; second, his inherited qualities influence his response to his environment; and third, his inborn tendencies influence the way others respond to him and thus influence his environment.

Many inherited characteristics, which are determined by the genes, are apparent at birth or soon thereafter, but others do not become apparent until later in childhood and adolescence, and some are not manifested until a person reaches old age.

From the time of birth, healthy babies show distinct marks of individuality which cannot be explained by any known factor in their environment. During the first few days they show characteristic differences in the intensity and tempo of their response to stimulation (Birns, 1962). As the weeks go by, one baby is characteristically active, another passive; one tends to be placid, another irritable. Children also differ in their sensitivity, the vigor of their demands, the extent to which they actively respond to human contacts, and in many other ways. As described by Shirley (1933) each baby is born with a "tough core" of temperamental qualities.[5] Each individual's personality has its physiological basis in the structure and organization of the nervous system and in the physical-chemical constitution of the body as a whole (Shirley, 1933).

A child's temperamental qualities are manifested in his response to his environment but they also shape his environment.[6] We see this when a baby who is actively responsive elicits a smile from others (who thus reinforce his good cheer), while a fretful and fussy baby elicits concern

[5] For studies dealing with this, see Gesell (1928), Shirley (1933), Blatz and Millichamp (1937), Buhler (1952), Chess, Thomas and Birch (1959), Berezin (1959), and Birns (1962).

[6] Mothers frequently find that the practices they used in caring for one baby have to be modified considerably in caring for another. A study by Berezin (1959) describes ways in which boarding mothers who have two or more infants in their care (awaiting adoption) have to adapt their methods of "mothering" to the individual characteristics of each infant.

and perhaps even anxiety in his mother (who thus may reinforce the child's fretfulness).

By the time youngsters reach adolescence, their original tendencies are so overlaid with the outcomes of their interaction with the environment that it is practically impossible for one who does not know their family background, and has not studied them since infancy, to surmise what these original tendencies might be.

INTERACTION BETWEEN GENETIC AND ENVIRONMENTAL FACTORS DURING ADOLESCENCE

Many facets of the adolescent's heredity do not appear until adolescent years. Genetic factors influence an adolescent's physical development (e.g., the rate of skeletal development, the onset of the menarche, the profusion of body hair, the timing and pattern of the "growth spurt," height, physique, the distribution of fatty tissue).[7] These physical changes influence the adolescent's perception of himself and the way others react to him.

Heredity and Height

Tables 1 and 2 show findings obtained in comparisons between the heights of parents and children. The first table is based on repeated measurements of the same children over a period of many years by Bayley (1954). "Mid-parent" height was computed by a formula which expressed, in one measure, the heights of both parents.

Table 2, from a study by Eichorn (1959), offers a kind of information that is very rare in developmental psychology, and it is included even though it deals with young children and adults rather than adolescents. The parents had been measured repeatedly from the time they were children until the time they were adults, and the children of these parents were measured repeatedly in infancy and during a five-year period.

The findings by Bayley and Eichorn indicate the importance of heredity as a factor in determining height. Bayley's study showed that the resemblances between parents and children in relative height are likely to be larger at the time the youngsters reach childhood and adolescence than at the time of infancy. While heredity is the "great master" in determin-

[7] Numerous studies dealing with genetic factors in physical development have been reviewed by Davenport (1923) and by Tanner (1955).

TABLE 3.1

CORRELATION BETWEEN MID-PARENT HEIGHTS AND
HEIGHTS OF THEIR CHILDREN *

Age	Boys		Girls	
	Number	Correlation	Number	Correlation
6 months	32	.35	29	.61
2 years	27	.36	23	.66
10 years	24	.60	24	.59
18 years	21	.58	17	.76
18 years	21		17	
	(father-sons)	.52	(father-daughters)	.64
	(mother-sons)	.44	(mother-daughters)	.52

* Adapted in abridged form from Nancy Bayley, "Some Increasing Parent-Child Similarities During the Growth of Children," *Journal of Educational Psychology* (1954), 45, 1–21. Reproduced by permission.

ing physical growth (Krogman, 1962), poor nutrition may prevent a person from reaching his full growth potential.

Other Manifestations of Heredity

More directly, in the psychological sphere, there is evidence that certain forms of mental illness which are not, in many cases, clearly manifested until a person begins to undergo the stresses of adolescent or adult life, may be influenced by heredity.[8]

As we will note in a later chapter, there are also certain intellectual attributes which more clearly show the influence of genetic factors when youngsters reach adolescence than was true in earlier years.

IMPORTANCE OF TAKING ACCOUNT
OF AN ADOLESCENT'S HEREDITY

There are several reasons why it is essential to consider the influence of heredity in adolescent development. Although we cannot change the

[8] A predisposition to the psychological illness diagnosed as schizophrenia, for example, which often is not clearly manifest until the teens or later, appears to be strongly influenced by genetic factors. When one member of a twin pair is afflicted, the chances are many times greater that the other also will be afflicted if the twins are identical (one-egg, uniovular—sharing the same genetic substance) than if the twins are non-identical (springing from two separate fertilized eggs) (Kallman, 1953; Slater, 1951). The greater likelihood that two identical twins will similarly be afflicted prevails even if the identical twins have been separated and have lived in different environments. See also Gottesman (1962).

TABLE 3.2

TWO-GENERATION SIMILARITIES IN HEIGHT
DURING THE FIRST FIVE YEARS *

Age in Months	Number	Correlation: Children and Parents as Children	Correlation: Children and Parents as Adults	Correlation: Parents as Children and as Adults
3–8	30	.18	.29	.61
9–14	29	.19	.12	.66
15–20	17	.52	.49	.69
21–30	24	.31	.40	.65
31–42	27	.27	.40	.66
43–53	18	.22	.39	.68
55–66	18	.67	.67	.83

* Adapted from Dorothy H. Eichorn, "Two-Generation Similarities in Weight, Height and Weight/Height During the First Five Years." Reported at Twenty-fifth Anniversary Meeting, Society for Research in Child Development, National Institutes of Health, Bethesda, Md., March 10, 1959. Reproduced by permission.

seeds from which adolescents sprang, much can be done to help adolescents to maximize their potentialities. Much can also be done to help the young people themselves—and their parents and teachers—acquire a realistic attitude toward inherited resources and limitations.

It is far more humane to have wholesome respect for heredity than to pretend it does not exist. Such respect can help to spare adolescents from blaming themselves, or being blamed by others, for conditions over which they have little or no control, such as early or late maturing, their physique, rate of growth in height. A proper regard for heredity can also help to relieve adolescents with inborn physical handicaps from the severe self-reproach some of them visit upon themselves.[9]

When the writer was an adolescent, one of his closest companions became ill with diabetes. This boy and his parents did not know that diabetes may be a genetic disorder, and insulin treatment had not yet been discovered. The illness was called "sugar sickness," and everyone in the community thought it came from eating too many sweets. So the boy wasted away and died "because" he had eaten too many sweets, and his parents had not prevented it. Here was tragedy compounded by guilt. The same self-accusations would not arise now that the nature of this illness, and the way to ameliorate it, are better understood.

[9] Youngsters suffering from physical disabilities or ailments, whether due to genetic weaknesses or unavoidable misfortunes, frequently blame themselves for their afflictions (Gips, 1956).

Today there undoubtedly are other afflictions, including afflictions in the sphere of personality development, for which people blame themselves and are blamed by others, which eventually may be found to be rooted in the inherited biochemical substance of those who suffer. Therefore it is essential to have a sober respect for the role an adolescent's genetic endowment has played and continues to play in determining what he is able to take from his environment and what he is able to bring to it. It is essential also to have a sober respect for what the environment can do to further or to impair the adolescent's welfare. Such respect is far more realistic and compassionate than an extreme environmentalist or an extreme hereditarian point of view.

SIGNIFICANCE OF KNOWLEDGE OF GENETICS FOR ADOLESCENTS

The author has observed, as student and teacher, that many adolescents are keenly interested in genetics from a personal point of view. They can relate some of the information to themselves. They can also weigh its meaning when they are looking for a prospective mate. The interplay between genetics and environmental factors is so intricate that no adolescent can foresee what a merger between his or her genes and those of another might bring forth. However, information about genetics may be helpful in assessing obvious signs of genetically influenced strengths or weaknesses.

The Body Image and Self-Evaluation

The adolescent's body and his physical traits have an important bearing on his picture of himself and on his idea of how he appears in the eyes of others. The effects of changes in size, build and strength, and contour on an adolescent's self-evaluation are in many respects as important as the changes themselves. Unfortunately, most of the authoritative studies of physical development have not included systematic parallel studies of the personal meaning of physical development.

The body image as described by Schilder (1935, p. 11) is the "picture of our own body which we form in our mind." This image plays an important role in a person's evaluation of himself, whether it is sketchy or comprehensive, and whether it comes close to being a mirror image or is a distorted picture.

From early childhood an adolescent has gained a growing familiarity with his body and his physical abilities. He has often, also, been reminded by others of the significance of size, physical appearance, and physical ability.

Long before the child is able to formulate the idea in words he seems to perceive himself as one who *can cause things to happen,* notably with his hands. With the further passage of time he *asserts himself* in his relations with others through his physical activities. Another important development is his growing capacity for *self-help*—such as feeding himself with a spoon. Such self-help is interwoven with growing independence. It is to a large extent through his increased muscular strength and coordination that the child outgrows his helplessness.

A child's use of his body, and perception of his body, is deeply imbedded in later stages of his evolving perception of himself. A youngster's continuing development in self-help and decreasing dependence on adults is influenced by his growth in strength, size, and physical ability. Many of his experiences in measuring himself come through vying with others in his physical activities.

The physical changes that occur in adolescence are superimposed on a vast number of experiences that have molded the young person's perception of his "physical self" and have impressed him with the importance of his physique and physical powers. His body image will be influenced also by experiences that have led him to regard himself as physically robust or weak, vulnerable to attack or capable of self-defense, able or unable to tolerate pain, etc.

When a youngster reaches adolescence there are many features of his physical make-up that he is consciously aware of, but there also are many he does not clearly recognize, or which have special meanings to him for reasons he does not apprehend.[10]

He may view himself as being far less physically attractive than others see him without being aware of what has led him to this view. Sometimes there is a considerable discrepancy between a person's image of himself and a photographic image. It is a revelation for some persons to observe a TV view or a home-movie of their appearance, posture, gestures, and facial expressions. Some persons have trouble in reconciling themselves to the appearance they make on the screen even after several viewings.

Discrepancies also appear in connection with still pictures. Some adolescents and adults never seem able to get a photograph of themselves that is "just right." The writer once questioned a group of students who

[10] The elements in a person's physical being which influence his behavior and attitudes but which he is not consciously aware of have sometimes been called his "unconscious body image."

had just received copies of pictures that would appear in their high school yearbook. Some thought the likenesses were fine; others did not. One good-looking boy pointed to a picture which was an exceptionally good likeness, except in his own eyes. "I don't look that good—just see for yourself. It doesn't show my freckles." Apparently the thing he had noticed most about his image in a mirror was his freckles. To him they were unbecoming and blurred his eyes to the handsome features of his face. A girl who disapproved of her picture very much pointed to it and said, "I don't look like that!" But at that instant her face showed an unbecoming expression of annoyance and distaste—almost the exact duplicate of what the camera had caught. When looking at herself in the mirror, she apparently had not noticed this sour expression.

The totality of a person's views and attitudes, whether or not he is consciously aware of their origins, profoundly influence his response to changes that occur during adolescence. On the other hand, these changes also require him to modify his body image or to fit what happens into a preconceived frame.

An adolescent's image of himself is likely to be influenced also by the way his peers appraise him. Ruff (1951) has pointed out that to be acceptable to one's peer group during adolescence one must not differ too much from others in physical appearance. If a youngster differs considerably he is likely to be avoided by others or to receive derogatory nicknames such as Fat Boy, Goon, Whale, Spider, Shorty, Short Stuff, Skinny, Four Eyes, Freckles, and Beaky (Orgel and Tuckman, 1935). Some other nicknames that call attention to a boy's masculinity may be a source of pride: Butch, Bull, Beefy, Slugger, Speed, Rabbit, and Slim (Habbe, 1935). Nicknames are likely to make adolescents keenly aware of the attitudes others have regarding their physical appearance.

The evaluations individuals give of their body (hair, complexion, body build, etc.) are more likely to resemble than to differ from their feelings concerning other aspects of themselves (morals, first name, popularity, life goals, moods, etc.) (Secord and Jouard, 1953).

Some of the features which young people report as having favorable or unfavorable effects on their self-esteem are shown in Table 3.3. This table shows the percentages [11] of youngsters from the fourth grade through

[11] The percentages probably would be much higher if the young people had been asked specifically to name physical characteristics instead of being questioned in more general terms.

college who, when asked to write compositions on the subjects "What I Like About Myself" and "What I Dislike About Myself" mentioned physical characteristics. Among the characteristics named most frequently were size, weight, and features of the face and head. At all grade levels from the sixth through the twelfth the number of girls who complained about their physical characteristics was larger than the number who spoke favorably about these characteristics.

In a growth study conducted at the Institute of Child Welfare at the University of California it was found that of ninety-three boys, at least twenty-nine were definitely disturbed by their physical characteristics at one time or another during an eight-year period (Stolz and Stolz, 1944). Five of the youngsters apparently faced a major problem of adjustment because of difficulty in accepting their physical characteristics. In a group of eighty-three girls, there were thirty-eight who gave evidence of being disturbed by their physical characteristics. The investigators regard this as a minimum accounting, for some of the young people might have been disturbed without bringing it to the attention of the physician who was in charge of the physical measurements.

Adolescents regard their appearance in complicated ways. We might expect that a girl will be pleased to be pretty and that a boy will be glad to see himself as handsome. However, one impressive thing about young people, when one gets beyond a surface acquaintanceship with them, is that some of them are disturbed by their good looks. The extremely pretty girl faces certain hazards and problems her plainer-looking sister does not. Others may try to exploit her or to gain prestige by being associated with her. She may become the object of competition for favor that is not founded on appreciation of her personality but rather on appreciation of the glamour of her looks. The pretty girl may also from an early age become a means of satisfying parental ambition so that she is "shown off." She will notice also that at times she gets special favors (such as special consideration from male instructors and traffic cops), and she may feel uneasy about this or even a little guilty. Nevertheless, in spite of such complications, most girls would probably prefer to be pretty.

Hazards such as these are perhaps not as prominent among boys, but boys, as well as girls, build on precarious ground if their appraisals of their own worth rest to an important degree upon the effects of their good looks on others.

TABLE 3.3

PERCENTAGE OF BOYS AND GIRLS AT VARIOUS GRADE LEVELS FROM THE FOURTH GRADE THROUGH COLLEGE WHO MENTIONED CERTAIN PHYSICAL CHARACTERISTICS WHEN WRITING COMPOSITIONS ON THE SUBJECT OF WHAT THEY LIKED AND DISLIKED ABOUT THEMSELVES *

"What I Like About Myself"

| | Elementary Grades | | | | | | Junior High School | | | | | | High School | | | | | | College | | | |
| | IV | | V | | VI | | VII | | VIII | | IX | | X | | XI | | XII | | Fresh.-Soph. | | Jr.-Sr. | |
Category	B	G	B	G	B	G	B	G	B	G	B	G	B	G	B	G	B	G	B	G	B	G
N	220	206	147	142	171	172	96	77	134	151	170	204	151	157	112	124	137	122	50	50	50	50
I. Physical Characteristics	15	19	22	30	12	30	14	13	29	42	23	35	25	37	17	19	15	20	40	28	20	38
A. General appearance	3	5	3	3	2	4	7	3	5	3	3	4	10	8	13	6	11	6	36	18	18	38
B. Size, weight	1	1	2	3	5	5	1	1	8	7	6	11	6	13	6	2	3	4	0	0	0	0
C. Body build	0	1	0	1	1	2	1	0	4	1	5	2	3	4	5	4	2	2	6	10	4	4
D. Features of face and head	10	14	14	25	8	23	6	13	13	35	11	25	9	26	4	12	4	14	2	6	4	4
E. Upper extremities	1	3	3	6	1	1	0	0	1	3	1	1	2	2	0	2	0	2	0	4	2	0
F. Lower extremities	2	2	2	2	1	1	1	0	1	3	2	3	3	5	2	2	0	1	0	2	0	0
II. Clothing and Grooming	16	27	12	26	12	28	14	12	13	25	13	23	17	11	10	15	9	6	10	34	24	20
A. Clothes	13	22	5	15	8	19	11	8	7	17	6	11	13	6	5	10	5	4	6	32	20	20
B. Grooming	5	5	8	11	2	8	5	4	4	8	3	9	3	4	4	4	7	2	4	4	8	4
C. Make-up, hairdo, haircut	5	6	1	3	3	4	2	1	3	5	4	2	4	3	1	2	1	0	0	0	0	0
III. Health and Physical Soundness	6	2	8	8	7	5	8	0	8	5	4	3	5	5	8	2	4	2	4	0	6	0

"What I Dislike About Myself"

Category	Elementary Grades IV B	IV G	V B	V G	VI B	VI G	Junior High School VII B	VII G	VIII B	VIII G	IX B	IX G	High School X B	X G	XI B	XI G	XII B	XII G	College Fresh.-Soph. B	G	Jr.-Sr. B	G
N	220	205	147	142	171	172	96	77	134	151	170	204	151	157	112	124	137	122	50	50	50	50
I. Physical Characteristics	11	16	17	30	17	41	17	26	24	48	32	53	27	44	13	32	10	30	12	20	8	12
A. General appearance	0	2	1	2	1	9	3	5	2	7	2	5	3	8	3	6	1	11	6	6	0	0
B. Size, weight	4	2	4	5	10	9	8	9	10	15	19	17	11	18	8	12	5	8	2	12	4	4
C. Body build	0	0	0	3	2	3	0	1	2	7	2	13	4	5	1	6	1	4	4	2	4	0
D. Features of face and head	6	11	10	20	6	20	4	12	8	26	12	35	13	24	4	11	3	11	2	4	4	8
E. Upper extremities	2	3	3	6	1	7	0	1	1	3	2	7	3	8	0	1	1	1	0	0	0	0
F. Lower extremities	0	0	0	4	1	6	0	1	2	5	4	8	3	9	2	1	2	3	0	2	0	0
II. Clothing and Grooming	4	10	7	5	4	9	2	8	4	7	3	10	1	3	3	2	4	2	0	0	2	0
A. Clothes	2	5	1	2	1	3	2	3	1	3	1	5	1	1	2	0	1	2	0	0	2	0
B. Grooming	0	0	4	2	1	0	0	0	1	1	1	0	0	1	1	1	1	0	0	0	2	0
C. Make-up, hairdo, haircut	1	7	2	1	2	6	0	5	3	5	2	5	0	1	1	0	1	1	0	0	0	0
III. Health and Physical Soundness	2	3	3	4	5	2	4	1	4	1	6	2	3	3	0	6	6	2	6	2	0	2

* Reproduced, by permission, from A. T. Jersild, *In Search of Self*. Bureau of Publications, Teachers College, Columbia University, 1952. Other categories pertaining to mental and emotional characteristics, personality traits, etc., are included in the complete table but are not reproduced here.

INTERPLAY OF PSYCHOLOGICAL
AND PHYSICAL FACTORS
IN PERSONAL APPEARANCE

Just as an adolescent's physical development has a psychological effect on his attitudes regarding himself and on the attitudes others have toward him, his psychological attitudes can have an influence on his physical appearance. In everyday speech we note that a person has a "hang-dog look"; he "looks cranky," "harassed," "worried," "gay," "happy," "twinkling," etc.

The relationship between an attitude and physical appearance is apparent when a person clearly is trying to falsify his or her appearance, as happens when a girl's dyed hair or false eyelashes give her an artificial look. It appears when an adolescent is almost defiantly sloppy in appearance. It happens also in somewhat more subtle ways when, for example, tight lips and tightly braided hair and a rather prim facial expression seem to go together with a rather stiff manner of acting and talking. We see it also when a girl, seemingly unable to accept her own femaleness, selects the styles that are most likely to cover her from view, such as high-necked blouses, or loosely cut clothes that conceal the shapeliness of her body.

The attention adolescent girls give to their appearance, including clothes and cosmetics, is related to other personal characteristics (Silverman, 1945). While girls in the age range from twelve to eighteen show a strong tendency to conform to prevailing fashions and to dress alike, there are many individual differences. The motivations most commonly underlying the girls' efforts to look well include a desire for approval, a desire for the internal satisfaction of feeling well-groomed, and a wish for sexual attractiveness. Silverman states that concern about appearance is purposive and is "rooted in the girl's life story." Girls who were rated as giving much attention to appearance seemed to have a higher estimate of themselves than girls who were rated low in appearance. Financial considerations were not of primary importance in influencing clothing and grooming practices, except that the wealthier girls were better able to afford luxury items, such as wrist watches and fur-trimmed coats.

In their dress and grooming, adolescent girls are usually quite style conscious and try to conform to the fashions of the day. However, within this framework, they try to modify current styles according to their own tastes and ideas of what is most becoming. Through varying her dress, hairdo and make-up, a girl expresses her individuality and experiments to discover effects that in her judgment are most fitting.

Some girls not only adopt current fashions but exaggerate them. This, at times, creates conflict between a girl and her elders. At a time when short skirts and low necklines are in vogue, parents and school officials may feel they should interfere as the hemline rises and the neckline falls. While the girl may need to be advised, it is important for her own development to have freedom of choice within the limits of propriety.

Adolescent boys, too, are style conscious, although less likely than girls to admit it. Many boys go through a phase when it is stylish to have no style. The boy scorns a nice suit and even a decent shirt. He cherishes old pants his mother would gladly burn. If none such are around he abuses a good pair of pants until they are battered down to a fine point of fashion. In some communities at present adolescent boys go through a phase of wanting to wear tight pants. Some boys look as though their pants are about to burst. But times change. Soon the boy who once looked like a tramp will deck himself in the best clothes he can get.[12]

[12] Psychological repercussions of early and late maturing, of physical characteristics associated with sexual development and motor development are discussed also in the chapters immediately following.

Chapter 4

Sexual
Maturation

Adolescents reach an important milestone in their sexual development when they are able to produce live germ cells.

Several terms are commonly used to describe the events that take place in the process of maturing sexually. One term is *puberty,* derived from "pubes," which, in one of its meanings, pertains to hair. One meaning of the term *pubescent* is to grow hair, or to grow hairy. Puberty refers to the appearance of hair in the genital area. In ordinary usage *puberty* denotes not simply the beginning of the process of sexual maturation but the whole process or completed process. This is the usage when the term is used to denote the earliest age at which "the generative power becomes established." Another term in common use is *menarche,* which denotes the beginning of menstruation. Still another term is *sexual maturity,* which sometimes is used as though it were synonymous with *puberty* and *menarche* in girls, although it is not. The menarche, or first menstruation, is an important event in a girl's life, but it does not necessarily mean that she is sexually mature in the sense of being able to produce fertile egg cells.

In boys there is no clearly defined event corresponding to the menarche in girls that may be used as a criterion of puberty. The basic criterion is the ability to produce well-formed, mobile, and fertile sperma-tozoa. There have been observations of the onset of puberty as judged by this criterion, but obviously it is difficult to conduct such studies on a large scale. In lieu of this, other criteria have been used. Among them are changes in the velocity of growth of certain dimensions of the body, change in velocity of growth of the penis and testes, and ratings of the characteristics of pubic hair, including the amount of such hair, its color, distribution, texture, and the eventual development of the kink or twist.

Physical Changes Preceding and Associated with Sexual Maturation

Many of the physical changes associated with the growth of adolescents are familiar to any casual observer, but students of adolescence will be interested in examining these in some detail.[1]

The chronological age at which any given development appears and the interval between the appearance of one feature and another vary con-siderably from individual to individual. Figure 4.1 from Greulich (1942) shows the approximate time order of some external changes associated with sexual maturation in boys.

The menarche in girls and the development of sexual maturity in boys are a culmination of developments in the endocrine system (ductless glands) beginning several years before puberty (Nathanson, Towne, and Aub, 1943). This observation is based upon studies of the secretion of sex hormones as determined by the analysis of urine. Such analysis revealed a small excretion of androgens (male sex hormones) and of estrogens (female sex hormones) by both boys and girls many years before puberty. At about nine years of age there begins to come a differentiation of boys and girls, with an increase in the ratio of androgens in the boys and of estrogens in the girls.

Girls show a cyclic excretion of estrogens about a year and a half be-fore the onset of the menarche. Thus, the rhythm of menstruation is fore-shadowed in the chemistry of the body before the first experience of menstruation and the establishment of the menstrual cycle. The increase in female sex hormones is more drastic and occurs within a shorter time span than the corresponding changes in boys (Nathanson, Towne, and Aub, 1943).

[1] Shuttleworth (1949) has provided a very instructive pictorial atlas of physical development in adolescence.

1. The accelerated growth of the testes, usually followed by that of the penis.
2. The appearance of a conspicuous growth of long downy hair on the pubes.
3. The appearance of long, coarse, rather straight pigmented hairs at, and lateral to, the base of the penis. These hairs are soon replaced by pubic hairs which are almost completely differentiated.
4. A marked increase in the amount of axillary perspiration.
5. The down on the upper lip, especially at the corners, becomes slightly longer, coarser, and darker.
6. Long, coarse down appears on the extensor surface of the proximal third of the forearm and on the lateral and dorsolateral surfaces of the distal fourth of the arm.
7. The beginning growth of rather coarse, slightly or moderately pigmented hair on the distal half of the legs and on the distal third of the thighs. This process is, for a time, farthest advanced on the extensor surface of the legs and on the flexor surface of the thighs.
8. Long down appears on the sides of the face, in front of the ears.
9. The pubic region becomes covered with a moderate to dense growth of definitive pubic hair. (The hair-covered area now has a concave or approximately horizontal superior border and it does not extend laterally onto the adjacent medial surface of the thighs.)
10. Short, fine, pigmented hairs appear in each axilla. (The axillary perspiration has now acquired its characteristic odor.)
11. The voice has deepened perceptibly.
12. Subareolar masses, when present, have usually attained their maximum size.
13. Pubic hair has spread laterally to, or onto, the adjacent medial surface of the thighs and terminal hairs are present along the linea alba. The penis and testes have attained almost their full adult dimensions.
14. A few terminal hairs appear on the sides of the chin and the upper portion of the cheeks just in front of the ears, and the hair on the upper lip becomes coarser and darker.
15. A few terminal hairs appear around the periphery of the areolae and over the sternum.
16. The adult type of hairline begins to differentiate on the forehead (calvities frontalis adolescentium).
17. Almost, or quite the full amount of terminal hair proper to the young adult is now present on the forearms, arms, legs, and thighs.

Fig. 4.1. Order of appearance of some external changes associated with sexual maturation in boys (From Greulich *et al.*, 1942).

In the study cited above an interesting association was noted between changes in sex hormone output in boys and other changes. While the study was in progress, parents and teachers reported a striking change toward masculinity in two boys. Chemical analysis revealed that while previously these boys had shown a preponderance of estrogenic (female) over androgenic (male) substances, they now, along with their increase in "masculinity," showed a shift toward an increased ratio of androgenic substances.

Other interesting findings concerning the relationship between behavior and the presence of the male hormone (androgenic material) are reported by Sollenberger (1940). Information was obtained concerning male hormone content and also concerning the interests and attitudes of several boys. There was a high correlation between hormone content and maturity of interests. As a further check, ten boys with high hormone content were compared with thirteen boys with low hormone content. A higher proportion of boys with a high male hormone content expressed interest in heterosexual activities, personal adornment, and strenuous competitive sports.[2]

Findings such as these are not surprising. They represent a line of inquiry dealing with the important relationship between psychological and physiological phenomena and give an indication of the complex forces that operate in the conduct of the individual adolescent. Two adolescents may be very much alike in the moral training they have received but differ considerably in the physiological factors that influence the intensity of their sexual drives. As a result, one faces a more serious problem in managing his sexual drives.

ONSET OF MENSTRUATION

Table 4.1 gives results from several studies dealing with the onset of menstruation. Investigators dealing with different groups of American children have reported somewhat different averages. The average girl reaches the menarche at about the age of thirteen years, but this "average" does not mean much, in view of the wide variations.[3] Table 4.1 shows that a small proportion of girls has reached the menarche before the end of the tenth year, while a small proportion has not reached the menarche before the age of sixteen, seventeen, or even eighteen years.[4]

THE MENARCHE AND FERTILITY

The beginning of the menstrual cycle does not necessarily mean ability to conceive a child. Limited evidence suggests that there may be a lag of as

[2] See also Dorfman, Greulich, and Solomon (1937).

[3] In a growth study of 300 white children conducted by the Fels Research Institute, representing a group that "is a fair cross-section of the white population in southwest Ohio" the average age at menarche was 12.9 (Reynolds and Wines, 1948; Reynolds, 1951).

[4] The average boy reaches a roughly corresponding point in his sexual development at about the age of fourteen and a half, but among boys also there are great individual differences.

TABLE 4.1 *

PERCENTAGE OF GIRLS IN VARIOUS SAMPLINGS OF THE POPULATION WHO REACHED THE MENARCHE AT SUCCESSIVE AGE LEVELS

Chronological Age at Menarche	Brush Foundation	Harvard Growth †	Chicago Laboratory School ‡	Hebrew Orphan Asylum **	Horace Mann Hebrew **	Non-Hebrew **
10 yr. to 10 yr. 11 mo.	3.5	3.2	1.0	1.1	3.4	3.4
11 yr. to 11 yr. 11 mo.	27.5	12.1	7.6	9.7	13.8	12.7
12 yr. to 12 yr. 11 mo.	35.0	33.5	23.0	22.7	31.9	31.8
13 yr. to 13 yr. 11 mo.	27.0	36.3	35.3	31.9	27.6	30.9
14 yr. to 14 yr. 11 mo.	6.0	10.5	25.3	27.0	17.2	12.7
15 yr. to 15 yr. 11 mo.	1.0	3.2	6.0	7.6	5.2	6.8
16 yr. to 16 yr. 11 mo.	—	0.8	1.6	—	0.9	1.7
17 yr. to 17 yr. 11 mo.	—	—	0.2	—	—	—
18 yr. and above	—	0.4	—	—	—	—
Number	200	248	487	185	116	236
Mean (yr.)	12.6	13.0	13.5	13.5	13.1	13.1
Sigma (yr.)	1.1	1.1	1.1	1.1	1.2	1.2

* From K. Simmons and W. W. Greulich, "Menarcheal age and the height, weight, and skeletal age of girls age 7 to 17 years," *Journal of Pediatrics* (1943), 22, 10.

† F. K. Shuttleworth, *Sexual Maturation and the Physical Growth of Girls Age Six to Nineteen*, Monograph of the Society for Research in Child Development (1937), 2, No. 5.

‡ E. M. Abernethy, "Correlations in Physical and Mental Growth," *Journal of Educational Psychology* (1925), 16, 458–466, 539–546.

** F. Boas, *Human Biology* (1932), 4, 307.

much as six years at one extreme to possibly no time lag at all between the menarche and fertility. The findings also suggest, although not conclusively, that the lag between the menarche and capacity to conceive is shorter for girls who reach the menarche at a later age than for those who begin to menstruate at an early age. In a review of the literature bearing on this point, Ford and Beach (1951) point out that menstruation starts in most girls before their ovaries are capable of producing ripe eggs and that egg production begins before the uterus is mature enough to support the bearing of a child. They report that relatively few girls are capable of reproduction before the age of fifteen years, and even then reproductive capacity will not be as great as it will be at a later time. (Table 4.2).

TABLE 4.2

PERCENTAGE OF WIVES IN TWO AGE GROUPS WHO CONCEIVED
DURING THE FIRST TWO YEARS OF MARRIAGE *

Number of Women	Age at Marriage	Per Cent Conceiving	
		First Year	First Two Years
700	15–19	13.71	43.71
1835	20–24	18.49	90.51

* Based on a study of age of first pregnancy in 2,535 Scottish wives studied by J. Mathew Duncan, reproduced in Ford and Beach, *Patterns of Sexual Behavior,* 1951, p. 172.

Limited findings also suggest the possibility that there is less variability in the age of onset of fertility than in the age of onset of menstruation.[5]

Even though, as indicated above, first menstruation does not provide an unquestionable criterion of puberty, it obviously is an important landmark in a girl's sexual development. It usually occurs several years before she marries or assumes the responsibilities of an adult. Moreover, the time lag between the menarche and adulthood has increased by virtue of the fact that the menarche comes earlier in the present generation than was true fifty or one hundred years ago (Mills, 1939; Jones, 1949b; Tanner, 1955).[6]

[5] For discussion of this subject see Ashley-Montagu (1946), Ford and Beach (1951), and Mills and Ogle (1936).

[6] This time lag is, if anything, greater in the regions of the world that lie within the temperate zones. Findings reviewed by Jones (1949b) indicate that girls tend to reach the menarche earlier in the temperate zones than in the northern polar regions or in the southern tropical areas. To what extent this difference may be due to the climate or better dietary conditions or other factors is undetermined.

Psychological Impact of Menstruation

Girls differ greatly in the extent to which they are prepared for their first menstruation and in their emotional response to it (Landis *et al.*, 1940).

It is likely that a girl's response to first menstruation will be affected by factors in her past life that have influenced her personality as a whole, her attitude toward herself as a female, her feelings about her mother, and her outlook on life in general (see, *e.g.*, Newton, 1955). The emotional effects of menstruation will be colored by the girl's tendency to be anxious or to feel guilty about the functions of her body. Her response will be influenced also by her tendency to feel confident about herself and her ability to meet what life has to offer, and by the freedom or restraint she feels with regard to discussing events in her life with others, notably her mother.

Girls differ too in their psychological reactions to menstruation after the menstrual cycle has become established. They vary in the extent to which they experience physical pain or discomfort, or changes in mood, such as depression, listlessness, and irritability. One theory about psychological reactions to menstruation is that they are related to the woman's acceptance or rejection of her status and role as a woman. According to this view, a woman who finds menstruation difficult may also be a woman who has difficulty in reconciling herself to other features of the feminine role, such as the thought of giving birth to children, caring for them, "mothering" them, breast-feeding them (see Newton, 1955).

There have been, in the past, many misconceptions and superstitions about menstruation, which have not been at all flattering to womankind. The vernacular referring to menstruation as a "curse" suggests that it is a symbol of unworthiness or punishment for sin. Hollingworth in 1914 gave an interesting account of views that had been held by laymen and by scholars on this subject. Such views ranged from statements to the effect that meat is likely to become tainted if handled by a woman during her menstrual period (construed, incidentally, as an argument against allowing women to become doctors or midwives) to the view that woman is subject to periods of physical incapacity and weakness that would prevent her holding a responsible position outside her home. In writings reviewed by Hollingworth it was even suggested that criminal law should take into consideration that a woman during a considerable part of her life should be looked upon as abnormal and subject to natural feeble-mindedness.

Views such as the foregoing are not accepted now, but it is interesting to observe that some persons at one time accepted them. The scientific literature on the subject definitely refutes the idea that a woman is less consistently efficient or reliable because of the menstrual cycle (see, *e.g.*, Hollingworth, 1914, and Bilhuber, 1927).

Contrasts Between Reproductive Functions of Males and Females

There is no regular happening in the sex life of a postpubescent boy comparable to the menstrual cycle in girls. Approximately every four weeks the girl is reminded that she is a potential mother. One of the thousands of egg cells contained in her ovaries ripens, and nature makes elaborate preparations for the conception of a child. When nothing happens, nature "empties the room" that has been prepared for a guest that did not come, and the process of ripening and preparation begins anew.

In the meantime, the boy's reproductive apparatus is also active, but in a more helter-skelter way. He becomes tumescent and detumescent several times a day; he has experience with nocturnal emissions and masturbation. But the activities of his reproductive organs are erratic compared with those of a girl. One day, or week, or month is for him much the same as the one before. There is no periodic crescendo of preparation for parenthood, no cycle to remind him each month that he is a potential father.

From a strictly biological point of view, a particular individual male is dispensable but the individual female is indispensable in the process of reproduction. A single robust man could supply enough sperm for artificially impregnating thousands of women. But it is not possible to hire a substitute for the individual woman's egg bank, or to take care of the process of ovulation, or to supply a substitute uterus for bearing her child.

These considerations should enhance the sexually mature girl's pride in her sex and the developments that have occurred during her adolescence. But many studies have found that young women seem, on the whole, to have more difficulty in accepting their femininity than men have in accepting their masculinity. The reason for this probably is that many girls perceive more disadvantages than advantages in their biological nature, and they perceive that in our culture men have more power and privileges than women.

DEVELOPMENT OF THE BREASTS

Breast development is the most important and most apparent of the secondary sex characteristics in the developing girl. There is considerable variability in the timing and outcome of this development (Reynolds and Wines, 1948). The breasts of most girls have progressed from the beginning bud stage to a more mature stage before the menarche. Breast development more often precedes than follows appearance of pubic hair, but in some girls the pubic hair appears first, and in some the two developments occur together.

In a group of girls studied continuously over a period of years by Reynolds and Wines (1948) the breasts developed from bud to mature size in about three years between the ages of eleven and fourteen. At any stage of development, breast size ranged from small to large. Breasts were classified as small, medium, or large in size and as flat, hemispherical, or conical in shape. Hemispherical contours were most frequent in all three of the size classifications.

ONSET OF PUBERTY IN BOYS

In one of the earliest large-scale studies of the onset of puberty in boys by Crampton (1908), characteristics associated with the development of pubic hair were used as criteria. The percentage of boys at various ages who were in the pubescent stage and the percentage of boys at successive age levels who had attained the postpubescent stage according to this criterion are shown in Table 4.3. This table is based upon (1) a study by Crampton (1908) of nearly 4,000 New York City high school boys early in the present century (98 per cent of the boys were American born, but 40 per cent of them had parents who had been born abroad); and (2) a study of 1,406 boys by Dimock (1937).

According to the criterion applied by Crampton, 60 per cent of the boys in his study had attained puberty by the age of 14.75 years, and 50 per cent had reached this stage sometime between age 14.25 and 14.75 years. In the population studied by Dimock, less than a third of the boys in the age range from 13 to 14 years had reached postpubescence, and almost two-thirds had reached this stage by age 15. In the latter study, as

TABLE 4.3

The first part of the table is based on a pioneer study by Crampton and the second on a study by Dimock which used Crampton's criteria, applied to 1,406 boys *

CRAMPTON DATA (1908)

Age	Percentage of Boys in the Pubescent Stage	Accumulative Percentage of Boys Who Had Reached the Postpubescent Stage or the Beginning of Puberty
12.25	16	2
12.75	25	6
13.25	26	18
13.75	28	31
14.25	28	46
14.75	24	60
15.25	20	70
15.75	10	85
16.25	4	93
16.75	4	95
17.25	2	98
17.75	0	100

DIMOCK DATA (1937) †

Chronological Age of Boys Between	No. of Boys	Prepubescent		Pubescent		Postpubescent	
		No.	%	No.	%	No.	%
10 and 11	106	104	98	1	1	1	1
11 and 12	227	188	83	32	14	7	3
12 and 13	347	215	62	86	25	46	13
13 and 14	280	112	40	80	29	88	31
14 and 15	240	32	13	52	22	156	65
15 and 16	115	2	2	9	8	104	90
16 and 17	67	0	0	0	0	67	100
17 and 18	21	0	0	0	0	21	100
Not given	3						

* From C. W. Crampton, "Physiological Age—A Fundamental Principle," I, *American Physical Education Review* (1908), 13, 141–154. Reproduced by permission.

† From H. S. Dimock, 1937, *Rediscovering the Adolescent*. New York: Association Press, p. 209.

Prepubescence means the period before there are any signs of puberty. In the pubescent stage, as here defined, there are pigmented hairs in the pubic region. In the postpubescent stage the pubic hair has a kink or twist and the scrotum is wrinkled. Crampton made microscopic examinations of secretions of some boys and found well-formed and mobile spermatozoa in boys who, according to his criterion, had entered the postpubescent phase.

in the former, we can infer that boys reach this stage sometime between their fourteenth and fifteenth birthdays.

Table 4.4 (based on a study by Ramsey, 1943) shows some results that were obtained when boys between the ages of ten and sixteen were questioned about developments associated with adolescence, including ejaculation, voice change, nocturnal emission, and pubic hair. Two hundred and ninety-one histories were obtained by personal interviews; 85 per cent of the boys were between the ages of twelve and sixteen. The data are not complete, for some of the boys were questioned before they had reached the age when the development in question would occur. Yet it is interesting to observe that about 2 per cent of ten-year-olds and about 7 per cent of eleven-year-olds reported that they had experienced ejaculation. From this it would appear that the capacity to have ejaculation appears, at least in some boys, very early in the adolescent period and before other prominent features of adolescent development have been clearly established.

According to Ramsey the first ejaculation occurred as a result of masturbation (as distinguished from nocturnal emission or other kinds of stimulation) in 75 per cent of the cases. The findings in Table 4.4, indicating a capacity for ejaculation at a rather early age in some boys, is in keeping with findings made by Kinsey, Pomeroy, and Martin (1948) in their study of sexual behavior in the human male.

TABLE 4.4 *

PERCENTAGE AT EVERY AGE-GROUP SHOWING PHASE OF
SEXUAL DEVELOPMENT

Age Group (in Years)	Ejaculation	Voice Change	Nocturnal Emission	Pubic Hair
10	1.8%	.3%	.3%	.3%
11	6.9	5.6	3.7	8.4
12	14.1	20.5	5.3	27.1
13	33.6	40.0	17.4	36.1
14	30.9	26.0	12.9	23.8
15	7.8	5.5	13.9	3.3
16	4.9	2.0	16.0	1.0

* Adapted from G. V. Ramsey, "The Sexual Development of Boys," *American Journal of Psychology* (1943), 56, 217–233. Reproduced by permission.

GROWTH OF THE MALE GENITAL ORGANS

In boys growth of the testicles usually is apparent earlier than growth of the penis. Table 4.5 shows changes with age in the length and circumference of the penis according to measurements by Schonfeld and Beebe (1942). As can be seen, the growth of this organ is rapid from about age fourteen to sixteen. The differences in size from one year to the next would probably be larger if boys were grouped according to age of reaching puberty. There is a close correspondence between the timing of rapid growth in height and rapid growth of the penis (Stolz and Stolz, 1951).

TABLE 4.5

LENGTH AND CIRCUMFERENCE OF THE FLACCID PENIS AT VARIOUS AGE LEVELS *

Age in Years	Length (cm.)	Circumference (cm.)
11	6.56	4.74
12	7.13	5.05
13	8.73	5.79
14	9.77	6.88
15	11.81	7.62
16	12.50	7.99
17	13.26	8.43
18–19	13.11	8.61
20–25	13.02	8.55

* Reproduced in abridged form, from Schonfeld, Wm. A., and G. W. Beebe, "Normal Growth and Variation in the Male Genitalia from Birth to Maturity," *Journal of Urology* (1942), 48, 759–777. Length measurements are from the dorsal pubopenile skin juncture to the tip of the glans with nonerect penis stretched to full length.

Psychological Reactions to Genital Development

Many boys are sensitive to the size of their genital organs, especially if they think they are small. Some boys with small organs shrink from athletics because they do not want to appear naked before others in the public showers. Differences in the size of the penis are especially conspicuous at ages thirteen through fifteen when many boys have reached the postpubescent stage and many have not. In the study cited above, at ages thirteen and fourteen the boys in the upper 10 per cent had organs that were at least twice as long as those in the lowest 10 per cent. But at the fifteen- to eighteen-year levels the difference was about 50 per cent.[7] The differences between the largest and smallest is more marked in the early and middle teens than in the late teens and early twenties.

Large variations such as these no doubt contribute to an important degree to the "feeling of being different" which afflicts many boys.

Although boys freely comment among themselves on this feature of their anatomy, they hesitate to discuss it with adults.[8] Yet is could be very reassuring to boys to discuss this with an understanding teacher. (Some physical education teachers encourage such discussion.) The mere fact of having an opportunity to reveal worries on this subject could be helpful.

It probably also would be reassuring to boys to know that there is a large normal variation in size; that the difference between them and others is not likely to be as large when they reach full growth as it is in the middle teens; that "manly men," regardless of bodily size and height, differ greatly in this respect; that there is no demonstrated relation between normal variations in the size of the male organ and attractiveness to the opposite sex (if there is any relation, it is more likely to be due to the young person's attitudes toward himself and women than to the actual size of his organ); that the boy's capacity, as a future husband, for love, tenderness and thoughtfulness will be far more important in marital sex relationships than the size of his genitals (La Mare, 1957).[9]

Apart from viewing his male organ as a symbol of manliness a normal adolescent boy is frequently reminded of his genitals. He has frequent

[7] Schonfeld and Beebe (1942) report the following measurements for those in the first and those in the 9th decile:

Age	First Decile	Ninth Decile
13	6.1 cm.	12.2 cm.
14	6.6	13.5
15	9.1	14.8
16–17	10.8	15.3
18–19	10.8	15.5
20–25	11.3	15.5

[8] Some boys have concern about their genitals which seems to parallel the concern some girls have about their breasts. But a girl has reminders of publicly accepted normal variations each time she looks at brassiere advertisements or goes shopping for lingerie. Boys have no corresponding open reminders that large variations are not abnormal.

[9] Statements such as these will not touch on the core of a boy's difficulty if he has deep-seated attitudes of self-rejection and then "attaches" these to a notion that his organ is not as large as he would like it to be. But with a teacher who has a talent for counseling, a discussion of this problem may become a point of departure for exploring the boy's attitudes regarding himself.

erections. These may occur at embarrassing moments in class or other times. Some adolescents go to great lengths to control their erections by turning their thoughts into somber channels. But often the organ behaves as though it had a will and personality of its own.

Other Puberal Changes

HAIR GROWTH

Changes in hair growth associated with puberty include the appearance of pubic hair and hair in the armpits and changes in the amount and distribution of hair on other parts of the body. Hair growth is notable especially in boys, who show rapid development of hair on limbs and trunk during adolescence.

Another change is connected with the shape of the hairline of the forehead. In immature boys this line is a bowlike curve, as in girls, but in most mature males the hairline is broken by a wedge-shaped indentation on each side. These indentations are a mark of maleness. In many men, as they grow older, the wedges become deeper and wider. (Men who are bothered by this progressive baldness would probably be glad to trade their wedges for a youthful hairline.)

SWEAT GLANDS

A part of the picture of puberal change is increased activity of the sweat glands in the armpits. The glands in this area are of a type also found in other limited areas of the body (the mammary, groin, genital, and anal regions), but they differ from the sweat glands that are generally distributed over the body as a whole. The development of these sweat glands (known as apocrine) appears to be related to the status of the reproductive system. The glands do not reach full development until puberty is well advanced. (An item of incidental interest is the opinion held by some investigators that these glands are related in the history of the race to the scent glands of some other mammals.)

VOICE CHANGES

The "change of voice" in boys is a commonly recognized feature of adolescent development. This change, like others, does not occur at any fixed age. Usually a deepening of the boy's voice is not noticeable until several other signs of sexual maturation have appeared. Figure 4.2 shows the range of tones correctly sung by children at various age levels through the age of ten, and by men and women.

Age	Tones
2 years ...	D E F G A
3 years ...	*C* D E F G(A)*
4 years ...	B *C* D E F G A B C
5 years ...	A B *C* D E F G A B C D
6 years ...	A B *C* D E F G A B C D E F G
7 years ...	A B *C* D E F G A B C D E F(G)†
8 years ...	G A B *C* D E F G A B C D E F G
9 years ...	F G A B *C* D E F G A B C D E F G
10 years ...	‡(F)G A B *C* D E F G A B C D E F G
(Boys ..	f g a b c d e f g a b c d e f g
(Girls ..	g a b c d e f g a b c d e f g a
Men ...	**(D)E F G A B C D E F G A B C D E F G A B C††
Women	C D E F G A B C D E F G A B C D E F G A

* Sung by 49 per cent of the children.
† Sung by 48 per cent of the children.
‡ Sung by 48 per cent of the children.
** Sung by 49 per cent of the men.
†† Includes the falsetto.

Fig. 4.2. Tones sung by 50 per cent or more of children and by adults. A few tones reproduced by slightly less than 50 per cent are shown in parentheses (Reproduced, by permission, from A. T. Jersild and S. Bienstock, *Journal of Educational Psychology* (1934), 25, 481–503).

The voices of girls also usually deepen somewhat during adolescence. As shown in Figure 4.2, women were able to sing several low tones that ten-year-olds could not sing, but they continued to be able to sing as high in the scale as the ten-year-olds. On the other hand, the men, while they had become able to sing a large number of low tones that ten-year-old boys could not sing, had also lost the ability to sing some of the high tones the younger males could sing. The gain in the low register is larger, however, than the loss in the high end of the scale.

The change of voice causes embarrassment to some boys. They go through a period when their voices are unstable; "breaks" may occur, with the voice suddenly rising or falling a whole octave. Changes may also be preceded by huskiness (Curry, 1946). Some who have enjoyed singing become self-conscious about it when their voices are in the process of changing. Some youngsters drop out of the school chorus or glee club while in the process of getting accustomed to the new qualities of their voices, and boys who once sang lustily in assembly or in church may, for a time, refuse to sing at all.

Some Psychological Effects of Early and Late Sexual Maturation

The timing of bodily changes during adolescence has an important psychological impact.[10] and differences in rate of growth may have different effects on boys and girls, especially in the early teens. A series of inquiries conducted in connection with a long-term growth study at the University of California (Berkeley) offers interesting findings on this subject. Jones (1949b) found that it is in many ways a disadvantage for a time for a girl to mature early, while for a boy early maturing brings several advantages.

The stresses of puberty face the early-maturing girl at an earlier age and seem somewhat sharper. She is relatively big and physically conspicuous. Although still a child of ten or eleven years, she has to anticipate and deal with the responsibilities involved in menstruation. Her size and proportions and the other characteristics that go with being more mature may make it difficult for her and other girls of her own age to accept one another on equal terms. Moreover, she is physically advanced at a time when most of the boys of her own age are still childish and unable to appreciate her physical qualities. The boys may even be somewhat wary in their attitude toward her. In addition, when her physical maturing is very precocious, she is not likely to have corresponding social or intellectual maturity. In that event, she will not be ready to associate with older girls who are similar to her in physical development. She may also have special conflicts, for her parents are likely to regard her as still a very young girl and to restrict her dating and her desire to dress like "older" girls.

The situation is not, however, always black for the girl who matures early. In a certain group it may be an advantage for a girl to mature early if the most popular and most influential members of the group are early maturers. Indeed, a girl who matures late may actually feel left out of

---

[10] Psychological aspects of sexual development, heterosexual relationships, and other urges and practices related to sex are also discussed in later chapters. Ways in which attitudes toward self and others are expressed through sexual interests and practices are discussed in several sections of this book, including those dealing with anxiety, personality development, and heterosexual relationships.

things, and even begin to be concerned about herself if other girls with whom she likes to associate mature early and she does not. In one such situation, a twelve-year-old girl had a difficult time. The half-dozen twelve-year-old girls with whom she had associated were blossoming out as young women. They told her they did not want her to go with them on the bus to the movies for she could not "look like fourteen." In their view it was harder for them to act convincingly in public as though they were at least fourteen or fifteen years old when this girlish-looking figure was with them.

In a later study in the California series (Jones and Mussen, 1958) early maturers and late maturers were studied at the age of seventeen. Few differences were found, at that later age, between the two groups, except that early-maturing girls showed "more favorable self-concepts," and early-maturing girls rated higher in popularity at age seventeen than they had rated in their earlier teens.

As already noted, the early-maturing boy is more likely to have an advantage than a disadvantage, both in the early and later teens. For a time he is relatively bigger and stronger than many other boys even though, later, some of these boys will reach him or outstrip him in both height and strength. As a bigger and stronger person he is likely to have a considerable advantage in competitive sports. At the junior high school level it has been found that boys who are sexually more mature are more likely to be chosen as athletic leaders (Latham, 1951). Moreover, the rapidly maturing boy has an earlier assurance of his maleness and a basis for feeling confident about his masculinity.

The psychological reactions to early and late maturing present an interesting illustration of the interplay between genetic factors, attitudes that prevail in the social environment, and attitudes toward self. Repercussions of having what boys regard for a time as an "inadequate masculine physique" associated with late maturing have been discussed by Schonfeld (1950). Schonfeld notes that many of the variations in puberal development that are frequently regarded as abnormal are "genetically determined physiologic variations in the process of development." But many slow-maturing boys whose organic development is well "within the limits of normal" are not free to wait for nature to take its course. "The attitudes of parents, teachers and playmates encourage prepubescent boys to take pride in their masculinity and frequently impose tyrannical standards of 'normalcy' without consideration for basic differences" among individuals.

During the second decade of life the attitudes of the companions of boys in Schonfeld's study "played a decisive role in formulating standards of masculinity." At this age all the boys had a great need for acceptance by their peers. Not only could they see for themselves that they differed from what the group regarded as normal but in addition they became targets of criticism and disapproval.

The youngster's own attitudes play an important role in the way he reacts to the standards set by others. "Being different to a child usually implies being inferior. . . . It is inadequate adjustment to being different that gives rise to the difficulty and not merely the actuality of being different" (Schonfeld, 1950, p. 50). Schonfeld noted that feelings of inadequacy persisted in some slow-maturing boys even when the physical differences that had made them feel inferior no longer existed. Hazards of this kind have been observed also by Stolz, Jones, and Chaffey (1937).

Some boys built defensive "compensatory mechanisms" to avert anxiety that would arise from full awareness of their self-contempt. A common defense was to swing toward "compulsive drives for dominance, mastery and power." However, when boys who were striving to attain superiority set for themselves goals that were impossible to achieve, their failures reinforced their convictions of being worthless.[11]

In a study by Jones and Bayley (1950) of ninety boys, the sixteen who were earliest in maturing were compared with the sixteen who were latest in maturing. Boys in the early-maturing group were rated as physically more attractive, less affected, and more relaxed when judged by observations of their behavior. When the boys rated one another on various traits, the early maturers tended to be regarded as more grown-up, more assured, and more likely to have older friends. In a later inquiry (Mussen and Jones, 1957), in the same long-term study, the sixteen boys who had been consistently accelerated in their physical development were compared at age seventeen with seventeen who had been consistently retarded, on the basis of their responses to a projective test (see Chapter 7). More of the late-maturing than the early-maturing boys gave evidence of an unfavorable view of themselves, more "feelings of inadequacy and negative self-concepts." In responding to pictures in the TAT test, "a significantly greater proportion of the late-maturers told stories in which the hero was rejected by parents or authority figures." The investigators point out that some parents may have been disappointed in their physically retarded sons, and the boys might interpret this as rejection.

[11] A study by Dimock (1937) likewise showed that boys below average in physical development had less wholesome attitudes toward themselves than boys with superior or average development.

In some cases, also, parents may have been reluctant to allow the slow-maturing boy to establish his independence, with resulting tension and increased parent-child conflict. A larger proportion of late maturers than early maturers also "displayed strong motivations to escape from, or defy, their parents." Relatively few of the early-maturing boys manifested feelings of being inadequate, rejected or dominated, or feelings of rebellion against their families.[12]

Behavorial, Emotional, and Moral Aspects of Sexual Development

In the adolescent's sexual development there is an interplay of all the important forces that affect human existence. Sex has an urgency of its own, but it is also intimately tied to nearly all other aspects of a person's strivings and his relationships with others. Sexual development is a meeting ground of the biological, psychological, and moral influences that shape an adolescent's life. It is also a meeting ground of the present and the past, for sex behavior has a history going back into early childhood.

Biological features of an adolescent's sexuality are present at birth. In early infancy there are evidences of special sensitivity in the genital zones. The psychological factors that affect an adolescent's attitudes toward sex also have a history going back into his early life.

The most direct and specific way in which sex enters into the adolescent's experience is in the form of a bodily hunger. Back of this hunger is the primordial urge of life to beget life. However, there is an additional large and complicated cluster of experiences connected with sex. Sex is associated in the boy's mind with his concept of his role as a male, and in the girl's mind with her concept of herself as a female. The psychological meaning sex has for the adolescent is likely also to reflect all or nearly all

[12] Fortunately not all boys who are slow-maturers are deeply disturbed about it, and according to Schonfeld (1950), those who are disturbed can benefit greatly from psychological help if it is made available. The picture, however, is so somber, and evidence of distress is so clear, that it calls for sympathetic concern by all who are responsible for the upbringing and education of adolescents. This is one reason why the author has maintained that those who can profit most from a study of adolescent development are adolescents themselves (1951). A course dealing with adolescence will not dispel the more severely ingrained personality problems. But good instruction and class discussion can do much to dispel the mystery, the mistaken ideas about what is normal and abnormal, and the self-reproach based on false premises. It can also do much to encourage boys and girls to acquire a deeper respect for one another, more sympathy and a stronger sense of responsibility.

the attitudes and tendencies linked to his personality as a whole, the attitudes he has regarding his own worth, and the attitudes he has toward others—his tendency to be self-confident or the opposite, his tendency to feel guilty about his desires; his tendency to be suspicious or friendly in his attitudes toward others.

In the healthy course of development in our society, an adolescent's sexual development becomes interwoven with his emotional development, resulting in a linkage of erotic desire and a feeling of tenderness.

SEXUAL INTERESTS, ATTITUDES, AND PRACTICES

When boys and girls reach adolescence, all of them have had experiences of one sort or another relating to sex. These experiences, when the adolescents were younger, included discovery of the anatomical differences between the sexes, an interest in childish forms of sex play, and curiosity about sex and reproduction (see, *e.g.,* Dillon, 1934; Isaacs, 1933; Conn, 1940; Levy, 1928; and Koch, 1935). Boys begin to have erections almost from the time they are born (Halverson, 1940). According to evidence presented by Kinsey and his associates, there are children, both boys and girls, who are "quite capable of true sexual response" before they reach adolescence (Kinsey *et al.,* 1953).

Experiences during Preadolescence and Early Adolescence

There are large individual as well as group differences in expressed sexual interests and activities, but there are some experiences and practices that are very widespread. In a study by Ramsey (1943) it was found that 73 per cent of the boys had had experience with masturbation by the age of twelve years, and 98 per cent had had such experience by the age of fifteen. Over half the boys in Ramsey's study had experienced nocturnal emissions, or "wet dreams," by the age of fifteen. Nocturnal emissions that occur during sleep come about without any deliberate action by the dreamer. A large percentage of boys had had ejaculations brought about by themselves or through sex play with others before they experienced wet dreams. By the age of thirteen, 38 per cent of the boys had been involved in homosexual play. Preadolescent sex play with girls or women appeared in two-thirds of the histories, and one-third of the boys had attempted heterosexual intercourse before adolescence.

Ramsey cites evidence from other studies tending generally to confirm his findings. The significant finding is that a large number of boys are active sexually in one way or another prior to adolescence.

Sex Activities in Middle and Late Adolescence

There is a great accumulation of findings regarding sexual interests and activities during adolescent years but, unfortunately, many of these deal with sex in a fragmented way. The monumental and well-known studies by Kinsey and his associates deal almost entirely with the physical (one might almost say the mechanical) aspects of sex experience. Kinsey and his associates give elaborate statistics about sexual "outlets" with little or no attention to the personal meaning of these outlets, their emotional and moral significance, and the interpersonal relationships (other than physical) existing between persons who mutually engage in sex activities.

Studies dealing with other facets of heterosexual behavior—such as dating, courtship, falling in love, early marriage—usually cover a somewhat larger personal and social context, but even some of these give more attention to statistics than to underlying psychological motivations (dating, courtship, and other heterosexual social activities will be discussed in a later chapter).

In the early teens there is a sharp upswing among boys, and a much more gradual increase among girls, in various practices and experiences.[13] The chief types of sex activity are masturbation, petting, sexual intercourse, and nocturnal sex dreams.

At the end of the teens it has been found or estimated that over 90 per cent of boys (unmarried) have practiced masturbation and that a majority carry on the practice regularly once or oftener per week.[14]

The incidence of this practice among girls is smaller. Studies in which female adults have reported about their adolescent activity have given percentages clustering from about 30 to 60 per cent, although some investigators have reported a much higher or lower figure. Kinsey reports that by late adolescence about two-fifths of girls have had experience with

[13] Findings showing the incidence of various sex activities should be interpreted with some caution, for the findings obviously depend on the veracity of those who are questioned, and (in retrospective accounts) on their ability to remember accurately. However, several recent investigations, employing varying methods and involving different populations, have shown a high degree of agreement on the points here under review.

[14] This statistic is from Kinsey (1948). Various other studies within the past few decades have reported that from about 90 to practically 100 per cent of males have engaged in the practice more or less regularly for shorter or longer periods of time (see Kinsey, 1948, and Reevy, 1961).

masturbation, but only about half of these are actively pursuing the practice at any particular time.

During recent decades there has been a marked change in what is said and written about masturbation. The horrid and brutal threats of depravity, sterility, and hell fire once repeated in books on "What Every Boy Should Know" have largely been removed. But there probably still is (or, at least, until recently there still was) a great deal of guilt and fear associated with masturbation. In a study of college men published in 1937, Pullias found that a majority of these had been told that serious physical and mental damage would result from masturbation, and a majority of them believed that some type of damage would ensue.

A thorough present-day study would probably reveal that the practice of masturbation is not regarded with such dread and guilt as once surrounded it in the minds of many adolescents. However, such a study would probably also show that masturbation often occurs in a context of anxiety, even though the fears concerning the practice, *per se,* are not as acute as they were in the past. Instead of causing fear it may be a result of fear—fear of sex impulses which, if uncurbed and unrelieved by self-stimulation, might lead a person into what he regards as more serious and threatening sex activity. In that event, the practice is a means of protecting a person from *physical* intimacy with the opposite sex and from establishing a relationship which might lead to *emotional* intimacy with the opposite sex.

Petting is one of the most common erotic activities during adolescence. Kinsey (1948) defines petting as ". . . any sort of physical contact which does not involve a union of the genitalia but in which there is a deliberate attempt to effect erotic arousal."

Petting as a means of erotic stimulation is almost as universal as masturbation among boys. Among girls, approximately 90 per cent have had the experience at the end of age 20 (Kinsey, 1948, 1953).

By age twenty-one, it appears that approximately twice as many boys as girls have experienced premarital intercourse (in the population as a whole, approximately one-third to one-half of the girls and approximately three-fourths of the boys have).

The incidence of premarital intercourse is far higher among those who leave school at the end of the elementary school period than among those who are headed for college or actually are attending college.[15]

---

[15] The percentages bearing on this situation have varied somewhat in different investigations (see, *e.g.,* Bromley and Britten, 1938; Finger, 1947; Ehrmann, 1952, 1959).

In weighing the meaning of the statistics dealing with sex activities it is important to note that many of the percentages represent "cumulative incidence"—namely, the proportion of persons who, up to a given age, have had this or that sexual experience at one time or another. A person is included in this cumulative percentage whether he or she has had the experience only once or regularly and often over a long period of time. In some respects this cumulative incidence figure gives a misleading impression. In several studies, including Kinsey's, the investigators not only report this "whether or not" statistic but also include statistics on how much or how often. The latter statistics show that within the group that has had sexual intercourse there are large numbers who have had the experience only once or a few times, indicating that there were periods of months or years during adolescence when no such sex activity took place.

A further note of reservation should be added: a large proportion of girls' premarital sex experience (especially among those who go to college) is limited to relations with boys whom they plan to marry.

Sex Activity of Boys Compared with Girls

As we have noted, adolescent boys are much more active sexually than adolescent girls. By the age of seventeen, according to Kinsey (1953) practically 100 per cent of boys had experienced orgasm, while about 35 per cent of girls had had a sexual climax. Boys and girls are more alike in petting—by age twenty-one, practically all members of both sexes have had experience with petting, but the practice is less frequent, on the average, and more sporadic, among girls.

Undoubtedly, there are cultural reasons for this difference. It reflects, at least in part, the "double standard." Boys have more freedom; girls are more carefully supervised; girls are warned against (and often frightened by) the threat of pregnancy out of wedlock. Both boys and girls tend to regard forbidden sex behavior as a more serious offense for girls than for boys. Boys are conventionally regarded as the ones who take the initiative in sex conduct. In a study by Ehrmann (1952) of dating behavior of college students, behavior ranging from holding hands to intercourse or attempted intercourse was initiated by the boys in about three-fourths of the instances when such behavior occurred (according to the boys themselves, 75.3 per cent and, according to the girls, 78.9 per cent of such advances). The boys and girls also agreed, to a marked degree, in their reports that when advances were stopped at a certain point it was the girl, far oftener than the boy, who was responsible. To a large extent, a girl is required to be "a conscience for two" in her dealings with boys.

Although cultural factors undoubtedly account for much of the difference between the sex behavior of boys and girls it also appears that there are physical differences in the timing of the sex drive. According to Kinsey, males apparently reach their peak sexual capacities in the mid-teens, while the female peak does not come until later. Even when there is freedom and opportunity for sex experience, it appears that the young male's drive is stronger. By the average age of fifteen the girls in the Kinsey group reported that they were having orgasm every two weeks if they were having any at all, while the average boy of the same age reported about five orgasms every two weeks.

Differences between boys and girls appear not only in connection with actively initiated sex behavior but also in connection with more passive sex experiences. Kinsey found that nocturnal emissions ("wet dreams") were far more frequent among boys than sex dreams resulting in a sexual climax among girls. A person cannot deliberately bring about a sex dream. Undoubtedly, strong inhibitions which may be at work even when a person is asleep can prevent them. But this difference between boys and girls suggests that the sexual mechanism can be triggered off more readily in boys than in girls, especially in early and middle adolescence.[16]

Social Issues Raised by Findings Regarding Sex Practices

It is apparent that in the sphere of sex there is considerable discrepancy between what society demands or condones and what individuals actually do. In commenting on this, MacIver (1948) states that 95 per cent of the male population engage with some regularity, or have done so, in sexual practices that are criminal offenses. If the laws were invariably enforced by males who do not break the law this means that 5 per cent of the male population would have to send the remaining 95 per cent to jail.

One issue that arises from findings concerning sexual practices is the question as to what might be the effect on adolescents when they read about these findings. Several studies dealing with the response of college students to the Kinsey reports were reviewed by Ellis in 1953. One group of college students expressed the view that the Kinsey report on men had more effect on their attitudes than on sex practices (Crespi and Stanley, 1848–49). Other studies do not convincingly indicate that awareness of

[16] This is supported by another curious finding reported by Kinsey: although sexual intimacies are more common at the lower than at the higher educational levels, a girl's educational level seems to have no bearing on the time when she begins to have sex dreams (if any).

the Kinsey findings will substantially change attitudes or have an appreciable effect on overt behavior.[17]

MORAL AND EMOTIONAL ASPECTS OF ADOLESCENT SEX BEHAVIOR

When adolescents tell about their sex activities many justify them with the remark, "Everybody does it." However, in view of the pervasive moral and religious restrictions and sanctions surrounding sex,[18] it is highly unlikely that anyone can avoid conflicts concerning sex by this bland announcement. Such conflicts do not arise only in those who overtly violate the moral code but also in many young persons who covertly do forbidden things in their fantasies. The conflict is likely to be especially acute, however, when it is compounded by fear of public disgrace and fear of disapproval by others. Conflict combined with fear apparently is more prevalent among girls than boys, for under a double standard of morality the girl is the one who is more likely to meet disapproval. Moreover, it is mainly she who must bear the burden of pregnancy out of wedlock. Statistics concerning illegitimate births give only a meager indication of how justified such fears may be, for such statistics do not include pregnancies that have been terminated or that have been legitimized by marriage. (In one group of girls who married before finishing high school, Burchinal [1959] found that about 40 per cent were pregnant before marriage.) Even if complete statistics were available, these would give only a small part of the story, for they would not tell of girls who feared they might have become pregnant as a result of an indiscretion but did not, or of those who are discreet but fear the thought of extramarital pregnancy.

[17] The Kinsey reports probably offer far less erotic excitement than many other influences to which young people are constantly exposed, including sexy movies, novels, and even illustrated advertisements in Sunday newspapers, not to mention the sex talk adolescents carry on with one another.

[18] There are codes regarding sex conduct even among those whose codes seem most unconventional (see, e.g., Whyte's 1943 account of "a slum sex code"). Actually, when young people make the statement, "Everybody does it," they may express not simply an excuse for sex behavior but, in some instances, a state of being unable to resist the social pressures brought to bear on them. In a study by Smith a large proportion of girls said they petted because of a desire to do so, but 30 per cent said they petted because others did it, 12 per cent said they lacked courage to resist, 12 and 11 per cent, respectively, said their motive was a desire to please the man or a fear of being unpopular. (These percentages are not mutually exclusive, for some girls gave several answers.)

In a study of the interests of 2,000 high school boys and a similar number of girls in problems relating to marriage and parenthood, Lantagne (1958) found that the subject of pregnancy rated highest in interest among the girls (it was eleventh on the boys' list). An interest in pregnancy problems cannot be interpreted as meaning fear of premarital pregnancy, but it is apparent that girls are considerably more concerned about pregnancy than boys.

Three-fifths of a group of single women and about half of a group of married women who took part in an investigation by Landis *et al.* (1940) reported that they had been the object of aggressive sexual advances by boys or men prior to the time they reached puberty. Over half of those who had had this experience reported emotional distress, including shock, worry, shame, fear of being found out, guilt, and extreme fright.

In a study by Jameson (1941), 21 per cent of a group of girls, juniors in college, reported that they had had shockingly undesirable experiences with boys during their college years. Although these girls did not hesitate to report that they had been shocked by the kind of advances men made to them, very few of them offered to describe these experiences.

Apart from acute emotional stresses, such as those described above, conflicts regarding sex arise when persons feel compelled, in spite of strong scruples, to have sex relations in order to be popular or to conform or to "prove" their masculinity or femininity. Emotional conflict is likely to arise, whether consciously recognized or not, whenever a person uses sex "dishonestly" to satisfy devious needs, such as a need for conquest, a desire to defy authority, a desire for revenge, a need to overcome feelings of inferiority, or a need to hurt others, or when he pretends a love he does not feel in order to persuade another to gratify his sexual desires.

SEX IN RELATION TO ATTITUDES TOWARD SELF AND OTHERS

There are complicated interrelationships between attitudes toward sex and attitudes toward self and others. Some of the child's earliest experiences of being rejected are connected with his sexual development. If a child's elders are anxious about sex, regard it as dirty, shame him when, for example, he plays with his genitals, the child is being taught to regard a part of his own person as something dirty and objectionable. When a child is taught to view his sexual nature with shame he is being taught to view a part of himself as shameful.

Sex may become entangled in other ways with attitudes the adolescent has about himself and others. A person's sex behavior (including his fantasies) may reflect other trends or traits in his personality: a tendency to be responsible or irresponsible; a tendency to be considerate, thoughtful, and tender in his relations with others or a tendency to be callous; a tendency to be compliant and conforming or rebellious.

The fact that sex is interwoven with all that goes into the making of a personality renders it difficult to interpret many of the research findings dealing with sexual behavior. To what extent, it might be asked, do the various forms of behavior reported by Kinsey indicate what is "natural" from a purely sexual point of view, and to what extent and in what ways do they reflect a mixture of motives? We need a more comprehensive approach to sex in relation to the personality as a whole to answer this question.

Chapter 5

Physical Abilities and Their Psychological Meanings

During late childhood and adolescence there is a more pronounced gain in muscular strength than in physical size. Measurements of strength of a group of young people over a span of years from age eleven to eighteen showed that four-fifths of an adult's strength but hardly more than one-third of his height is acquired after the age of six years (Jones, 1949a).

Through gains in strength, speed, and capacity for coordinated movement that occur during adolescence, the body reaches or almost reaches the maximum development of its physical powers. The peak of ability in some performances may be reached even before the period usually covered by the term *adolescence* has been completed.

During adolescence many persons reach not only their peak performance in several motor activities but also the peak of their desire to be active. Many begin to show a strong decline in their desire for being physically on the go at the middle and toward the end of adolescence. This differs from their behavior in early childhood years. One mark of childhood is a strong desire to be active. One of the most stable marks of maturity is a strong inclination to sit down.

Girls "mature" in this fashion earlier than boys, except, perhaps, in their interest in dancing. As we shall see later, girls also reach their maximum capacity for physical activity earlier than boys. But boys begin to slow down a bit and to curtail the number of their play activities as they reach the end of the teens. They are likely to confine their activities or to specialize much more than they did when they were ten or twelve. Even the boy who still knocks himself out on the college football field (while the girls, seated, look on) is likely to be much more sedentary between games and practice periods than he was in high school or in the elementary grades. (Men, as a group, seem to cling more to the memory of their active childhood years than women do, but most of them do so vicariously by watching others play the games they used to play themselves.)

Growth Trends in Motor Performances of Boys and Girls

Some measurements of motor development are shown in Figures 5.1–5.4. These measurements were made by Espenschade (1940) in a study in which the same boys and girls were tested repeatedly over a period of several years. Figure 5.1 shows performances in a test of jump and reach. Figure 5.2 is based on a test of the distance those tested could throw a twelve-ounce ball. Figure 5.3 shows speed of running a 50-yard dash, and Figure 5.4 shows distance of a broad jump. In all these performances the boys excelled the girls, and in most of them the boys were still showing appreciable gains from one half-year to the next. The girls, instead of improving from one half-year to the next, made a poorer record in three of the performances when tested at age sixteen, or a short time thereafter, than they had made in tests when they were younger. Differences between boys and girls were less marked, however, in a test for accuracy in throwing at a target.

In other words, the superiority of boys is less when it involves precision of movement. Moreover, in dealing with performances that call for skillful coordination rather than speed or vigor of movement, it is likely that the difference between boys and girls, if there is a difference, will depend more upon the amount of practice they have had than upon any special advantage that goes with being a boy or a girl. This is illustrated in a study by McFarlane (1925). Tests designed to measure "practical ability" were given. Some of the tests called not only for manual skill in fitting various mechanical parts together but also for the ability to per-

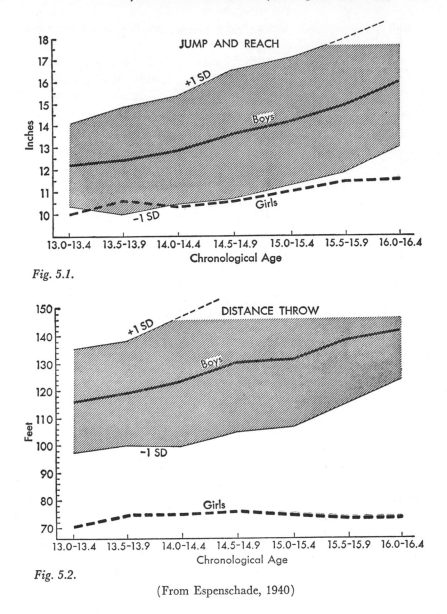

Fig. 5.1.

Fig. 5.2.

(From Espenschade, 1940)

ceive or to grasp what the parts added up to or what could be made of them. Two tests involved pieces of wood which, when fitted together, produced a wheelbarrow and a wooden cradle. Two tests required the fitting together of pieces of cloth to produce a girl's dress and a boy's coat. An other test called for speed and precision in inserting a steel plunger into a succession of sockets.

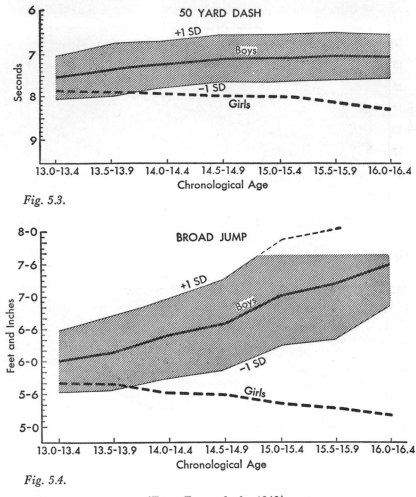

Fig. 5.3.

Fig. 5.4.

(From Espenschade, 1940)

The boys were superior to girls in putting together a cradle and wheelbarrow, but girls were superior to boys (and to a greater degree) in all comparisons in making garments out of pieces of cloth. In the test with the plunger there was little difference. In other words, in activities in which the girls presumably had had more practice than the boys, they not only equaled but surpassed the boys. This suggests that many of the sex differences that are found in motor and mechanical activities are due not so much to a genuine sex difference as to a difference in amount of interest, experience, and practice.

We have noted that boys continue to show an interest in physical activities after many girls have begun to show a sharp falling off in such interests. In junior and senior high school, girls frequently ask to be excused from gym classes. In one large school population (Lund, 1944) there was an increase of 400 per cent from the seventh to the twelfth grade in girls' requests for excuses due to alleged physical disability. However, this increase was due to changes in interest and motives rather than to an increase in illness or other kinds of physical disability. The social interests of the girls apparently were not in accord with what was demanded or offered on the gymnasium floor. Among the reasons given were a lack of physical inclination to take the exercise, concern about the effect gym work might have on the the hairdo and make-up, fear of developing big muscles, and unwillingness to change clothes.

Relationships Between Mental and Physical Growth

At practically all age levels the individual who is above average in one major feature of his make-up is more likely to be above than below average in other features. Positive correlations have been found between mental ability and certain physical measurements. However, among normal children the correlations between mental ability and bodily size, and between intelligence and motor ability, while positive, are low (Abernethy, 1936). Within the normal range of intelligence, the correspondence between mental and physical growth is so low that youngsters who are homogeneous in mentality will be very heterogeneous physically.

In a study of 800 boys who resided in institutions for the mentally defective, Flory (1936b) found that mentally deficient boys were from two and a half to three years later in attaining pubescence (as determined by the presence of pubic hair and hair in the armpits) than boys in the general population. Morons matured earlier than imbeciles and imbeciles earlier than idiots.

Relationships Between Physical Ability and Popularity

Relationships between motor performance and other traits, as shown by a group of California boys who cooperated in a growth study in which various measurements were made at half-yearly intervals from age eleven to age eighteen, are shown in Tables 5.1 and 5.2. The "gross motor scores" were based on a series of athletic performances such as are commonly involved in playground games. Popularity was based on a measure of reputation with classmates. "Good looks" were also determined by classmates' ratings.

Popularity was more closely linked with physical strength and skill in athletic activities than with intelligence and school achievement. Also, there was a higher correspondence between strength and popularity than between popularity and socioeconomic status. An athletic boy from the "wrong side of the tracks" was likely to be more popular than a non-athletic boy from the "right side."

TABLE 5.1

MOTOR PERFORMANCE CORRELATIONS WITH OTHER DEVELOPMENTAL
TRAITS IN BOYS *

	Total Strength (Grip, Pull, Thrust)	Gross Motor Scores (Track Events)
Chronological age	.39 ± .06	.18 ± .07
Skeletal age	.50 ± .055	.36 ± .06
Height	.65 ± .04	.40 ± .06
Popularity	.30 ± .07	.39 ± .06
"Good looks"	.21 ± .07	.38 ± .06
Intelligence	−.17 ± .07	.05 ± .08

* Reproduced from a study by P. A. Bower by H. E. Jones. *Motor Performance and Growth*, University of California Press, 1949.

TABLE 5.2

CORRELATIONS OF STRENGTH AND OTHER TRAITS WITH POPULARITY
(BOYS)*

Variable	Correlation
Dynamic strength	.39 ± .06
Static strength	.30 ± .07
Maturity (skeletal age)	.15 ± .07
Height	.07 ± .08
Social status (home rating)	.05 ± .08
Intelligence	.04 ± .08
School achievement	.03 ± .08
Chronological age	.00 ± .08

* Reproduced from a study by P. A. Bower by H. E. Jones. *Motor Performance and Growth*, University of California Press, 1949.

Observations such as the foregoing are significant from the point of view of understanding adolescents and the way they appraise one another. Adults rating adolescents are likely to give more weight to intelligence and school achievement and less to strength and athletic ability than young people do. In the view of some adults, therefore, adolescents follow a system of values which is superficial.

The observations above do not, of course, show anything approaching a perfect correspondence between social acceptance and strength or athletic ability. Other characteristics obviously are important. For instance, Jones (1949) points out that the prestige boys attach to physical characteristics, especially strength and the masculine meaning of strength, is likely to vary in different social groups. However, the high value placed on athletic ability stands out sharply in quite diverse communities.[1]

Values Attached to Athletic Ability

In a study conducted in a large high school in Brooklyn, New York, Tannenbaum (1959) asked eleventh-graders to record their attitudes toward hypothetical students with various combinations of (1) athletic ability, (2) brilliance, and (3) studiousness.

The eleventh-graders were asked to mark each hypothetical student on the basis of a list of fifty-four traits. (Twenty-seven of these traits had been rated as desirable by a large percentage of high school students in a preliminary study; nineteen as undesirable; and eight received a divided vote and were treated as "neutral."

Table 5.3 shows that the nonathletic was consistently rated lower than the athletic, by girls and boys. Students who had good scholastic records, or whose parents were above average in education, did not differ significantly from other students in placing a high value on athletic ability.[2]

When adolescents place a very high estimate on athletic ability and a low estimate on studiousness, they are reflecting attitudes common in adult society. The athletic star is honored more than the hard-working scholar. However, individual adolescents have varying motives for up-

[1] Tannenbaum (1959) has reviewed a number of studies on this subject, including writings by Americans and Europeans who have discussed evidences of "anti-intellectualism" in the United States.

[2] In the same study, results from small samplings of adolescents with varying ethnic backgrounds in other urban and rural communities did not differ significantly from those shown in Table 5.3.

TABLE 5.3

AVERAGE RATINGS MADE BY ELEVENTH-GRADERS OF THE SOCIAL
ACCEPTABILITY OF EIGHT HYPOTHETICAL STUDENTS *

	305 Girls		310 Boys	
	Average †	Rank	Average	Rank
Brilliant, nonstudious, athletic	31.36	1	25.28	1
Average, nonstudious, athletic	29.04	2	23.14	3
Average, studious, athletic	26.10	3	22.27	4
Brilliant, studious, athletic	23.66	4	23.83	2
Brilliant, nonstudious, nonathletic	14.27	5	9.24	6
Average, nonstudious, nonathletic	10.68	6	10.61	5
Average, studious, nonathletic	8.86	7	8.02	7
Brilliant, studious, nonathletic	1.58	8	2.83	8

* Reproduced by permission from Tannenbaum, A. J., 1959, "A Study of
Verbal Stereotypes Associated with Brilliant and Average Students," unpublished
Doctor of Philosophy dissertation, Teachers College, Columbia University.
† The maximum possible range of scores was from +46 to −46.

grading the athlete and downgrading the bright, studious nonathlete.
Some perhaps envy the diligent student, especially if he is bright. It is
likely also that some young people who give a low rating to studiousness
are knowingly or unknowingly expressing rebellion against teachers and
the meaninglessness, to them, of what they have to memorize at school.
Whatever the varying motives might be, however, it is clear that the
athlete has high prestige.

On the other hand, even though the high esteem accorded to physical
ability and athletic skill is impressive, there is something artificial about
it. The athlete is honored more than he is emulated. Educators who are
interested in promoting physical fitness, rather than simply in whipping
a small minority of students into a winning team, frequently deplore the
general unfitness of a large proportion of young people. In a study of
1,000 students entering a midwestern university, Cureton (1943) found
a large proportion were lacking in ordinary physical skills. Fourteen
per cent were classified as soft, flabby, with undeveloped physique; 24
per cent could not jump an obstacle waist high; 26 per cent could not
chin themselves five times; 42 per cent could not skin the cat; 64 per cent
could not swim fifty yards. In another larger college group of 2,628 men,
40.5 per cent could not run a mile in seven minutes; [3] 52 per cent could
not do twenty leg-lifts and sit-ups in succession.

[3] Older readers might wonder why anyone would *want* to run a mile in less
than seven minutes. But speed in running is very important in most of the sports

There are many schools in which, from the viewpoint of some adults, the prestige system is dominated too much by athletics. An athletic program (or any other program) that throws the spotlight on a few stars can do an injustice to those who do not make the grade.

The value adolescents place on athletic ability may, however, have a democratizing effect if it is not the dominant or only standard applied in judging the worth of the individual student. In a school where scholastic ability is an important criterion for judging a student's worth, there will be many students who will be judged unworthy by that standard even though, in other respects, they are very worthy. If, however, in this school, students are judged also by athletic ability, there will be an opportunity for a larger proportion of students to have their abilities recognized. In the group of good scholars there will be some who belong to the group of good athletes; but it is more likely that many students will belong to only one of the groups, for there is only a low correlation between motor ability and academic ability.

Motor ability does not seem to be distributed according to "social class" or socioeconomic status to the same extent as intellectual ability. Jones (1949a) compared children of high socioeconomic status within his total group with children of low status. The first three years of the study coincided with three years of severe economic depression when many of the "low" families lived on drastically reduced budgets and some depended upon public relief. Although, as Jones points out, other studies have shown that children of higher socioeconomic status tend to have an advantage in height and weight (Sanders, 1934), the findings in Jones's study still indicate that motor ability cuts across socioeconomic lines to a greater extent than does intellectual ability.

Personal Implications of Physical Ability

The meaning of having or lacking the kind of strength and athletic ability that is highly valued in a group has been brought out in very personal terms by Jones (1949a) in the study cited above. Jones compared the ten boys who stood lowest in ability with the ten who stood highest.

The boys selected as "strong" were, more often than not, well favored

---

that bring athletic acclaim. Moreover, other skills in the above list are advantageous in other ways. Ability to jump a waist-high hedge might be very handy for an enterprising young man, and ability to swim fifty yards could make the difference in staying alive or drowning.

when evaluated in terms of other aspects of their personalities. The group of boys who were poor in tests of strength presented a different picture. The lower ten were socially as well as physically weak, usually they were not so much disliked as ignored by their classmates. When records of their personal adjustment were examined, only one of the ten showed up in a distinctly favorable light. Three had approximately average scores in "total adjustment," but showed evidence of persisting tension and conflicts arising from inferiority. Six of the boys had records that seemed definitely to reveal maladjustment, especially at the end of adolescence. One boy, for example, fell from being about average in popularity to a very unpopular position at a time when physical differences between his associates and him were most marked. At age fourteen and a half he was regarded by his classmates as unfriendly, listless, lacking in humor about himself, immature, inactive in games, unwilling to take a chance, and afraid to fight. He did not easily accept this loss in social esteem. Although he took no part in games, he showed an increase in restlessness; and although he was judged to be less friendly, he was more talkative and attention-seeking. Actually, he did not want to be less friendly, but he was immature and ineffective in his use of social techniques.

Another boy described by Jones also suffered a decline in prestige, but the decline in his case came later, partly because he had a natural buoyancy that helped him for a time. At the age of fourteen and a half he was still above average in popularity. But three years later he was rated low in popularity. He was no longer regarded as friendly by his classmates. He no longer stood out as a person who seemed to enjoy himself in most situations; he had less humor, and was looked upon as immature. His reaction, like the reaction of the boy mentioned above, was to become more bossy, restless, talkative, and attention-getting. But he was "not one to be held down by adversity," so he also showed a tendency to become more aggressive ("enjoys a fight") and more daring "always ready to take a chance at things that are new and unusual"). Both these boys, Jones points out, were exposed to similar adolescent stresses, from causes that were in part the same, but their reactions to these stresses were an outgrowth in part of their earlier personality tendencies. One of them who already was a fighter became the "fightingest" boy in the group. The other, who was previously timidly inclined, became the least aggressive of the group in situations that required initiative and physical enterprise.

The fact that physical skills have great prestige value suggests that troubled and unaccepted adolescents might benefit from a systematic program to improve skills. Though this is probably true, it is stated too simply. More would be required than merely to patch certain skills onto an already existing personality structure. A boy's tendency to join in activities or to stay passively on the side lines is not determined simply by the factor of skill. Whether or not he enters into sports will be influenced by his willingness to rub elbows with others, his ability to enter easily and freely into social contacts, his aggressiveness, his willingness to face the possibility of being roughed up a bit. The tendency to enter in vigorously or to stay on the fringe is influenced also by the boy's ability to tolerate the idea of being tested, being defeated, making mistakes.

In one study in which "actives" and "fringers" were compared (Cowell, 1935), it was observed that lack of desire or ability to take part in the physical education program may be tied to characteristics such as shyness, sensitivity, a tendency to be upset by defeat and to shrink from new ventures. In another study, Fauquier (1940) cites findings and opinions that support the theory set forth by Adler (1929a) that it is not just by chance that a person joins in this or that game or sport. According to this theory, a person's choice of a certain activity, his approach to it, and the importance he attaches to it tell something about his attitudes regarding himself and his relationships with others. From findings in a study comparing "aggressive" and "submissive" boys, Fauquier concluded that play habits are not isolated and disconnected elements in a boy's personality that may be molded and manipulated at will. Rather, play habits are symptoms reflecting a larger and more complicated system of thinking, feeling, and acting.

Play activities may give expression to a desire for novelty, adventure, and excitement. They may express a need for social approval, attention, status, and recognition, or they may spring from an urge for a sense of mastery, power, success, and achievement (Dimock, 1937).

In view of the fact that participation in physical activities is linked with pervasive tendencies within the personality, it is apparent that a program designed to help individual youngsters must be varied and flexible. This would hold true especially in a program designed to help shy and troubled youngsters. Instead of demanding a standard of excellence that is beyond the reach of a large number of youngsters, such a program would recognize levels of ability so that youngsters would be aware of achievement and improvement even though they were far from a perfect performance. It would not have a lopsided emphasis on a few sports, such as football and basketball, nor would it center entirely on competitive activities. This would require teachers or leaders who were sensitive to differences in interest and temperament and who were able to tolerate a wide range of achievement. It would require teachers who could identify with individuals at various levels of skill and who were not seeking by proxy to work out some of their own unmet needs to be glamorous stars.

This would mean, among other things, that the instructor might encourage one youngster to strive to reach the peak of form while trying to get other youngsters to participate regardless of form. Also it would mean that in an activity such as square dancing the immediate goal might be to help one person improve his timing and rhythm while helping another person to grip his partner as though he really meant business, even though he was still somewhat inept in going through the steps. There is perhaps no other single department of the high school that offers greater opportunity than the physical education program for studying the individual student, his style of life, his potentialities for being spontaneous and free, his hesitancies and lack of self-confidence, his need to vanquish, or his need at all costs to avoid defeat or to avoid a contest in which he might look awkward.

But to realize the potentialities for helping young people in the quest for self-discovery we need an emphasis different from the one students often see as prevailing in many schools.

part three | Thought and Fantasy

Chapter 6

Mental Growth

During adolescence normal young persons advance on many intellectual fronts. They gain in intellectual capacity and power. They increase in their ability to grasp relationships and to solve problems of increasing complexity and difficulty. They acquire a greater capacity to deal with abstract ideas. They grow in abilities commonly measured by intelligence tests. And they continue to gain in breadth of knowledge, depth of understanding, judgment, and common sense. With a little encouragement many of them also seek to understand themselves and others.

Intellectual Ability and Self-Evaluation

By the time youngsters in our society reach adolescent age, they have been reminded on countless occasions of the tremendous value of mental ability. Through the school years their mental abilities are continually put to the test. Over and over again they are given a grade or rating—by their teacher, by their peers, and by themselves.

At school they discover that they are quick, average, or slow learners as compared with others. Unless they have become discouraged and have given up the struggle, they vie with others to finish first or to be the best. In most schools, teachers give more weight to the kind of intellectual achievement that enables a person to learn academic assignments than to all other aspects of the child's life and personality. In the usual school, a young person uses and tests his intellectual powers in a highly competitive situation in which the ultimate test of a student's worth is his ability to digest and, on demand, disgorge impersonal academic information. In the day-to-day work of many classrooms there are opportunities, to be sure, for the student to voice an individual turn of thought or to write original compositions that have a personal flavor. But when the chips are down, there is little opportunity for a student to put the stamp of his own mentality on the mass examinations which give the official verdict regarding the worth of his mind.

Many curious things happen when young people test and assess the properties of their minds in this competitive way. We might expect that those who are average or below, the "also-rans" in the academic marathon, would have a low opinion of their own worth, while those who lead the pack would glow with pride. But several studies have shown that there is a relatively low relationship between self-esteem and performance on the usual mass-produced measures of intellectual achievement (see, e.g., Smith, 1932; Spivack, 1956). Apparently there are many reasons for these findings, and there is more to them than meets the eye. An ironic twist is that many people who are exceptionally able feel inferior. One apparent reason for this (although not the only reason) is that these people do not measure themselves against the average but compare themselves with their most able peers. Such a comparison is likely to be unfavorable, for not all can reach the peak. An extremely bright person who feels inferior is, in a sense, like a pugilist who has lost a bout for the world championship and feels he is no good, even though he can outfight every person on the globe—save one.

In the case of young people with more modest abilities, many, it seems, develop an armor of resistance, rebellion and denial to protect themselves from reminders that teachers view them as second-rate.[1] There are many measures they can take, however, to enhance their conscious self-regard. Some who are not able to win acclaim for their minds are able to win approval for their participation in sports, social activities, and other nonacademic pursuits.

In addition to influencing his conception of who and what he is, the

[1] Defenses of this sort will be discussed in a later section.

adolescent's evaluations of his own intellectual ability will influence his hopes concerning who and what he may become. If he is convinced that he is stupid, this conviction is likely to close many avenues of life to him that might in reality be open. Even in the late elementary grades, he may look upon himself as one who cannot take a full academic program in high school and should not even think about going to college. When his thinking is dominated by this idea, he is likely to shut off lines of vocational choice which he might otherwise consider and about which he might daydream.

On the other hand, the person who is confident about his mental ability can plan and dream on a more expansive scale. The "inner world" in which he moves in his fancies and his thoughts is larger. He can freely give play to imagination about entering this or that occupation. He can see himself in a cap and gown along with the best of them. He can conceive of himself as being more or less at home in any group because he has the ability, so he believes, to move in any intellectual circle into which his interests may lead him.

In the growing person's picture of his mental abilities there will, of course, be varying degrees of realism. He may be canny in his judgment of his ability, or he may be underrating or overrating himself. But whether or not the estimate is realistic, it will have a vital influence on the growing person's outlook on life.

Trends in the Growth of Understanding

As a young person matures intellectually, changes occur in his thinking and concept formation.

INCREASED ABILITY TO GENERALIZE

The normal adolescent is able to generalize far better than he could when he was a young child. The younger the child, the more his thinking is likely to be restricted to specific things. As he grows older, he is able to think in more inclusive terms. This was illustrated in a study (Jersild and Tasch, 1949) in which children were asked to name "three wishes." In Grades I to III, 80 per cent of all wishes dealt with specific material objects or possessions. At Grades VII through XII, only about 30 per cent of the wishes were of this character. The young girl wished, for example, for a new dress, a new hat, and new shoes. The older girl includes a "whole new spring outfit" in one wish and then has two wishes to spare.

While the younger child views things on a *perceptual* level, the older child views them more on a *conceptual* level. For instance, in studies of children's reactions to a war situation (Kimmins, 1915–1916 a and b; Bender and Frosch, 1942; Preston, 1942; and Jersild and Meigs, 1943), it was observed that younger children described war in terms of specific happenings, such as the damage that had been done by bombing. Children near teen-age, on the other hand, saw the war in terms of larger concepts: the damage from a particular bombing was not just an isolated episode, but a sign of danger yet to come.

INCREASED ABILITY TO DEAL WITH ABSTRACTIONS

When children reach the adolescent period, most of them are able to think not only in general terms but also in abstract terms to a greater degree than was true at an earlier age. They are capable of a greater amount of learning involving *symbols* rather than *concrete things*.

The younger child is likely to prefer to deal with a type of problem that goes like this: "In Farmer Brown's barn there are two horses and four cows. How many animals are there in the barn?" At a later age he will tackle a problem that involves the same quantities, but more abstractly, such as: "If X is two and Y is four, how much is X plus Y?" This increased ability to deal with abstractions is recognized by practices in teaching that have to do with quantities. It has been customary, for example, to assume that the typical child becomes ready for thinking in the abstract terms of algebra by about the age of thirteen or fourteen.[2]

The ability to deal with the abstract appears in connection with *qualities* as well as quantities. It is especially important in connection with the growing person's search for meaning. Much that goes into the convictions and commitments which constitute a person's view of life must be formulated in abstract, intellectual terms, if formulated at all. Note the phrasing here: "if formulated at all." A person can have an

---

[2] This assumption works out pretty well in practice, although there are some youngsters who are unable to handle the more difficult problems in algebra at the age of fourteen who probably could do so if given a little more time to mature, say until sixteen or seventeen; and there are some youngsters who never become ready to handle algebra.

effective philosophy of life without being able to define it precisely in intellectual terms. He can be loyal, for example, without being able to give an abstract definition of loyalty. However, to the extent that a person wishes to grasp, in general intellectual terms, his own beliefs and values or wishes to clarify for himself some of the meanings he holds, to that extent, ability to think abstractly about qualitative concepts is essential. And if he is seeking to communicate his thoughts and feelings to others, to share them, and to catch the meaning of the values others embrace, it is necessary to be able to comprehend the meaning of abstract concepts and to express such meanings in words.

One aspect of the ability to deal with abstractions is an understanding of symbols. An illustration of the development of this understanding appears in a study of the ability to grasp the meaning of cartoons. Shaffer (1930) devised a scale for measuring the ability of young people in Grades IV through XII to interpret the symbolism in ten cartoons dealing with social, political, and economic problems. In Grades IV and V (corresponding roughly to ages nine to eleven) many children simply gave a literal description of what the drawing contained, while in higher grades there was a considerable increase in abstract interpretations.

One cartoon, depicting the need for public support of education, showed a man (citizen) passing a crumbling school building. In Grades IV, V, and VI over half of the children either gave a simple descriptive response (such as, "Schools should have better buildings"). In Grades VIII through XII from 62 to 84 per cent of the children gave abstract interpretations (such as the idea that education needs public support).

INCREASED ABILITY TO DEAL WITH THE CONCEPT OF TIME

As children reach the ages of eleven and twelve, they show an improvement in their ability to conceive of the past. As they approach the teens, they show an increased understanding of, and preoccupation with, the future.

In early childhood, it is apparently easier for children to comprehend the idea of the immediate past, such as yesterday, than to comprehend the near future, such as tomorrow (Friedman, 1944a). Even so, it is not until approximately the ages of eleven to thirteen that the majority of children grasp the abstract idea of the historical past (Oakden and Sturt, 1922; Bradley, 1947). At the sixth-grade level (which is close to the beginning of adolescence for many children), the understanding of time concepts is still incomplete.

Understanding of time concepts has been measured by tests of the meaning of terms descriptive of time (medieval, B.C., etc.); locating historical events on a time line; placing in proper sequence the times of Lincoln, Washington, Columbus, and the mother of the person taking the test (Friedman, 1944b). Responses to such tests show a gain in understanding of time until the tenth grade, when young people reach about the same level of understanding as that shown by the average adult.

Although the ability to anticipate the future, to imagine what might happen in it, to plan for it, begins to develop in childhood, it comes into play especially during adolescent years. Building a perspective about the future requires greater mental maturity than building a perspective concerning the past.

Adolescents' ability to grasp and apply the concept of the future in a personal way has not been studied systematically. However, the ability is revealed indirectly when adolescents plan for vocational careers and show a realistic appreciation of how their present activities serve goals that cannot be realized until a future time.[3]

Ability to deal with the concept of the future is especially important as adolescents make the transition from childhood to adulthood. In making this transition the enterprising adolescent anticipates adult status long before he actually is an adult. Adolescents show evidence of anticipating this future status as adults when they make idealistic plans for bettering the society in which they live.

INCREASED ABILITY TO DEAL WITH IDEAS WITHOUT IMMEDIATE PERSONAL INVOLVEMENT

The younger the child, the more he is concerned with things in which he is directly involved. As he becomes older, he becomes increasingly able to be concerned about conditions that do not even indirectly affect him in any obvious way. His thoughts encompass not only himself and his immediate family but also people in the world at large.

Some facets of this ability are well established in a large percentage of children as they approach adolescent years (Baker, 1942). At the sixth-

[3] Much of what the adolescent is required to learn has meaning only if he is able to view it as an investment in the future.

grade level the topics youngsters talk about in "free discussion" periods at school range far beyond happenings at home or in the immediate community. Intellectually, young adolescents are to a greater degree citizens in the larger world of adults than they were in the early or middle elementary school grades. To some extent, however, this interest is deceptive and artificially induced by their teachers. Youngsters who in class avidly discuss the political situation in the Middle East are unlikely to give this topic a passing thought when they converse with each other outside the classroom. But at any rate, they are able in the classroom to play the inellectual game on a more expansive scale than when they were younger.

INCREASED CAPACITY FOR LOGICAL THOUGHT AND COMMUNICATION

As youngsters approach the adolescent period, they become increasingly able to carry on a discussion in which there is a "meeting of minds" on a single theme (Baker, 1942). This enables young people not only to share their thoughts but also to argue about them, test them, and, in the process, examine the rationale of their own thinking. According to Inhelder and Piaget (1958, p. 341), the young adolescent's interest in spinning theories, speculating, and expressing ideas about various and sundry issues in the world about him represents an important phase of his transition from childhood to adulthood. ". . . each one has his own ideas (and usually he believes they are his own) which liberate him from childhood and allow him to place himself as an equal with adults." Inhelder and Piaget view the early teens as a period when decisive changes occur or have occurred in the nature of children's thinking.[4] Some other investigators view these changes in thinking as occurring in many children before adolescence. But, whatever their timing, it is instructive to examine them.

One important attribute of a normal adolescent's thinking is his ability to keep a concept in mind and to apply it abstractly. This enables him to apply a principle in theory without having to make concrete tests along the way. It also enables him to keep a variable in mind without being distracted by other variables. For example, having grasped the principle of specific gravity and the idea of density of matter, he will be able to foretell that a penny will sink if placed in water, even though it is small, and that a cork will float, even though it is much larger than a penny.

[4] Since Jean Piaget's classic studies of the development of thinking have been based mainly on work with preadolescent children they will not be reviewed here.

Likewise, having grasped these principles he will be able to calculate how much water a 6 x 6 x 6–inch cork will displace from knowing the amount displaced by a 3 x 3 x 3–inch cork.

Another important attribute of a normal adolescent's thinking is his ability to become aware of his thought processes and to retrace the steps in his thinking. He does this when, in the example just cited, he tests the accuracy of his solution to the problem with the 6 x 6 x 6–inch cork by reviewing the formula that he appplied in arriving at the solution and checking the correctness of his arithmetic; but he does not actually have to go through the motions of finding a big cork and putting it in a container of water.

The adolescent reaches a further important achievement when he is able to keep an abstract idea in mind as a hypothesis and trace where it would lead even if it is contrary to known fact. This enables him to deal with the problem of "if." Having grasped the idea of weightlessness (suspension of the law of gravity) he can answer the question: You need the strength of both your arms to hold up a child so he can watch a parade. What happens to the child if you have an uncontrollable urge to scratch your leg and, in the same instant, the law of gravity is suspended?

He reaches an even greater achievement when he is able to keep an abstract idea in mind while examining the logical consequences of a line of thought, even though the idea is not only contrary to what he thinks is a fact but also contrary to what he desires to believe. When able to do this, he can tackle a problem such as: Assuming your teacher is *not* biased, as you think she is, how would that change your ideas about the mark she gave you on that examination?

The ability to keep an abstract idea in mind as a hypothetical constant, as an idea that is conserved in spite of all competing perceptions and prejudices, is a powerful tool. It enables the adolescent, potentially, to grasp the logic of science, to assimilate the discoveries made by others, and, if he is bright, to launch on discoveries of his own. It enables him, potentially, to view ideas and issues in the human area from the standpoint of another person. It enables him, potentially, to question his own ideas and attitudes from an objective point of view. The human mind reaches supreme heights when it is able to examine its own operations.

From a strictly cognitive or intellectual point of view, an intelligent adolescent possesses a latent capacity for taking a thoughtful view of his own subjective experiences. He is not likely to employ this capacity effectively, however, unless it is nurtured and cultivated. We will discuss this matter in a later section.

PLEASURES OF THE MIND

Besides being potentially a powerful tool, the mind of the normal adolescent can also be a source of joy. Among the significant satisfactions in life are "pleasures of the mind"—the excitement of being curious, the thrill of discovery, the triumph of finding an answer to a puzzling question or mastering a challenging problem. Most adolescents, as young children, eagerly sought these pleasures. They scarcely had learned to talk before they came forth with a barrage of questions: What? How? Why? Where? They also began to speculate, to venture forth with answers of their own. ("Behold the Child among his new-born blisses, See at his feet some little plan or chart.")

However, as time goes on, the eager questioner is likely to become more and more silent. At school his curiosity seems more often to be blunted than sharpened. He loses his zest and begins to act "as if his whole vocation were endless imitation." At the adolescent level, a large proportion of youngsters show less appetite for the intellectual fare at school than they did when they were younger (Jersild and Tasch, 1949).

Adolescents who lack interest and whose thinking is not challenged by what they are taught at school are likely to have poor academic records —which is serious enough—but they are likely also to suffer from more profound limitations. A person who is constantly labeled as a failure, or who is constantly on the edge of failure, lives in a depressing emotional climate.

Even youngsters who manage not to fail may lack the sense of achievement which contributes to mental health. Almy (1962, p. 470–71) points out that schools have failed in their mental health role when youngsters find no intellectual stimulation at school and are "without commitments, with little sense of personal challenge, beset by apathy." According to Almy, teen-agers who are in this state "spend their days in waiting," begun when they were much younger, when they were waiting to graduate from elementary school. They go on "waiting to graduate from high school, and then waiting for college, or waiting for marriage, or waiting for a job that involves waiting for quitting time. Then they wait for the coming of their children." When schools fail to provide a challenge for these children they, in their turn, ". . . will carry on the endless waiting, the endless round of meaningless activity."

To realize the mental health potentials of the intellectual part of the school's program, according to Almy, it is essential not just to get a youngster to learn to repeat the correct answers for academic questions but to help him understand the meaning of these answers for him. Without such understanding, learning is a mechanical exercise, an academic goose-step. But when youngsters are able to perceive a personal meaning in what they learn, the enterprise of learning and thinking comes alive. There is a quickening of the intellect and, to that degree, a greater animation in the youngster's whole life.

Growth in Ability As Measured by Intelligence Tests

The kind of mental ability measured by commonly used intelligence tests continues to "grow" until about the age of twenty and beyond, although the rate of growth is not as rapid during the late teens as during earlier years. The amount of change varies also according to the kind of mental task being done.

Figure 6.1 shows results obtained when the Army Alpha Test was given to persons at various ages from ten to sixty in several New England communities. The figure shows the results for the composite test, consisting of eight parts. It reveals a gain from year to year to about the age of twenty. It also shows the beginning of a gradual decline shortly thereafter, but concerning this decline we will have more to say at a later point.

Table 6.1 is based on a study by Freeman and Flory (1937) of a group of boys and girls who were tested annually from the age of eight to the age of seventeen. The table shows the annual increase in scores on four parts of the intelligence test. As can be seen, each succeeding year showed a gain over the preceding year, but the gains became smaller as the young people moved on into the teens. It is also apparent, however, that the young people were still gaining at the age of seventeen, when most of them dropped out of the study. Some of the individuals represented in Table 6.1 were retested after they had left high school and had spent a year or more in college. The average score at 17 years of fifteen boys was 245.7; on a later test at an average of 18.7 years, the average was 277.5. There were eleven girls who earned an average score of 246 at the age of 17 and an average of 278.8 when tested at an average age

TABLE 6.1

ANNUAL INCREMENTS ON THE FOUR PARTS OF TEST AND ON THE TOTAL TEST ADMINISTERED
TO THE SAME GROUP OF CHILDREN ANNUALLY FROM AGE EIGHT TO AGE SEVENTEEN *

Tests	Ages									
	8–9	9–10	10–11	11–12	12–13	13–14	14–15	15–16	16–17
Vocabulary	6.25	5.81	6.23	4.89	3.72	3.31	3.85	3.95	2.01
Analogies	3.62	5.35	4.83	3.90	4.67	4.56	2.91	1.16	.38
Completion	5.31	6.84	6.31	8.05	6.45	5.99	6.95	4.78	2.96
Opposites	3.59	3.90	4.90	4.53	3.80	2.22	3.59	2.47	.34
Total Test	18.85	21.62	22.27	22.20	18.17	15.80	18.26	11.61	5.58

* Adapted from F. N. Freeman and C. D. Flory, *Growth in Intellectual Ability as Measured by Repeated Tests*. Monographs of the Society for Research in Child Development, 2, No. 2, 1937.

[121

of 18.7 years. These limited findings indicated that mental ability, as measured by these tests, continued to increase at the college level.

In the study just referred to, those who were below the average in this particular population continued to make proportionately the same amount of gain during the teens as those who were average. The authors suggest that this indicates the slowly developing child can profit proportionately as much as the bright child by prolonged schooling. They point out that this may not hold, however, for extremely dull individuals.

Other findings dealing with trends in the growth of intelligence are shown in a study by Thorndike (1948), based on two or more tests and retests of about one thousand persons ranging in age from thirteen and a half to twenty. The findings indicate that in individuals still attending school, "Ability to achieve on a standard type of paper and pencil test of intelligence or scholastic aptitude continues to increase at least until age 20 and probably beyond" (p. 15). Thorndike computes the approximate age at which growth *theoretically* might cease by statistically projecting beyond the age of twenty the facts known about mental growth up to the age of twenty. According to one method of calculation, the probable point at which no more growth would take place is twenty-five years, nine months; according to another method of computation, it would be reached at twenty-one years, six months. Thorndike points out that these values are highly speculative, yet they emphasize the point that, according to the results he obtained, mental growth as usually defined would probably continue beyond at least the age of twenty in a population such as the one he studied.

THE ROLE OF HEREDITY
AND ENVIRONMENT

Studies of the development of young people as they enter and go through the adolescent period emphasize the influence of both heredity and environment on intellectual ability.

One of the most impressive investigations in this area is a long-term study of adopted children by Skodak and Skeels (1949), begun with about 300 children in the 1930's. In 1946 it was possible to locate 100 of the children who, with their adoptive parents, were willing to cooperate in a final phase of the study. The investigators regard these 100 as representative of the original 300.

If the environment has an appreciable influence on I.Q., one would expect to find evidence of this in adopted children. Adoptive homes are usually chosen with great care. Careful selection is possible because usually the number of couples desiring to adopt children greatly exceeds the supply. The chances are that voluntary adoptive parents will try to provide as favorable an environment as possible. In addition, adoption agents usually try to "fit the child to the home"—they try, for example, to place a child whose background suggests he might be "college material" with adoptive parents who have a college background. Such "selective placement," if based on sound evidence, would have the effect of producing more similarity between adopted children and their adoptive parents than could be expected by chance.

On the average, the adopted children in the Skodak and Skeels study consistently maintained a higher intellectual level "than would have been predicted from the intellectual, educational or socioeconomic level of the true parents." This indicates that a favorable environment promotes intellectual growth.[5] However, the Skodak and Skeels study also shows that there is no uniform relationship between the environment and children's mental test scores. There was practically a zero correlation between the mental test scores of the children and the educational level of the adoptive fathers and mothers. On various tests administered from about the two-year level to an average thirteen-and-a-half-year level, the correlations between the scores of the children and the educational level of the adoptive mothers ranged from .03 to .10; the corresponding correlations with adoptive fathers ranged from .00 to .06. On the other hand, when the adopted children had reached an average age of thirteen-and-a-half years old, the following correlations appeared when their performance was compared with their true parents from whom they were separated as infants:

Mental test scores of adopted children and *mental test scores* obtained by their true mothers: .38 and .42.[6]

Mental test scores of adopted children and *educational status* of their true mothers: .31, .32.[6]

[5] By contrast, children who are kept in institutions providing a bare minimum of care are not likely to rise above their predicted level but, if anything, are likely to show an impairment in their language development and mental test scores (Skeels, Updegraff *et al.*, 1938).

[6] The two coefficients are based on the children's scores on the 1916 and 1937 revisions of the Stanford-Binet scale. Mental test scores were available for sixty-three of the mothers; information about educational status was available for ninety-two mothers.

These correlations between the performance of the adopted children and their "true" mother's educational level are interesting when compared with findings in a study by Honzik (1957) of children reared by their own parents. Honzik found these correlations between children's mental test scores and the education of their parents:

"Own" children, aged 12–13 and "own" fathers' education: .39; "own" mothers' education: .38.
"Own" children, aged 14–15 and "own" fathers' education: .37; "own" mothers' education: .35.

It is interesting to note that there was a significant relationship be·tween the mental test scores of adopted children and the test scores of their "true" mothers. And it is noteworthy also that the educational status of the true mothers, from whom the children had been separated as infants, gave a better prediction of the children's I.Q.'s than the educational status of the adoptive parents with whom the children had lived most of their lives.[7]

This intriguing finding is not easily explained. There is no way that the educational status of an adopted child's true parents can directly influence the child's I.Q. However, while the educational status a child's true parents attain obviously is influenced by environmental factors, such as family tradition and income, it is likely also to be influenced by their intelligence. To the extent that this is true, the resemblance between the intelligence of adopted children and their true parents' educational status indirectly reflects the influence of the genetic factors which produce a resemblance between the intelligence of adopted children and the intelligence of their true parents.

On the side of heredity, a great accumulation of evidence indicates that genetic factors have a substantial influence on a person's potential level of intellectual ability.[8] The evidence which shows that the environment makes a difference is also impressive, especially from studies of children who have been transferred from a definitely substandard setting to a more stimulating one.[9]

[7] Lawrence (1931) found that the correlation between the intelligence of orphanage children and the socioeconomic status of their parents from whom they had been separated did not decline with age but tended to be slightly higher in the case of children over eleven years old than in the case of children under the age of eleven.

[8] For an extensive review of studies in this area, see Fuller and Thompson, 1960.

[9] See, e.g., Skeels, Updegraff et al. (1938); Klineberg (1935, 1938); Lee (1951).

Available evidence indicates that an improvement in mental functioning is far more likely to appear when youngsters who had been deprived of intellectual nurture are placed in a stimulating environment (Skeels, Updegraff *et al.*, 1938) than when youngsters in a moderately good environment are shifted to a setting that provides richer opportunities (Pritchard, Horan and Hollingworth, 1940).

One aspect of a youngster's development that is influenced by the environment is his verbal ability, which has a high correlation with scores on mental tests. Children differ greatly in their aptitude for mastering the use of words, but word meanings obviously are learned, so individuals who have had poor learning opportunities are penalized on a mental test. They may show a large discrepancy between achievement in some academic subjects and their intelligence test scores.

When large discrepancies such as these occur, it is likely that a person's academic achievement, especially when it involves mastery of abstract ideas, is a truer gauge of his intellectual power than his performance on a mental test. But an opportunity to demonstrate this power is not easily available to students who are advised against taking a college preparatory course, or are denied admission to college, primarily on the basis of their mental test scores.

A long-term study of an older group of adolescents deals with the effects of continued schooling on intelligence (Lorge, 1945). In this study 131 boys were tested in 1921–1922, at the age of fourteen, and again twenty years later, in 1941, at the age of thirty-four. In the meantime, some of these people dropped out of school at the end of the eighth grade, some dropped out during high school years, some completed high school, and some completed one or more years in college. When classified according to similar I.Q.'s at the age of fourteen, most of the groups that continued their formal education longer had higher average scores at the age of thirty-four.

The kind of ability measured by intelligence tests was affected by schooling. More schooling led to a gain. We have no precise way of determining whether such gains mean a general increase in intellectual power or just an increase in ability to perform the specific tasks demanded by an intelligence test. Lorge points out that intelligence tests are, to a large extent, built on tasks that are emphasized at school. They deal with information, reading, vocabulary, arithmetic, reasoning, computation and the like. "Insofar as the tests favor the kinds of things taught in school, they will tend to favor people who have had the greater extent of schooling." This is quite an advantage, for whatever might be the nature of the gain "it can be interpreted as meaning better ability in dealing with the intellectual environment" (Lorge, 1945, p. 490).

However, in this study it was apparent that there are large differences in intelligence that cannot be attributed to schooling. Although persons with more schooling had higher average intelligence scores at the age of thirty-four than similar persons who had had little or no schooling after the age of fourteen, there still was a high degree of correspondence between the scores earned at fourteen and those earned at thirty-four, whether or not the persons had continued their schooling. A high-scoring boy who leaves school at fourteen is likely in his thirties to have a higher score than a low-scoring boy who continues in school for several years. But while schooling is likely to raise the general level to some degree, it is not likely to raise a below-average rating to a far-above-average rating; much less is it likely to change the least able into the most able.[10]

IMPLICATIONS OF THE CONTINUATION OF MENTAL GROWTH INTO THE LATE TEENS AND EARLY TWENTIES

The fact that young people continue to grow in intelligence up to and beyond the age of twenty has important implications for education and for planning a vocation or a career. One implication is that there is a rather long period during which young people might test their abilities so far as academic learning is concerned. If a boy does not have the mental ability to master algebra at the age of fourteen, it does not follow that he is forever barred from learning algebra. As a result of continuing mental growth, he may have the ability to master the subject at sixteen or eighteen. (On the other hand, if we assumed that mental growth ceased at about fourteen, fifteen, or sixteen [as was assumed in the past], we would pretty much have to conclude that if he did not have the necessary ability at about the middle teens he would never possess it.)

The same implication probably holds with respect to many other school subjects, including the learning of subject matter in the areas of physics, chemistry, biology, and other branches of science. Some individuals, who were not fully able to master these subjects in the early or

10 The boys in Lorge's study were measured with a test of abstract intelligence at fourteen and with two other tests in 1941. The correlation between intelligence test scores in 1921–22 and the two tests administered in 1941 was, respectively, .64 and .62.

middle teens, might later be able to do so by virtue of the mental growth that continues into the late teens, for even if their I.Q. remains constant their mental age will increase.

The full implications of findings in recent years to the effect that growth in intelligence continues until the age of twenty or beyond, instead of ceasing at the age of sixteen, if not before, have not yet been explored. It is quite possible that there are many young people who do not seem to be "ready" for the conventional college program at the age of seventeen or eighteen, or who give up or are thrown out, but who might be ready to tackle this program at twenty or twenty-one or later.[11]

CONSISTENCY AND CHANGE
IN RATE OF MENTAL GROWTH

How accurately can the intelligence of a person during the early, middle, and late adolescent years be predicted from tests given at an earlier age? How consistent is a person's rating on intelligence tests likely to be during adolescent years? These queries touch upon the general question of the constancy of the I.Q. We have already anticipated a partial answer to these questions in the account above of findings obtained when Lorge tested young people at the age of fourteen and again twenty years later. Although, as noted, there were changes in intelligence test ratings during the twenty-year period, and these changes tended to favor the boys who had continued their schooling, there still was a high correspondence between scores earned at the age of fourteen and those earned at thirty-four.

Further evidence bearing upon this question has been offered by Thorndike (1947) and others. In an analysis of several thousand test records, Thorndike compared scores obtained by young people at the end of high school and scores obtained by the same group at varying intervals prior to that time. In 600 cases the data provided comparisons with tests given ten or more years prior to the test given at the end of the high school period. Thorndike concluded that tests given at various times during a child's high school career are about equally accurate in foretelling what his score will be at the end of the high school period. In other words, a test given in the freshman year of high school seems to give prac-

---

[11] Many college instructors have maintained that young people who enter military service after high school gain more from college after this delay than they would have gained at an earlier age.

tically as accurate a prediction of a person's score at the end of the senior year as does a test given, say, sometime during the junior or senior year. A test administered in the ninth grade gives almost as accurate a forecast of scores that will be obtained at the end of the senior year as do tests administered only a few months before the end of the senior year. Tests administered during upper elementary grades also give a reasonably accurate statistical prediction of scores at the end of the high school period, but the accuracy of the predictions is somewhat lower. The correspondence between test results at one age and a considerably later age was influenced both by the length of time elapsing between the two tests and also by the particular tests used.

The findings in Thorndike's study imply that as far as the factor of intelligence is concerned, it is possible to give a student substantially as accurate guidance concerning his educational plans at the beginning of his high school course, and perhaps even in the upper elementary grades, as at the end of the course.[12] Such consistency means that substantial changes in score are the exception rather than the rule.

While there is consistency in group trends in mental growth there also are individual variations in the pattern of growth. This was brought out in an investigation by Bayley (1949) in which forty children were tested and retested from early infancy through most or all of eighteen years. Bayley's findings show, as other findings have shown, that the scores children earn on tests given before the age of two do not at all provide an accurate prediction of what the same children will do later on. But test scores become more stable and consistent as children move beyond the preschool period. In the span of years from eleven to eighteen, the correlations between tests separated by an interval of three or more years were not materially or consistently different from correlations obtained between tests separated by an interval of only a year or two.

Bayley advances the theory that as the individual approaches a mature level, or as he comes nearer to the limits of growth in a particular process, fluctuations are likely to be less marked than during an earlier period. As children approach the ceiling, their rate of growth tends to become more stable.

There were some young people in Bayley's study who, during the eighteen-year span of the investigation, tended to be *labile:* they varied from time to time, showing a heightened quickening or a slowing in rate of growth. Other children tended to be relatively *stable,* manifesting

[12] See, also, Bayley (1933, 1940), Honzik (1938), Anderson (1939), Goodenough and Maurer (1942), Ebert and Simmons (1943), and Bradway (1944).

fairly steady progress without spurts and lulls in the growth process. There were other children who, at different periods and for varying lengths of time, appeared to be both labile and stable. For example, a child might be very stable in his intelligence test ratings for several years and then become labile, showing considerable change from test to test. Just what trends such as these might mean Bayley does not have sufficient evidence to tell, but she does point out that, at least within her limited population, the tendency toward lability or stability did not seem to be tied to adult intelligence level.

CHANGES IN INTELLECTUAL FUNCTIONS AFTER ADOLESCENCE

As we have noted, intellectual ability in the average or slightly above-average person as measured by mental tests probably reaches its peak at approximately the early twenties. Now we might ask, what is the trend in intellectual ability after the early twenties?

One of the early investigations dealing with the problem of mental decline was a study by Jones and Conrad (1933) in which the Army Alpha tests were given to persons in New England communities at various age levels from ten to sixty years. Table 6.2 (which is an abridged table) shows the scores at selected age levels on various subtests constituting the total Army Alpha test. According to the results in this study, some of the subtests of the Army Alpha showed a decline with age between the twenties and the fifties. An outstanding exception was the subtest dealing with general information. From the results of this carefully conducted study, it appeared that there is a decline with age in some of the functions or operations involved in what we call intelligence. However, the extent and nature of the decline are still questionable, and the need for further research is indicated by another study (Owens, 1953) using the same tests.

The population in Owens' study consisted of 127 men who had been tested with the Army Alpha, Form 6, as a college entrance test in 1919 and who were tested again about thirty years later, during 1949–1950. In this study there was a retesting of the same population at different ages, as distinguished from the Jones and Conrad study, which tested different populations at different ages. Instead of showing a decline in score during the thirty-year period, as might have been predicted from earlier findings, the individuals in Owens' study showed an increase in the total Alpha

TABLE 6.2

SCORES IN SUBTESTS OF THE ARMY ALPHA INTELLIGENCE TEST AND IN THE TOTAL TEST AT VARIOUS AGE LEVELS *

Alpha Subtest	Age						
	10	14	18	22–24	30–34	40–44	50–54
1. Oral Directions	3.7	5.8	7.2	6.8	6.0	6.2	5.9
2. Arithmetical Problems	5.0	7.1	9.6	9.6	9.1	9.1	8.5
3. Common Sense	4.2	7.5	9.7	8.9	8.5	8.2	7.3
4. Opposites or Vocabulary	5.1	10.3	14.3	13.5	14.0	16.6	14.5
5. Dissected Sentences	6.2	10.1	12.4	12.8	11.3	11.8	10.9
6. Numerical Completions	4.9	7.7	8.5	8.3	7.7	7.7	6.9
7. Analogies	9.7	16.1	18.3	16.4	14.2	12.6	10.8
8. General Information	8.1	14.2	19.7	18.0	20.1	21.4	21.0
Total Alpha	44.4	75.7	97.0	91.8	87.0	92.2	81.3

* Adapted from H. E. Jones and H. S. Conrad, *The Growth and Decline of Intelligence: A Study of a Homogeneous Group Between the Ages of Ten and Sixty*, Genetic Psychology Monographs (1933), 13, No. 3.

score. The increases in some subtests were substantial, and there was no significant decrease in score on any subtest.

Owens raised many questions as to the meaning and interpretation of these results. Among other things, it may be noted that his population consisted of persons who went to college (80 per cent of them finished four or more years of college), while the Jones and Conrad population was a more nearly random sampling of the population at large. It is possible that those who went to college and who were interested in co-operating in such a study thirty years after they had entered college had a stronger motivation to do well on the test than those in a random sampling of the population. It is also possible that they were involved in daily intellectual activities of a kind that might keep them mentally alert and in better trim to do the kinds of tasks required by an intelligence test. It is possible, furthermore, that there has been a change in the general cultural setting that might make a fifty-year-old person of today more alert and testwise than was true of a fifty-year-old person two or three decades ago.

Another study bearing on this subject was conducted by Corsini and Fassett (1953), who tested over one thousand adults at various age levels on the Wechsler-Bellevue test. In their study, as in the Owens study, there was no general decline in intelligence from early to late maturity but instead a downward trend in performance on some subtests (those containing visual and motor factors) and an upward trend on subtests containing material depending on continued learning.

Interesting findings concerning the level of mental ability persons maintain as they grow older have been reported by Bayley and Oden (1955). Over a thousand adults, who were above average in intelligence when tested at an average age of about thirty years, were retested several years later. There was a high correlation between the test and retest scores, and all groups who took part in the study showed an increase in the average scores on the retest. The findings indicate that in this large group of superior adults there is strong evidence that the kind of intelligence tested by means of a "concept mastery" scale continues to increase at least through fifty years of age.

In other studies in this area, it has been found that older persons are more likely to show a decline in performing mental tasks that have a time limit and call for *speed* than on untimed tests allowing the one who is being tested to draw upon his fund of knowledge at his own pace. An indication of a decline in speed with age in certain operations is shown in Table 6.3. This table presents the results of testing individuals at different age levels (a different group at each level) on an instrument for which there was no time limit (CAVD) and on two tests that had a time limit, the Army Alpha and the Otis intelligence tests. Those who took part in the study were equated, so that all three age groups had approximately the same score on the test on which there was no time limit. Table 6.3 indicates that, on the speed tests, those in the age range from twenty to twenty-five did better than those in the age range from twenty-seven to

TABLE 6.3

AVERAGE SCORES OF THREE AGE GROUPS ON THREE INTELLIGENCE TESTS. THE GROUPS WERE EQUATED ON THE CAVD (COMPLETION, ARITHMETIC, VOCABULARY, DIRECTIONS) WITH NO TIME LIMIT, AND TESTED ON THE ARMY ALPHA AND THE OTIS WITH A TIME LIMIT *

Age	CAVD	Army Alpha	Otis (20-minute limit)
20–25	405.3	149.6	44.4
27–37½	405.7	142.3	39.3
Over 40	405.5	128.7	33.4

* I. Lorge, "Psychometry: The Evaluation of Mental Status as a Function of the Mental Test," *Journal of Educational Psychology* (1936), 27, 100–110.

thirty-seven and a half on the tests with a time limit. Further, those in their late twenties and thirties did better than those in their forties or beyond. The differences, as can be seen, are quite pronounced, although it must be noted that again we are dealing with three different groups of persons rather than with a single group of persons tested some time in their early twenties, again in their early thirties, and again in their forties and beyond.

Another difference that has been noted is that the older adults have greater difficulty than the younger ones in forming entirely new associations than in performing intellectual tasks to which they have long been accustomed. In a study by Gilbert (1941) a group aged between twenty and twenty-nine and a group aged sixty to sixty-nine, who had about the same intelligence level as measured by a vocabulary test (vocabulary has usually shown a high correlation with general intelligence) were tested on their ability to remember a Turkish-English vocabulary (Turkish was new to all of them). The older group earned scores 60 per cent lower than those of the younger group. However, when tested on memory span for digits (the number of digits a person can reproduce correctly immediately after one presentation), their performance was only 8.5 per cent poorer than that of the younger group.

The older persons either had difficulty in forming entirely new associations, such as would be required in learning the Turkish equivalent of English words, or were less interested in making the necessary effort. It was also found, incidentally, that the brightest older adults retained their ability to master new materials better than older adults who were not so bright. (This is in keeping with other findings pertaining to aging in relation to brightness.)

In some studies, there is evidence that the older person's speed is likely to vary with the kind of intellectual task. When asked to make a decision or to solve a complicated problem within his own area of specialization, the older person is less likely to show a loss in speed than when asked to deal with tasks that are not part of his customary mental activity. The older person's loss of speed seems to be most pronounced in performances that are artificially contrived, such as managing complicated patterns of lights and switches, or performances that require flexibility, such as shifting back and forth from addition to substraction instead of completing a set of addition problems and then a set of subtraction problems.[13]

When we observe differences such as these between older and younger persons, we may well ask what these differences mean. Has the older person actually slowed down and suffered a substantial decline in ability to learn new things? Or is there a difference in his attitude and approach so that he feels less inclined to hurry, and less concerned about mastering an assignment given to him by someone else? There is need for further research in this matter, but whatever may be the underlying condition, the mental operations of an older person are different in some ways from what they were when he was younger, and this may have an important bearing on the way the old regard the young and the young regard the old.

Young people are often impatient with what seems to be the cumbersome working of the older person's mind, especially in adapting to new things. What the youngster takes for stubbornness may actually be slower uptake. Likewise, when the oldster complains about the young person's newfangled ideas, or objects to new features in the schooling of the young or to new viewpoints on economic or social or philosophical problems, the

[13] Studies by Clay (1954), Kay (1955), and others, dealing with experiments in this area, have been reviewed by Jones (1959).

difference may spring not so much from the fact that he is prejudiced against the new as such but that it is harder for him, now that he is older, to get interested in new ideas.

Superior and Gifted Youth

Young people with I.Q.'s of 120 or 125 or above who are commonly labeled as "superior," comprise from 5 to 10 per cent of their age group. Persons within this group with I.Q.'s of 135 to 140 and above, who are commonly labeled as "gifted," represent from 1 to 3 per cent of the total population.

A bright adolescent is an important social asset. The present age of science, technology, and complicated social engineering requires good brains. In commenting about this, Neel (1960) states, "Not all of us are born with the intellectual endowment which permits us to master higher mathematics, nuclear physics, electronics, advanced chemistry, or certain aspects of economics, sociology or medicine." Neel estimates that "certainly less than 10 per cent" of individuals in our population are "inherently capable of making the really original contributions in these fields on which our national well-being depends." This estimate of 10 per cent is no doubt arbitrary, but it highlights the social importance of mental ability.[14]

Brightness is obviously also an important personal asset, although many adolescents, when evaluating themselves, emphasize other qualities more than their intelligence. They are more likely, for example, to mention their emotional and social characteristics than their mental abilities when describing what they admire in themselves (Jersild, 1952). There are, however, two qualifications that should be made. First, young people who go to college (and probably also high school students who are bound for college) place a higher premium on intelligence than those who do not intend to go to college. Second, many young people probably attach more importance to intelligence than they openly admit.

Even when young people do not express pride in being bright they are likely to go to great lengths in resisting the idea that they may not be as bright as they would like to be. This appears indirectly in a study in which students and their teachers gave their opinion as to why students fail in

[14] There are those who believe that much latent talent remains undiscovered and uncultivated, especially in underprivileged sections of the population (see, e.g., Bond, 1960).

high school subjects (Gilbert, 1931). In making a check list of reasons for failure, teachers gave the highest rating to "lack of brains." By contrast, "lack of brains" ranked eighth in students' accounts. Students marked such items as "laziness," "dislike for the subject," "hard to study at home," "sickness," "shows and parties" as more important than lack of ability as reasons for not succeeding in schoolwork. Students were more inclined than teachers to attribute difficulty in schoolwork to a physical weakness (sickness) or a moral weakness (laziness) than to lack of mental ability.

Many facts have been established concerning typical gifted adolescents.[15] Most of them were "gifted children," whose brightness showed forth at an early age. Most of them come from homes that are above average or at least average in socioeconomic status (although there also are many very bright youngsters in lower socioeconomic groups [Drews, 1957, 1961]). They are above average in size and health. Compared with other youngsters they usually have more favorable attitudes toward school. They are more concerned than the average with abstract ideas. They have more interests and hobbies than children of average intelligence (Abraham, 1957). They are above average on tests of emotional adjustment, honesty, and moral judgment. (However, their superior standing on such tests may be due in part to greater shrewdness in guessing what the tester regards as the "right" answer.) Many of the personal and social qualities in which they excel are characteristic of persons in the socioeconomic level from which a majority of the gifted come. The good showing they make in a number of characteristics may therefore be linked with their family background rather than solely with their high I.Q. (Bonsall and Stellfre, 1955).

Gifted young people demonstrate the principle that in human development "correlation rather than compensation is the developmental rule": to him that hath, much is given. But there are many exceptions. Bright adolescents, on the average, do superior schoolwork, but many are "underachievers" (Goldberg, Gotkin, and Tannenbaum, 1959). The correlation between I.Q. and academic achievement in high school is about .60 (Thorndike and Hagen, 1961)—a respectable correlation, but far lower than would prevail if each youngster's schoolwork were on a par with his intelligence test score. Although they are, on the average, superior in tests of adjustment, some bright children bear the scars of old wounds, acquired when they were resented or misunderstood by their

[15] See Terman (1916), Terman and Oden (1940, 1959), Hollingworth (1926, 1939), Strang (1956), Dunlap (1958), Goldberg (1962).

teachers and rejected by their schoolmates.[16] Many suffer from feelings of inadequacy in spite of their high ability (Smith, 1932). In Terman's classic long-term study it was found that at age forty or fifty, individuals who had been in the gifted group excelled the average to a more marked degree in scholastic and vocational success than in social and emotional adjustment (Terman and Oden, 1959).

Extremely bright youngsters may actually appear to be misfits and oddballs when thrown in with an average group of peers (or teachers), especially when they are aggressive in asserting their cleverness or have interests others can neither understand nor share. They themselves cannot help but become aware that they are in some ways different from others.

Gifted young people face many hurdles. They face the boredom and monotony of the usual school situation. They run the risk of developing poor work habits in high school that will plague them when they face stiffer competition in college. They face the difficult task of acquiring harmony between their intellectual precocity and their social and emotional development.

For some, the greatest problem is to avoid "selling out," as it were, to the intellect while sacrificing their capacity for feeling. In a study recently completed by the writer and his associates, this problem was mentioned by many bright persons, and more often by women than by men (1962). A person who easily masters the usual academic skills, and is honored for this ability, can be lured, so it seems, into placing his or her chips on this success, while neglecting other resources.[17]

THE BRIGHT "UNDERACHIEVER"

The so-called underachiever is one whose work at school is distinctly poorer than might be expected from his score on an intelligence test. The problem of underachievement becomes especially baffling when bright students fail, or are constantly on the margin of failure, or show a sharp discrepancy between their mental test ratings and academic performance.

[16] Hollingworth (1926, 1939) gives illustrations of this.

[17] One of the women in the study mentioned above expressed her regret about having gone "all out" for the intellectual by saying, "From now on I want to be a woman, not just a brain." Many other bright women voiced the same sentiment, and many men expressed a corresponding aspiration—a desire to be more tender and compassionate. They were not saying that brains and warmth of feeling are incompatible. Rather, they were saying that a highly intellectual person runs the risk of becoming a detached person.

Underachievement among gifted youngsters frequently becomes most apparent in early high school years (Terman, 1947).

The first question that might be raised about the "underachiever" is: According to what standard, and whose standard, is he an underachiever? Maybe he is so labeled because he is not eager to meet the usual academic requirements but is using his mind in his own way. If so, the idea of "underachievement" exists primarily in the minds of teachers who want everyone to learn what they teach and the way they teach it.

History records many examples of persons who did not do well at school but made great names for themselves. If a bright "underachiever" is carving out a destiny of his own, he may be a wiser and more mature person than the one who doggedly gets high marks in all his school subjects. But the situation is not so simple. Many underachievers, while failing or doing marginal work at school, are not finding success or satisfaction by other routes. In the Terman study, it was found that gifted individuals who were least successful in their occupations as young adults included a large proportion of persons who had a history of underachievement in high school.

Many studies have been made of bright underachievers on the assumption that, since their I.Q.'s are high, the reason for their lower-than-expected school performance must be due to nonintellectual factors— their personal and social characteristics. In several studies it has been found that underachievers show more signs of personal maladjustment than persons who do well at school, but the findings as a whole are conflicting and inconclusive (Raph and Tannenbaum, 1961).

There is some evidence that bright underachievers, on the average, receive less constructive discipline and less intellectual encouragement and support at home. In a review of studies in this area, Raph and Tannenbaum (1961) note that students with a record of successful academic achievement tend to come from the higher socioeconomic and educational backgrounds, and from homes where there has been an emphasis on cultural pursuits. However, some youngsters who are good achievers come from homes in the lower socioeconomic and educational brackets. A study by Kahl (1953) indicates that low-status youngsters are more serious about schoolwork and have higher aspirations when their families are interested in "getting ahead" than when their parents are satisfied with their low status. According to Goldberg (1962, p. 19) it appears that "within a given socioeconomic stratum a family's attitude toward their occupational status has a greater influence on the achievement expectations of the sons than does actual class membership."

Several investigators have also found that many underachievers come from disrupted homes. One special circumstance that has been observed in some boy underachievers is a lack of identification with their fathers (Kimball, 1953; Goldberg, 1959; [18] Gowan, 1955).

Findings regarding the home throw some light on the relationship between underachievement and a young person's family situation, but they leave much unexplained. Many successful students come from what appear to be unfavorable home environments, and many unsuccessful ones have what appear to be desirable backgrounds.

In view of the varying findings, Raph and Tannenbaum (1961, p. 19) state that good or poor personal adjustment or desirable or undesirable home conditions do not, *per se,* account for expected achievement, or for underachievement at school. "Despite the voluminous work done in this area, we do not as yet have a clear profile of traits that distinguish underachievers from their comparably able peers who live up to scholastic expectations."

How, then, can we account for the fact that many young people with high I.Q.'s are underachievers? One answer is that perhaps the label of "underachievement" often is a mislabel. The concept of underachievement rests on the assumption that there should be a substantial correspondence between a person's I.Q. as measured by a standard intelligence test and his success in academic subjects, and it implies that when schoolwork is not up to expectations the reasons must be nonintellectual (poor emotional adjustment, poor motivation, unfavorable home conditions, etc.). But, as we have noted, the evidence that nonintellectual factors are responsible is not conclusive.

Even when a relationship seems to exist between poor achievement and emotional stress we cannot take for granted, without further evidence, that the former is due to the latter. Some underachievers have hostile attitudes, for example, but this does not prove that their hostility is responsible for poor work at school. Unless there is evidence to the contrary, it is just as reasonable to assume that their hostility is a result of their experiences at school as to assume it is the cause of their lower-than-expected performance. Even evidence which indicates that some who do not do well at school come from homes that are not "achievement-conscious" is open to various interpretations. When parents of a youngster who does

---

[18] There are far more underachievers among boys than among girls. This is in keeping with other findings showing that boys far outnumber girls in language difficulties, reading difficulties, and "problem behavior" at school.

poorly at school do not seem to set high standards before him, the reason may not be that they are unconcerned, but that they have become weary or discouraged, or regard it as futile or unkind to keep hammering away at him, or the reason might be that they value other achievements more than academic achievement.

The lack of clear evidence as to why students with favorable I.Q.'s do not achieve up to expectations has led some investigators to question whether such students actually *are* underachieving. It is possible that the expectations placed on them by others are unrealistic, based on a misconception of the power of a high I.Q., and of the varied abilities measured by the test on which an I.Q. is based.

There are many components or "factors" [19] of intelligence, and an I.Q. is usually derived from the composite score on a test that includes several subtests (such as vocabulary, ability to perceive relationships, information, reasoning from given facts). A person may earn a high I.Q. and still be quite uneven in his abilities on these subtests. A person's performance on the sampling of intellectual tasks used to determine his I.Q. does not necessarily indicate how well he might (or should) do on other intellectual tasks.

In discussing this point, Goldberg (1962) notes, for example, that intelligence accounts for only a small portion of the individual differences students show in their ability to learn a foreign language. She questions whether a bright youngster who fails French or Spanish should automatically be regarded as an underachiever. In spite of his high I.Q. he may simply lack the kind of intellectual ability involved in learning a foreign language. Goldberg likewise points out that intelligence test scores account for "only a modest portion" of individual differences in ability in mathematics.

These observations regarding the limitations of the I.Q. as a basis for foretelling what a student will do, or prescribing what he should be expected to do, in school subjects, do not negate the importance of intelligence test scores. They do emphasize the point, however, that there are intellectual qualities which the typical intelligence test does not measure. They also underline the point that unless we know more about an adolescent than is told by his mental test rating, we should hesitate to belabor him, or his parents, if his achievement is below expectations.

[19] In a discussion of components of the intellect, Guilford (1959) comments, "With about 50 intellectual factors already known, we may say that there are at least 50 ways of being intelligent."

Varieties of Intellectual Functioning

Two people with similar I.Q.'s may differ greatly in their intellectual performance and in the way they apply their minds. This holds true even among adolescents with very high I.Q.'s. One is glib, one is profound. One scintillates, another is unimaginative. One can excel all comers on a TV quiz program, "throw the book," so to speak; another might respond in a clumsy fashion to a rapid-fire quiz but comes forth with novel ideas of his own. One moves in a conventional, logical way toward finding the correct answer to a problem; another speculates, introduces new ideas of his own and evolves novel solutions.

It appears that the typical intelligence test measures an adolescent's ability to give the right answers that already have been established by others rather than his inventiveness, his ability to come forth with an *original* answer that goes beyond what is known.

Studies by Guilford (1959) of the structure of intelligence provide a clue to tests that might better identify adolescents with a talent for originality than the intelligence tests now commonly used. Guilford identifies "five major groups of intellectual abilities": (1) *cognition*—"discovery or rediscovery or recognition"; (2) *memory*—"retention of what is cognized"; (3) *convergent thinking*—using information in a way that "leads to one right answer or to a recognized best or conventional answer"; (4) *divergent thinking*—thinking "in different directions, sometimes searching, sometimes seeking variety"; and (5) *evaluation*—through which we "reach decisions as to the goodness, correctness, suitability or adequacy of what we know, what we remember, and what we produce in productive thinking."

CONVERGENT AND DIVERGENT THINKING AND CREATIVITY

The distinction between *convergent* and *divergent* thinking is especially noteworthy. In divergent thinking, as compared with convergent thinking, there is more flexibility, originality, a greater flow of ideas, more ingenuity. The course of divergent thought is not confined to the information at hand; it goes beyond what is obvious and apparent. In convergent thinking, thought is more channeled or controlled in the direction of finding one correct solution. In divergent thinking there is less conformity to a fixed pattern, more freedom to strike off in new and different directions, more of a disposition to consider several possible answers and novel solutions. Divergent thinking draws more upon creative abilities than does convergent thinking. Although creativity is an elusive quality, psychologists in recent years have made progress in identifying and measuring some of the properties of a creative mind.[20]

Among the characteristics of creativeness are "adventurous thinking" (Bartlett, 1959) which enables a person to get off the beaten track; initiative in pursuing new lines of thought; sensitivity to problems; flexibility (as in divergent thinking); a rich flow of ideas; originality. The creative person ventures, takes risks, makes novel assumptions, questions rules and authority, enjoys trying out a hunch, takes the risk of venturing into what others regard as absurd or silly.

An interesting study of adolescents by Getzels and Jackson (1960) is an outgrowth, in part, of Guilford's work on divergent thinking and creativity. Over 400 students in a high school were tested by means of conventional intelligence tests and also on a battery of tests of creativity. From the total population the investigators singled out two groups for special study: a *high creativity group* of 26 students (students in the top 20 per cent in creativity) and a *high intelligence group* (28 students who were in the top 20 per cent in I.Q., compared with students of the same age and sex, but not in the top 20 per cent in creativity). They then compared these two groups with each other and with the remaining students in the school.

The high-I.Q. group (average I.Q., 150) and the high-creativity group (average I.Q., 127) were equally superior to the total population in standardized school achievement tests. But beyond this there were many interesting differences. In response to a series of stimulus-pictures, the high-creativity group greatly exceeded the high-I.Q. group in giving unexpected endings, in humor, incongruity, playfulness, and stimulus-free themes (mentioning details of happenings not obviously apparent in the pictures).

Getzels and Jackson state that the kind of divergent thinking involved in creativity is not well sampled by the usual intelligence test items. In the

---

[20] Guilford's work on the complexity of mental operations, and notably his distinction between divergent and convergent thinking abilities, has done much to stimulate inquiry into creativity. See Guilford, 1959. See also Guilford, 1950; Guilford *et al.,* 1951; Guilford *et al.,* 1952; Guilford *et al.,* 1960; Torrance, 1959a, 1959b, 1962; Getzels and Jackson, 1960.

same vein, Torrance (1962, p. 4) states "traditional tests of intelligence are heavily loaded with tasks requiring cognition, memory and convergent thinking." He also states that to assess abilities involved in creative thinking, it is necessary to develop and administer tests which are different from those commonly used to measure mental ability and intellectual achievement. Among the shortcomings of the traditional instruments, according to Torrance, are an overemphasis on traditional academic values, and lack of differentiation between talent, creativity, and conformity.[21]

Youngsters who have been identified as high in creativity, on the basis of tests and criteria that have been developed to date, are, in many respects, nonconformers. Torrance (1962) and Getzels and Jackson (1960) give many pithy illustrations of unconventional thinking in creative youngsters. Such thinking apparently often is not admired by teachers, and it may even be disconcerting. In the Getzels-Jackson study teachers showed a greater preference for the high I.Q. group than for the high creativity group. If we may believe legends about creative thinkers in the past, they also often had to swim against the tide, or, as Kierkegaard puts it, "come up against the wind."

When students in the Getzels and Jackson investigation were asked to name their vocational interests, a large proportion of the high-creativity group mentioned unusual occupations (adventurer, inventor, writer) while a large proportion of the high-intelligence group mentioned conventional occupations (lawyer, doctor, professor).

A promising start has been made in identifying and measuring creative abilities more adequately than these have been measured in conventional intelligence tests. Tests of creativity have been developed more recently than the standardized tests of I.Q.; they have not been used on the same massive scale; they have not been tested, as have I.Q. tests, by longitudinal studies of large numbers of persons through childhood, adolescence, and into middle age. The work that has been done in identifying and measuring creativity, however, supports Guilford's statement that "the multiplicity of mental abilities seems well established"

---

[21] A low degree of emphasis on divergent or creative thinking apparently also prevails in the teaching of school subjects. In a survey by Torrance (1962) social studies teachers in high schools were asked to list the three most important objectives in the teaching of units or courses in their subject-matter area. When classified according to Guilford's five groups of mental abilities the following results appeared: emphasis on *cognition,* 70.7 per cent; *memory,* 5.3 per cent; *convergent thinking,* 18.7 per cent; *divergent thinking,* 1.7 per cent; *evaluation,* 3.6 per cent.

(1959, p. 479). It also strengthens the view, held by many authorities, that in searching for talented adolescents and in awarding scholarships, it is better to use a multidimensional measure of intellectual abilities and temperamental qualities than to rely entirely on the I.Q.

Training of the Gifted

Gifted adolescents of today are the persons who will influence our destinies tomorrow. Although they have a great amount of ingenuity in finding their place in life, even extremely bright persons need proper nurture to achieve their full potential.[22] Terman and Oden (1940) noted that having an I.Q. in excess of 140 or 150 did not seem to add much to the achievement of the persons whom they studied in early adult years. This does not mean that those with I.Q.'s many points above 150 did not have a greater potentiality for achievement. Rather, according to Terman and Oden, it is likely that we have not learned in our educational system to bring the highest gifts to fruition.

The education of the gifted places a heavy responsibility on the school (but the same can be said regarding the education of the average student or the education of the handicapped). Many expedients have been used to provide for the gifted. These have consisted primarily in manipulations in the academic area, such as rapid promotion, provision of special classes, and what has been known as an "enriched" academic program. Each of these expedients apparently has both merits and shortcomings. The policy of segregating the gifted in special classes has been used widely. However, the mere fact of placing bright students in separate groups does not necessarily produce a higher quality of achievement or personal development. The provisions that are made to challenge their abilities and to encourage them to use their unique talents apparently are more important than simply to place them in a separate group (Eckstrom, 1959; Goldberg, Passow et al., 1961).

Even if the best program of training is provided, however, it may fall

---

[22] For a discussion of some of the achievements of intellectually gifted children and some of the problems they face, see Terman et al. (1925); Hollingworth (1926); Burks, Jensen and Terman (1930); Cox (1946); Witty (1930 and 1951); Terman and Oden (1940). For a discussion of plans and provisions for the education of talented youth, see Cruickshank and Johnson (eds., 1958); Passow, Goldberg, Tannenbaum and French (1955); and Goldberg (1962).

short if it emphasizes only academic knowledge and skill. Observations bearing on this point are made by Hollingworth (1942) in a study of young people with exceedingly high I.Q.'s (180 or more). These observations indicate that a young person does not become intellectually great by the sheer force of a high I.Q. He may be brilliant, but unless in time his brilliance is combined with other qualities of mind and heart he will not become wise. He may scintillate on a quiz program, but unless he becomes committed to a search for knowledge that has meaning for him, his knowledge is not likely to have much meaning for anyone else. There may be a magnificent sweep in what his mind can encompass, but unless he combines his cleverness with courage and compassion he will not be a hero in the search for truth. To get the maximum personal satisfaction and social usefulness out of their gifts, bright adolescents need to gain a healthy respect for the unique abilities that set them apart from others as well as for the motives and feelings that make them akin to others. They need (so this writer believes) to be encouraged to use their bright minds to understand themselves. This need is not met simply by having them learn five or ten times more academic material than is mastered by the average student. In the management of his personal affairs, a person can be just as foolish in five languages as in one (Kubie, 1954a). A student who has read ten books in an "enriched" course can be just as blindly moved by grievances, guilt, fears, and self-reproach as an ordinary student who barely manages to learn what is in one book. A bright mind can soar to great intellectual heights and still be fettered by unrecognized earthy emotions. Murphy (1945) expressed this thought when he said, "The towering genius of the great scientist often lapses into childish babbling as he turns to problems in which his personal desires give structure to his thought."

What is the meaning of this for the psychology of adolescence? Mainly, that we should try, as far as possible, to give bright young people, as well as other young people, an opportunity to develop their own potentials, to realize as fully as possible the resources latent within them.

All adolescents, whether richly or modestly endowed, have something in common: the growth process is strong within them; within their own limited domain they are capable of breaking new trails of thought; they are able to learn to see the old and familiar in a new light; to discover something within themselves and within their relationship to others that might enable them to take a more enlightened and productive approach to their present circumstances and to their future.

Interplay of Thinking and Feeling in Insight into Self

One of the finest tributes one can pay an adolescent (or an older person) is that he is "wise to himself," "doesn't fool himself." Although insight into self is generally held in high regard, our knowledge concerning how much insight the typical adolescent attains, or what he *might* attain, is very meager. Nonetheless, the subject is so important that it deserves attention in a book on adolescence.

Insight means to see into, to be aware. The writer has searched widely to get a simple definition of insight but the search has not been fruitful. One reason probably is that insight is a very personal kind of enlightenment with many individual variations that cannot be covered by one general definition.

Insight is usually something a person possesses to a greater or lesser degree rather than something he either has or has not. It may be very articulate in the sense that a person can "intellectualize" and express it fluently in words, or it may operate as a canny form of unspoken self-appraisal. It may spring from a sudden jolt or surprising discovery, but it is more likely to come through a slow process of exploration. It may even come as an incidental afterthought, or seemingly out of nowhere, when least sought.

COGNITIVE AND NONCOGNITIVE ASPECTS OF INSIGHT

When insight into self is formulated as an explicit idea it involves cognition—an intellectual comprehension of an inner state. However, an adolescent cannot acquire insight by sheer intellectual effort such as he uses in learning a logical syllogism.

This is one of the baffling and oftentimes exasperating aspects of insight. A person may be intellectually aware of a facet of himself—a personal asset he might use or a fault he would like to correct—and still not be able to do anything about it. Acquiring an insight involves a mobilization of emotion as well as thought, and the emotional involvement may range from acute agony to an uneasy but unshakable state of perplexity. The emotional component will also include great satisfaction when a person makes what to him is an important self-discovery.

It is absorbing to observe, as sometimes with good luck one can, that an adolescent may get a thrill of satisfaction even when he discovers a facet of himself which, *per se,* usually is regarded as unfavorable, such as characteristics which have offended his peers. A junior high school student from a poor neighborhood, who seemed to have gained much from a course dealing with adolescent problems, once told the writer with a pleased grin, "I ain't learned nothin' in this class but I sure get along better with other kids." And then he told how he was "on" to characteristics that had made others dislike him, but which he previously had attributed to others.

The fact that the process by which a person acquires insight into himself involves a complicated blend of thought and feeling makes it very difficult to predict when insight might occur, or how it came about when it does occur. Studies that have explored insight by experimental methods have, in general, been quite unrevealing.[23]

ADVANTAGES OF INSIGHT
AND LACK OF INSIGHT

A temporary advantage of a *lack* of self-insight is that it makes a person free to *externalize* his problems. He can regard his difficulties, and even his aspirations, as residing in outside circumstances or in other people. He has many grievances, let us say, but this does not mean that he is hostile—it is "they" or "it" or "life" that gives offense. If he is adept at this, he is able to disavow responsibility for himself.

There are conditions under which lack of insight is a blessing. One prevails when an adolescent's limitations are so dire that to realize them fully would leave him in a state of complete despair. It is better for him to live with an illusion than to go into a state of hopelessness; for the possibility remains that on a future day he might have more strength to face realities.

The major advantage of self-insight for a person who has the courage and strength to acquire it is that he can use his resources in a realistic way. Such insight may even enable him to regard qualities as assets which he once regarded as faults. An adolescent who once blamed him-

[23] A number of studies in this area have been reviewed by Wylie (1961). Experimental studies of insight are not likely to be fruitful if insight is regarded as a form of logic or clever divination or is defined primarily as a person's awareness of faults that others see in him, as the equivalent of "adjustment," or as something that can be assessed by a jury.

self for not trying to be best at everything may discover that he is wise in not trying to knock himself out by competing with everyone.

Even when insight does not dispose of a problem it can do much to soften its effects. This happens when a person makes a discovery about the nature of his moods. A boy who has had unaccountable spells of feeling depressed or a girl who now and then has weeping spells may discover that these moods are most likely to occur some time after occasions when their feelings were hurt but they pretended there was nothing to be angry about. Having gained insight into this sequence, the person might anticipate a melancholy mood—and thereby blunt it. Or he might take steps to prevent it by deliberately trying to be alert to his feelings at the moment they are aroused instead of ignoring or swallowing them, and then feeling miserable afterward.

Insight consists not only in recognition of personal limitations or faults but also in awareness of assets. This needs to be emphasized, for often in everyday life (and sometimes even in psychological literature) insight is regarded as primarily denoting that a person perceives faults in himself which others also perceive. Actually, an adolescent's sagacity in realizing his good qualities is just as important, and in many ways more productive, than ability only to discern his frailties.

An adolescent who is wise to his assets and limitations avoids the error of constantly overestimating or underestimating himself. His expectations are reasonably realistic. This spares him from being carried away by hopeless dreams. It also spares him from setting his sights so low that he does himself an injustice.

In informal interviews with adults about their adolescence the writer has found many persons who regretted that they underrated themselves during middle and late adolescent years. One person, for example, recalled that at about age nineteen he calculated that it would take him ten years to complete his professional education, while earning his own way. It took only five. He figured that at thirty he might be earning $3,000 a year. When that time came he actually earned several times that much. He did not try to date the girls who attracted him most, believing he would not be attractive to them.

This young person who thus underestimated himself was pleased, of course, when his fortunes turned out much better than he predicted. But as he moved into adult life he was slow in making a more realistically favorable self-estimate, and he lost thereby. His undervaluation of himself was costly even in financial matters. His first car was a poor secondhand one (the best he thought he could afford), and when he had to turn it in soon after for a better one, he lost money that he could have saved had he bought a better car at the start. Later he built a house, planning it on a small scale; but soon thereafter he had to spend much more to get it enlarged than it would have cost had he planned a larger house from the beginning.

DIFFICULTIES IN ACHIEVING SELF-INSIGHT

We might expect that the adolescent would know himself well for he has had a long time to get acquainted. However, self-knowledge seems to be more difficult to acquire than other forms of knowledge. A person with a brilliant intellect can encompass vast areas of learning and still have little insight into his own motives or habits of thought.

The barriers to achieving self-insight reside in the culture as well as in the individual himself. In the intellectual climate of most schools it is not easy to pursue a search for knowledge of self.

Apart from cultural barriers to the idea of self-examination there are conditions within the individual himself that make self-examination difficult.

Slow Development of Ability to View Self Objectively. In his early childhood the adolescent did not, as far as we can judge, have the power to reflect upon the nature of his feelings or his thoughts. He was swept by anger and fear long before he could detach himself from his emotion and ask, "What's going on here?" He reached conclusions without being able to retrace the steps of his reasoning. He formed opinions without being able to examine the process of thought leading to them. Young children have less capacity for reflective thinking than an older person. However, it also appears that young children vary greatly in their ability to view themselves objectively.[24]

Gaps in Recall of Earlier Development. Another obstacle to self-understanding in an adolescent (or older person) is the gap between what he remembers and what happened in his earlier life. The typical adolescent does not have conscious memories of happenings in his life prior to about the age of three and a half years (Dudycha and Dudycha, 1933a, 1933b). By that time he has had a vast number of experiences that influ-

[24] The writer once heard a tired four-year-old child, just home from nursery school, announce: "Don't bother me, I'm in a bad mood." This seemed to show a certain amount of self-scrutiny.

ence his mental outlook and his ideas and attitudes toward himself and others. Even the memories an adolescent can trace back to the years after three and a half are fragmentary. And they may be erroneous. For, as we have noted earlier, a person's memories are likely to be *selective*. They give more of an indication of what a person now is—and the rationale he has built to justify or explain his present state—than of actual happenings in his earlier life that determined what he now is.

This is a barrier to self-knowledge, although it is not, in itself, an insurmountable barrier. As long as the effects of past experience persist in the present there still remains a possibility of examining them, even though each person has a strong disposition to preserve rather than to question and revise his interpretation of his past.

INCENTIVES FOR SELF-EXAMINATION

Although there are barriers to self-examination there also are incentives for breaking down these barriers. Persons who deal with troubled individuals repeatedly emphasize that they can count on a strong impulse to grow, a striving toward wholeness and health even in persons who, at the same time, are resistant to such strivings (see, *e.g.,* Rogers, 1942; and Horney, 1945, 1950).

In another chapter we note how a person, in spite of being committed to "strategies" that protect him from facing the nature and meaning of his anxiety, still feels promptings to get rid of these strategies. The person who is compulsively competitive feels an urge, at times, to relax, to join in spontaneous fellowship with others. The person who has tried to protect himself by withdrawing, by remaining aloof, still possesses an urge for intimacy with others. Such promptings and urges give a person a glimpse of something that might be. Such a glimpse is, in itself, a nascent form of insight. It may lead to a more profound insight if a person ventures to follow his urge.

Promptings leading to a new perspective on oneself are often greatly bolstered by another incentive, namely, a desire to escape from suffering. Unrealistic attitudes regarding oneself are burdensome and self-defeating as well as painful. When a person can get an inkling of the relief that might come from "seeing through them" and "working through them," he has a strong inducement to seek a realistic view of himself. A person who feels this inducement is most likely to find a happy outcome if his own strivings are aided by encouragement and help from others.

Chapter 7

Fantasies,
Daydreams,
and Dreams

The imaginative life of the typical adolescent is rich and colorful, but it is not often that he lets others get a glimpse of it. Every glimpse that he gives reveals something important about himself.

The adolescent is a veteran in the world of fantasy. He has gone through many phases in the development of his ability to imagine. Early in his childhood he learned to deal with the images of things in place of the things themselves. He learned, in his imagination, to go places and do things and enter into experiences without having to be there in the flesh. Some adolescents even went through periods, when they were younger, when it was hard for them to tell the difference between the fancied and the real. Some of them had imaginary companions so vivid and so similar to the substance of their own inner life that they were hardly aware of their make-believe quality. Many adolescents also found thrills and adventure in daydreams of a "continued story" sort during their preschool and early elementary school years.

As they move toward adolescent years children lose some of the capacity they once had for becoming absorbed in imaginings so vivid as to seem almost real. As a child grows in understanding and awareness, the

150]

realities of life and of his own experience intrude upon his make-believe. It becomes harder for most young persons, as they reach adolescence, to lose themselves completely in the vicarious kind of living that fancy can supply. Yet in adolescence, as earlier, the typical young person has a rich fantasy life that continues to serve many of the functions imagination served in earlier years. These include both a kind of daring venture and a kind of retreat, both a constructive means of dealing with life's problems and a means of evading them.

Functions of Imagination

Through his imagination the adolescent, like the younger child, can leap over the barriers of time and space. He can transcend the limits of his own powers and vastly extend his reach. In fancy he can venture into many experiences that are not open to him in his actual life. He can be a great singer or actor, a soldier or a statesman. He can live in splendor even though his actual circumstances are drab, live a glamorous life even though his everyday existence is dull, find companions who respect and admire him even though in everyday life he feels lonely and unaccepted. In daydreams the boy can woo and win the most wonderful girl, and the girl can love and be loved by the ideal boy.

When we thus speak in opposites, contrasting the fantasy of what might be and the reality of what is, we are dealing with a common form of imagining, but only one form. While daydreams offer a means of escape from unpleasantness, the adolescent's imagination is not just a means of fleeing from a real to an unreal world. Imagination serves many functions that are important in connection with the adolescent's aspirations and plans. In his imagination he is, with varying degrees of directness, coping with issues in his life. Through his imagination he struggles with unresolved problems from his past. He strives to meet demands that press upon him from within and from without. He gives structure to his hopes for the future.

FANTASY AS A FORM OF SOLACE

Even when the adolescent's daydreams seem to be an unrealistic kind of wish-fulfillment and escape, these dreams are not completely idle. He is perhaps doing the best he can to make the conditions of his life tolerable.

It is possible that his life would be unbearable if he were unable, in his fancy, to find relief from the confines of the present. There are times when he can make life livable through fantasy when actual circumstances are such that he feels beaten, rejected, and hurt. In the bleakest moments of life he is able in his imagination to picture a better day (unless he has become completely discouraged). So those whose lot is harshest find it is possible, in the worst extremity of suffering and near-despair, to enjoy a refuge through the imagination. And there are those who probably would say, if they could clearly formulate the thought, that if they could not dream they might as well die.

FANTASY AS A REMINDER
OF UNREALIZED ASPIRATIONS

While an adolescent's fantasies may bring a kind of comfort, they also, in some instances, may serve to underscore his discontent without relieving it. This happens, for example, when an adolescent has daydreams of pleasure or glory or success far beyond anything he could ever achieve, then feels miserable or angry with others or himself, because of the vast difference between drab reality and his glorious dreams.

Fantasy does not create desire, but it may, by giving a kind of imaginary substance to desire, leave a person with a deeper feeling that something is amiss. For example, an adolescent who longs to be recognized and accepted may desire to be a singer. If he plans to try for the glee club, and imagines himself a member of the glee club, his imagining is tied to a desire and a plan within reach of any youngster who has a moderately good voice. But if, regardless of whether he has a good voice or even a mediocre voice, he leaps in his fancies beyond the idea of singing as one of a chorus and sees himself as a soloist, and not just an especially good soloist, but a new Caruso, he moves far from reality. He may become so absorbed in this image of himself that he does not even try out for the glee club. In his fantasies he lives in a world that is not just more glamorous than the one in which he actually lives but completely divorced from it.

It is likely that large numbers of adolescents (and probably also adults) now and then take flight into such a word in their fancies, but on the whole they stay in touch with the realities of life. The more an adolescent's most compelling ideals, as embellished by his fancies, are removed from anything he can ever possibly be or achieve, the less likely he is to find something rewarding in the good things of life that lie within his reach. His fantasies take the place of reality but leave him empty-handed. And where such a discrepancy between the real and the ideal exists, there is likely to be some sort of disorder in the emotional life, perhaps in the form of anxiety, perhaps in the form of grievances against others or oneself, perhaps in the form of discouragement and apathy.

FANTASY AS A FORM OF THINKING

One of the very useful functions of the imagination is to help the young person see his exertions of the moment in a larger perspective. It enables him to take a panoramic view of life, to fit the present into a context linked with the past and extending into the future. If he is making some progress but also has great difficulty in his struggle for independence, he can imagine the day when he can earn his own keep, make his own decisions, and enjoy a kind of freedom his present life does not afford. Similarly, when he is working on assignments in school that, taken by themselves, are boring and meaningless, his labors become lighter when, in his imagination, he can see his present work fitting into an ambition that he might realize at a future date.

One function imagination plays in the lives of some young people is to give them an opportunity for a kind of role-playing. In his imagination the boy can picture himself in the role of a doctor, a mechanic, or a farmer. The girl can picture herself as a teacher, a nurse, a singer, or a social worker. The young person is likely to add a little more drama and color to these roles than they actually possess. Yet the process of acting out this or that role in fantasy has a serious purpose. It is a kind of thinking. The process of projecting himself into a role may help the adolescent in making important decisions.

FANTASY AS AN AID
TO PROBLEM SOLVING

A young person's imagination is helpful not alone through what it anticipates for the future; it is helpful also in facing the problems of the present. This is underscored by the fact that not all daydreams are pleasant. Many have a painful quality. Such a painful quality exists when, for example, in his fancies a young person struggles with an immediate, pressing problem. His fantasies may give play to his presentiments and his fears. Through his imagination he can "try out" the worst that might happen if, for example, he does not work harder or if he is caught cheating or if someone he admires and whose good opinion he prizes greatly should look in upon him at an unguarded moment. When he gives play to his resentments in his imagining, the experience is not a very pleasant one, although through fancies concerning what he might do to protect himself from those who abuse him, or what he might do to avenge himself on those who have done him wrong, he is struggling with a real problem. The one who has meekly submitted to injustices may in his fancy see himself asserting his rights and through this dream get a better glimpse of what his rights are and the means he might use to fight for them. He might then go on and assert himself in a healthy way.

In many daydreams dealing with present problems there is a nice blend of the real and the imagined. The particular episodes into which the adolescent projects himself in his imagination—when, in anger, he stands up for himself or when, in fear, he copes with what is frightening— may be very fanciful, but the anger and fear are very real. Even the imaginary representation is not entirely fanciful, for in exploring ways of dealing with his problem the person may find a solution that can become an actuality. Moreover, an imaginative activity that goes one step beyond fantasy into an actual acting-out of something in an imaginary setting— such as occurs in role-playing—may lead a person to a deeper insight into himself and a better solution of some of his problems.

Of course, an adolescent's fantasies may at times be so far removed from anything real, and he may wander off repetitively into such impossible and fantastic plots, that he is almost completely divorced from reality. But we might find, if we could look into the mind-wanderings of the typical adolescent, that his imagination is a handmaiden to his problem-solving and that some of his fancies bear fruit.

RELEASE OF EMOTION IN DAYDREAMS

Through his daydreams an adolescent can experience emotions and concerns about which he does not freely speak or even deliberately think.[1] In

[1] The relationship between imagination and feeling was emphasized in an early study by Libby (1908), and has been the subject of a study by Sanford and his associates (1943). Symonds (1949) has given an excellent review of historical developments in the use of projective techniques, through which the adolescent can express his fantasies.

his revery, hostile impulses may appear which in his ordered thought he would thrust out as bad and utterly forbidden. He may, for example, picture a disliked teacher as being involved in an accident—perhaps a fatal accident—and in so doing he is, in a sense, in his fancies, killing off his teacher. Similarly, in his fancies, he may give play to sexual desires he would not ordinarily deliberately plan. Again, he may imagine others in the act of doing something he cannot allow himself to do. Hostile impulses and other desires that are expressed have something real about them, even when clothed in make-believe. It is because of this that the adolescent, like the adult, can often discover more concerning what he "really is like" by catching himself in the middle of a daydream than by going through the process (usually futile) of making a list of his "good" and "bad" qualities.

THEMES OF ADOLESCENT AND POSTADOLESCENT MAKE-BELIEVE

Themes appearing in the daydreams of older adolescents and adults are shown in Table 7.1, based on a study reported by Shaffer and Shoben (1956), which included a group of college undergraduates (64 men and 131 women), with a median age of twenty-one years, and a group of graduate students (83 men and 112 women), with an average age of twenty-eight years. As can be seen, there is a high degree of resemblance between the older and the younger groups. Many themes are frequently named, such as performing mental feats and being successful in a vocation. In both groups a large proportion reported past and present daydreams with a sexual theme. A large proportion also reported daydreams in which there was an element of worry.

Projective Methods

The term *projective techniques* covers a number of methods that have been used to stimulate a flow of thought and fancy that may reveal something about a person's inner life. These methods take advantage of the fact that the experience a person has, for example, when listening to music, or when looking at a picture, is determined in part by what he projects or reads into what he is hearing or watching. Similarly, one might see a distant cloud as the fleece of a lamb, or as a cold snowbank,

TABLE 7.1

THE OCCURRENCE OF TYPES OF DAYDREAMS AMONG TWO GROUPS OF STUDENTS *

Percentage of Students Reporting Each Type

	Ever?				Recently?			
	Undergraduate		*Graduate*		*Undergraduate*		*Graduate*	
	M	*W*	*M*	*W*	*M*	*W*	*M*	*W*
1. Physical Feat	91	60	96	58	30	3	13	2
2. Physical Attractiveness	89	95	94	96	34	63	17	56
3. Mental Feat	88	92	89	90	48	42	47	61
4. Vocational Success	100	98	99	93	81	69	78	64
5. Money or Possessions	100	97	94	95	69	66	51	52
6. Display	78	76	90	83	22	16	19	19
7. Saving	89	63	90	66	14	5	14	8
8. Grandeur	67	48	63	39	11	7	6	0
9. Homage	81	72	81	66	16	13	24	18
10. Sexual	97	96	96	89	74	73	63	71
11. Death or Destruction	39	44	60	46	9	9	10	9
12. Martyr	70	79	64	62	9	15	10	12
13. Worry	92	89	87	91	45	56	49	50
14. Other Types	63	53	52	51	30	20	24	23
15. Repeated Daydreams	89	93	83	87	48	51	36	47
Median Number of Types	13	12	13	11	5	5	4	5

* From L. F. Shaffer and E. J. Shoben, Jr., *The Psychology of Adjustment*, p. 206. Boston: Houghton Mifflin Co., 1956. Reproduced by permission.

or as the beard of an aged man. Again, in looking at a farm scene, one person thinks of long, hard hours of toil, another of fertility, yet another of the joy of tilling the soil. In making up a story about a certain subject one person gives his tale a happy ending while another's story ends in misfortune. The theory underlying the use of projective techniques is that when persons thus respond they are revealing something about themselves, and in so doing may reveal aspects of their feelings and their character that they themselves do not clearly recognize.

An early contributor to projective methods was Rorschach, who devised the famous "ink blots" comprising the Rorschach test (1942). This test consists of a set of cards, each one of which contains a large "ink blot." The blots vary in contour and include some that are in black and white and others containing several colors. The person to whom the test is given is asked to tell what each blot might be or what he sees. There are standard directions for giving the test, and elaborate criteria have been worked out for interpreting the results.[2]

Pictures have also been widely used as projective techniques in studies of adolescents as well as of older and younger persons. One of the pioneers in the use of pictures as a projective technique was Murray (1938), who developed what is known as the TAT (Thematic Apperception Test).[3]

CONTENTS OF ADOLESCENT PROJECTIONS

A study by Symonds (1949) gives a wealth of information concerning the projections of adolescents. Symonds used forty-two pictures, which an artist had prepared according to a set of specifications by Symonds. One showed a boy carrying a suitcase: he might be seen as one who is running away or going on a journey or seeking a job, etc. Another showed two boys, one well dressed and one who apparently had had an unfortunate experience, sitting together and looking worried and disconsolate. One picture showed a kneeling woman looking intently through a keyhole. In

[2] For discussions of the Rorschach test see, for example, Beck (1937), Rorschach (1937), Klopfer (1937), Krugman (1940), Klopfer and Kelley (1946), Klopfer et al. (1956), Ames and Learned et al. (1952), and Blum, Davidson, and Fieldsteel (1954).

[3] Other projective procedures include play techniques, role-playing in what is sometimes called a "psychodrama" (see, for example, Moreno, 1946); drawing and painting (see, for example, Alschuler and Hattwick, 1943), including the drawing of a human figure (see Machover, 1949). For general discussions of projective procedures see Frank (1949), Symonds (1949), Abt and Bellak (1950), and Anderson and Anderson (1951).

another picture a girl was shown walking upstairs, with shadows suggesting that it is nighttime; the clock shows the time as about three-thirty, and a shadowy figure is standing at the head of the stairs.[4]

Symonds obtained responses to his forty-two pictures from twenty boys and twenty girls at the junior and senior high school levels. The opening statement of the directions given to those who took the test read: "This is a test of creative imagination. I want to find how much imagination you have. Here are some pictures which I am going to show you one

TABLE 7.2

"PSYCHOLOGICAL" THEMES OCCURRING IN THE RESPONSES GIVEN BY
FORTY ADOLESCENTS TO FORTY-TWO PICTURES IN THE SYMONDS
PICTURE-STORY TEST *

Themes	By Cases			By Occurrences		
	Total	B	G	Total	B	G
Aggression	40	20	20	1,562	988	574
Eroticism	36	17	19	459	286	173
Negative Emotion;						
Depression	29	15	14	349	187	162
Anxiety	28	14	14	310	130	180
Altruism	28	14	14	401	198	203
Success; Ambition	25	11	14	268	156	112
Repentance;						
Reform	24	14	10	305	217	88
Positive Emotion	22	10	12	193	78	115
Excitement	18	12	6	312	247	65
Escape	16	11	5	136	107	29
Thinking; Decision	16	9	7	248	118	130
Morality; Goodness	15	8	7	112	58	54
Jealousy	13	5	8	52	23	29
Concealment	10	5	5	119	55	64
Wrong; Badness	10	7	3	81	60	21
Guilt; Conscience	10	3	7	58	19	39
Yearning; Wanting	7	3	4	54	19	35
Fatigue	6	2	4	31	17	14
Craziness	5	3	2	33	24	9
Waiting	5	1	4	25	3	22
Dreams; Daydreams	4	2	2	15	8	7
Miscellaneous				376	142	234
Total				5,499	3,140	2,359

* From P. M. Symonds, *Adolescent Fantasy*. New York, Columbia University Press, 1949. Reproduced by permission.

[4] Figures 7.1, 7.2, 7.3, and 7.4 reproduce four of the pictures used in Symonds' study.

by one and I want you to make up a story on each picture." The directions then proceed to give more specific instructions to the respondent
and indicate some of the questions he should seek to answer.

In treating his results, Symonds made a distinction between what he
calls "psychological" and "environmental" themes, arbitrarily defined as
follows: What you do to another person is psychological; what another
person does to you is environmental. Tables 7.2 and 7.3 show the frequency with which various themes occurred in the young people's
responses when these were classified into various categories under the
two headings.

Erotic themes appeared in stories told by thirty-six of the forty young
people, but there were few instances when these were openly expressed as

TABLE 7.3

"ENVIRONMENTAL" THEMES OCCURRING IN THE RESPONSES GIVEN BY
FORTY ADOLESCENTS TO FORTY-TWO PICTURES IN THE SYMONDS
PICTURE-STORY TEST *

Categories	By Cases			By Occurrences		
	Total	B	G	Total	B	G
Family Relationships	40	20	20	1,595	766	829
Economic	38	20	18	632	370	262
Punishment	33	18	15	614	484	130
Separation; Rejection	32	18	14	397	185	212
Accidents; Illness;						
Injury	28	14	14	297	189	108
School	28	15	13	251	122	129
Social; Gangs	21	9	12	130	70	60
Place of Residence	17	8	9	98	56	42
Appearance	13	3	10	75	15	60
Strangeness;						
Unusualness	12	8	4	125	85	40
Discussion; Advice	10	7	3	54	33	23
Age	10	5	5	46	23	23
Gossip	8	5	3	55	31	24
Entertainment	7	3	4	41	23	18
Work	7	3	4	39	15	24
Night	4	2	2	25	12	13
Food; Eating	4	3	1	22	16	6
Mail; Writing	4	2	2	14	7	7
Miscellaneous				294	211	83
Total				4,804	2,713	2,091

* From P. M. Symonds, *Adolescent Fantasy*. New York, Columbia University
Press. 1949. Reproduced by permission.

sex. Twenty-four mentioned marriage, twenty mentioned boy-girl situations and relationships, thirteen referred to friendship, and eight spoke directly about love and falling in love. The theme of love was expressed in episodes relating to dating, auto rides, marrying, and living happily thereafter. The stories about love usually dealt with social relationships rather than physical contact.

Every adolescent boy and girl studied by Symonds told at least three stories in which there were themes of aggression ranging from mild criticism and rebuke to robbery and murder. Even the boys and girls who gave the appearance of being mild and gentle in real life, told stories filled with destructive violence. Symonds observed that a boy would sometimes gasp with surprise when a story he had told was repeated to him; he would act as though he had expressed violence without fully recognizing its nature at the time, and as though he were now annoyed and anxious about it.

The way an adolescent ends a story in which he has given play to his imagination in response to a picture is of special significance, according to Symonds. Many of the adolescents in his study consistently gave happy endings to their stories. Only a few permitted endings to be tragic or fatal. However, when a person characteristically finds a happy ending (as in the ending of fairy tales where "they lived happily ever after"), one cannot assume that he is more hopeful or that the ventures of his life usually take a happier turn than is true for those who do not always seek a happy ending when they let their imaginations go. The happy ending may even denote a feeling of guilt. Symonds points out, for example, that there are adolescents who permit themselves to create an aggressive story (in a fantasy, for example, about a boy in a speeding car who knocks down a woman), but do not permit themselves to end the story on a harmful and destructive note. Some adolescents allow themselves aggressive fantasies and then make some kind of amends at the end so that no drastic damage is done, as though they felt the need to be aggressive but also felt guilty about their aggressiveness.

An interesting finding in this study was that while adolescents expressed guilt when they had given play to their aggressive fantasies, they did not, in general, express guilt when they had gone into the theme of love. This may be due to the fact that in themes of love the young people did not let their fantasies go as far as they did in expressing themes of aggression.[5]

[5] It is interesting to observe that adolescents "let themselves go" more freely in projecting passions leading to violence than in projecting passions that lead to

In this study of adolescent fantasy, Symonds noted some differences between boys and girls. Boys are more direct and, in a sense, more primitive in expressing their passions than girls. Boys, for example, more often gave stories with themes of violence, death, crime, and murder. The girls also voiced aggression, but they tended to show it by disobedience, resistance, rebellion, and coercion, rather than through more violent means. One somewhat unexpected finding was that boys more frequently brought in themes of love or falling in love than did girls. Girls, on the other hand, more often brought in themes pertaining to friends and children.

When older and younger adolescents were compared, it appeared that the younger people seemed to be freer in expressing hostility without feeling guilty. The older individuals in the study tended more often than the younger ones to show disappointment, and to voice concern about the future. The older ones seemed also to show greater seriousness by bringing in themes of *wondering, thinking,* and *musing.*

The fantasies pertaining to school that were expressed in Symonds' study are especially interesting, and they are in keeping with many other findings, cited elsewhere in this book, concerning the meaning, and frequently the meaninglessness, of school in the life of the adolescent. As revealed through their projections, adolescents did not regard school as a particularly happy place. According to Symonds, punishment and the threat of failure hung over many of these adolescent storytellers when they spoke about school. In their stories the adolescents seldom showed affection for their teachers, but pictured them more often as stern, threatening, and avenging.[6]

Twenty-eight of the forty adolescents in Symonds' investigation took part in a follow-up study in 1953–1954, thirteen years after the original inquiry (Symonds and Jensen, 1961). These twenty-eight persons, in 1953, ranged from twenty-five to thirty-one years in age.

A substantial number of the stories told by these persons in 1953–1954 were, in general, quite similar to those they told thirteen years earlier, but there were some notable changes. There was a *decrease* in

---

making love. As we will note in a later chapter, when young people directly (rather than projectively) express their moral judgments, they regard some forms of sex misconduct as a more serious offense than murder.

[6] It is possible that the students who happened to take part in this study tended to be somewhat more melancholy in their view of school than the typical high school student, although there is no good reason to think so, for in selecting persons for the study an effort was made to obtain volunteers who were typical, neither predominantly bright nor dull, nor considered to be "problem" children.

themes dealing with violent aggression or punishment for aggression.[7]
There was an *increase* in themes dealing with depresssion and guilt.

As adolescents, these persons had had many hopeful fantasies, but
thirteen years later there were many "undisguised expressions of disappointment, discouragement and dejection." This shift had been fore-
shadowed in the 1940 study, for at that time the older adolescents
emphasized discouragement and disappointment more than the younger
ones. Symonds and Jensen regard the increase in depressive themes as
signifying two tendencies. One is disillusionment about adolescent hopes.
The other is a shift from an outgoing form of aggression (fantasies of
violence and crime) to "aggression turned inward" in the form of "self-
recrimination, and feelings of inferiority, discouragement and hopelessness."

According to Symonds' interpretation, many of the persons in this
study confirmed, in their actual conduct as adults, the fantasy themes
they had expressed as adolescents. In some instances the resemblance
between adult conduct and earlier fantasies was striking. Six girls, in
adolescence, expressed fantasies which "depicted strong hostility toward
mother figures." Three of these later married against their mother's
wishes and in spite of "vehement protest." A boy who had expressed
hostility toward father figures in adolescence directed his hostility against
bosses in later real life; he had had ten different jobs since leaving school,
and he left most of them following a quarrel or disagreement with the
boss. Symonds and Jensen describe several other similarities between
earlier fantasies and later conduct. However, many fantasies were not
borne out, and the evidence is not firm enough to show how well and in
which instances an account of adolescent fantasies will predict what will
happen in later life.

Dreams

The adolescent's dreams, like his daydreams, have their roots in his past
experiences and in the current happenings of his life. But even though
the dreams of adolescents, like the dreams of children and adults, are
built on the substance of everyday experience, they often seem to belong

[7] In 1940, fifteen of the persons, as compared with six in 1953, told stories
about criminal death. The total number of stories dealing with crimes against persons or property, or criminal death fell from ninety-seven in 1940 to thirty-one in
1953.

to another existence, as though springing from a personality different from that of the dreamer. Because of this, an adolescent will sometimes speak of his dreams in an amused and offhand way as though they were not of his own making.

Yet his dreams, if their nature could be understood, would be very revealing to him and to others. He is the producer of the dream and the main actor in the drama that the dream unfolds. If the dream expresses the fulfillment of a wish, it is a wish welling up within him that is being fulfilled. If there is violence in the dream, as when he dreams of someone being shot or run over, it is he, directly or by proxy, who pulls the trigger or produces the vehicle that knocks someone else down or that knocks him down. When he dreams of wild beasts, these beasts seem like creatures from another world, yet they are *his* beasts, and what they do are of his doing. If there is terror in his dreams, the terror resides in him. If the policeman comes in the dream to take someone else to jail, it is he who summoned the police and it is he who conjured up the jail and it may also be he (through the person of one of his characters) who is being taken to jail. The ledge on which the dreamer walks, the bogs through which he flounders, the pleasures he enjoys are contrived by him. When, in his dream, someone dead comes to life, or someone living appears as dead, it is he, within the world of the dream, who gives life and takes it away.

The simple yet very significant fact, of course, is that the adolescent's dream is *his* dream.[8] This fact is rather obvious, yet it is difficult to fathom its meaning.

SLEEP AND DREAM PATTERNS

Important discoveries by Dement and Kleitman and their associates have opened a promising new approach to the study of dreaming in childhood, adolescence, and later years (Aserinsky and Kleitman, 1953; Dement and Kleitman, 1957a, 1957b). These investigators, using a device that measured eye movements during sleep, found that rapid eye movements

[8] Students who wish to inquire more deeply into studies of dreams are referred to Freud's classic work on dream interpretation (English translation, 1950), and the writings of Jung (1953) and Bjerre (1925, 1936). References to recent outstanding contributions by Dement and his associates will be given in a later section. Hall (1953) has made studies of thousands of dreams collected with the help of college students. For further discussions see Fromm (1951), Gutheil (1951), Hadfield (1954), and Schonbar (1959).

and dreaming often go together. Sleeping laboratory subjects who were awakened at times when rapid eye movements occurred usually were able to tell of an ongoing dream; if awakened at times when their eyes were quiescent they rarely reported a dream.

Eye movements during dreams range from frequent and pronounced movements, when a person seems to be very actively involved in his dreams, to virtually none at all, in a dream in which the dreamer apparently is a more passive spectator.[9]

Persons who claim they seldom or never dream are able to report dreams if artificially awakened at the moment when a recording device shows that rapid eye movements are occurring. Studies by Goodenough *et al.* (1959) and Antrobus (1962) indicate that those who say they rarely dream ("nonrecallers") probably dream as much as those who say they often dream ("recallers"). The difference between those who say they often dream and those who say they seldom or never dream apparently is not in amount of dreaming but in ability to recall dreams after a night's sleep.

The sleep and dream patterns of adolescents (aged fourteen to eighteen years) and younger children have been compared with adult patterns in a study by Roffwarg, Dement, and Fisher (1962). In young adults the "dream time per cent" (fraction of total sleep time during which periods of rapid eye movements occur) usually ranges between 20 and 25, with an average of about 22. The average dream time per cent shown by a small sampling of adolescents was 18.5, with a range from 14 to 25 on individual nights. It appears that the adolescent dreams during a somewhat smaller per cent of his sleeping time than adults. Adolescents seem to dream about as much as children in an age range from five to thirteen years (who also showed an average dream time per cent of 18.5). The investigators (p. 10) state their "expectation that there would be an increase in the per cent of dreaming at puberty along with the general upsurge in sexual drive at the same time was not borne out."

[9] Dement and Kleitman made the further discovery that rapid eye movements characteristically occur during a certain sleep cycle as revealed by recordings of brain wave patterns by means of an electroencephalograph (EEG). They believe that the onset of, duration and ending of, a dream can most readily be ascertained from the brain wave pattern, and that simultaneous recording of both brain waves and rapid eye movements "gives a highly reliable picture of the patterns of dreaming during a night of sleep" (Roffwarg, Dement, and Fisher, 1962). For other studies dealing with eye movements as related to dreaming see Dement and Wolpert, 1958a, 1958b.

Fig. 7.1. From P. M. Symonds, *Adolescent Fantasies* (Columbia University Press, 1949). Reproduced by permission.

Fig. 7.2. From P. M. Symonds, *Adolescent Fantasies* (Columbia University Press, 1949). Reproduced by permission.

Fig. 7.3. From P. M. Symonds, *Adolescent Fantasies* (Columbia University Press, 1949). Reproduced by permission.

Fig. 7.4. From P. M. Symonds, *Adolescent Fantasies* (Columbia University Press, 1949). Reproduced by permission.

Although they retained some characteristics found in younger children, adolescents' sleep-dream patterns in many ways resembled those of young adults. During the later parts of a night's sleep, periods of rapid eye movements lasted longer in the adolescents than in the younger age group, and closely resembled the duration of corresponding periods at the young adult level. However, the younger adolescents sometimes differed from adults in the earlier part of a night's sleep. In adults, a brief period of rapid eye movements typically occurs at about 60 to 80 minutes after the onset of sleep. Younger adolescents frequently "miss" this period. In preadolescent children, likewise, the first period of rapid eye movements commonly shown by adults is also usually delayed. The investigators believe this arises from the fact that children and young adolescents are physically more active than adults and require a larger period of heavy sleep to take the edge off their bodily fatigue before they enter a "light sleep" cycle when dreaming is most likely to occur.

The discoveries made by Dement and his associates open up great new possibilities for studying dreaming and dreams at the moment they occur, in adolescents and older and younger persons. They give access to dream material of persons who ordinarily forget their dreams.

CONTENTS OF DREAMS

In the study of dreams a distinction is commonly made between what is called the manifest and the latent content. This is in keeping with Freud's theory that a dream has meanings that are concealed or disguised and that cannot be ascertained simply by literally taking the dream, as remembered, at face value.

Judging from scattered accounts, there is a large degree of resemblance between the manifest content of themes of adolescent, preadolescent, and postadolescent dreams.[10] Among the frequent themes are everyday activities; recreational activities; traveling by automobile, by bus, air or train, or on water; dreams of frightening events; fighting or other forms of violence. In a study by the writer and his associates (Jersild, Markey, and

[10] The manifest dream content in childhood and young adulthood has been studied more systematically than the content of adolescent dreams. Dr. Calvin Hall has a huge collection of dreams, but according to a personal communication, his data about adolescents are comparatively limited. He does, however, offer some interesting information about adolescent dreams in his book published in 1953.

Jersild, 1933), preadolescents (aged eleven to twelve years) reported considerably more dreams involving prestige, achievement, and independence than did younger subjects. It seems likely that such dreams would increase in frequency during adolescent years.

Dreams about relatives are frequent. The relatives appearing in the dreams of young people in their teens and early twenties are fathers and mothers more often than other members of the family (Hall, 1953).

According to Hall, about four out of ten characters in dreams are strangers. He regards strangers in dreams as representing "the unknown, the ambiguous and the uncertain." He maintains that the characters most likely to appear in dreams, whether strangers or relatives, represent "focal points of unresolved conflict." This theory would account not only for the appearance of strangers in adolescents' dreams, but also for the presence of parents at a time when young people are struggling for independence and are often at odds with their parents.[11]

In Hall's collection of dreams there were very few dealing with events or striking happenings in the world at large (such as dreams about the atomic bomb at the time it was first exploded in Japan). The dream, instead, is likely to deal with the dreamer's personal world, intimate emotional concerns, and personal conflicts.

Hall notes that dreams ending in nocturnal emissions, which account for only a small proportion of all dreams, occur most frequently in the late teens and then diminish with age. In some sex dreams, there is an obvious sexual contact or physical approach. But in others there is little or no manifest sexual content in the main part of the dream; the ejaculation at the end seems to come as a non sequitur, if the dream is viewed solely from the viewpoint of its manifest content. Such dreams illustrate Freud's theory of the "psychic censor"—a person's superego or conscience standing so vigilantly on guard against forbidden impulses and acts that even during sleep, when inhibitions are likely to be more relaxed than in waking moments, he cannot permit himself openly to dream his desires but pursues them in a disguised way.

---

[11] The idea that dreams represent unresolved conflicts suggests that dreams are a symptom of trouble and implies that if a person were untroubled, he probably would not dream. This is questionable, at least from the point of view of many persons who tell about dreams that are serene, blissful, and distinctly pleasant. It may, of course, be that "a pleasant dream" represents a temporary or seeming resolution of a conflict. What seems more likely, in the author's opinion, is that dreams may reflect the whole spectrum of a person's emotional life.

DREAMS AS AN AID
TO SELF-KNOWLEDGE

Dreams potentially offer a rich source of information about adolescents in general, and they could also provide the individual adolescent himself with valuable insights. Often, however, it is very difficult, and it may seem impossible, to decipher the cryptic message they tell.[12] At the present time, dream interpretation is more an art than an exact science, and judging from writings on the subject, even "experts" are often baffled by their own dreams and the dreams of others. There are, however, some rudimentary principles which might help a student of adolescents, or adolescents themselves, in making a start toward studying the meaning of dreams.

One principle is that although dreams are often very complex there are some aspects which frequently can be observed in simple form. These include: the mood or emotional tone of the dream; the underlying theme or themes; the "problem" with which it deals; the "solution" it offers or fails to achieve; the elements of conflict it contains; the thread of continuity that runs through several dreams during a single night or dreams that recur again and again over a longer period. Another feature that often stands out clearly is the general drift or direction of movement in a series of dreams. A series of recurring dreams about missing the bus, for example, may "move" in the direction of more and more difficulty in getting there on time, or more and more instances of making it, at first barely, and then with ease, followed by no more dreams about catching a bus. Likewise, a series of dreams about animals may start with dreams about menacing creatures which become more menacing with

---

12 In the writer's opinion, far more could be done to tap this source of self-knowledge than commonly is done. This opinion is based on the view that the general tendency to ignore dreams, or to treat them as capricious hallucinations, does not spring solely from the fact that dreams are hard to understand, but also from a general tendency in the culture to ignore the subjective dimensions of life. It is not dreams alone that are shunted aside as unworthy of serious attention. Daydreams, fantasies, the vagrant feelings and thoughts of waking life, surges of anxiety, and countless other currents in the psychic stream are likewise commonly ignored. The writer believes that if massive cultural resistances to self-inquiry were removed, children, adolescents, and adults could acquire far more astuteness than they now possess in probing into the secret reaches of mental life, as represented in dreams, fantasies, and other vagaries of the mind.

time, or which, as the series continues, are mastered.[13] Dreams that include automobiles may begin with some in which the dreamer is a passenger in a car, careening at a dizzy pace, and end with the dreamer in the driver's seat, in complete control of the vehicle. We can suspect that a person has a conflict about asserting himself if, in one dream after another, he plays a passive, inadequate role; or that he fears men and regards them as hostile if his dreams repeatedly depict men as aggressive (Hall, 1953, gives examples of such recurrent dreams reported by an eighteen-year-old adolescent).

Another principle is that a person may be able to find meanings in dreams if he tries not to be deceived by characteristics that make dreams seem bizarre and full of nonsense.

DREAMS CONTRASTED WITH
WAKING FEELINGS AND THOUGHTS

There are many deceptive characteristics of dreams. If these are viewed casually, they are likely to obscure the meaning of a dream, but if examined more carefully they may be revealing.

The Appearance of Opposites. Dreams sometimes contain just the opposite of what seems to be happening in reality. The timid adolescent boy dreams that he fights the town bully. In such dreams the action seems farfetched, yet when viewed from the standpoint of an adolescent's own strivings such dreams are not so farfetched. In his fancies, the timid boy may have had an angry impulse to thrash the bully.

Exaggeration. Dreams often seem to exaggerate the "point." Fighting, destruction, dismemberment, and terror frequently are more violent than anything that occurs in waking moments. Dreams sometimes are brazen. An adolescent girl who, in actual life, is just a little daring in her choice of a low-cut party dress may, in her dreams, appear in a very daring costume, or perhaps with no dress at all. Such exaggeration makes

[13] In one such series related to the writer, the first dream was about a stable full of wild, black threatening horses; after many further dream encounters with these horses, there came a dream in which the dreamer, in full command, was driving a team of horses. At the end of the series came a dream in which the horses, once so menacing, had been reduced to a single horse—a Shetland pony, at that— pulling a heavy load, but doing so successfully. The dreamer, on awakening, was struck with the thought: "I guess that little horse is me."

dreams seem unreal. Yet it might be possible to detect in the dream a hard core of truth.

Illogical Features. The dream, instead of following the logical sequence of ordered thought, is often completely (or at least seems to be completely) illogical. Events that seem out of place and actions that are incongruous are brought together. Events in real life that were separated by many years are thrown together, as when a new acquaintance is seen in a setting that occurred a long time ago. However, when a dreamer in waking moments examines these incongruities he may find that they have an underlying thread of meaning.

Displacement. The phenomenon known as *displacement* often occurs in dreams. The young person who has had a quarrel with his mother may dream that he is fighting with his aunt; the dreamer who is questioning the authority of his father may dream that he argues with a teacher or a preacher. Such displacement in dreams may obscure the meaning of the dream, yet similar displacements of feeling often occur also in waking life.

Condensation. Another phenomenon that occurs in dreams is *condensation:* a little detail in the dream may embrace a large meaning. This happens, for example, if a young person who is in the habit of dawdling and leaving tasks unfinished has a dream in which he should be fully clothed but neglected to put on one of his socks. The symbol of the missing sock may stand for a weakness that perhaps worries him and appears in many ways in his everyday life.

Problem-Solving and Restorative Functions of Dreams. As we have noted above, dreams have been viewed as an effort to resolve conflict. Many writers, while viewing dreams as an effort to resolve problems, also view the dream as a means of revealing latent strengths and resources for health and happiness.

Hadfield (1954) maintains that dreams are an attempt to restore the personality to wholeness and to health. According to him, they release emotions that should never have been repressed and that, having been repressed, produce inner conflict.

According to Bjerre (1925), dreaming represents a useful, creative, life-affirmative force. In this sense, the dream can have a curative value.

The idea that dreams have a curative and constructive value seems farfetched when we consider that many dreams seem to deal with violence, destruction, and fear. However, an interesting bit of evidence in support of the theory that dreams serve a useful purpose comes from one of the studies made by Dement (1960).

Eight persons underwent a laboratory experiment in "dream deprivation": they were awakened when eye-movement and brain-wave recordings indicated they were in the act of dreaming. Persons whose dreams were thus interrupted during several consecutive nights showed an increase in dream "attempts"—had to be awakened progressively more frequently as night after night went by. They apparently were trying to "make-up" for lost or interrupted dreams. During waking hours they showed psychological disturbances such as anxiety, irritability, and difficulty in concentrating. These psychological changes disappeared after the dream deprivation period ended. In a "recovery" period, when dreams were no longer interrupted, their dreaming time rose above normal for a time—they apparently were still trying to "catch up."

During a series of "control" nights, following the dream deprivation period, several of the subjects were awakened during periods of nondreaming. These forced awakenings occurred as often as the forced awakenings that had been imposed in the main experiment. Forced awakenings during periods of nondreaming did not produce an increase in dream "attempts" or in psychological after-effects during the day. This indicates that the changes occurring when dreams were interrupted were due to dream deprivation and not due to being awakened.

Another bit of evidence regarding the utility of dreams appears in a study by the writer and his associate of the dreams reported by 300 children aged five to twelve. At all age levels more dreams were classifiable as "unpleasant" than as "pleasant." When the youngsters were asked, "Do you wish you would never dream?" 47 per cent said they preferred to keep on dreaming, 33 per cent said they wished they would never dream, and the remaining 20 per cent were undecided or gave equivocal replies. This finding suggests that many youngsters regarded their capacity for dreaming as an asset rather than as a burden, even though a large proportion of the dreams they remembered on the spur of the moment were "troubled" dreams.

Dreams may serve both as warnings and as indications of methods of solution. They may remind the dreamer that he is still able to struggle, and this helps to keep hope alive. A dream may give an almost ecstatic picture in which a greatly desired goal is achieved, and such dreams, according to the view under discussion, may have an uplifting and inspiring effect.

THE LANGUAGE OF DREAMS

Many images which appear in dreams may not be the ones the dreamer would prefer to use in his waking thoughts. The visual image of an open or closed door, for example, may symbolize meanings which could be more readily understood if they appeared in words that could be heard or read. The language of a dream is often a picture language.

Sometimes dream imagery may appear as almost a literal kind of symbolism. For example, a boy who was angry at being rebuffed by a girl with the nickname "Chick" dreamed that he ran over a chicken while driving a garden tractor.

The "language" of the dream may take the form of signs that are like metaphors or other figures of speech. We use many metaphors in everyday speech. We say, for example, that we have the *key* to this problem; let us keep an *open mind;* I am in *deep water;* let us not *close the door* to new ideas; *quick as a flash;* he is *up to his neck* in trouble; *catch it on the wing;* I am *in the dark;* he is *playing with fire.* We also have various metaphoric expressions for states of feeling such as I feel *trapped, empty, stuck, lost, caught in a jam, torn between* two desires. The metaphor of the door (which may be open or closed or stuck) or of the empty space, of being lost, of being in the dark, etc., is common in dreams.

In commenting on the use of metaphors, Hadfield (1954) points out that the metaphors in ordinary speech as well as in dreams may be mixed, and he cites a fragment from a speech by a member of Parliament to illustrate this point: "I smell a rat, I see it floating in the air, but mark my words, I will nip it in the bud."

DREAM SYMBOLISM

The "language of the dream" is, as we have pointed out, often a wordless language, just as a musical symphony or a painting is wordless. There have been many theories concerning the interpretation of dream symbolism. Freud and his followers have especially emphasized sex symbols in dreams. Actually, dreams are so complex, and the play of imagery in the dreams so varied and so personal, that we cannot assume that a certain symbol (such as a snake or a ship) has a certain fixed meaning. The same symbol may mean different things in the dreams of different persons or even in the dreams of the same person and, according to some views on the subject, the same symbol may have several meanings even within a single dream.

Even if it were established that certain dream contents have a fixed and universal symbolic meaning the problem of untangling the dream would still remain. Each dream is a personal document, uniquely inter-woven with the dreamer's life. For this reason, dreams must be examined in the context of the dreamer's own experience. Someone else's interpreta-tion of his dream material has no significance whatsoever unless he him-self can grasp a personal meaning, can fit the pieces together in a way that clicks in his own mind and makes sense to him. A practicing psychol-ogist who has made an intensive study of his own dreams and the dreams of others, and knows all that has been written in the books, will usually avoid making a bookish, didactic interpretation of another person's dreams.

EXPLORATION THROUGH
FREE ASSOCIATION

The common practice when a person seeks to explore his dreams with professional help is to draw on his own "free associations"—snatches of feeling and thought that come to his mind, fragments of old memo-ries, ideas and recollections that, on the surface, may seem to have no logical relationship at all with one another or with the content of the dream.

The process of free association, as noted elsewhere in this book, is very different from the usual exercise in logic. It is a kind of search, with no fixed notion where the search will end and no idea in advance of what might be found. It is far more akin to the "divergent" than the "con-vergent" forms of thinking described in the preceding chapter. But it is, if anything, even more *divergent* than the thinking there described—for the thinker is not even *trying* to think, in the usual sense of that term. He does not have an anticipated answer. He does not give an orderly struc-ture to his ideas. Instead of directing his thoughts, he follows the vagaries of his mind. This might be called the cogitation of a lazy mind were it not for one thing: the person who undertakes it is seeking; he makes a plunge into the unknown.

DREAMS AS A STIMULUS
FOR SELF-DISCOVERY

In the preceding chapter we cited authorities who maintain that schools place too much emphasis on conventional thought patterns and too little on original, imaginative, unconventional forays of thought. In the writer's opinion, dreams might provide the starting point for an even more venturesome endeavor—a kind of thinking that is not only divergent and creative but self-revealing, in the sense that it leads a person to a clearer view of divisive and conflicting elements in his existence. In the writer's opinion, dreams can provide a challenge to self-revealing thinking. In dreams conflicting, scattered, disorganized, and chaotic fragments of life are combined within one drama. On surface appearance, the dream is even more fragmented and confused than the experiences of life from which it springs. But it offers a means of self-discovery when examined through a process of free association. This kind of thinking is within the power of practically everyone. In their daily lives, adolescents do a great deal of thinking of this sort, but usually in an aimless way. Often the chain of free association is broken when a young person's thought brings up unpleasant recollections, or leads him into forbidden or suppressed desires. The process often stops at the very point where a bit of self-discovery might be achieved.

The process of free association is a kind of thinking that can be cultivated. A person who is undergoing therapy practices this kind of thinking when he comes again and again to the brink of self-revelation and retreats, and then through other routes comes to the same brink again and again, until finally he takes the plunge. This kind of thinking through free association can also be cultivated by a person working by himself.

Practically nothing has been done in schools to encourage thinking by free association and to discover what it might produce. It would be a revolutionary thing in education to introduce this kind of thinking by way of a study of dreams. It would require a radical departure from the usual academic undertakings, a revision of teacher-training programs, a great amount of courage, and a great deal of exploring and experimentation. But the day might yet come when inquiry into the "inner world" of dreams and fantasies will be regarded as a respectable endeavor.

part four | Emotional Development

Chapter 8

Introductory: Love, Affection, and Joy

To understand the adolescent it is important to know what he does and thinks but it is even more important to know what he feels. The more we seek to understand the adolescent's world the more necessary it becomes to look into his feelings—his pride and shame, love and hate, hope and discouragement, and his fears.

Adolescents themselves emphasize the importance of emotions. When young people report what they admire or dislike about themselves, they mention emotional characteristics more often than their physical characteristics or their mental ability (Jersild, 1952).

This chapter and the three that follow will consider the meaning of emotion and will deal with various emotional conditions, such as love and affection, anger and hostility, fear and anxiety.

Conditions Underlying Emotion

To be emotional means to be "moved." An emotional experience usually involves *feeling* (such as the feeling of fear), *impulse* (such as an impulse to flee), and a *perception* of what it is that gives rise or seems to give rise to the emotion. Sometimes these elements of the experience are so vague that a person cannot clearly identify them. In another chapter we shall notice that the impulses, feelings, and perceptions may be so clouded and ambiguous (as under some conditions of anxiety) that a person has no distinct notion of what is happening to him or why he feels as he does.

During adolescence, as at all times of life, the conditions that give rise to emotion are as varied as the conditions of life itself. Emotion is involved in everything in which the adolescent is involved. Emotion occurs in the adolescent's life when his desires are fulfilled, or when he is blocked or thwarted in his efforts, or when he is harmed or threatened with harm. Emotion is aroused by any happening that touches upon the adolescent's view of himself, any occurrence through which he discovers his talents and his limitations, and any event that threatens to contradict a view he has of himself. Among the circumstances that are most potent in arousing emotion in the adolescent are those that collide with his pride in himself or the expectations he places upon himself or those that arouse misgivings concerning himself.

Concealment of Emotion

Prior to adolescence a young person has gone through many emotional upheavals and storms, in addition to experiencing the quieter currents of emotion that flow through all the tides of his life. He has also gone through long and rigorous schooling in the art of hiding or blunting or disguising his feelings. This means that if we seek to understand the adolescent we must not only observe the emotions he openly reveals but also try to fathom emotions he has learned to conceal or to deny.

When adolescents conceal their feelings, or falsify their expression of emotion, they may do so knowingly or unknowingly. They knowingly suppress emotion when, for example, they definitely feel anger but think it is prudent not to show it. This is conscious control of emotion. Conscious control may occur by suppressing any sign of emotion, or pretending a different feeling, as when a person who is angry deliberately appears conciliatory.

The process of snuffing out emotion is more complete when a person is not just controlling his overt expression of feelings but is himself unaware of them. Such a condition prevails when a person who is affronted acts in a conciliatory way but has no conscious feeling of anger. He feels, instead, that his *real* experience is a desire to please the one who has abused him. When an affront which naturally would produce anger is thus shoved aside, as though it did not exist, but still leaves a mark that the person is not aware of, we say it is *repressed*. It is down but not out. When the anger which has been banished from awareness still rankles, but in ways undetected by the angry person, it is labeled "unconscious." According to the theory of repression, any emotional impulse, such as anger, fear, love, or desire, may thus be excluded from awareness. A person who knowingly suppresses his feelings is concealing something from others; a person who unwittingly represses his feelings is concealing something from himself.

The influences that lead an adolescent to alter, suppress, or repress his expression of emotion reside both within him and in the culture. Two influences from within are especially important. First, changes that occur in the natural course of development lead to many changes in emotional response. The growing child becomes increasingly able to cope with many conditions that once disturbed him. With increased ability he can take in stride many things that once produced anger or fear. As his language ability develops he has less need to strike out in anger or to cry. Also as he grows older he is better able to view things in a larger perspective, to bide his time, to make allowances.

Another condition within the youngster himself which influences both the nature of his feelings and his expression of feelings is conflict. Various impulses and motives clash with one another and lead to a different emotional outcome than would emerge if only a single motive were at work. Conflict prevails, for example, when his anger at his parents collides with his fondness for them or when his desire to assert himself is blocked by fear.

There also are powerful forces in the culture that lead adolescents to disguise or repress their emotions. For one thing, the adolescent has been reminded again and again throughout childhood that he should not show his feelings. As a child he was told not to cry; and so the adolescent, and notably the adolescent boy, seldom cries even though the conditions of his life are such that he might weep if he felt free to show his feelings.

From early childhood adolescents have had fears, but they have been told not to show them. They have been told by adults that there is "nothing to be afraid of." Peers have admonished them not to be "fraidy cats." So they are often afraid without openly showing it. It is a strange paradox that in adolescence, as in adult life, it often takes more courage to show fear than to conceal it.

From early infancy all adolescents have known anger, but they have learned that it is dangerous to show anger openly, and many adolescents were taught, as children, not simply to hide their anger but to fear it and to feel guilty about it.

Likewise, most adolescents have had the experience of loving, as well as being loved, but many of them have learned to conceal even this worthy emotion. Quite apart from their own tendency to become less demonstrative in showing their feelings, youngsters are under pressure from others in childhood and adolescence to control their open expression of affection. It is "babyish" for an older child, especially a boy, to caress others or to seek a caress. A youngster is likely to be jeered if he tenderly avows that he loves a playmate or a teacher. There are strong taboos against affection both on the playground and in the classroom.

The prohibitions against a display of affection are also strengthened, as youngsters grow older, by fears about the intermingling of tenderness and sex. Many youngsters who gladly accepted a little hug or pat from their teachers in nursery school would be flabbergasted if a high school teacher hugged them (and the teacher probably would be embarrassed if observed in the act). Because of such taboos, many persons recoil more from tenderness than from anger.

When tenderness is taboo it is, as we have noted, due in part to the fact that sex is taboo; and sex is taboo, in part, because society, of necessity, must impose some sexual restraints. But what often seems to happen is that tenderness becomes a forbidden emotion while sexual impulses survive. Such a fatality of tenderness has occurred when sex is more closely linked in the adolescent's mind with the idea of aggression and exploitation than with the sentiment of love.

The conditions of life that make it necessary (or seem to make it necessary) for young persons to conceal or tone down their emotions may strike so deeply that they not only conceal emotion from others but, as we have noted, lose touch with it themselves. This happens, for example, when they doubt whether they really should be angry or affectionate or afraid.

This process of suppression and concealment of emotion often goes far beyond what is prudent or essential. Much of the blunting of emotion in children takes place because adults in their upbringing were taught to conceal and fear their emotions. One consequence is that adults often are disturbed and become anxious when children cry or are frightened or show anger. They may basically be kindhearted people but feel threatened by another's show of feeling. They hurriedly tell a child not to cry or not to be afraid or angry without giving him a chance to express, and themselves a chance to discover, why he is upset. In so doing they cut themselves off from the child and curb the child's right to his own feelings.

As a result, by the time a person reaches adolescent age the "natural" quality and flow of his emotions have frequently been overlaid with many pretenses and distortions. So if we center our attention only on the emotion shown by the adolescent and take this emotion at face value, we are likely to miss much and to make some radical mistakes. There are aspects of adolescent emotion that we can understand only to the extent that we are willing and able to see beyond the adolescent as he now is and to reconstruct, as it were, the child he once was. In trying to fathom how an adolescent might feel, it is necessary for adults to endeavor to look beneath the surface of their own emotions and to draw as fully as they can on the emotional experiences they had during adolescence and childhood.

Love and Affection

An important feature of the adolescent's emotional life is his capacity for affection for others, and another is his capacity for receiving affection from others. The ability to accept affection is as essential as the ability to give it. As the young person reaches emotional maturity, the distinction between giving and receiving becomes harder to make, and the two are often merged.[1]

ORIGINS OF AFFECTION

The importance of affection has been brought home to the adolescent from the time of earliest infancy. He begins life as one who is helpless. Affectionate behavior from others is closely linked to his physical survival and affectionate behavior from others is an important factor in his psychological well-being. Also, in early childhood, he himself goes out to others with affectionate pats and caresses.

One theory concerning the origin of love is about as follows: The

[1] Aspects of affection are also treated in other sections, including those dealing with parent-child relationships, relationships between friends, and between members of the opposite sex, and compassion as a component of emotional maturity.

primary needs of the child are those connected with his animal wants—his need for food, drink, and protection against the elements. It is satisfying for a child to have these needs gratified, and this influences his feelings toward those who gratify them; they are a part of the total situation in which gratification occurs. Feelings arising from gratification become associated with certain persons and conditions. A child eventually loves his mother because he originally liked her milk and the comfort she provided.

Another theory concerning the origin of love is that it is not just a by-product of the gratification of animal wants but an inherent and primary element of human nature. According to this view, it is as "natural" to love and to seek love as it is to eat.

In discussing contrasting views, Sorokin and Hanson (1953, p. 99) summarize evidence supporting the idea that there is an "enormous power for creative love, friendship, and nonviolent and nonaggressive conduct in human affairs and in social life."

Among the best-known current discussions of the origins of love are Harlow's (1958, 1962), based on a study of monkeys, some reared by their own mothers and others by mechanical substitute mothers. Many of Harlow's monkeys have been studied from infancy through adolescence and are now sexually mature.[2]

In one experiment four baby monkeys received their milk from the artificial breast of wire mothers and four received milk from cloth mothers, but all had access to both a wire and a cloth mother. The infants fed by wire mothers, as well as those fed by cloth mothers, spent far more time with the cloth mother. They would rush to her when frightened, use her as a secure base from which to venture out to explore the surroundings, cling to her, seek comfort through contact with her. According to Harlow (1958, p. 676), the "contact comfort" a baby can derive from a mother is much more important than the mother's milk in the development of affectional responses.

The artificially reared monkeys seemed to thrive as babies, but as they passed through adolescence and reached maturity a different story emerged (Harlow, 1962). They failed, or had difficulty, in developing normal social relationships, normal affectional relationships, and normal

[2] There is a fascinating similarity between human and monkey babies in their response to mothering. As they grow older, they normally show strong affectional ties. Harlow believes that his data regarding social and affectional development in monkeys "have almost total generality to man" (1962, p. 5).

sex behavior with other monkeys. Males and females did not mate as monkeys normally do. Many fought viciously with each other, and even those who attempted sex behavior did so in an infantile and "unreproductive" way.

Eventually, after much effort had been made to overcome their lack of sexual responsiveness, a few of the artificially reared monkeys became mothers. But Harlow reports that this success in imparting "the priceless gift of motherhood" to these monkeys was a "Pyrrhic victory," for the mothers who had never known a real mother of their own were "helpless, hopeless, heartless mothers devoid or almost devoid of any maternal feeling." These studies indicate that monkeys apparently need the lively give and take between themselves and other monkeys when they are young in order to develop their social, affectional, and sexual potentialities.

Human babies have not been reared by wire or cloth mothers, but many are reared with a minimum of "mothering." Among these are institution-reared foundlings, orphans, and children from broken homes. Findings in studies of such children have varied greatly. Some investigators report that babies separated from their mothers are likely to suffer from severe impairment, such as emotional shock, apathy, lack of ability to become emotionally attached to other human beings, along with general developmental retardation (see, *e.g.,* Spitz, 1951). Other investigators have reported that the factor of being reared in an institution does not, in itself, produce emotional disaster or other drastic impairments (see, *e.g.,* Rheingold and Bayley, 1959, and Dennis, 1960, and a review by Casler, 1961).

Although findings in studies of mother-deprived children vary greatly, some generalizations can be made. One is that children differ greatly in their tendency to become desperately attached to a single mother or mother figure and in their ability to respond to substitute mothers. Children reared in institutions that provide less mothering than youngsters commonly receive at home differ greatly in their all-round development and their emotional responsiveness, just as home-reared children do (Rheingold and Bayley, 1959).

A child can apparently develop his capacity for friendliness and affection even though he receives far less attention than the average youngster, but it probably is impossible for him to develop this capacity with *no* friendly contacts. (Even a child in a crowded, understaffed institution has human contacts, which must seem friendly and gratifying to him, when he is fed, bathed, clothed by attendants who are hurried, but not unkind.[3])

There is every reason to believe that the foundation for loving and being loved in adolescence is built in early childhood. Unfortunately, our knowledge as to how firm or frail this foundation must be is very limited. We also have limited knowledge about how ingenious and resourceful children can be in building affectional ties even under adverse circumstances, or about how dim the spark of love might be and still remain alive.

THE SUBSTANCE OF LOVE

Adolescents who are able to love possess a priceless gift. When they are loved in return they taste one of life's greatest joys.[4]

Among the important ingredients of love are tenderness; feeling in another's behalf; an impulse to cherish and protect. Genuine love is freely given, without ulterior motive or purpose—"love seeketh not her own." Love includes acceptance—acceptance of others in spite of their shortcomings, but this does not mean that love must be blind to faults, or condone them, or leave them unreproved. The one who loves sometimes is "cruel only to be kind."

THE EFFECTS OF LOVE

Evidence from personal testimony and from a number of studies dealing with practical effects of a loving attitude in social relationships has been reviewed by Sorokin and Hanson (1953). They cite illustrations and findings in support of the position that love and kindness can stop aggression and enmity; that love begets love and hate begets hate; that love is

[3] Evidence that children seek and need affection and will go to great lengths to establish bonds of affection appears in a study by Freud and Dann (1951). These investigators describe a small group of refugee children who were bereft of their parents; they were rootless, homeless and moved hither and yon in infancy. Lacking any stable parent substitutes from whom to receive affection and on whom they could confer their affection, these children acquired strong attachments to one another. They used each other as their "real love objects." When finally placed in a settled refuge they were, at first, antagonistic to adults, but intensely loyal to one another.

[4] Wenkart (1949) speaks of the adolescent's first sharing of love with a person of the opposite sex as a "revelation."

an important factor in human vitality and longevity; that there is in love a therapeutic force, a power to cure (here they cite, among other matters, the importance of a friendly and accepting attitude on the part of the therapist); that love is linked to the mainspring of life and that without the manifestation of biological love-energy in the care parents give their children, man would die out; that love has a creative and integrative power in the life of the individual (here they mention the warping of the growth process shown by unloved and rejected children); that love has a creative power in social movements; that love constitutes the supreme and vital form of human relationship.

Where there is love there is freedom—freedom to venture far out, to take a chance of making a mistake without paralyzing fear of punishment, freedom to feel the sweep of other emotions. There also is freedom to think large thoughts.

Goldfarb (1943) found that adolescents who apparently had suffered from being reared in an institution showed restriction in the intellectual as well as the emotional sphere. Youngsters who lacked spontaneity and freedom to form emotional ties with others also showed a lack of freedom in their thinking. They were lacking in ability to assume what Goldstein and Scheerer (1941) have called the "abstract attitude." They tended to think concretely rather than conceptually.

ADOLESCENT LOVE

The most dramatic instances of adolescent love occur when adolescents fall in love with a person of the opposite sex and are convinced their love is "true." Some writers have questioned how true an adolescent's "true" love actually is. (We will consider this in a later chapter.) Adolescents are also at times swept with other loving sentiments—for their parents, their home, the family cat or dog (and, in an earlier day, they felt tenderly about their favorite horse). Unfortunately, very little systematic research has been made of adolescent love. Even the studies of adolescents' experiences of being in love with the opposite sex offer only a meager amount of information.

Although our information about the sway of love in the life of adolescents is limited, such glimmerings as we have indicate that to love and to be loved is supremely important in their lives. We see this when even a delinquent will suffer in loyal devotion to his gang. We see a striving for loving when young people feel and express an impulse for doing idealistic things. Their idealism may be visionary and a mixture of many motives. But the germ of love is there when a young person feels an impulse to give of himself and not just to take.

Joy

The joys of adolescence have received less attention from research workers than anger, fear, and other forms of "problem behavior" that involve distress rather than pleasure. Yet in writings on adolescence one can discover a great deal of joy if one reads between the lines.

Each advance in a person's growth adds to the possibilities of life and opens the way for new or richer satisfactions. When things go well we can assume that the adolescent often experiences joy, as when he is warmly accepted as a companion, when he falls in love and his love is reciprocated, when he is successful in ventures that are important to him, in and out of school, when hopes he long has held are realized, when he is respected for his maturity and appreciated as one who not only can carry added responsibilities but can also be granted new privileges, when he makes a discovery of talents and abilities and qualities that emerge during adolescence or when these are especially noticed and appreciated by others.

Some of the joys that adolescents have themselves described as being outstanding in their lives are listed in Table 8.1. The material in this table was drawn from accounts young people wrote when asked to describe one of the happiest days of their lives. The information would be more meaningful if it had been possible to explore a little more deeply into why the happenings were regarded as being especially pleasing.

The table includes younger children as well as adolescents in order to show certain age trends. It can be noted that as children grow older they give less attention to holidays, birthdays, and the like, and that the people in the middle and late teens mention self-improvement and benefits befalling others more than younger children do. Boys mention sports and going to places of amusement more than girls, and girls mention companionship and social relationships more than boys.

Leisure Time Pleasures

A large proportion of adolescents' leisure time pleasures are enjoyed in company with others. Many of these pleasurable activities are described in Chapter 12.

TABLE 8.1

FREQUENCY OF RESPONSES IN VARIOUS CATEGORIES WHEN CHILDREN
DESCRIBED "ONE OF THE HAPPIEST DAYS OF MY LIFE" *
(The values represent percentage of children giving one or more responses
in each category.)

	Grades 1–3 Ages 6–0		Grades 4–6 Ages 9–12		Grades 7–9 Ages 12–15		Grades 10–12 Ages 15–18	
	Boys	Girls	Boys	Girls	Boys	Girls	Boys	Girls
Number	363	331	309	343	282	290	159	171
Receiving or having or otherwise enjoying material things, gifts, toys, money, living quarters	8.7	8.1	10.4	7.2	10.1	4.5	5.6	3.1
Holidays, festive occasions, birthdays, Christmas, etc.	39.1	40.5	32.4	38.9	6.3	10.1	0.6	6.5
Sports, games, hiking, hunting, bicycling, etc.	10.2	6.4	9.1	5.5	12.4	5.8	13.0	7.3
Going to miscellaneous places of recreation, going to camps, traveling, going to resorts, to parks	9.6	9.0	10.1	11.4	9.7	13.9	30.2	6.9
Self-improvement, success in school, educational opportunity, evidence of vocational competence, getting a job	2.4	2.3	2.9	1.9	4.8	4.1	13.6	15.9
Happenings connected with school, including last day, end of school, going to a certain school	3.6	3.4	5.4	4.3	14.0	11.1	7.0	5.4
Relationship with persons (explicitly described), companionship, being with certain friend, return home of relatives, etc.	7.7	15.9	8.0	15.8	10.5	22.0	8.7	19.9
Residing in, moving to, a certain city or community	1.3	1.0	0.8	2.9	0.9	2.9	1.4	5.0
Benefits befalling others, or mankind in general, including end of war	0.6	0.8	3.2	2.8	2.2	2.6	7.9	9.7

* Reproduced, by permission, from A. T. Jersild and R. J. Tasch, *Children's Interests*. Bureau of Publications, Teachers College, Columbia University, 1949. The table omits several categories, including hobbies, movies, and radio programs, art activities, and so forth, mentioned by only small percentages of children.

Boredom. The condition of boredom that prevails when there is an absence of joy or zest has not received much attention in research studies, except indirectly and by inference, even though it is an affliction that often is widespread among adolescents. We may assume boredom, ranging from mild to acute discomfort, when students lack interest in their work at school, "hang around" with nothing to do, or get into scrapes in order to stir up excitement. Boredom in the form of a kind of uneasy restlessness seems often to occur among young people who are relatively unpopular with others (see, *e.g.,* Laughlin, 1954). In studies of delinquents it likewise has been found that they, as compared with nondelinquents, are under considerable pressure to be "on the go" and in need of distractions (see, *e.g.,* Healy and Bronner, 1936).

The adolescent who is bored a great deal of the time is probably also a person who often is anxious or resentful. His boredom may be due in part to the barrenness of his environment; it may also occur because he does not have the freedom to throw himself into interests of his own choosing, or he feels ill at ease when left to himself as though he were unable to enjoy or even to endure his own company in solitude.

Chapter 9

Anger
and Fear

Adolescents, like younger and older persons, are often angry and often afraid. Fear and anger are both aroused by conditions that threaten or seem to threaten the adolescent's well-being—his physical safety, comfort and welfare, plans and desires, pride, or anything that he values and wishes to protect. When threatened by conditions he feels able and willing to oppose, the young person responds with anger. When he is over-whelmed, or does not trust his strength, the adolescent is frightened, and retreats. Anger and fear are interrelated in complicated ways with one another and with other emotions. An adolescent may be angry but afraid to show it. He may be angry about being afraid. Fear may appear in the guise of anger, and anger may be imbedded in other feelings, such as depression and self-pity.

Anger

It is through his anger that an adolescent most sharply asserts his demands and interests. But he has gone through a long series of experiences that determine how his anger will be provoked and how it will be expressed or suppressed. The basic conditions that arouse anger remain much the same throughout life, but there are changes with age in the particular circumstances that provoke it. Many obstructions that made the child lose his temper have little effect on the adolescent. Some threats that aroused fear when he was smaller arouse anger now that he is older. But his anger continues to be evoked by thwarting of his actions or intentions, and by any assault on his self-esteem.

When we try to understand anger in the adolescent it is easier to identify what it is that makes him angry than to tell *why* it makes him angry. To inquire into the why it usually is necessary to study an adolescent over a period of time.

When a young person's temper flares often and easily we may suspect that he is overly sensitive, that he tends to feel abused because of the past, or that his self-regard is shaky.

But if the adolescent displays what seems to be the opposite trait, showing no anger when most persons would be angry, we can also suspect that something is wrong. He may be afraid of showing anger to others. He may be afraid of the meaning his own anger has for himself. He may have surrendered the right to demand from others the kind of respect and consideration any human being has a right to demand. But if he seems to have surrendered this right it is likely that even when he appears outwardly calm and serene he is angry within.

CONDITIONS THAT AROUSE ANGER

During adolescence anger is most often provoked by persons rather than things. There are many unavoidable frictions in the give and take of everyday life. There also are thwartings and restraints imbedded in the culture. These are transmitted by individuals, frequently by parents.[1]

High school students who responded to a check list (Block, 1937) reported a large number of conditions in the home that aroused anger. Among them were rules pertaining to dress and grooming, close supervision, differences between parent and child with respect to what is correct (for example, the use of lipstick). Nagging and restrictions of

---

[1] For accounts of anger and conditions causing annoyance and friction at the high school or college levels, see Anastasi *et al.* (1948), Block (1937), Gates (1926), Hicks and Hayes (1938), Meltzer (1933), and Stott (1940).

various sorts were also checked with high frequency. (Other details of this study are reviewed in the discussion of parent-adolescent relationships in Chapter 11.)

Many adolescents are annoyed not only by specific parental practices but also by parental traits and habits (Stott, 1940).

At the college level, Williams (1950) found that anger was frequently aroused by what students regarded as unjust criticism by parents, being treated like a child at home, clashes of opinion with parents, and troubles with brothers and sisters.

As a child grows older, and as his relations with persons outside the home become increasingly important to him, there is an increase in the frequency of annoyances pertaining to persons other than his relatives (just as nonrelatives play an increasing role in his everyday joys and satisfactions). Older adolescents, for example, more frequently than younger persons mention nonrelatives in what they dislike outside of school (Jersild and Tasch, 1949).

In a study of 250 junior high school pupils aged eleven to sixteen years, Hicks and Hayes (1938) found, by means of interviews and other methods, that the following circumstances most often made the youngsters angry: being teased, someone being unfair to them, things not going right, sarcasm, and bossiness. It appears that the young adolescent is especially likely to be angered by behavior of others which, as he sees it, reflects unfairness and lack of consideration and respect.

Grievances connected with school are reported more frequently by adolescents than by younger children. In a study by the writer and Tasch (1949), there was an increase in the early teens, and an even larger increase in the late teens, in the proportion of individuals who mentioned persons when describing what they *disliked most* at school. The percentages of persons rose from 5.5 in the primary grades to 29 per cent in the senior high school. A large proportion of responses concerning what was disliked most included an element of resentment. Much of this change was due to an increased dislike of teachers (rising from 0.1 per cent in the primary grades to 17 per cent in the senior high school). In this study, young people of adolescent age also reported more annoyance with rules and duties prescribed at school than did youngsters in the elementary grades, but the differences between the younger and older groups were not as large as the differences in mention of persons at school. At the college level, Anastasi *et al.* (1948) found that students who kept diary records of their emotional experiences reported that schoolwork constituted 12.7 per cent of all anger situations.

CONDITIONS THAT INCREASE
SUSCEPTIBILITY TO ANGER

Adolescents, in common with others, are likely to become angry more readily if they are hungry or tired (Gates, 1926; Young, 1937). Stratton (1929) found that adults who had a history of illness during childhood tended to be somewhat more subject to anger than persons who had no history of serious illness.

To understand the meaning of an adolescent's anger in his relationships with people it is important to consider not only what people are doing to him but also what he expects or demands of them. Teasing, which frequently arouses anger in the adolescent, illustrates this point. One youngster teases out of spite, another in a spirit of fun. One youngster who is teased may be amused, another may become very angry. The teasing that arouses anger may be of a malicious sort that would anger anyone, or it may be of a playful sort that would rile only a rather thin-skinned and insecure person.

When adolescents are thwarted or provoked by another person, such provocations are most likely to be anger-arousing if the other person is intentionally provoking or if he is *perceived* as being intentionally provoking. When a person perceives another as being deliberately offensive he views himself not only as justified in his anger but also as justified in retaliating or seeking revenge.[2]

ANGER AND INJURED PRIDE

The adolescent is likely to resent any kind of assault upon his pride and self-regard.

Any experience of failure may produce shame, but there are two conditions involving shame that are especially wrath-producing. One condition is linked to demands placed on the adolescent by others. The other is tied to demands he makes upon himself.

Shame containing an element of resentment is especially likely to occur if the adolescent again and again is thrust into situations where he fails. Some adolescents face such conditions day after day, at home or at

[2] This cognitive aspect of anger provocation, and other elements involved in anger, have been discussed by Kaplan and Goodrich (1957).

school. Failure has a bitter taste. It has been called a kind of "psychic poison." Failure is no less bitter to an adolescent just because, as seen by someone else, it was his own fault that he failed. Indeed, failure that the youngster blames in whole or in part upon himself is probably often the most bitter of all. Moreover, failure does not lose its sting just because it is repeated again and again. When we consider how frequently, in the lives of many adolescents, the experience of failure at school is repeated, without any good coming from it or any growth ensuing from it, it is easier to understand why it is that some young people lash out in acts of vandalism and other forms of violence or go about sullenly as though consumed with hate.

DIRECT EXPRESSIONS OF ANGER AND HOSTILITY

A young child goes through a phase when he is quite free to show his rage openly and violently by thrashing out, making angry outcries, kicking, pushing, and biting. However, by the time young people reach adolescence, especially if they have been reared in what are known as "middle-class" homes, it is not often that they show their rage so openly, and in most groups in our culture adults seldom come to blows when they are angry. In a study by Richardson (1918) it was noted that in about six hundred instances of anger reported by twelve adults, no blows were struck except among "those persons who have the correction of children." (It is interesting to note that many adults who would not think of striking one another do not mind taking a poke at a child, especially if the child is a little beyond infancy and a little short of adolescence.) It is, of course, fortunate that adolescents do not go about slugging each other as freely as they might like, for they could cause serious injury. Yet it is also true that there are many ways of giving vent to anger that are more damaging in the long run than a slap on the cheek or even a sock on the jaw.

Crying

Crying and ranting are other methods of directly displaying anger that usually decline with age, although girls continue to be given the privilege of crying much more freely than boys.[3] This difference in freedom to cry

[3] The most primitive and natural way for infants and young people to show anger, or any other distressing emotion, is to cry. Even later in life, when men are

probably accounts in part (although only in part) for the fact that boys far more often show their resentments in more aggressive ways. Such aggression at school is commonly regarded as "problem behavior." Boys showing "problem behavior" outnumber girls about four to one. (For a review of studies in this area, see Ullman, 1952.)

In the management of anger, boys often face a dilemma, especially if they are being annoyed by girls or women. When exasperated to the point of rage a big boy is not supposed to weep, nor is it manly for him to hit a female, even if she happens to deserve a clout or two.

Verbal Aggression

Most adolescents have acquired many ways of making a verbal "attack" such as name-calling, belittling and sarcastic remarks. One method of verbal attack is to call attention to the desirable qualities of someone else. Other methods include gossip, tattling, slander.

Teasing. Teasing is a common device for expressing hostility. It can be developed into such a fine art that the blame for a quarrel is placed not on the teaser but on the one who is teased when at last he loses his temper and strikes back.

Swearing. Swearing is another obvious way of giving vent to anger. Some boys do not begin to swear in earnest until they reach adolescence, even though swearing is a rather childish thing. Youngsters who have scruples against profanity often builds a vocabulary of polite swear words. Due to social taboos against swearing by women, girls often weep in situations where boys use profanity.

CONCEALED, DELAYED, OR CIRCUITOUS EXPRESSIONS OF ANGER

The training adolescents have received in curbing the impulse to show anger is one of the most impressive features of their education. One result is that the typical adolescent has learned a great variety of devious ways

seeking, through therapy, to "get in touch with their true feelings" they frequently go through a phase when they allow themselves to weep openly in a manner they have not permitted themselves to do since they were children.

When men and women who have rigidly schooled themselves not to weep finally break down and cry, it seems sometimes as though a dam had burst and that they had made an important step toward recapturing long suppressed or repressed emotions.

of venting anger and hostility. But often his success in curbing his anger is deceptive, and often it is gained at a high price. Evidence that he has not really succeeded in smothering his rage appears when he "blows his top" because of some trivial annoyance. The little annoyance touches off anger that has been smoldering for a long time.

"Stored Up" Anger

Some who tolerate annoyance without becoming angry at the moment feel anger later as a delayed reaction (which is more healthy than not to feel it at all). A young person may be unjustly criticized at school, for example, but it may not be until that evening, or the next day, that his anger "hits" him. His anger comes too late for him to do anything directly about it, and so he may seethe within himself and "take it out" on himself, perhaps losing his appetite for supper and getting a bellyache in the bargain.

A tendency to "store up" anger—not feeling its sharp edge at the moment of provocation, but then being riled by it later—appears frequently among adults (Jersild *et al.,* 1962), and we may assume it occurs often among adolescents also. "Stored up" anger appears when a person who has been offended without striking back thinks up a "snappy comeback" an hour or a day (or even some years!) after the occasion.

Anger in Fantasies

Anger frequently shows itself in fantasies and daydreams. The angry one has images of revenge, of someone else coming to grief, of scenes of personal triumph that put the offending person in his proper place. Fantasies expressing aggression were frequently noted by Symonds (1949) in the study of adolescent fantasy reviewed in Chapter 7.

Aggressive fantasies are often so violent and lurid that the adolescent would be mortified if the fantasies could be projected on a screen for others to see. They sometimes envision acts of revenge so stark that the adolescent would recoil from the thought of acting them out. This happens, for example, when a young person lets his mind wander into the possibility of an accident befalling someone he resents.

The label "death wish" has been given to fantasies in which someone is imagined to have died or is imagined to be in a situation that might cause death. Studies of adolescent fantasies, particularly by means of projective techniques, indicate that such imaginings are quite common. Often when such imaginings occur, they are checked before the final blow falls. Moreover, an adolescent or a person at any age who has such fantasies is likely, if he gives them a second thought, to avow to himself that he did not really mean to kill. If he describes such imaginings to others, he is likely to maintain that they are just idle and meaningless flights of fancy. In a sense they are meaningless, for, fortunately, few such fantasies are enacted. They represent impulses which seldom are carried over into a deliberate plan or scheme to do harm. But the fact that the impulses are there, even if in a somewhat embryonic form, is significant, and it can be extremely self-revealing if a person will allow himself to examine his fantasies.

According to some who have made a study of fantasies, it is also possible that these imaginings serve a purpose. This has been summed up in the quip, "A death-wish a day keeps the doctor away."

Violence by Proxy

Adolescents, like persons of other ages, have at their disposal a vast amount of "ready-made," substitute aggression. They can revel in violence by way of television, movies, and reading matter. In many television shows, there is an orgy of killing.

Obviously, we cannot assume that a person who watches killing on the screen would like to be a killer himself. Yet we can say that when a viewer seeks out a program in which people are killed wantonly and in cold-blood, or under a thin pretext of preserving law and order, he is at least a passive participant in the carnage. Even though, on the conscious level, it would be morally repugnant to him to commit homicide, he would not be a passive participant in scenes of violence unless these in some way appealed to impulses that are latent within him.

Displaced Anger

When an adolescent does not feel free to express his anger directly against his offender, he will, like an adult, frequently direct his anger at someone or something else. He may turn against objects, for example, smashing something when angered by a person whom he does not want to attack openly. (In some areas a great amount of such displaced anger is manifested by broken bottles, smashed windows, and other forms of destructiveness.) Or he may direct his anger against animals, as when he hurts the family cat, or cruelly crushes ants or bugs underfoot. He may turn his anger against other persons, as when he hits a boy after being angered by a girl, or thrashes a younger sibling after being angered by an older one, or makes blistering comments about the milder of his parents after having been angered by the sterner of the two. He may turn his anger, induced at home, against school, or turn school-induced anger against those in his home.[4]

One way of giving vent to hostile impulses in a disguised way is to ally oneself with causes, to join militant groups, or to take violent sides in political disputes. Through championing a cause the adolescent may give play to his hurt feelings, his need for vindication, or his impulse to take revenge, although none of these motives is obvious to him nor perhaps to those who observe his behavior.

When the adolescent speaks out against injustices that have been visited upon farmers or laborers or businessmen, he may, in roundabout fashion, be crying out against injustices that have been done to him. When he identifies himself with a minority group, seeking to befriend this group or to champion the rights of that group, his actions may constitute an indirect attack on those whom he opposes and also an indirect plea for sympathy and support for *his* minority interests. (Of course, devotion to a cause or to the interests of a group, whether powerful or downtrodden, may be a wholehearted and genuine thing rather than a displacement of personal problems, as in the examples above.)

One thing that makes the championing of a cause so convenient an expression of hostility for both adolescents and adults is that in the guise of promoting a certain idea or principle, a person can make harsh comments about others without being guilty of an obvious personal attack.

As noted in another chapter, displaced hostility may take the form of prejudice. Other expressions include antisocial acts, rebelliousness at school, and sexual promiscuity of a sort that hurts others.

Projected Hostility

One way of dealing with anger and hostility is to externalize it, to impute it to others. When a person does this he convinces himself that it is others who are angry, bitter, and unfair and that his own anger, if he is aware of it, is righteous indignation and a necessary defense against others who are at fault. It is usually less uncomfortable, for example, when one is in a bad mood, linked to some conditions within oneself, to attribute the difficulty to someone or something else. In so doing, the adolescent, in a sense, locates his anger outside himself. A high school student who is not easy to get along with may, for example, discuss his problem in getting

[4] Because of displaced anger an adolescent may behave quite differently at home than at school. He may be very aggressive in one setting, and seem quite serene in the other. As a consequence, parents and teachers do not see him in the same light. When this happens, parents and teachers have difficulty in understanding each other's views concerning the youngster.

along with others, and the bitterness this problem arouses, as though the problem were entirely due to others. When a person thus externalizes his anger he disowns responsibility for it.

Under some conditions it is a merciful thing that a person can, by this means, escape from some of the bitterness of his own rage. When he is angry there is a need to attach blame somewhere, and if he cannot blame someone or something else, the only one left to blame is himself. There are young people whose lives at times are so filled with bitterness that it would be almost intolerable for them to face this bitterness as something located entirely within themselves. So the ability to externalize anger serves in a way to protect a person from facing realities within himself that might involve him in overwhelming feelings of guilt and self-reproach.

The Feeling of Being Abused. Externalized anger is frequently manifested in grievances. Often an adolescent seems to be full of grievances, speaking and acting as though he were an especially abused person. The grievances and the feeling of being abused may show, for example, in a chronic complaint against his background, his school, his community, certain persons in the neighborhood, or those belonging to particular racial or religious groups. All adolescents have been, and are, to some extent abused by others and by the limitations within their own circumstances of life. Many of their complaints and grievances are therefore justified. We are not now, however, speaking of grievances of this sort. Instead, we are speaking of grievances through which the young person finds a whipping boy for his own resentments.

It is important to remember, however, that once an adolescent has a grievance, whether it is based on realistic grounds or not, his grievance will influence what he sees and hears. So a grievance can nourish itself. If the adolescent has a grievance, his perceptions will be affected. He may see a smile as a smile of contempt, even though the smiling person is actually friendly. He may perceive an assignment at school as another evidence of unfairness, when actually it is not so intended. Even when someone speaks to him in a kindly way, he may distort the intention and respond as though the person were simply using friendliness as a device for additional abuse.

When a person has a grievance, every intellectual process may be influenced. He may be selective not only in what he perceives but also in what he remembers. He may remember when he was punished, forgetting the times he was treated with kindness. He may remember an act of unfairness that happened long ago, forgetting the many occasions on which he has been treated in a fair and even a very favorable way. It is because of this fact that what a person recalls, when he tells the story of his childhood or of happenings that occurred only a month or a year ago, may reveal more about his current attitudes toward himself and others than about past events.

In dealing with an adolescent who carries a grievance it is very difficult for an adult to see beyond it and to perceive, in a sympathetic way, the total operation in which the adolescent is involved. From the adolescent's own point of view, a long-standing grievance is completely justified. The more convinced he is that his grievance is justified, the more difficult it will be for others to understand his complaints. Moreover, an adolescent with a grievance is likely to arouse resentment in others. Everyone has a natural tendency to become annoyed and defensive in dealing with someone who complains chronically and apparently unreasonably.

Parents, teachers, and fellow students are likely to argue with the one who has a grievance. They cannot be blamed for this, but the simple fact is that argument will not help the one who feels abused to see the light. He is more likely to be helped if he can, at an odd moment, get a glimpse of himself. This sometimes happens when a person with a grievance has sounded off so violently in a discussion that even he can hear an echo of his anger. Such a glimpse of self is more likely to occur in a situation in which he is accepted and does not quickly have an opportunity to reinforce his grievance by arguing with someone who is quick to argue with him.

A person with a grievance can also sometimes get what almost amounts to a revelation by hearing a playback of a recording made while he was voicing his grievances. There is no guarantee that insight will result from this device, but it is an example of one way in which a person may see or hear himself from a little distance and get a glimmering of attitudes that ordinarily are so acutely felt and so vigorously defended that it is impossible to look at them objectively.

ANGER DIRECTED AGAINST SELF

There is a close interweaving of anger directed against the adolescent by others, anger directed by him against others, and anger directed against himself. His tendency to be angry will be influenced strongly by his attitudes toward himself, but these attitudes in turn will be influenced by the attitudes others have shown toward him. He is likely, for example, to be "angry with himself" if he fails to live up to his expectations, but these expectations have been influenced by what others once expected of him.

Much of the exasperation one sees in the behavior of the adolescent arises from a lack of tolerance for his own limitations. He may become angry, for example, if he expects to find an answer to a problem and then finds no answer.

His demands on others are likely to have much in common with the demands he makes on himself. If he is intolerant of his own stupidity, he is likely to be intolerant of stupidity in others. But if he is intolerant of his own stupidity, or what he regards as stupidity, this is an attitude he has acquired. So we have a triangular situation: he tends to visit on others what he thinks was visited upon him and what he now also visits on himself. This may not invariably hold true, but it provides an important key to understanding the adolescent. If we see him from the point of view of one side of this triangle we can make a pretty good guess concerning the other two sides.

Anger directed at self may take many forms. It may appear in a tendency to be severely self-critical, far beyond what is reasonable or helpful. We may suspect self-directed hostility when an adolescent again and again blames himself for a mistake long after the event is over but does nothing in the meantime to remedy the mistake or to avoid repeating it. One adolescent, for example, who seemed to have a large amount of anger directed against himself, was given a chance as a freshman to take the leading part in a high school play, and then he hesitated so long that the part was given to someone else. He then became so involved in blaming himself for having missed this opportunity that he missed other opportunities to take part in subsequent plays.

A self-critical attitude may be so strong that the young person will not even try to make the team or the honor roll or be accepted by the group he admires, on the grounds that he does not really deserve it and perhaps, unwittingly, because he would be bitter in his self-accusation if he should try and fail.

Sometimes when an adolescent directs his anger against himself he may do so because he has learned that it is safer to blame himself than to blame others. Anger directed against self may also occur because he has learned through being the butt of constant criticism and complaint to adopt the view that if anything goes wrong it is his fault.

Another way, according to some authorities, in which hostility directed against self may be expressed is in psychosomatic illness. The theory here is that some allergies, unaccountable headaches, and other aches and digestive upsets have a "psychic" origin, a feature of which is unresolved hostility. The physical pain is preferable to the pain of self-hate experienced as such.

Yet another sign that is probably often an expression of anger turned inward is a tendency again and again to get into various self-punishing scrapes and difficulties, including accidents. According to this view it is not entirely "accidental" when a person repeatedly does things that get him into trouble, such as openly defying a friendly teacher when he has nothing to gain by his defiance, or when he continually gets injured by banging into things or stumbling on the stairs.

THE RIGHT TO BE ANGRY

We have noted in many parts of this discussion that it is difficult for adolescents to face the meaning of their anger. They are not dealing with anger in a forthright and constructive way when they recognize their tendency to become angry but feel guilty about this tendency. An adolescent may be completely justified in feeling remorseful about a particular outburst of anger; his anger might have been out of proportion to the occasion, or it might have inflicted more hurt on another than he intended, or it might have been regrettable in other ways. But when he deplores his tendency to become angry, his susceptibility to anger, he is deploring an essential element in his nature. He is repudiating an emotion that is unavoidable and inescapable in the normal course of life. He is, in effect, denying his right to be a human being.

In a study by the writer (1952), 18 per cent of a group of 1,600 junior and senior high school students singled out their temper or tendency to become angry when writing compositions on the theme "What I Dislike about Myself." At the college level (200 students) the per cent was 19.5. If these persons had been asked specifically about their anger it is probable that a far larger number would have deplored their anger. On the other hand, only about 3 per cent mentioned anger in describing what they liked about themselves, and in practically all instances this represented approval of their ability to control their anger. In the general population it is only an exceptional person who will express approval of himself for having the capacity to become angry and for being able to feel and show anger when it is justified.

Repudiation of the right to be angry goes far beyond simply deploring anger that people are aware of; it occurs also when people disavow anger, project it on others, feel and express hostility without recognizing it for what it is (by way, for example, of snobbery and malicious gossip) or are so threatened by anger that they suppress it before they have felt its full surge.

It is far healthier for an adolescent to be realistic in acknowledging his anger than to deny that it exists, and to accept the fact that he is bound to become angry rather than to deplore himself for being endowed with the ability to become angry.

To grant oneself the right to be angry is quite different from blindly giving way to anger by punishing others or oneself and then condoning such conduct. The right to be angry does not mean a right to strike out in rage against everyone and everything. It does not mean that the angry one should be permitted to indulge in unrestrained violence. The right to be angry does mean, however, that a person does not always have to blunt his anger before it has a chance to develop, or punish himself through feelings of guilt because he has had angry impulses.

The more realistically a young person can accept his anger the more likely it is that he will use anger in ways that are healthy and constructive and in ways which, in the long run, add to his own well-being and the welfare of others.

When an adolescent is able thus to accept anger to some degree as something inherent in the human struggle, he will be better able to perceive how other persons' hurts and strivings are revealed through anger. And if he can now and then look objectively at his own anger it may give him a revelation of himself.

It is unfortunate that the process by which such a revelation might take place is so often blocked at home and at school. It is, of course, necessary to block the adolescent when his anger becomes so violent that it is damaging to others and to himself. But it is helpful when an adolescent's elders try to hear him out when he is angry, thus availing themselves of his anger as a way of understanding him and indirectly as a way of helping him to understand himself.

Fear

Adolescents have undergone a long series of developments that influence the ebb and flow of their fears. Some earlier fears have been outgrown, though some are likely still to persist. Many new fears have arisen by virtue of the threats and allurements that go with adolescent development itself.

All adolescents, like all adults, are more or less frightened at times. Some of them experience fear only on occasions when they happen to run into danger. Some have recurring fears that are touched off again and again by happenings in their daily lives or by dreams or by their own trends of thought. Some experience states of dread lasting days or even weeks at a time. Some struggle with fears that arise out of the problems of life. No one who throws himself into the possibilities of life can live without fear. The only way to evade fear is to surrender to fear, as happens when a person is so afraid that he does not daringly reach for what the present or an uncertain future might bring.

In this section we will consider some of the fears of adolescence as they can be observed or as they have been described under the name of fear or some other term. In the next chapter we will move on to the topic of anxiety, which in some ways is related to fear but which, as we shall see, incorporates more than we usually mean when we speak of the fears of everyday life.

SOME COMMON "FEARS"

At the time they are about to enter the teens, many children report fears in one or more of the following categories: animals; painful situations; danger or threat of bodily accidents and injuries; fears arising during dreams; fear of ridicule; fear of failure; "bad" people, such as robbers and kidnappers; dangers associated with the dark or being alone in the dark; imaginary creatures such as ghosts; reminders of characters met in stories, movies, radio programs, and the like (Jersild and Holmes, 1935). Youngsters in their teens report fewer fears of domestic animals than preadolescent children and more fears of physical harm (other than through attacks by animals, Winkler, 1949).

Studies of the "worries" of young persons of high school or college age add several items to this list. In one such study, high school students, in naming problems they were "most concerned about" (Bonar, 1942), listed getting a job, preparing for a vocation, war problems (this was in the early forties), school problems, and social problems. When a person says he is very "concerned," it does not necessarily mean that he is clearly afraid; but some kind of uneasiness and probably a certain amount of apprehensiveness are involved.

Among the "worries" reported by college freshmen in a study by Lunger and Page (1939) were worries about not being as successful as they would like to be, hurting the feelings of others, impressions made upon others, not working hard enough. Relationships with others and attitudes toward self figure prominently in these "worries." Fears and worries about relationships with others (reputation, popularity, relations with the opposite sex, etc.) are common among both boys and girls, but are reported more frequently by girls (Angelino *et al.*, 1956). Among the items marked most frequently on a check list of "worries" in a study by Marsh (1942) were the following: selecting a suitable vocation, feelings of inferiority, getting enough sleep, lack of self-confidence, finding a purpose in life, concentration, complexion, building a philosophy, having the blues, moodiness, budgeting time, being overweight.

In many ((perhaps all) of these "worries" there seems to be an element of emotional conflict: a desire for getting more sleep, for example, apparently clashed with motives that kept the person from going to bed or from falling asleep. In worry over "being overweight" there may be conflict between a craving (or perhaps a compulsion) to eat and a desire for a trim figure. In other words, there is more involved here than a fear of this or that danger in the external environment. Many of these "fears" are symptoms of complicated personal problems.

As indicated by these reported fears, many young people of high school and college age are apprehensive about their personal limitations, their ability to appear well in the eyes of others and their ability to measure up to their own standards or to the standards by which others judge them. In a study of fears recorded in diaries by college girls, Anastasi *et al.* (1948) found that the largest number of fears centered on schoolwork (40.2 per cent). The second largest number (30.8 per cent) related to "inferiority and loss of prestige." An interesting finding in this study was that schoolwork was decidedly more often reported as producing fear than anger (40.2 per cent of the fear-arousing situations as compared with 12.7 per cent of the anger-arousing situations). A deeper examination of many of the fears listed above would probably reveal that they contain an undercurrent of anger. Fear is a painful emotion, and when the cause of it is attributed to persons, these persons are likely not only to be feared but also resented.

In a study dealing mainly with older adolescents and young adults of college age (Jersild and Holmes, 1935), many persons reported that they were still troubled by fears carried over from childhood years. The 303 persons who took part in the study gave written descriptions of over a thousand "fears" they recalled from childhood, and, of these, 349 were described as still persisting. This does not necessarily mean that about a third of the fears of childhood carry over into late adolescence and young adulthood. These college students probably had forgotten many of their childhood fears; and it is possible that many apprehensions of childhood were replaced by other similar "fears" (such as fear of not doing well in one's job as a "replacement" for fear of failing at school).

The most frequently reported childhood fear was fear of animals, and about half of these fears were described as persisting in late adolescence or early adulthood. Another frequently mentioned childhood fear was of accidents and injuries, and over a third of these were described as still persisting. Two-fifths of the fears pertaining to personal failure, inadequacy, or ridicule that were described as arising during childhood were identified as still persisting. Other "fears" carried over from childhood into late adolescence with less frequency but still in considerable number were fears associated with dangers in the dark and fears pertaining to robbers, kidnappers, and other criminal characters.

As we shall see in the next chapter, many of the "fears" reported by children, adolescents, and adults might better be regarded as evidences of anxiety than as apprehensions concerning specific dangers.

EXPRESSION AND CONCEALMENT OF FEAR

Adolescents are adept at disguising their fears, and their expression of fear may take many forms. The form that is easiest to detect is an outright show of fright, as revealed by running, clutching, calling for help, trembling, or obvious efforts to avoid or escape. There are moments in the lives of everyone when a situation is so frightening that fear is openly shown.

But fear may be concealed behind a manner suggesting just the opposite of fear. A frightened person may show anger which serves as a means of protest or counterattack, designed to blunt the experience of fear or to protect him against having to face a frightening situation. A simple form of this appears when a person is afraid of going to the dentist and snarls with anger when he is reminded that he should go.

Fear may also appear in the guise of extreme mildness and conformity. The extremely "good" adolescent may be a frightened person who uses his goodness as a means of protecting himself from fear of punishment, disapproval, or rejection.

"IRRATIONAL" FEARS

As in earlier childhood, a large proportion of the fears reported in adolescence are "irrational" in the sense that the fears are quite out of proportion to the dangers that actually exist. Many bright young people "fear" that they will do poorly on examinations even though they have always done well and have no real reason to think that they will not continue to do well. Such irrational fears, although centered on an external danger, are symptoms of conflict. They fall under the heading of anxiety, a condition we will examine in the next chapter.

Chapter 10

Anxiety

To understand adolescents—or persons at any stage of life—it is essential to come to grips with the concept of anxiety, for this concept provides a key to much that is baffling in an adolescent's conduct.

Anxiety has many facets which cannot be encompassed in any simple definition. We will, however, begin with a very general statement and then add to it as the chapter proceeds.

Anxiety prevails when a person is at odds with himself. It can be defined in very general terms as a persisting, distressful psychological state arising from an inner conflict. The distress may be experienced as a feeling of vague uneasiness or foreboding, a feeling of being on edge, or as any of a variety of other feelings, such as fear, anger, restlessness, irritability, depression, or other diffuse and nameless feelings.

The underlying conflict springs from a clash between incompatible impulses, desires, or values. Such a conflict prevails when a person is angry but is afraid of giving offense. Likewise, it exists when a person is eager to be popular but has strong scruples against doing what is necessary to become popular.

Anxiety exists as a conscious state when the anxious person is aware of the nature of his conflict and the ways in which the conflict affects his feelings and his conduct. But it has unconscious elements when the anxious person does not recognize what is troubling him, or realize why he feels as he does, and is unaware of ways in which his behavior is influenced by his anxiety. When a person who is afraid of disapproval goes out of his way to please people and then resents the fact that he has allowed others to take advantage of him, his anxiety is on a conscious level as long as he is aware of what is happening. But the anxiety has unconscious elements if this person sees himself as one who is very generous rather than as one who is afraid and if he does not recognize that it is he who invites others to take advantage of him.[1]

A further characteristic of anxiety is that it precipitates strategies or defenses for coping with the distress and inner conflict.

Examples of Adolescent Anxiety

The sketches which follow illustrate some aspects of adolescent anxiety.

Our first example is an adolescent boy who felt anxious about expressing his own opinions. He was in a school where everyone was encouraged to "speak his mind." But he was unable to speak out, even when he disagreed with something others had said. He wanted to disagree openly, but had strong inhibitions against opposing someone else. So during periods of "free" public discussion he was silently engaged in a battle which left him in a "nervous" and sullen mood after the discussion was over.

As a child and preadolescent he had been taught not to be "pushy" or outspoken in any way that might offend others, and he was chastised for not heeding this lesson. For example, one time he was severely scolded by his father for frankly telling some adult neighbors that they had taken unfair advantage in a business deal. His father privately agreed with him and felt incensed about the business deal, but was mortified by having the boy express this opinion outside the family circle. Thus, the idea of

---

[1] The labels "normal" and "neurotic" are used by some writers in discussing anxiety. Broadly speaking, a person beyond the stage of early childhood has "normal" anxiety (also referred to as "objective" or "uncomplicated" or "realistic" anxiety) when he consciously recognizes the nature of his conflict, is aware of the feelings connected with it and seeks to resolve it, as best he can, in a thoughtful, constructive way. By contrast, a person is said to have "neurotic" anxiety if he is not aware of the underlying conflict, does not recognize why he feels as he does, and uses "unconscious defense mechanisms" or "pseudosolutions" in dealing with the conflict.

speaking out frankly in public became associated in this boy's mind with disapproval and with the idea that taking issue with another person's opinions would be construed as a personal attack and would provoke retaliation.

This adolescent boy was aware of the conflict between his desire to speak out and his fear of doing so, and to that extent his anxiety was on the conscious level. He did not, however, recognize the irrational nature of his inhibition against speaking-out. His inhibitions were a carry-over from an earlier situation in which being outspoken actually was reproved by others. In his present situation, where being outspoken was encouraged, he was "unconsciously" acting out an old fear.

The anxiety here would have been farther removed into the "unconscious" if the boy had managed to repress his awareness of his fear of speaking-out. Such repression would occur, for example, if he no longer experienced his inhibition against speaking-out as a fear but regarded it as a virtue, an evidence that he had the good sense and strength of character to keep his mouth shut when all around him were babbling.

Our next example is that of a girl in her late teens. She was attracted to a certain boy and had fantasies about some day marrying him, but these fantasies threw her into a conflict. He belonged to another religious faith, and she realized her parents and the family tradition she had absorbed were opposed to such a union. Therefore, she was both drawn to the boy and driven to reject him, and this was reflected in her actions. At times she tried her best to charm him. But at other times she said and did things to make him feel inferior and miserable—such as reminding him that he had little money, or disparaging his friends. She finally "resolved" her conflict by telling him, in a painful scene, that they would have to stop seeing one another because of the difference in their faiths. He accepted this verdict, and did not try to see her again. But her conflict was not actually resolved. Despite many feelings of guilt and shame, she continued for a time to try to get in touch with him again.

This sketch, and the others here reported, illustrate elements of what has been referred to as "normal" anxiety as well as characteristics of "neurotic" anxiety.[2]

---

[2] Actually, the use of the label "normal" in contradistinction to "neurotic" in describing anxiety is an unfortunate use of terms. "Normal" pertains to the norm; it is a quantitative label, denoting the usual, typical, or average. The inappropriateness of the terms is apparent if we imagine a community in which 51 per cent suffer from "neurotic" anxiety. In this community "neurotic" anxiety is "normal." However, the distinction between the two kinds of anxiety is a meaningful one, even though the labels are not good.

In this anxiety situation, the girl was conscious of a realistic cause for concern: she was aware that marriage with the boy would wound her parents and that a marriage between persons with different religious backgrounds might not turn out well. On the other hand, there were aspects of the total anxiety situation which she did not understand: why, for example, in spite of her strong religious views, she was attracted to a boy belonging to another faith. She did not recognize that the attraction was, in effect, a rebellion against her parents.

When she attacked the boy's pride in order to make him feel inferior she was using tactics which writers about anxiety have called "unconscious defense mechanisms." The attacks served two "purposes" which she did not recognize at the time. First, they were a form of revenge: although she was fond of the boy she also resented him, for her attachment to him caused her much anguish. Second, by hurting his feelings she was inviting him to become so offended that he would have nothing more to do with her. If he left the scene, she would no longer have a tangible reminder of the conflict which centered around him.

The details of our next example are drawn from extensive interviews with a postadolescent young man who had strong sexual urges and strong inhibitions against them. On the conscious level he had a conflict between his sexual desires and his conscience, a conflict that is quite common in adolescent boys and girls.

Following an episode of relatively mild sex play with a girl, he suffered acute anxiety. Because he had strong moral scruples about sex, he felt anguish and remorse about what he had done. Yet, he still had the desires which had led him to yield to temptation, and these were a continuing threat to his moral scruples.

To cope with this conflict he developed defenses against it. These were to a large degree unconscious in the sense that at that time he did not perceive the relationship between these defenses and his conflict about sex. His main defense was to use his ambitions for success as a means of protecting himself. He resolved to work hard and to save his money to pay for his schooling. This resolve meant that he could not have dates because, as he saw it, he could not afford them. Having no dates meant that he was to that extent protected from the danger of intimacy with any girl.

In his struggle with anxiety this adolescent did many contradictory things, as anxious people often do. He could not help being attracted by girls, but in his fantasies he preferred girls whom he regarded as "out of reach" because of their wealth and popularity. When such girls were friendly toward him, indicating that perhaps they were not out of reach, he retreated. At the same time he built up in his fantasies a dream girl, a girl so glorious that no one could be the living model. This dream girl helped to protect him from becoming infatuated with a real girl.

Although he pictured himself as having too humble a station in life to be attractive to girls who attracted him, he also pictured himself as one who could get girls to "fall" for him. He bolstered this with the further thought that he did not want to break a girl's heart. So, as he saw it, he must be careful not to show an interest in any girl who might fall in love with him.

The record of this adolescent shows other aspects of anxiety. There was an hiatus between his public and private behavior. In the eyes of others he was sexually "pure" and he was admired for his success in schoolwork. (This is what is known as a "secondary gain" from defenses against anxiety.) But in his fantasies he was far from pure. Further, although a feeling of guilt was the *leitmotif* underlying much of his behavior he was also, perversely, self-righteous. For a time he took a strong stand against social dancing; according to his "reasoning" it was too erotic. Yet dancing would have been a rather innocent activity compared with his own erotic fantasies.

Anxiety-Producing Stresses in Adolescence

It is quite generally agreed that unresolved childhood problems play an important role in the anxieties that prevail in adolescence and later periods of life. Likewise, it is probable that a person will continue to use the maneuvers for coping with conflicts that he used as a young child.[3] However, each period of life brings issues that are new in the sense that a person faces possibilities and responsibilities that differ from those he

---

[3] Conditions that produce anxiety in infancy and early childhood have been described by Freud, whose contributions have inspired those who accept his views and, perhaps even more, those who do not. Other trail-blazers in recent times are Horney (1939, 1945, 1946, 1950) and Sullivan (1947, 1948, 1953). An earlier pioneer in the exploration of anxiety was Kierkegaard, whose contributions we will consider in a later section.

An adequate discussion of the background and childhood beginnings of adolescent anxieties would require a book-length account, which is not feasible here. For a review of theories regarding anxiety the reader is referred to May (1950), and Hoch and Zubin (1950). The writer has given a condensed account in previous books (see, *e.g.*, 1960 and 1955).

has faced before, or must make choices he has not been required to make at an earlier time; and these issues may precipitate anxiety or aggravate an earlier tendency to be anxious.

Everything that an adolescent for the first time recognizes about himself, every venture that he accepts or declines, every decision he makes, may threaten earlier ideas, perceptions, and attitudes he has acquired regarding himself.

In planning his career and surrendering some of his earlier fantasies about his future, the adolescent faces issues which previously were not pressing. Many young people are confronted for the first time with facts about themselves and their background (the social status of their family, their religion, their ethnic origins, and their prospective earning power) which may produce serious conflicts.

The young person who struggles with the problem of whether or not to continue his schooling faces a conflict which could not come to a head until the teen-age years.

As noted in Chapters 3 and 4, the course of physical growth itself has many emotional repercussions in adolescence, such as the stresses connected with early or late maturing, adolescent obesity, concern about development of the genitals and secondary sex characteristics. In the sphere of sex, he has urges and faces temptations, choices, and hazards which are more critical than his earlier experiences with sex. In his interpersonal relations he faces problems of independence-dependence, conformity-nonconformity, and self-assertion–self-negation.

In the pages immediately following we will consider some facets of anxiety and some sources of conflict-producing anxiety that are especially significant at the adolescent level (although not confined to the adolescent level).

ANXIETY AND SELF-DETERMINATION

As we have noted, an adolescent faces numerous choices and must make many decisions. The process of choosing sometimes involves little more than an objective calculation of the advantage or disadvantage of one alternative compared with another. But often the adolescent's choice involves something more profound, for he is, in effect, "choosing himself" —making decisions about what he is, who he is, and what he might become.

The interplay between anxiety and the self, notably "choosing oneself," was discussed over a century ago by Kierkegaard, a Danish philosopher who anticipated many ideas which have been incorporated into psychoanalysis and psychology.[4]

According to Kierkegaard, a unique attribute of man is his *awareness of possibility*. His awareness of possibility includes and is intimately interrelated with *awareness of freedom:* freedom to seize what is possible or to reject or evade it, freedom to choose one alternative rather than another. Without freedom there would be no inner conflict, but where there is freedom—awareness of possibility—anxiety is inevitable.[5] The freedom of which he speaks is the freedom everyone knows as a personal experience when he perceives the possibilities that lie before him and is convinced that he can make a choice and is convinced also that he is free to change his mind. This freedom, from the point of view of a person's own experience, is a psychological reality. Even if a person adopts a philosophy of determinism and regards everything that happens as a link in an unbreakable chain of cause and effect, he cannot escape from the idea that he is responsible. He cannot shake off the feeling that he has freedom. It is within the boundaries of this freedom that human beings weigh alternatives, debate with themselves, feel guilty. It is within the boundaries of this freedom that they "choose" themselves, or "will" to be themselves by seizing or evading possibilities for realizing their potentialities. In so doing they have a hand in creating what they are and what they might become. They can venture, or play it safe. They can assert themselves or drift with the crowd. Without choice there would be no conflict, without conflict there would be no anxiety.

Kierkegaard vividly describes anxiety as a painful experience and describes how a person can learn from it or try, in vain, to escape from it. Encounters with anxiety offer opportunities to acquire greater self-awareness, greater strength within oneself, larger vistas of freedom or possibility, a more realistic interpretation of life, more inward "certitude," and increased power to deal with anxiety. On the other hand, individuals may try to evade the challenge of "possibility" and their freedom to make commitments by attributing everything to fate, or by trying

[4] References to anxiety and man's predicament in facing the choices that lie before him appear in many writings by S. Kierkegaard which have been translated into English by Walter Lowrie, including *Either/Or* (1949), *Stages on Life's Way* (1940), and, notably, *The Sickness Unto Death* (1941) and *The Concept of Dread* (1944).

[5] Kierkegaard uses the term "Angst," which several translators have translated as "dread." "Anxiety" as used in this book is a more appropriate translation of "Angst" than "dread."

to shut themselves off, adopting rigid beliefs, resorting to superstition, or taking refuge in conformity or in academic abstractions.

Throughout his writings, Kierkegaard describes many of the symptoms of self-negating efforts to deal with anxiety that are prominently discussed today. In his own language he speaks of what we currently call "the organization man," the person who seeks safety and security in conformity, in "outer-directedness." He also often speaks of what we currently refer to as the "man in the ivory tower"—the person who amasses knowledge and spins abstract theories that are purely academic, with little or no personal meaning.[6]

ANXIETY AND INTERPERSONAL RELATIONSHIPS IN ADOLESCENCE

We have described anxiety as resulting from an "inner conflict." A conflict of this sort, residing within the person himself, is sometimes referred to as "intrapsychic"—within the psyche of a particular individual. But the conflicts which underlie anxiety arise in a social context; they are both intrapsychic and interpersonal.

To realize his potentialities it is essential for an adolescent to maintain his integrity as an autonomous, self-directing individual, but it is also essential for him to develop his resources as a social being. He has attributes which can be expressed only through his relationships with others and he has needs which can be fulfilled only through intimate association with others. Some of the conditions that produce conflict in the adolescent's interpersonal relationships have been described by Harry Stack Sullivan (1947, 1948, 1953).[7]

Prior to adolescence, according to Sullivan, a young person has gone

---

[6] In one passage, Kierkegaard speaks of a speculative philosopher who found a new proof for the immortality of the soul, "then came into mortal danger and could not produce his proof because he had not his notebooks with him" (1944, p. 124).

[7] In Sullivan's account (1953), anxiety in adolescence, and the consequences of such anxiety in the young person's personality development, have a history extending back to infancy. According to Sullivan, the mother or "mothering person" communicates her anxiety to her infant child through a process of empathy— "emotional contagion and communion"—before the youngster is consciously aware of what is going on. She also induces anxiety through gross or very subtle acts or signs of disapproval. According to Sullivan, the self comes into being through a child's endeavor to cope with anxiety-inducing disapproval and to preserve the feeling of security, self-approval and self-esteem which comes with approval.

through a vast number of experiences that influence his "self-system"—what is incorporated within it and what is excluded from it by "selective inattention," "dissociation," and other means. The self-system a young person already has established includes attitudes toward self and toward others which influence his reaction to people and events during adolescence. But in the process of maturation, during preadolescent and adolescent years, two developments occur which can add a deeper dimension to the young person's interpersonal relationships and also result in new occasions for insecurity and anxiety.

One of these developments, according to Sullivan, is a need for (and, all being well, a capacity for) interpersonal *intimacy*. The other is what Sullivan calls "maturation of the lust dynamism" (1953, p. 279). "Lust is the felt aspect of the genital drive" (1953, p. 295).

The need for intimacy normally first appears in preadolescence, according to Sullivan. The young person who, as an infant, had an inherent need for tenderness from the mothering person now is able to bestow it and share it and has a need to do so. Intimacy, in Sullivan's account, means emotional closeness with another—*collaboration,* love. Intimacy involves mutuality, "an intimate exchange with a fellow being" (p. 246). "It is a matter of *we*" (1953, p. 55). The need for intimacy is at first best-fulfilled, according to Sullivan, through relationships with a member of the same sex—a chum.

A young person may face "disasters" in connection with the need for, and fulfillment of the need for, intimacy, if the timing of his development is out of step with that of other persons with whom he might establish an intimate relationship. In discussing this, Sullivan calls attention to the well-known fact that young people differ markedly in their rate of maturation. This may cause disturbance in a young person's interpersonal relationships if, due to a slower rate of development, he has no need for intimacy when most of the other persons of his age have this need.[8]

With the development of a "need for lustful satisfaction, which is connected with genital activity in pursuit of the orgasm" (1953, p. 264) there is (all going well) a growing interest in achieving intimacy with a member of the opposite sex. In connection with this development there are several circumstances that may lead to a disturbance in interpersonal relationships—with consequent anxiety.

[8] One form of failure in achieving intimate interpersonal relations is seen in the condition of loneliness. Loneliness, according to Sullivan, is a phenomenon encountered only in preadolescence and thereafter. "Loneliness in itself is more terrible than anxiety" (1953, p. 262), and as a "driving force" it may compel people to seek companionship even though they are intensely anxious.

One source of difficulty is that "our culture provides us with singular handicaps for lustful activity . . . , lust promptly collides with a whole variety of powerful dynamisms in the personality" (1953, p. 266). Disapproval by others of a child's early interest in his genitals and his impulse to play with them lead him to regard his genitals as bad. They are a part of his person which the child is taught to repudiate. They are not incorporated into what he regards as his approved and worthy self. Consequently, at adolescence his sexual desires may clash with his self-system. To accept his sexuality he must, in effect, revise his "self-system." He must incorporate into it, as worthy and approved, a part of his person which he previously regarded as unworthy and unapproved.

According to Sullivan, conflicts in connection with sex do not arise simply from a clash between the adolescent's desires and his conscience. There may be an equally serious or perhaps more serious "collision" between the adolescent's intimacy needs and his sexual needs. In discussing ways of dealing with this conflict, Sullivan notes the widespread tendency among boys to distinguish between "good girls" and "bad girls." The "good girls" are for friendship and for a future state of marriage; they are the ones who "can satisfy a person's loneliness and spare him anxiety" (1953, p. 269), while "bad girls" are persons who can satisfy his lust. But this does not solve the conflict. For the "bad girls" are, in his eyes, unworthy. As long as he views sex as an unworthy part of his own nature and is unable to integrate his lust with his need for intimacy his relationships with the "bad girls" represent an unworthy aspect of his own personality. According to Sullivan, the adolescent cannot consort with them without loss of the self-approval and self-respect which are his security against becoming anxious.[9]

Sullivan discusses masturbation as one means young people use in trying to resolve their conflicts about sex and intimacy. Masturbation can relieve sexual tension, but according to Sullivan, "There is no way that I know of by which one can, all by oneself, satisfy the need for intimacy, cut off the full driving power of loneliness . . ." (1953, p. 271). Through masturbation a person may reduce his sexual tensions to such a degree

[9] Sullivan centers most of his attention on the adolescent boy. But he clearly implies that similar conflicts and anxieties arise in girls, although girls tend much less than boys to divide members of the opposite sex into bad persons who can satisfy their sexual desires and good persons with whom they can satisfy their need for intimacy. Anxieties of girls and women who have repudiated their femininity and sexuality and who have difficulty in establishing a relationship of mutual tenderness with a male have been discussed elsewhere by the writer and his associates (1962).

that he is not impelled to break the "barrier" which keeps him from integrating his sexual needs and his need for intimacy. Sullivan regards such masturbation, as distinguished from incidental and occasional autoerotic performances, as a profoundly serious "warp" in the personality. Although Sullivan does not specifically mention anxiety in this context, he clearly implies that a continuing practice of masturbation is both a manifestation and a source of anxiety when it is used to prevent a mature integration of a person's sexual capacities and his capacity and need for having an intimate relationship with a member of the opposite sex.[10]

ANXIETY DUE TO CONFLICT BETWEEN COMPETITIVE STRIVINGS AND NEED FOR GROUP MEMBERSHIP

In a historical and theoretical discussion of anxiety, combined with a study of thirteen adolescent and postadolescent girls, May (1950) offers a theory of anxiety which takes account of conflicts between a person's need to become both an independent, autonomous person and at the same time a contributing and accepted member of his social group.

According to May, the growing child learns and adopts as his own the "prestige goals" that are dominant in the culture. These prestige goals are "a means of gaining security." In our present culture, according to May, social prestige goals chiefly take the form of a high valuation of individual competitive success in all spheres of life. Prestige gained through competitive success is an aid to security, for it is accepted as a proof of one's power in one's own eyes and in the eyes of others, it is "identical with self-esteem and self-worth" (p. 217).

But the struggle for competitive success is beset by inherent difficulties. Since success in competition "is always relative to the success of others,

---

[10] Findings in a study by the writer and his associates (1962) underscore some of Sullivan's ideas as reviewed above. In this study, 200 teachers—most of them well beyond adolescent years—who had undergone intensive psychotherapy, told what therapy experience had meant to them. One of the most interesting outcomes pertained to anxiety in relation to tenderness and sex. Practically all of those who thought, on entering therapy, that they had a problem in connection with the physical aspects of sex, or felt their problem was too much guilt about the physical aspects of sex, became convinced that their basic problem was one of establishing a close, intimate relationship with a person of the opposite sex. Men, more often than women, claimed that they had suffered from, and overcome, a divorcement between eroticism and tenderness or affection (what Sullivan refers to as lust and intimacy), but a large proportion of women reported a similar problem, and a similar outcome.

it is insatiable" (p. 217). And since it involves a striving to triumph over others, it augments hostility within the social group. Instead of furthering an individual's capacity to relate himself to others, it isolates him and sets him apart from others. So the means a competitive, prestige-seeking person uses to achieve security defeats security, and this leads to anxiety. Such anxiety involves a person in a "vicious circle" of added efforts, further isolation from others, anxiety, and increased competitive striving.[11]

The girls included in May's study were unmarried mothers, half of whom were in their teens. These girls were facing a crisis and May points out that "one might reasonably have expected that the girls' chief occasions of anxiety would be social disapproval or guilt. But this was not the case. The predominant occasion of anxiety reported by the girls was competitive ambition—*i.e.*, whether they would measure up to cultural standards of 'success' " (p. 152).

ANXIETY ARISING
FROM REPRESSED GUILT

Underlying practically all the decisions and commitments made in adolescence are ethical or moral issues: what is right or wrong, better or worse, from the adolescent's own point of view or from the point of view of other persons. A person is likely to be anxious when his conscience or "superego" is overly "severe," driving him to repress wholesome promptings of his nature and to strive for a perfection which is beyond human reach. Such a person is assailed by guilt that goes beyond the limits of healthy remorse. But a person can also become anxious if he goes to the other extreme by repressing feelings of guilt which cannot go unheeded if he is to satisfy the needs and follow the teachings which impel him to be an accepted member of society. Mowrer (1950, 1953) states that the conflicts which cause anxiety involve moral or ethical issues (a point that is mentioned also by some other writers). He maintains that anxiety arises from unconscious, repressed, repudiated guilt.

Here is another thread in the complicated skein of anxiety in adolescence and other periods of life: a person can become anxious if his morals demand more of him than any human being can attain or if he

---

[11] May does not regard the "stringent form" that the goal for individual competitive success takes in our society as an "immutable attribute" of human nature but as a cultural product.

tries to side-step moral responsibilities which no person, as a member of the human race, can successfully disavow.

Defenses Against Anxiety As a Source of Further Anxiety

Since anxiety is a painful state it will induce measures to bring relief. One way of trying to relieve the pain is to face it—to learn from it, to move through it, to come up against it as one who pushes forward against an adverse wind. But this is not an easy thing to do at any stage of life, and it is especially difficult for a young child. As a consequence, the anxious person seeks to evade and side-step anxiety by many means. In Kierkegaard's account a person tries to escape anxiety by surrender to "untruths"; Freud speaks of repression, and Sullivan of "dissociation." These endeavors aim at excluding the underlying conflict from awareness, as a means of avoiding or allaying, rather than facing it. These are makeshift defenses, for although they may, for a time, blunt the sharp impact of anxiety, they do not resolve it.

The defenses a person adopts to blunt or evade conflicts that underlie his anxiety involve him in new conflicts. Accounts of the struggle with anxiety that are especially revealing have been offered by Horney (1939, 1945, 1946, 1950). Horney describes strategies for dealing with anxiety which probably every thoughtful person can perceive in himself and others at some time. These strategies at first are used by a person as a means of protecting himself, but they may become so strongly entrenched within the personality that they persist even when the danger that gave rise to them no longer prevails. According to Horney, a further condition of anxiety arises when these strategies are threatened, as happens when they conflict with reality or with one another.

One strategy a person may develop in trying to survive in a threatening environment is to *move against* others, not in open warfare but by means such as becoming competitive, seeking to surpass others, to outdo them, and to rise above them in sports or in schoolwork or in business or in romantic conquests or in any area of his life.

Another strategy, according to Horney, is to *move away* from others: to withdraw, to remain aloof and detached. We see this strategy when we see an adolescent who has no spontaneity, when the ecstasies of life seem not to stir him and the sorrows leave him unmoved. A detached person may go through the motions of being interested in others but his feelings are not suited to his actions and his thoughts. He remains emotionally removed. Bookishness may be a form of detachment when it is not something freely chosen but a means of keeping aloof from the flesh and blood of human existence. A detached adolescent may go through the motions of making friends without actually moving emotionally close to anyone or allowing anyone to come close to him.

A third strategy, according to Horney, is *moving with* others: a policy of compliance, conformity, and self-effacement. The compliant one moves with the tide. He yields. He tries to placate and appease. At the adolescent level, the compliant one may be the "good" person who is ready to let others direct what he should do or learn or think, or is even ready to let others use him as a "doormat." A compliant, appeasing adolescent may be the one who always cleans up after a party while the others are at play, or the one who always puts a coin in the parking meter while other fellow passengers saunter off.

Horney does not regard any of these forms of conduct *per se* as a mark of anxiety. There are times when a person spontaneously or deliberately competes, or complies, or holds himself aloof, and the same person may use one or the other of these strategies at different times and in different situations. But these forms of conduct are "pseudosolutions" or "neurotic" when a person is driven blindly to employ them as a defense.

To the extent that a person lives according to such "pseudosolutions" he is playing an assumed role. They do not reflect what he would be and do if he were free to use his resources and to draw on them in an unfettered manner.

RATIONALIZATION OF "PSEUDOSOLUTIONS"

According to Horney (and in keeping with positions taken by many other writers) the person who has adopted devious means of coping with an anxiety-producing environment will cling to them tenaciously. He will try to feel comfortable about them. He will use his powers of reasoning and imagination and his capacity for rationalization to convince himself that the adjustments he has made are a genuine part of his real character. So he may persuade himself that his great urge to outdo others is a kind of strength, thus avoiding the painful awareness that there is no zest or verve in his competitiveness but that it has, instead, a compulsive quality. The one who uses compliance as a strategy may see himself as a noble and generous person, rather than one who has a blind need to efface himself and to surrender his own rights and wishes. The person who is detached may see himself not as one who is cutting himself off from the emotional currents of life but as one who is able to go it alone, a strong, reasonable individual with a great capacity for looking at things objectively.

According to Horney, strategies used as a defense against anxiety become integrated into what she calls the "idealized self" to the extent that a person is convinced that they are genuine.

The strategies and the idealized view of self that is built around them make trouble when they outlast the occasion of their need. Then anything that threatens to expose or undermine the "solutions" a person has contrived, anything that threatens the idealized image, is likely to arouse anxiety. Anxiety occurs when the idealized image is threatened by the realities of life. There is the danger of being found out by oneself and others. There is also the danger of strategies conflicting with each other or with the promptings of the healthy part of his nature.

For example, an adolescent who habitually takes the course of being a compliant appeaser is bound now and then to feel a surge of revolt against this style of life. He will feel at times that others are taking advantage of his good nature. He will have an impulse to rebel against his own tendency to let himself be pushed around. There will be moments when he feels a defiant uprush of anger. But it is threatening and anxiety-producing to have such a war within himself. The anger, even if brief, and even if directed outwardly, is very disquieting to one who has a confirmed view of himself as a genial and peaceable person. The anxiety may be so painful to the appeaser that he drives himself even more desperately to make what he regards as the "good part of his nature" prevail. We have in such a drive a form of goodness that is demonic.

In like manner, the adolescent who uses aggressiveness as a strategy and who has built an image of himself as a strong, unsentimental, enterprising person may have misgivings that threaten this view of himself. There are times when he would like to rebel against his driving need to compete with others. There are times, too, when his potentialities for compassion and friendliness clash with his aggressive impulse to move against people. This is threatening and anxiety-arousing.

The detached person is also bound to meet threats to his detachment. An adolescent who has a strongly entrenched habit of holding himself aloof from others is likely to retain a potentiality for emotional closeness with other persons. He may face the danger of falling in love, the danger of desiring an intimate and tender attachment to another person. Perhaps he feels a strong sweep of indignation against conditions at home or at school, which he usually has regarded in an aloof way. If so, there is collision, conflict, and anxiety. Some young people (and older people) with a strong tendency toward detachment go through periods of intense anxiety when they take an overt step toward a relationship with others, such as becoming engaged.

Evidences of Anxiety in Adolescence

It would not be possible to make an exact estimate or measurement of the prevalence of anxiety in adolescents without making a prolonged study "in depth" of each individual in a large, representative group. One difficulty is that anxiety that involves repression and "unconscious" defenses is not recognized for what it is. However, findings that have emerged from studies of what has been called "manifest anxiety" indicate that the typical young person is aware of, and will report, many personal problems that probably should be regarded as symptoms of what some writers refer to as "neurotic" anxiety. In a study of about two thousand college students, Taylor (1953) applied a test of "manifest anxiety" containing fifty items. The number of symptoms a person could report ranged from zero to fifty. The average score was about fifteen.

When persons of high school and college age are studied by means of projective tests such as the Rorschach and TAT (referred to in Chapter 7), the typical person gives responses which, according to the interpretation schemes that have been devised for these tests, represent symptoms of conflict and a more or less disturbed state of mind (see, *e.g.,* Frank *et al.,* 1953).

From such evidence as is available it can be assumed that anxiety is widespread among adolescents. Probably all have what has been called "normal" anxiety, and a large proportion probably are burdened with mild or with severe forms of what has been called "neurotic" anxiety.

In trying to perceive and assess symptoms of anxiety one must remember that they are as numerous as the frailties, perversities, and inconsistencies of human behavior. Symptoms of anxiety often crop out in behavior that seems sullen and "ornery," that is annoying to others, in behavior that seems queer. Many of the symptoms have been touched upon in earlier sections, but it is useful to review these symptoms and to note others that have not previously been mentioned.

We may suspect that an adolescent is anxious if he responds in a way that is out of proportion to the occasion or "overreacts" by being greatly upset by little things; if he is bitterly angry at something that seems trivial; if he is plagued with guilt beyond the limits of genuine remorse; if he has worries or fears that are "irrational" in the sense that his worries are quite out of proportion to any overhanging threat, or he is afraid of dangers that actually do not exist, and continues to be afraid in spite of reminders from his own experience that there is nothing to fear.

We may also suspect that an adolescent is anxious if he "underreacts," if he shrinks from any show of anger when anger is justified, or is apathetic and unmoved in situations where normally a person would feel joy or apprehension or grief.

An adolescent is probably suffering from anxiety if he has unaccountable moods, such as being depressed or having sudden outbursts of crying for no apparent reason or feeling "out of sorts" and edgy without knowing why.

Anxiety probably prevails if an adolescent seems to be driven by compulsions. There are many of these: an unrelenting compulsion to compete; an unaccountable urge to repeat acts that previously have brought him into trouble and which, from a rational point of view, he knows will get him into trouble again. An adolescent has compulsions which probably signify anxiety when he is in "a fever of activity," has an urge to rush hither and yon, is unable to sit still or to relax, as though he cannot bear the thoughts that spring up in an unoccupied moment.

An adolescent is probably suffering from anxiety also if he acts distinctly "out of character," if he has mild and friendly ways but now and then does things that are unnecessarily cruel.

It is also likely that an adolescent is anxious if he is exceedingly rigid in his attitudes, is self-righteous, markedly smug, prudish, or dogmatic.

An adolescent is also probably in the grip of anxiety if he imposes impossible standards on himself, if he expects more of himself than anyone could possibly demand of him, and then deplores himself for not living up to these standards.

We can assume that practically every young person who is backward in his studies is also anxious to some degree. It is likely that he has been made to feel that it is his own fault if he does not do well. So he may feel guilty, as though one part of him were blaming another part of him about not living up to the expectations placed upon him by others. Or he may feel guilty and also feel a strong resentment toward those who fail him, but yet be in conflict about this resentment.

At the adolescent level there are already those who seem to be anxious to the point of despair. We may suspect that a state of despair or near despair exists in the adolescent delinquent who does desperate things, as though bent on destroying himself.

On a milder scale, anxiety probably prevails when adolescents complain bitterly about their parents and find serious fault with them. (This is discussed in a later chapter.) It is not easy to feel anger at a parent without also having a guilty notion that one should be a dutiful and loyal child. Anxiety probably prevails among young persons who have turned against their background, their upbringing, the social group in which they were reared, the religious or racial group into which they were born. When a person turns against his home and the environment and the traditions in which he was reared, he is turning against something that is part of himself. Unless he resolves this conflict in some way, he will probably be anxious to some degree.

In emphasizing the prevalence of anxiety in this way we are not simply trying to paint a gloomy picture of human existence. Actually, if anxiety prevails more gloom results from denying or concealing it than from trying to face it.

Anxieties and Other Problems Revealed by Ratings, Clinical Studies and Reports by Adolescents Themselves

Studies of adolescents have revealed that large numbers of them suffer from personal problems which may be an expression of anxiety or a source of anxiety. These studies indicate that at high school and junior high school levels many disturbances, such as inability to get along with others and a considerable amount of self-rejection, exist among the youngsters (see, for example, Fleege, 1945; Hertzman, 1948; and Spivack, 1956).[12]

In a study by Pope (1943) 2,000 high school students wrote essays on the subject of their personal problems in which they mentioned about 7,000 problems. Many of the students expressed their problems in terms of their difficulties in dealing with the external environment, without mentioning, and perhaps without recognizing, that some of these diffi-

[12] Among the investigations in this area are studies by Rogers (1942) and Ullman (1952). Other studies dealing with emotional problems in childhood and adolescence have been reported by Pope (1943), Powell (1948), Hertzman (1948), Havighurst and Taba (1949), Symonds and Sherman (1949) and Elias (1949).

culties might reside within themselves rather than outside themselves. (Adults show a similar tendency to externalize their problems, Gurin, *et al.*, 1960). Almost half the students mentioned problems in their relationships with their teachers. Problems expressed as relating more directly to their own emotional adjustment, in such terms as feelings of "inferiority" or feelings of "superiority," were mentioned by 11 per cent.

In a survey of the problems of over 5,000 high school youth Elias (1949) found that 20 per cent or more of the young people named problems in each of the following categories (as phrased by Elias): "Being able to talk to people"; "How to develop self-confidence"; "Daydream too much"; "Having a desirable personality"; "Losing my temper"; "Wanting people to like me"; "Hurting people's feelings"; "Making something of myself"; "Concerned about the future"; "Choosing a vocation"; "What job best suited for"; "Don't know what I really want." Many students in this study, as in the study by Pope mentioned above, named problems pertaining to school, such as being unable to concentrate, not studying enough, being unable to express themselves well. The median student reported from 15 to 19 personal problems.

Frank and his associates (1953) conclude from an investigation, in which projective techniques were used to explore the personality development of 300 high school and college girls that these girls showed evidence of "more frequent and more severe emotional disturbances" than the investigators had anticipated. Problems appeared especially in the area of interpersonal relationships, giving rise to "preoccupation with personal perplexities, feelings and fantasies." There was evidence of a great deal of unhappiness and tenseness especially among some younger groups of adolescent girls representing "widely differing social-economic levels and ethnic-cultural backgrounds."

Heath and Gregory (1949), in a study mentioned in another chapter, found that among 259 "healthy, 'normal' students" at the college level, 90 per cent either raised problems they wished to discuss, or presented problems which members of a research staff recognized as difficulties.

One of the most extensive and exacting studies that has been made of the mental health situation in the adult population which adolescents will soon join is the "Midtown Manhattan Study" (Srole *et al.*, 1962). According to the judgments of a team of psychiatrists, 18.5 per cent of the persons in the sample could be rated as mentally "well." Over a third of the persons were rated as having "mild" symptoms from a psychiatric point of view, and another 21.8 per cent were classed as having "moderate symptoms." Persons with "marked" and "severe" symptoms and those diagnosed as "incapacitated" were all regarded as having impaired mental health: the impaired group included 23.4 per cent, or almost a fourth of the sampling.[13]

In the study just cited, as in other studies (see, *e.g.,* Gurin, 1960), it was noted that only a small proportion of adults who suffer from psychological ailments seek, or are inclined to seek, psychological help. In this respect older adults do not differ much from young persons of high school or college age. In the population at large there are millions of persons who would not hesitate for a moment to go to a dentist with a toothache, or to a doctor with a fractured arm, but who would not, when emotionally distressed, think of seeking professional help. One consequence of this attitude is that troubled adolescents, as they go about their task of growing up, bear their emotional burdens in solitude. Most of them keep a lonely vigil with their troubles.

The fact that adolescents have many personal problems must be weighed against the fact that most of them manage to carry on in their daily lives and to assume adult responsibilities. But the fact that so many problems exist raises challenging questions. To what extent are these afflictions inevitable? To what extent are they perpetuated by the fact that large numbers of troubled persons, in keeping with the traditions of our culture, do not even consider the idea of seeking help? To what extent might the burden be lightened if we had an active concern in education about the emotional welfare of children and adolescents rather than a widespread policy of ignoring this aspect of life?

[13] Srole and his associates review findings in other large surveys, including a survey in Baltimore and an Army study, and conclude that their findings are not exceptional.

part five | The Adolescent's Social World

Chapter 11

Parents,
Home,
and Family

The adolescent's relationships with his parents may be viewed as a three-act drama. In the first act the young adolescent continues, as in earlier childhood, to need his parents; he is dependent on them; he is profoundly influenced by them. He begins, however, to become more keenly aware than he was before of his parents as persons. Increasingly he is absorbed in the larger world outside the home. He begins, in a psychological sense, to leave his home to move into this larger world in which he eventually must reside as a self-directing adult.

The second act of the drama might be called "The Struggle for Emancipation." To achieve stature as an adult the adolescent must outgrow his childhood dependency on his parents. He must renounce major allegiance to his parents and be able to shift his allegiance to prospective mates. Eventually, he must be prepared to assume the role of a parent. Although the struggle for emancipation sometimes is a relatively quiet campaign in which the adolescent steadily assumes more and more responsibility for himself, often the campaign is turbulent, full of conflict and laden with anxiety both for the adolescent and for his parents.

In the third act, if all has gone well, the struggle subsides, as the young person takes his place among adult peers. But the drama has not ended, for the influence of his parents extends into adult life. Many persons who, in their teens, rebelled against their parents' ideas and attitudes adopt these same ideas and attitudes as their own when they enter their twenties (Bath and Lewis, 1962); and many persons keep assessing and reassessing the view they have of their parents and their feelings about their parents several decades after adolescence is over (Jersild, Lazar, and Brodkin, 1962). Some retain undercurrents of bitterness toward their parents; some acquire a deeper feeling of tenderness; some, when they have children of their own, for the first time appreciate or recognize what their parents meant to them.

Importance of Family Relationships

The importance of family relationships is emphasized when adolescents tell about their early lives. Findings bearing on this point will be reviewed in later sections. The role of the family also is emphasized to a marked degree when adults view their adolescence in retrospect. Several times, while teaching a graduate course on the psychology of adolescence, the author has asked students to write an account of conditions and events which, in their judgment, were most helpful or most trying and burdensome during their adolescent years. These accounts have regularly mentioned the home and relationships with parents more than any other single factor. A tally of one sampling showed that over 90 per cent referred to home life, naming such matters as family accord or discord, problems relating to discipline, authority, grievances against parents, help received from parents in time of stress, etc.[1]

Increased Awareness of Family Characteristics

During preadolescent and adolescent years youngsters become more aware of and sensitive to conditions in the home and characteristics of the family that might affect their own pride and prestige: the physical appearance of their parents and siblings; the condition of the furniture; the habits and manners of their parents and brothers and sisters, the social and economic status of the family. Some adolescents show a strong re-

[1] The next most frequent category (mentioned by 84 per cent) included relationships with peers.

formist spirit, especially if they are ambitious and eager to have their family (and themselves) look well in the eyes of others: Father should not laugh so loud at his own jokes; Mother should be more tidy; sister Mary should improve her mind instead of reading movie magazines.

The impulse to reform, while it is not displayed by all adolescents, may be so strong for a time that the youngster is hard to live with. This is especially so if the youngster's criticisms touch on matters concerning which his parents or other members of his family already feel inferior or defensive.

Outgrowing Childhood Dependency on Parents

Adolescents and young adults are achieving independence when they strike off on their own, establish their own living quarters, begin their careers, and earn their own keep. These steps are relatively simple from a purely practical point of view.

Outgrowing psychological dependency is more complex. The roots of psychological dependency are deep-seated. Often they have hidden or unconscious elements. Adults may be financially self-supporting (and even support their parents) and yet be subservient to their parents in childish ways. Such dependency may prevail even when young people openly rebel against their parents or defy them. But when young persons continue into adult life to go out of their way to defy their parents it probably means that they have not "severed the silver cord": they would not need to be defiant if they were not still struggling, perhaps blindly, against parental domination.

It should be noted that emancipation from one's parents is not the same as repudiation of them (although, in the struggle to take command of their own affairs, many young people go through a phase of repudiating their parents). A person who is thoroughly emancipated can feel affection for his parents, cherish worthy ideals they have taught him, and heed the Commandment "Honor thy father and thy mother." The essential element in emancipation is the freedom, desire, and ability to take responsibility for one's own thoughts, feelings, moral judgments, and practical decisions. The emancipated person may seek advice from his parents, but he will not allow his parents to dictate his decisions. He respects his parents' moral values, but he measures what is right and wrong by his own convictions and not simply in terms of what he thinks his parents will approve or disapprove.

When adolescents strive to achieve independence and emancipation from their parents they are gradually but drastically reversing a pattern of behavior they showed in their infancy. The infant clings to his parents, he desires to have them close at hand, and during a stage of infancy, babies cry when their mothers leave them alone. At a later stage, they protest when parents go for an outing, leaving the youngsters in the care of others. One of the commonest and severest fears of young children is fear of separation from parents. But in adolescence the child who once was afraid his parents might abandon *him,* now, in effect, sets out to abandon *them.*

EARLY STEPS TOWARD INDEPENDENCE

When conditions are favorable adolescents can make important strides toward independence during preadolescent years, such as getting part-time jobs through their own initiative; taking complete responsibility for spending or saving the money they earn; pursuing interests and hobbies of their own even though these are quite different from the interests of their parents; deciding to go to summer camp (if their parents can afford it) even though they anticipate spells of homesickness.

On a more subtle level, preadolescent and adolescent youngsters are moving toward independence when they are free to raise questions about their parents without regarding such questioning as disloyalty, or feeling guilty about it. They may, for example, question their parents' practical judgment or political beliefs.

OBJECTIVE AND SUBJECTIVE ASPECTS OF RELATIONSHIPS WITH PARENTS

An adolescent's relationships with his parents, like all other interpersonal relationships, includes both objective and subjective elements. The objective elements are those that are manifest and out in the open. The subjective elements are more subtle and elusive. They may be unrealistic from an objective standpoint. For example, a young man was convinced he had deeply disappointed his father when he chose a career different from the one he thought his father had preferred for him. He stuck to his choice, but he had an uneasy foreboding that some day he would feel overwhelming remorse about having defied his father. It was not until his late twenties that he realized his father was proud of him and happy at the progress he had made.

In this instance, the son imputed wishes to the father which the father did not have. He *perceived* his father as disappointed when actually the father was not. And as long as his ideas about his father's wishes, whether distorted or not, plagued his conscience, he was, in effect, still an unemancipated person.

Acquiring a Realistic Image of Parents

Over the years the youngster builds a conception of his parents, their standards, their view of him, their expectations. This conception is realistic to the extent that he sees them as they are. But the image is distorted if he misperceives them because of his own needs and limited understanding. He may perceive them as more perfect than they ever could be, as holding higher standards for him than they do, or as being more disapproving than they actually are.

It is probably inevitable that the adolescent as a child acquired an unrealistic image of his parents. While he was small and helpless, they were big and strong. In the child's eyes they seemed almost omnipotent. It is not easy for an adolescent to cut omnipotent parents down to size, even if the parents themselves never make any pretense of being omnipotent. His parents were also powerful figures in a moral sense, since it was they who judged what was right and wrong, and they who punished or rewarded.

Young people have taken a long stride toward independence when they are able to acquire an increasingly realistic perception of their parents.

There is an intricate relationship between a person's image of his parents and his image of himself and between attitudes toward parents and attitudes toward self. As a consequence, anything that leads a person to examine, or to change, one dimension of this relationship is likely to lead to an examination and change in the other.

The fact that attitudes toward parents and attitudes toward self are intertwined emphasizes the poignancy of the struggle adolescents undergo when they rebel against their parents. This struggle is not just a tug-of-war between a young person and his elders; it involves a battle within himself.

Changing the Model

In striving to achieve emancipation many youngsters for a time renounce their parents as models and choose entirely new models. In several studies (see, *e.g.,* Hill, 1930, and Havighurst *et al.,* 1946) it has been noted that as young people move toward and into adolescence there is a decline in the proportion who name their parents as their heroes or ideals. In early adolescence quite a few name glamorous or distinguished characters. It is as though they were leaving mom and dad to run away with someone else. This, on the surface, seems like gross unfaithfulness. But it is part of the drama of growing up.

Changing the Primary Objects of Love

The parents, from whom young people must seek to become independent, were also (in most instances) the first objects of the adolescent's love. To realize their potentialities as adults, young people must shift the primary objects of their love—from parents to prospective mates, and ultimately to the spouse. Later, their love must also embrace their childen.

There are conflicting views concerning the nature and intensity of this aspect of emancipation. Those who literally accept the Freudian theory of an Oedipus complex regard the final renunciation of a person's primary love object as involving, for many young people, a cataclysmic struggle. The young man must, in effect, psychologically divorce his mother, and the girl her father. They cannot do this in cold blood (Levy and Monroe, 1938). A person cannot leave a lover just by turning on his heel. To break away and to establish his freedom to seek other love objects, he must justify the break. In the process, according to some writers, many adolescents go through a period when they deplore and disdain the parents whom they once adored. If this occurs, the young person, while seeming to turn against his parents is actually struggling to discard something within himself.

According to those who do not accept the theory of the Oedipus complex, emancipation is not primarily a struggle with a sexual problem. Large numbers of psychologists, psychiatrists, and psychoanalysts deny the theory that children universally develop a sexual attachment to the parent of the opposite sex. They do recognize, however, that there usually are strong emotional bonds between children and their parents and that young people face a struggle when these hinder them from forming emotional bonds with others.

CONTINUATION OF DEPENDENCY
BEYOND THE TEENS

The struggle for self-determination is still going on in the lives of many young people after they have finished high school and have gone on into college or a job. Lloyd (1952) indicates on the basis of a study of about a thousand students belonging to five colleges in a southern state that a large number had failed to attain "emotional emancipation" from their parents. Sherman (1946) obtained responses from over four hundred university students to a questionnaire dealing with "emancipation status." The items on the questionnaire covered matters such as dependency on parents for help in meeting personal problems, a tendency to daydream or to think a lot about the parents back home, freedom to think or do things whether or not parents approved. The emancipation scores ranged from seventeen (least emancipated) to fifty-eight (most emancipated) with a maximum possible score of sixty; the average score was forty.

How far a person of college age has gone toward achieving emancipation will depend, of course, on how strictly we define emancipation. The criteria of being a free and self-determining person could be made so stringent that hardly any adult at any age could be regarded as having become emancipated from his parents. At any rate, according to the findings cited above, the typical college student is not a completely emancipated person.

Homesickness

In some circumstances homesickness is a sign that the adolescent has not won emancipation from his home or is still actively struggling to become emancipated. We say "in some circumstances" because homesickness is not in and by itself a mark of weakness or dependency. The person who is homesick has at least ventured far enough away from home to become homesick. It is unlikely that a person who feels emotionally attached to the home folks can at any stage of life leave them for a rather long space of time without feeling some twinges of homesickness, at least during the early stages of his absence.

Nor does the fact that a person has *not* been homesick mark him as an independent person. There are some persons who are so dependent on the home that they will not even take the risk of becoming homesick by leaving to take a trip or to go away to school or camp or college or to take a job. There are some adolescents and young adults whose dependency on the home is so great that they have trouble in facing the thought of leaving home.

Among the experiences involved in being homesick are loneliness, feeling strange and lost, feeling sad, unhappy, and depressed (see McCann, 1941, 1943; Rose, 1944, 1947). Homesickness may also involve irritability and a tendency to be hostile.

When a person is homesick we assume that he is longing for the home from which he is separated, and this raises the question, What specifically is he longing for? When this question was raised with a number of homesick college girls who were interviewed by Rose (1947) many answers were given, including longing for the father and the mother or for friends that were left behind, their own room, the home atmosphere, the freedom and privacy of the home, pets that had been left behind, and the like. Many of the girls, in telling what they longed for, did not give much information, and Rose states that the vagueness of the answers suggests that homesickness perhaps involves more dissatisfaction with the conditions under which the person is living at the moment than a longing for what the person left behind.

Homesickness in some instances seems to be linked to feelings of inadequacy. Rose (1947) points out that the one who is homesick may feel insecure in dealing with new social relationships. There are some who repeatedly become homesick even though they do not seem to have a great desire for being with persons belonging to their homes.

Homesickness sometimes involves feelings that are closer to anger than to sorrow. Rose noted, for example, that some of the college girls felt irritable or hostile during episodes of homesickness. Even the feeling of being "depressed," which often occurs in homesickness, may include an element of anger. When this is the case the homesick person may be quite as much aggrieved as grieving. His homesickness may involve an element of protest against having to leave his home as well as protest against the people and the conditions where he now resides.

DIFFICULTIES PARENTS FACE IN ''LETTING GO''

Adolescent emancipation is not simply a problem for the son or daughter —it is also a problem for parents. Some parents find it difficult to "let go" of a child. Ever since the youngster was an infant they have had him in their care. The habit of watching over him is strong, and the desire to continue to do so is also likely to be strong. It is especially hard for parents to let go an offspring in adolescence if they have not gotten into the habit of gradually allowing the youngster to have more and more freedom and self-determination.

There are other circumstances that may make it hard for a parent to let a child "grow up." A mother who has given her all for her children may become anxious at the prospect of being without a mission in life. A parent who has lived his life through his children, so to speak, seeking through them to achieve, by proxy, pleasures he has never enjoyed or ambitions he never realized, may be very troubled when his offspring want to go on their own way.

A parent who has leaned on his children for emotional support, using them as though they were as much *his* parents as he theirs, may feel insecure and abandoned at the thought that his offspring are now moving on into other relationships. Again, a parent who has not been realistic in facing the fact that he is getting older may feel threatened by the reminders of age that come when his own children are becoming adults and want to enjoy the privileges of adults.

Methods of Maintaining Parental Domination

There are many ways a parent who is unwilling to let his adolescent son or daughter grow up tries to keep a hold on the young person. One way is to be very forbidding, denying the adolescent the right to meet persons of the opposite sex, or the right to venture out on his own, or the right to go out and earn money.

Another way is to appeal to the gratitude and loyalty of the offspring: I have done so much for you, now you must stay near me and do things for me. Still another method is to belittle, to try to undermine the young person's confidence in his ability to do for himself. Yet another technique is to overwhelm the youngster with gifts and with help, doing everything for him and thereby implying (although perhaps not consciously) that he really cannot do much for himself.

A parent may also try to maintain control by pleading for sympathy, saying that he is lonesome (so the young one will not stay out late when he goes courting), or that he needs extra help around the house or on the farm or in the business. If he is well-to-do he may use bribery, saying in effect, if you remain as home-loving a boy or girl as Mama or Papa would like you to be we will give you something special: if you go to college in your home town rather than go to a place some distance away we will pay you an extra allowance; if you settle down in your home town we will let you have the upstairs rooms as your home, or build you a house on the vacant lot next door. (Sometimes the motivation for these actions may be wise and good, both from the parents' and from the adolescent's point of view, but that is not the kind of motivation we are here considering.) In extreme cases, a parent who wishes to maintain a hold on his son or daughter may resort to invalidism, claiming that his health is so precarious that his offspring must stay at home and take care of him (implying, perhaps, that if he should die it would be the fault of his ungrateful son or daughter).

POSTADOLESCENT REASSESSMENT OF PARENTS

While achieving independence many adolescents have a less favorable image of their parents than they had before, but in the end, if all goes well, they see them more kindly as well as more realistically. In many instances this does not occur until some years beyond the adolescent period.

Mark Twain alludes to this when he said, "When I was a boy of fourteen my father was so stupid I could scarcely stand to have the old man around, but by the time I got to be twenty-one I was astonished at how much he had learned in the last seven years."

The finding that many persons continue the process of re-evaluating their parents and relationships with them into the twenties and beyond appears in a study by the writer and his associates (1962) of two groups of teachers and graduate students, ranging in age from the twenties to the late forties. One group consisted of 111 teachers who had undergone therapy; another included 58 persons who served as "controls." They were asked whether during the past four years, or during the period of therapy, their attitudes or ideas concerning their parents had changed in the direction of: (1) "Recognizing, in a manner that helps you to understand yourself better, faults or weaknesses in one or both parents." Sixty-three per cent of the control group answered *Yes;* 41 per cent said that this had occurred to *Some* extent and 22 per cent reported it had occurred to a *Marked* extent. In the therapy group the corresponding percentages were *Yes,* 96 per cent; to *Some* extent, 25 per cent; to a *Marked* extent, 71 per cent. In response to another question, 62 per cent of the controls and 67 per cent of the therapy group reported a change in the direction of "Liking one or both of your parents better." (The respective percentages reporting that this change had occurred to *Some* or a *Marked* extent were: controls, 29 and 33 per cent; therapy group, 34 and 33 per cent.)

The Role of Parental Affection in an Adolescent's Upbringing

The experience of being loved, and of loving, is one of the essentials of healthy human growth. The affection parents and their offspring have for one another is seldom (probably never) unmixed with other emotions. But a strong foundation of parental love during childhood gives the youngster an invaluable resource as he embarks on his adolescent career. And continued assurance of his parents' love is an invaluable asset during adolescent years.

The adolescent who is loved for his own sake does not constantly have to calculate how to procure or retain the good will of his parents. He can put his trust in his parents' good will, even when he is at odds with them and sorely tries their patience. The young person who can count on his parents' love has greater freedom to venture, to explore, to be himself, to find himself, to test his powers, to cultivate his own judgment in making choices and in weighing one possibility against another in planning his future. He has leeway to make mistakes, such as one who treads new ground is bound to make, without having to fear they will be fatal. He is likely to be more immune to shattering guilt than the one who is unloved.

The adolescent who is realistically confident of his parents' love is spared many burdens. In a clash of wills with his parents, he can directly fight for his rights as he sees them without also having to fight a rearguard action of grievance or revenge.

LIMITATIONS IN THE POWER OF PARENTAL LOVE

While parental love accomplishes much for an adolescent it obviously cannot accomplish everything. Parental love does not protect the young person against disappointments and errors of judgment. It cannot cure any inherited weaknesses that the adolescent might have. It cannot forfend the malice of persons with whom the adolescent deals outside the home, or eliminate prejudice. It cannot guarantee good conditions at school. Loving parents cannot spare the young person from temptation. They cannot control the accelerator when he drives a car. Their moral example may help him, but it alone cannot keep him from falling in with bad companions. They cannot rid life of all the conditions that lead a young person into folly, grief, or disaster.

An adolescent may have loving parents and still be a lonely creature. Conditions in the culture, described in Chapter 8, which compel people to conceal and suppress their feelings, bear down upon his parents and also on him. As a consequence, parents with the most affectionate intentions may be unaware of their child's innermost feelings, and he of theirs. Loving parents would like to assuage their child's sorrow, allay his fears, and comfort him when he is hurt. But they cannot try to relieve distress when they do not know it exists.

The gulf between the private "inner" dimensions of life and what is permissibly and openly displayed is one of the tragedies of human existence. It separates man from man, woman from woman, men and women from each other, parents from their children and children from their parents.

THE UNLOVED OR "REJECTED" ADOLESCENT

The lot of adolescents who are unloved or rejected by their parents is a hard one. Unless they can find substitute parents or crumbs of affection outside the home they must face life's uncertainties and hurts without help from others, and they must reach for what life might offer with no one to guide or encourage them. They must depend on their own unaided resources. They face a world in which many hands are raised against them and no close-by hand raised in their defense.

Every human being has probably had some experience of feeling rejected—at home or elsewhere. His feeling of being rejected may have been well-grounded; others may have intentionally rejected him. Or the feeling may have been based on a mistaken perception of the intentions of others—he may have felt cast out by others who had no intention at all of rejecting him. But whether or not it is well-founded, the feeling of being rejected is bitter.

Most of the studies dealing with the role of lack of affection on the fortunes or misfortunes of adolescents are of an *ad hoc* variety. Studies have been made, for example, of adolescents who are emotionally disturbed, or delinquent, or who are failing at school, to discover conditions in their upbringing that might account for their misfortune.

In a number of studies the evidence seems to show that many adolescents who are having a hard time come from an unfavorable home background—broken homes or homes in which one or both parents did not give affection, or were actively rejecting. Studies of this sort tell a moving story, but one must be cautious in interpreting them.

When an adolescent is in trouble his parents are also likely to be distressed. The account they give of their past will be colored by this: the parents may feel guilty and accuse themselves, or they may be hostile and blame the adolescent. The troubled adolescent, likewise, will see his past through the darkened glass of his present distress. Unless there is other evidence, we cannot know how the trouble began. The parents and the youngster may all have been caught in a web of fate, an adverse heredity or an adverse environment, or a combination of these, which none had the power to surmount.

One difficulty in obtaining an adequate measure of affection, or as it is also referred to, wholehearted *acceptance,* and its opposite, *rejection,* is that these conditions cannot be assessed simply by noting overt behavior. It is possible to observe whether an unfeeling parent cruelly beats his child, openly neglects, scorns, derides, and humiliates him. But such stark cruelty and rejection are not typical. The usual family muddles along with less harshness than this. Judging by many surveys, it is not just the exceptional home but also the usual home that produces persons with serious problems.

While parents' overt actions can be observed, inferences about their intentions or feelings must be made cautiously. In a study in which the interactions between children and parents at home were observed, Lafore (1945) noted that parents who have good intentions differ greatly in the way they deal with their children. An observer who simply watches their overt behavior could easily be misled into labeling one parent as accepting and another as rejecting.

The predicaments parents and children face likewise need careful examination to be understood. For example, parents of a sickly child, or of a dull child who is failing at school, face a very different situation than that confronting parents of a child who is robust and bright. Again, by way of example, one parent may be indulgent and, on the surface, appear accepting; the other parent may find it necessary to counterbalance this indulgence by being more stern than he or she otherwise might want to be—and, on the surface, seem to be rejecting.

The nature of the young person's demands on his parents likewise require careful attention. Anna Freud (1955) in a warning against loose usage of the concept of rejection notes that no matter how devoted a mother might be, she cannot meet all the boundless demands made by a child. She is speaking about young children, but the same principle no doubt also applies to adolescents and their parents.

A youngster may perceive himself as being rejected regardless of what his parents' actions or intentions are. He may make demands his parents cannot possibly meet, or voice desires which no wise parent would grant, and see his parents as rejecting him when they refuse him. On the other hand, a youngster may perceive himself as receiving loving care regardless of his parents' actions because his need for their affection is so strong that he does not perceive unkindnesses that are obvious to others.

When a youngster perceives his parents as loving or unloving, they actually *are* so from his standpoint, even if no one else agrees. Ausubel and his associates (1954), in a study of the role of a child's perception, state that although parent behavior is an objective event in the real world, it affects the child's development "only to the extent and in the form in which he perceives it. Hence, perceived parent behavior is in reality a more direct, relevant and proximate determinant of personality development than the actual stimulus context to which it refers."

The same thought was expressed earlier by May (1950) in a discussion of the effects of parental rejection. He says, "In impact upon the child, there is a radical difference between rejection as an *objective* experience (which does not necessarily result in subjective conflict for the child), and rejection as a subjective experience. The important question psychologically is whether the child *felt himself* rejected." [2]

Whatever the source of feelings of being rejected, these feelings have

[2] Findings touching on various facets of the way in which children view their parents or think their parents view them, as compared with children's views regarding themselves have been reported by Beier and Ratzeburg (1953), Helper (1958), Jourard and Remy (1955), and Manis (1958). The findings are not as revealing as they might be, for they consist mainly of reports of responses to paper-and-pencil tests and do not show how a child's reported views influence his attitudes and behavior and his interactions with his parents in day-to-day life.

In a review of various studies that have been done, Wylie (1960) notes that some evidence suggests that the child's conception of himself is similar to the view of himself that he attributes to his parents. There also is limited evidence indicating that the child's level of self-regard is associated with his parents' reported level of regard for him.

many other consequences, such as grievances and feelings of being abused. In our discussion of anger in Chapter 9 we noted that when a youngster has an established grievance he is likely to find evidence to support it. His grievance is confirmed by scoldings which an unaggrieved youngster might take in stride. When parents are impatient, or refuse a request, they "prove" his point.

Fortunately, in spite of this self-affirming tendency, grievances are often temporary and are washed away in the give-and-take of family life. But if they are not, deep resentments, that carry over into adult life, may result.[3]

Parental Acts Which Annoy Adolescents

Within the family circle, practically every detail of daily life is a potential source of annoyance to adolescents—and to parents. A large proportion of adolescent complaints against parents arise in connection with the young person's desire for independence and his wish to act and look grown-up.[4]

In a study of conflicts between adolescents and their mothers, Block (1937) obtained responses from over five hundred junior and senior high school boys and girls to a list of fifty complaints. Among the complaints checked by the largest percentages (over 60 per cent of the adolescent boys and girls) were the following:

Pesters me about my table manners.
Pesters me about my manners and habits.
Holds my sister or brother up to me as a model.
Scolds if my school marks are not as high as other people's.
Objects to my going automobile riding at night with boys.
Insists that I tell her what I spent my money for.
Won't let me use the car.
Insists that I eat foods that I dislike, but which are good for me.

[3] It seems that such resentments are quite common among adults without being recognized by the ones who hold them. It is not unlikely that an adult has unresolved resentments against his *own* parents if he has a punitive attitude toward *other* parents.

[4] Sources of friction between adolescents and their parents have been described by Block (1937), Stott (1940a), Anastasi *et al.* (1948), Lloyd (1952), and Connor *et al.* (1954).

There were many other complaints, such as the mother deciding what subjects the young person should take at school or what job he or she should plan for. About half the boys reported that mothers teased them about their girl friends and two-thirds of the girls reported that mothers teased them about their boy friends.

In a study by Block (1937) girls checked a larger number of complaints than boys. Girls frequently complained that their mothers spent too much time at bridge parties and the like and were seldom home (checked as disturbing things by 78 per cent of the girls, as compared with 29 per cent of the boys). Moreover, girls also objected, more than the boys, to what the mother did when she was at home.

Among the difficulties girls mentioned especially often as compared with boys were the following: nagging by the mother; objecting to persons of the opposite sex with whom the adolescent chose to go out; nagging about little things; insisting on investigating places to which the adolescent went for parties. Connor et al. (1954) also found that a large number of conflicts between parents and daughters centered on dating and choice of boy friends.

It is easy to understand why mothers (and fathers, too) would be concerned about the possibility of their daughters falling in with bad company, or getting a bad name, or becoming involved in sexual intimacies. If any harm should come from such matters it is likely that the girl would suffer more than the boy. When parents are anxious about a daughter, it is difficult for them to trust her, or to put her on her own responsibility and give her the freedom she feels she has the right to demand.

It is also understandable, however, that girls resent the fact that they are given less freedom and are held more strictly to account than boys. Girls resent the fact that there is a double standard of sexual morality, that society judges them more harshly than boys for various kinds of misconduct.

In a study by Stott (1940a) involving several hundred adolescents living on farms, in small towns, and in a city, it was also noted that the girls criticized their parents more than did the boys. In this study, fathers were criticized more frequently than mothers for personal habits (personal conduct includes items such as smoking, drinking, swearing, driving the car too fast, and the like). Mothers were criticized more often than fathers for matters related to discipline and control and for their tendency to overwork and sacrifice themselves. In these groups, the adolescents living on farms complained most about discipline and control. City dwellers relatively more often had complaints about their parents' personal habits and temperamental traits.

Mothers are more likely than fathers to be the ones who punish the adolescent (Stott, 1940b). To the extent that these findings hold true for adolescents at large it appears that it is the mother more than the father who takes the greatest personal responsibility for the young person and is, in a sense, closer to the young person as a friend, confidante, disciplinarian, and (from the adolescent's point of view) a nuisance.

A large number of the complaints about parents voiced by young people of high school age also appear at the college level. In a study by Heath and Gregory (1946) of 259 college sophomores, one of the most troublesome problems these boys reported was that of strained relationships with parents. The most frequent problem in this area was in the category "antagonism to parents, family criticism" (reported by 69 persons).

The Harassed Parent

Even when the family situation is as good as human affairs permit, parents of adolescents face problems for which they have no good solution.

Changes in customs and manners and in economic conditions from one generation to the next mean that adolescents are likely to demand privileges and rights which their parents did not demand in their youth. But this difference between the generations accounts for only a small portion of the problems that beset parents.

Parental Anxiety. Parents cannot help but be anxious at times about their offspring's safety and well-being. From a sheer statistical point of view, many of the worries parents have about adolescents are more "real" than their worries about younger children. Parents of younger children frequently worry that their youngsters will have physical accidents—through drowning, fire, poisoning, injury in traffic, etc.; but in most instances, fortunately, their worries are not verified by disaster.

On the other hand, when parents worry about hazards connected with adolescents and the automobile, the actual accident statistics bear them out. More than that, grounds for worry come right to their own and neighboring homes. A father whose son had just completed the teen years reported that every teen-age boy within his own and his son's acquaintance had had a mishap with automobiles, ranging from arrests for

speeding and reckless driving to minor or serious smash-ups and colli-
sions. Likewise, in the area of sex, Kinsey's findings, and statistics
regarding illegitimate births, and the high incidence of marital difficulties
among those who marry in their teens all proclaim that parents have
reasonable ground for concern. When parents of adolescents worry, they
are not flying in the teeth of reality—they are concerned about hazards
that actually exist.

Parental Feelings of Being Rejected. When adolescents are at the
peak of their search for independence and self-direction, parents often
feel that they are being rejected. Rightly or wrongly, they may think that
the adolescent is intentionally trying to hurt their feelings when he
pointedly ignores them, criticizes them, repeatedly does "foolish" things
which they urged him not to do. The adolescent seems not to "want"
them any more when he refuses to join the family at a picnic, shows little
interest in being with the family at holiday celebrations which he once
eagerly looked forward to, has no desire to accompany the family on a
vacation. Parents are likely to feel "left out" when their adolescent child
is much more swayed by the opinions of his peers than by the judgment
of his parents.

If parents could view the situation dispassionately they would realize
that the adolescent who seems to be rejecting them is actually struggling
to grow up. The young person probably is not being unfeeling or cruel
just for the sake of hurting them. If they could view the matter objectively parents might even welcome seeming acts of rejection as a sign
of healthy growth. But it is difficult for parents to be that objective, especially when they have tried for years, and are still trying, to give their
child as much devotion as they can.

Parental Feelings of Failure. Many parents have a feeling of failure
when their adolescent children are critical of them, get into scrapes,
flounder or seem to be bewildered, confused or emotionally distressed.

Parental Feelings of Guilt. Any real or imagined "failure" in the
upbringing of adolescents or any mishap that befalls the adolescent is
likely also to stir up feelings of guilt in parents, especially if they have
high standards for themselves and their offspring. Such guilt feelings are
nurtured by much of what they read and hear about the responsibilities

and shortcomings of parents. These feelings of guilt are reinforced by feelings of helplessness when parents face dilemmas that are almost impossible to resolve. When parents of adolescents "let down their hair" they can list many such dilemmas.[5]

Parents are told they should not control their adolescent children's lives, but they are also told they should prevent late parties, early dating, early marriage, speeding, drinking, and sex misconduct.

They are admonished not to impose "middle-class" pressures for success on their children, but if their youngsters do poorly in school it is "because the parents have not set proper standards at home."

Parents are exhorted not to make undue sacrifices—Mama should not have to wear the same coat for six years so Mabel can have a new one every year. But at the same time they should also spare Mabel from the humiliation of being the only girl wearing "old clothes."

There is no adolescent foible or misfortune, ranging from reckless driving to pregnancy out of wedlock, that has not been attributed to the fact that parents have been too lenient or too strict, too overprotecting or too rejecting, too solicitous or not solicitous enough, too aggressive or too passive in asserting their masculinity or femininity, too weak or too domineering.

In rearing their adolescent children parents not only face confused and frequently smug and guilt-provoking advice from experts, but they also frequently feel that they stand alone, with little or no moral support from anyone else. In many communities parents are disunited while adolescents seem to present a "united front" in what they demand. There is hardly anything an adolescent wants to do which he cannot truthfully support with the claim, "But other kids are allowed to do it." This claim would probably be more true if the adolescent said that *some* instead of implying that *all* other youngsters have the privileges he demands. But the claim, no matter how it is phrased, adds to the difficulty a parent faces when he tries to use his own judgment and desires to lay down firm rules.

In the author's opinion, the lot of parents and adolescents would be much easier if all who pass judgment on them or make pronouncements about them would respect the multiplicity of factors that determine human behavior.

[5] The author vividly recalls the roar of agreement voiced by a group of parents —all college graduates—when one parent exclaimed: "Nothing you do is right. You're damned if you do and damned if you don't."

REACTIVATION OF PARENTS' UNRESOLVED PROBLEMS

A parent's anxiety about the problems that confront his adolescent son or daughter is intensified if these problems touch on unresolved problems of his own. Probably every parent, to some degree, is vulnerable on this score. Adolescents face issues in the area of sex; so do a great many seemingly "well-adjusted" adults. Adolescents must make decisions with regard to the work they will do in adult life; many adults feel regret about or dissatisfaction with the occupational choices they made. It is important for an ambitious adolescent to prepare himself to "get ahead"; in the adult population, there are vast numbers of persons who are vigorously competing and endlessly trying to "get ahead." Adolescents of marriageable age must make choices as to the person they wish to marry; judging from divorce statistics and studies of marital discord, a large proportion of adults apparently have second thoughts as to whether they made the right choices.

Parents as Confidants

Some parents succeed better than others in becoming the confidants of their children (White House Conference on Child Health and Protection, Committee on the Family and Parent Education, 1934). Boys and girls often find that they can confide more readily in their mothers than in their fathers.

Children who feel free to confide in their parents showed better adjustment than those who do not confide, when adjustment is determined by such criteria as social compliance, emotional stability, desirable character traits, and obedience in the classroom. These findings suggest that the confider also tends to be a conformer. Moreover, there was also some evidence, but not conclusive evidence, that children who in school are rebels or unruly somewhat more often come from homes in which there was not a confiding relationship between the parent and the child.

While it is valuable for an adolescent to have someone with whom to share his perplexities, it cannot always be assumed that persons who are most intimate and confiding will face the hurdles of adolescent development most successfully. The person who is confiding may be one who is depending to an undue degree on his parents and is prolonging his dependency on them.

TABLE 11.1

PERCENTAGE OF CHILDREN AT VARIOUS GRADE LEVELS WHO REPORTED THEY "TALK TO MOTHER OR FATHER" OR "TALK TO A FRIEND" IF WORRIED ABOUT SOMETHING *

| | | Grade in School | | | |
		VI	VIII	X	XII
Girls	Father or Mother	81	68	56	43
	Friend	1	10	24	37
Boys	Father or Mother	61	63	48	51
	Friend	8	10	14	23

* Adapted from C. M. Tryon, *UC Inventory I, Social and Emotional Adjustment,* Institute of Child Welfare, University of California, 1939.

DIFFICULTIES IN COMMUNICATION

In many situations it would be good if youngsters and parents alike could openly express their feelings to one another. But it is difficult for them to do this. One reason is that an open avowal of feeling—a youngster's feeling, for example, that his parents are unfair—is likely to sound like an accusation. A more important reason is that the feelings parents and their offspring have about one another often are mixed and unclear.

Several illustrations of this appeared in a study by the writer and his associates (1962). One woman felt as a child and as an adolescent that her mother basically disapproved of her. Disapproval usually causes resentment, but as a child and adolescent this person did not recognize resentment (which later, as a young adult, she was able to detect). Instead, she felt unworthy and guilty, and she strove endlessly to win her mother's approval. Even if she had been able to tell about her guilt her mother might not have been able to understand. The mother would quite likely have felt a wave of guilt herself, or perhaps annoyance. In such a situation it would be hard for either the daughter or the mother to talk freely and to get to the heart of the matter, although, in spite of this, after a painful scene or two, it is likely that the mother and daughter might be able to communicate more freely and establish a closer relationship.

The Value of an "Outsider's" View

When youngsters reach adolescence they and their parents have been swimming in the same emotional stream so long that it is difficult for them to examine the stream. To ask them to do so is almost like asking a fish to get out of the water and examine the eddies and currents in his native pool. For this reason it is often more valuable for adolescents, and their parents as well, to confide in an outsider than to try to confide in one another.

The outsider may be a psychiatrist, psychologist, teacher, or counselor who has a gift for helping others. The outsider is not personally responsible; he or she is less likely to be threatened or to feel accused. He or she, if gifted with some understanding, can help clarify confused feelings, and bring them out into the open. An outsider may be far more able to help someone else than to help his own kin, much as a doctor can trust his hand to be more steady and can be more confident in his judgment when he operates on someone else's son or daughter than when he operates on his own.

Parental Satisfactions

Although adolescence is a time that tries the souls of even the most doughty parent, it also brings great satisfactions when things go moderately well. Parents see a new creature unfolding before their eyes, yet this new creation retains fond and familiar traits of an earlier day. In the physical sphere alone it is fascinating to watch a child shoot up.

It is even more rewarding, although baffling, to take part in the drama that goes on when the young person more and more insistently claims the rights and privileges of a young adult. In spite of all the misgivings he has about what Junior does when alone in the family car, Papa can sit back and let Junior do the driving. Mama, although she frets about her daughter's dress and grooming, can also get a thrill from her daughter's becoming appearance, and she may even turn to her daughter for advice. It is gratifying when son or daughter or both urge Ma and Pa to take it easy, go on a vacation, and when son tells Pop not to worry about clearing the snow from the driveway—he will do it. It is more intensely gratifying when adolescents take decisions into their own hands and, in spite of parental misgivings, do a good job of it.

The process through which parents adapt themselves to the fact that their children are "grown up" is beset by many trials, but one must look far to find anything more heart-warming than the end product when all turns out well.

Chapter 12

Adolescents and
Their Peers

A young person's relations with his own age group become increasingly important as he advances from infancy toward the adolescent years. During adolescence a person's dealings with his peers become even more significant. When he leaves adolescence and becomes a young adult, all other adults are his peers, at least in a legal sense. He must find his place in a society that includes not only his own age group but adults who, although older than he, are on a par with him as voters, citizens, parents, job-holders, and in many other ways.

Adolescents' relations with their peers are important in connection with all aspects of their development, as we have noted in earlier sections of this book. In this chapter and the next we will focus more specifically on these relationships.

In many respects, adolescents have a society of their own, overlapping with, and yet distinct from, the larger society in which they live. There is a great amount of "ganging up" among them. Some belong to an organized gang, with a name, rigid rules and clearly defined "power structure"; but such adolescents constitute only a small minority. In the more typical situation, adolescents operate as a loosely organized but powerful confederation. Through this, adolescents exert an influence on each other and pressure on their parents.

Adolescents in concert with each other, to a large extent, determine what "goes." They influence the moral climate, decide the proper way to dress, develop their own lingo and rules of etiquette.

Adolescents as Preceptors. Much of the education adolescents provide for one another comes through an opportunity to test their views and theories. Such a test enables the young person to "think out loud" and to observe how others react. In their conversations, adolescents often advance extravagant ideas. In the guise of expressing what seems to be an impersonal theory they have an opportunity to express ideas which have important personal meanings—ideas about themselves, parents, teachers, persons in authority, personal problems, attitudes about sex, ideas concerning relationships with the opposite sex, ideas about schooling, about joining the military service, and a host of other issues.

In order to express their attitudes and views, they have to formulate them so that others can understand and respond, and this is an incentive to formulating them as clearly as they can in their own minds. In adolescence, as in earlier childhood, a person's thinking is sharpened and clarified, by the need to formulate his private thoughts in language and logic that *others* can understand. Others are not likely to get the drift of his thoughts if he, himself, has not formulated them in ways that are clear to him.

Escape from Loneliness

Adolescence is not only a time of intense sociability but, for many, a time of loneliness. Adolescents live in solitary isolation when they cannot share their concerns with others and when the only close companions they can find are those who dwell within their own imagination. There are many conditions in adolescence—and adult life [1]—that cut persons off from one another. We have discussed some of these in earlier chapters dealing with the ways in which young persons and adults conceal their feelings and thoughts from one another.

Loneliness occurs not only in those who physically are alone. It can

[1] Almost all adults who were interviewed informally in a study by the writer (1955) spoke of being lonely to a small or large degree. In response to a more formal written inventory, about half of a group of 229 respondents reported one or more conditions of loneliness as representing a "problem" in their lives.

occur in its most acute form when a person is in the midst of a crowd, joining in the banter and enforced sociability. Some adolescents feel their loneliness most vividly when they are at a party or dance. A boy and a girl can dance together for hours in what seems to be a close contact. But physical closeness does not, in itself, bring psychological closeness. Unless there is a bond, a feeling of intimacy and tenderness, each may feel as lonely as ever, or perhaps even lonelier, for the contrast between the superficially friendly motions and the deeper unrequited needs is magnified.

In adolescence, as in later periods of life, individuals try to build barricades against loneliness. They become joiners. They sing the sorority and fraternity songs. They clasp their hands together and cheer for the team or for the "cause." But the glitter and the formal wrappings of "togetherness" do not fulfill the deeper need, the yearning, longing, and hope which underlie a person's loneliness. One of the great rewards of a close friendship in adolescence is that it helps the young person to escape from the pangs of loneliness.

Friendships among Adolescents

The most important peer relationships are those existing between close friends. The factors which draw two adolescents together into a close companionship are complex and not well understood. From ordinary observation one can note, however, that in some companionships the relationship is that of leader and follower. Some companionships appear to have an ulterior purpose, as when one youngster ingratiates himself with a popular member of the group as a means of gaining prestige and the other youngster "uses" him as though he were a convenient, unpaid servant.

The most meaningful companionships, however, are those in which two young people share one another's company as equals, feel at home with each other and feel free to confide their innermost thoughts and feelings to each other. In such a relationship there is trust, there is no need to pretend, no necessity for being on guard against betrayal of shared secrets. Adolescents who have a relationship of this kind can reprove each other without condemning each other.

A friendship of this kind is likely to occur between two persons who are more alike than dissimilar in some of the more obvious characteristics, such as intelligence and socioeconomic status. But there are subtleties underlying the affinity which these measures do not reveal. Two friends may differ in ways that one might expect to keep them apart. For example, one of them may have much stronger moral scruples than the other.

When an adolescent finds a "real" friend he possesses something very precious. He is not only tasting the joys of companionship but he is also discovering himself. To the extent that he is able, he brings out, for open display, doubts, resentments, and concerns of many kinds. In the process he may gain a deeper assurance of his own worth. He may discover feelings which he hardly knew he, or others, possessed—and be able to express them in a way he ordinarily would not allow.[2] (He may also expose himself to the sorrow of parting, but the sorrow of parting from a friend is likely to be outweighed by the value of having had a friend.)

One characteristic of a close companionship is its effortlessness. There is no need for the usual formal and superficial social amenities. Even when the companions have been separated for weeks they can easily slip back into their old relationship as though they had seen each other just an hour ago.

Another characteristic is that close companions can tolerate silence. They may chatter at a great rate one moment and then go through long periods when no one says anything. This is in sharp contrast to the behavior of persons who are "friends," but only in a formal sense. When such "friends" get together, silence is usually insufferable. We see this contrast more among the older adolescents and adults than among the younger persons. In a typical gathering of two or twenty older persons who are "friends," silence produces anxiety—if it ever occurs. The atmosphere is pierced with remarks by this person and then another chimes in. Often, in such a gathering of "friends" there is a grim undercurrent of competitiveness. Among those who have the good fortune to find mutual friendship of a more personal kind, however, periods of silence do not arouse anxiety.

But there are other marks which also differ from the usual behavior among persons who are "friends" in a formal way. One of the most conspicuous marks is an outspokenness such as would have provoked a duel among nonfriends in the days when knighthood was in flower. This appears more often among boys than among girls. One can almost meas-

[2] In a companionship between two boys in their late teens, reported to the author, a time arrived when one had to move to a distant place. The boys were roommates. In the middle of the night before the leave-taking, one of the boys awoke and heard his companion crying. Without revealing that he was awake he also began quietly to cry. These boys were robust, masculine characters who ordinarily would never allow themselves to cry in public.

ure the depth of the companionship between boys by the epithets they now and then good-humoredly hurl at one another. One of the milder ones appears in the salutation: "Well, how are you, you horse's neck?"

Social Acceptance, Rejection and Isolation

There is a wide range in the extent to which individual adolescents are regarded as acceptable members of their peer group. At one extreme, an adolescent may be very popular—highly regarded by all and disapproved by none. At the other extreme, an adolescent may be extremely unpopular—disapproved by everyone. Between these extremes, there are many gradations: the adolescent may be generally accepted and respected; he may be accepted as a group member who is neither winsome nor obnoxious; he may be ignored and isolated as one who deserved no notice, or he may be an outcast, actually excluded from any friendship with his peers.

One of the systematic ways of getting information about the extent to which an adolescent is accepted or ignored or rejected by members of his group is what is known as the *sociometric* method (Moreno, 1934, 1954; Jennings, 1937, 1947). Each person writes the names, for example, of individuals whom he would like to have as seat-mates or as close friends or as guests at a party in his home. Sometimes, also, each person is asked to name those he definitely does *not* care to have as companions. Another procedure is to provide each member with a list of all other members of his group and ask him to rate each one on a scale ranging from a high degree of acceptance to complete rejection.

When choices have been made, it is possible to raise many interesting questions, such as: Who is chosen most or least often? Who chooses whom? To what extent do various persons choose those who also choose them, or choose those who do not choose them? Are the choices heavily centered on a few popular members of the group, or are they widely distributed? Is there evidence that there are several little cliques or social islands within the group? [3]

Information obtained by means of the sociometric technique can be shown graphically in what is called a *sociogram*. An example of a sociogram is given in Figure 12.1.

Several other methods have also been used to gain information concerning popularity, leadership, and other indications of the extent to

[3] Studies using sociometric methods appear widely in the literature on adolescence. Many such studies are published in the journal *Sociometry*.

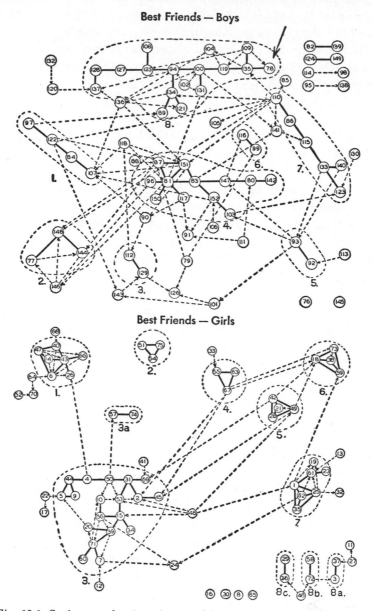

Fig. 12.1. Sociogram showing choices of best friends by boys and girls in the California Adolescent Growth Study (From Harold E. Jones, *Development in Adolescence*. New York: Appleton-Century-Crofts, 1943, p. 43).

which members of adolescent groups admire or disdain one another. One procedure that yields interesting results is a "Guess Who" test. This contains brief sketches of personal traits—such as, here is a person who always is fair, here is a person who always has to have the last word— and the members of the group are asked to write in the names of persons in the group whom such descriptions fit.

CHARACTERISTICS OF ADOLESCENTS WHO ARE WELL LIKED

Many characteristics of adolescents who are regarded as most acceptable and least acceptable by members of their group have been listed. Such lists are a little misleading, of course, since it is usually a person in his totality rather than just a certain one of his traits that attracts or repels others. However, it is worth noting some of these traits.

One characteristic frequently named in a person who is liked is that he likes others.[4] Another frequently mentioned characteristic is a certain kind of freedom and spontaneity and willingness to enter into things, which may be described in terms such as "active in games," "you can have fun with him or her," "willing to take a chance," "initiates games and activities." Another quality frequently noted is a kind of liveliness, cheerfulness, and gaiety described in terms such as "enjoys a joke," "is cheerful and happy." Fairness and good sportsmanship also are often named as qualities of persons who are liked. Frequently also, qualities are mentioned suggesting that the well-liked person is relatively "natural" and free of pretense: he or she is "not conceited," "enjoys a joke on himself." Tidiness, neatness, and cleanliness are also sometimes mentioned, as are qualities such as "seems to come from a good home."

Several investigators have found that there is a positive relationship between social acceptance and intelligence, and between social acceptance and academic achievement. But, intelligence and academic achievement do not influence social acceptance as much as some other characteristics do (e.g., Jones, 1949a; Bonney, 1946; Latham, 1951; Laughlin, 1954; and Ryan and Davie, 1958).

---

[4] For studies bearing on this subject, see Jennings (1937), Bonney (1943c), Kuhlen and Lee (1943), Neugarten (1946), Potashin (1946), Shoobs (1947), Kuhlen and Bretsch (1947), Northway and Wigdor (1947), Polansky et al. (1950), Foshay (1951), Bretsch (1952), Feinberg (1953), Cannon (1958), Gronlund and Anderson (1957), Feinberg et al. (1958), and Ryan and Davie (1958).

In a study by Jennings (1947) it was noted that those who were named far more frequently than the average when sociometric choices were made tended to be persons who had qualities that brought people together in constructive ways: those who could contribute to the flow of ideas and who made good suggestions about activities; who could initiate and plan; who had ingenuity of a sort that would help the group to make good use of time or to have an interesting time. In other studies it has been noted that the young person who is good in athletics is more likely than not to be popular (Jones, 1949a, and Feinberg et al., 1958).

It has been observed (Jennings, 1947) that young people who are not frequently chosen and who are either isolated or rejected show many forms of behavior having the effect of drawing people apart rather than bringing them together. Kuhlen and Collister (1952) noted that ninth-graders who were failing in school and who were generally not well adjusted socially tended to be unattractive, poorly groomed, lacking in social "know-how," withdrawing, shy, and unhappy. Other terms which adolescents themselves use in describing peers they reject are pesty, noisy, conceited, silly, and effeminate (Feinberg et al., 1958).

The general trend of the findings concerning adolescents who have a low level of acceptance within the group or who are ignored or rejected by members of the group is that they often, in the privacy of their own lives, are rather moody, troubled, and distressed. It has been observed, for example, that those with low social acceptance often seem to show symptoms of insecurity; many of them seem to be troubled by problems in their home environment and to be absorbed by difficulties in their own lives to such an extent that they lack the freedom to enter into lively give-and-take with others.

The characteristics adolescents admire or dislike in one another were investigated by Tryon (1939) in a study in which responses were obtained from a large group at an average age of twelve years and again at the age of about fifteen. The findings showed certain differences between the evaluations made by boys and girls, and also changes in values between the ages of twelve and fifteen, notably among girls. At twelve years, the girls described as most acceptable the kind of person who was rather quiet, gracious, conforming, and inclined to be nonaggressive. At fifteen years, on the other hand, the girls expressed less admiration for sedate and demure behavior and considerably more admiration for liveliness, ability to entertain, and a tendency to be active, and the qualities of being a good sport and attractive to boys. Boys were more consistent in their evaluations from twelve to fifteen years. At the earlier age they expressed most admiration for boys who were skillful, daring, and leaders in games. At fifteen years, prestige for the boys still appeared in large measure to be determined by physical skill, aggressiveness, and fearlessness. In only one pair of traits was there a marked reversal on the part of boys in this group. At twelve years, being unkempt in appearance tended to be regarded more as a positive than as a negative quality, but at fifteen years this characteristic was disapproved.

In this group of young people the traits that made boys attractive to girls also tended to rate high as traits giving a boy prestige within his own sex group. On the other hand, there was not so much overlapping between qualities that made a girl attractive to the opposite sex and admired by her own sex. Tryon makes the point that more demands are placed on girls than on boys for flexibility and for the capacity to readjust their values. However, Tryon also suggests that the fact that most of the girls, during the period of the study, had passed through the pubescent period, while probably less than half of the boys had done so, also had made a difference.

CONSISTENCY IN SOCIAL ACCEPTANCE

There is likely to be a great similarity from year to year in the extent to which a person is accepted by his peers during the preadolescent and high school years.

At the elementary school level it has been noted that in some groups social acceptance scores remain almost as constant from year to year as the scores the children earn on tests of intelligence and academic achievement (Bonney, 1943a and 1943b). In a study by Laughlin (1954) children rated one another while in the sixth grade and again when they had moved on to the seventh grade in a junior high school. There was a marked tendency for youngsters to maintain their popularity ratings even after they had moved to the upper school, where there was a good deal of mixing of populations from the various elementary schools.

Repeated sociometric ratings over periods of one, two, and three years were obtained in a study of high school students by Cannon (1958). The social acceptance scores showed a high degree of stability (correlations ranged from .61 to .91 on various tests). In retests of high school students' choices of leisure-time companions Wertheimer (1957) found correlations ranging from .55 to .71 when comparisons were made over periods ranging from eight to twenty months. It is possible, however, that as a result of the shifts in group membership that occur when adolescents leave high school and go to college, there may also be a shift in the ratings they receive (see, *e.g.,* Horrocks and Wear, 1953). The data on this question, however, are not very adequate.

ACCEPTANCE AND SOCIAL ADJUSTMENT

A youngster who has qualities which make him acceptable to his peers obviously has many advantages. He is likely to be more serene both in his individual life at school and in his social relationships outside of school than the one who is rejected by others. In a study of over 2,000 adolescents, Feinberg (1953) found that young persons who were accepted by others had, on the whole, a more favorable view of themselves than the rejected ones, and that they have better relationships with their parents and teachers.

For many youngsters, high or low acceptance by peers in late childhood—or the personal qualities that are responsible for high or low acceptance—has a significant bearing on how the youngsters will fare in high school. This is shown in a study by Gronlund and Holmlund (1958) who examined the high school careers of children who had a high or low sociometric status as determined by tests administered when they were in the sixth grade.[5] The records of these persons seven years later showed that 82 per cent of the high-status pupils, as compared with 45 per cent of the low-status pupils, graduated from high school. About three times as many pupils in the low-status group as in the high-status group dropped out of high school.[6] Gronlund and Holmlund point out that their findings do not show whether lack of social acceptance was a direct cause of pupils' dropping out of school or a factor related to other causes. In the high school, a considerably larger number of those who had been most accepted than those who had been least accepted by their sixth-grade peers joined clubs and organizations, participated in varsity sports and held positions of leadership in the school.

[5] In the sixth grade each of 1,073 pupils named five persons whom they preferred as seat-mates, as play companions and work companions—fifteen choices in all. Pupils who received twenty-seven or more choices were designated as high-status pupils and those receiving three choices or fewer were designated as low-status pupils.
[6] The difference in intelligence between the two groups (high-status average I.Q. was about 109; low-status about 101) was not large enough to account for this difference in number of drop-outs.

DISCREPANCIES BETWEEN PERSONAL
AND SOCIAL ADJUSTMENT

Although the adolescent who is highly accepted by his peers is a social success, we cannot take for granted that good social adjustment, as indicated by high popularity ratings, means good "personal adjustment." Neither can we assume that a low degree of acceptance by peers is a sign that an adolescent is personally maladjusted. To judge the meaning of high or low acceptance by peers it is essential to consider the standards and values the peers are applying. As we have noted elsewhere, adolescents place a higher value on athletic ability than on intellectual ability. Yet in adult life, an individual is likely to find that good brains are an important personal and social asset.

To assess the meaning of high acceptance by peers it is also necessary to consider the price a person has paid for it (see, *e.g.,* Wittenberg and Berg, 1952, and Mill, 1953). A young person who takes extra pains to win popularity may be one who lacks confidence in himself. He may be one whose assurance of his own worth is so weak that he must endlessly strive to prove, by way of hard-won popularity, that he is a worthy person. Among those who win a high degree of social acceptance on a sociometric test, there are some who are "seriously disturbed" (Northway and Wigdor, 1947).

The fact that high acceptance by peers does not in itself reflect or produce a kind of mellow friendliness and friendly attitude toward others is shown in a study by Foshay (1951). He noted that children with high peer acceptance sometimes were quite inconsiderate of children with low peer acceptance or of children who were new in the classroom. On the other hand, in the groups studied by Foshay, children with high peer acceptance tended to be considerate of other children with high acceptance.

ADULT JUDGMENTS CONCERNING
THE POPULARITY OF ADOLESCENTS

The characteristics that influence the extent to which an adolescent is accepted or rejected by other youngsters are sometimes not easy for adults to detect. An adult is likely to misjudge an adolescent's standing with his peers if he sees the adolescent entirely from the viewpoint of adult goals and standards. Adults who judge an adolescent mainly in terms of the respect and deference he shows toward them may be using a standard that has little meaning when adolescents judge each other. If an adolescent has qualities that make him well liked by his peers, he probably will also impress adults as a likeable person, but there are many exceptions to this (see, *e.g.,* Gronlund, 1953).

In one study in an institution (Fauquier and Gilchrist, 1942) it was found that teachers and house parents, when asked to judge who were the leaders among the boys, identified less than 50 per cent of those the boys themselves named as leaders.

Bonney (1947) found that high school teachers were more successful in identifying students who were well accepted by other students than in identifying those who were poorly accepted. He also found that teachers tended to overrate students who were outstanding in class but lacked skill in interpersonal relations. They also overrated students who were courteous and responsive to teachers but possessed unfavorable traits not so noticeable to teachers. Teachers tended to underrate students who did not respond well to the academic situation but who were proficient in their relationships with a clique or select group of youngsters. They also underrated individuals who antagonized teachers but were well liked by students.

Competition

An important feature of the adolescent's relationships with other persons is the way he competes with others and the needs in his life he tries to fill by competition with others.

DEVELOPMENTAL USES AND VALUES OF COMPETITION

The typical adolescent has had a great amount of experience as a competitor. Most adolescents began during the preschool period to compare themselves with others. Many of them at the age of four or thereabouts began to keep an eye on what others did and tried to outdo them or at least to do as well.

Much of a child's growing perception of himself comes about through comparing himself with others. His developing conception of who he is, what he is, what he can do, depends in part on opportunities to observe

264] The Adolescent's Social World

what others do and what others are. One way of testing his strength and ability is to vie with others. Competition serves an important *developmental* purpose when children and adolescents try out their growing powers in spontaneous competition with others. Some competition of this sort is inevitable, and as long as it is an aid to realistic self-discovery it is healthy. Competition is also healthy when it is undertaken in a spirit of fun and when it adds to a person's zest for life.

It is also good for a youngster to compete if that is necessary in order to safeguard his own self-interest in a realistic and equitable way. It is a sign of good health if a youngster sees to it that he gets his chance even if it means that he has to vie with someone else to get it, vigorously strives to get his proper share of things to work with, and actively seeks, in dealings with adults, to get the attention that is his due.

ADULT MODELS OF COMPETITION

Competition is not only a *developmental* phenomenon but also a pervasive *cultural* condition in the adolescent's world. The American adolescent (in common with adolescents in large areas of the world) is surrounded by an adult society that is saturated with competition. People compete for attention, for posesssions, for power and prestige. They compete in the sphere of love and sex.

Most adolescents emulate the competitiveness that prevails in the adult world. For example a class discussion at school is often a competitive marathon (as discussions frequently are at the adult level). In almost every group, some adolescents are especially adept and aggressive in this kind of competition. They watch their timing, plunge in to have their say when a previous speaker has barely closed his mouth. In the meantime, other members of the class, equally competitive but less adept, silently make speeches to themselves.

UNHEALTHY ASPECTS OF COMPETITION

We have noted some of the healthy uses and constructive values of competition. Competitiveness can also be employed in unhealthy ways. Competitiveness is unhealthy when it is not employed as a form of venturesome self-discovery but functions instead as a symptom of low self-esteem: a person suffers from low self-esteem when he must endlessly "prove" his worth by surpassing others. It is unhealthy when it is self-defeating. A person is a victim of self-defeating competitiveness when his need to excel others is so strong that he is unable wholeheartedly to enjoy any activity or experience for its own sake. A competitive person is also defeating himself when, in struggling to be viewed as a success in the eyes of others, he antagonizes the very persons whose good opinion he is trying to win (we noted some aspects of this in the discussion of anxiety in Chapter 10). The most serious self-defeating aspect of competitiveness is that the one who must incessantly prove his worth by excelling others can never really succeed. He may win many battles, but he continually wages a losing war. The adulation he seeks from others can never serve as a substitute for confidence in himself.

There are many other contrasts between healthy and unhealthy competition. A person who is the master of his competitiveness uses it discriminately. Whether he competes for the fun of it (in a friendly game of bridge) or for an ulterior purpose (such as competing with others in an examination to qualify for a promotion), he chooses where and how and when he will compete. He also chooses not to compete when there is no reason to do so, and he does not enter contests that are outside his field of competence. A compulsive competitor, on the other hand, is often indiscriminate. He plunges in, even when he has nothing to gain—other than to gratify his need to get attention. He tries to impress people whose opinions really do not matter. It is difficult for him to listen to a conversation without horning in. He is constantly making a mental comparison between himself and others.

Competition is unhealthy too when it is a symptom of an underlying attitude of hostility. A person's competitiveness is hostile when he gloats over others, when he not only has a desire to excel but to destroy (as distinct from the anger that often arises spontaneously in the heat of eager competition). Such hostility is compounded by deceit when the competitor pretends he is competing in sportsmanlike fashion while looking for opportunities to violate the rules of the game. Competitiveness with underlying hostility is frequently carried on by persons who, when competing by proxy as spectators, cheer when a member of the opposing team is hurt, jeer when an opponent-by-proxy comes to grief.

An underlying streak of hostility appears not only when a competitor manifestly expresses animosity toward others but also when he shows a politely callous disregard for the feelings of others. Such callous disregard is almost inevitable when a person has a relentless impulse always to compare himself with others and to outdo them. One of the mildest but most common forms of callous competition is manifested by the person who is an inveterate bore in conversation. If someone has a toothache he cannot give himself time to sympathize with the sufferer, but he is quick to recall a humdinger of an ache he once had; or he breaks in to announce that his teeth have always been perfect or that he has the best (or the poorest) dentist in six counties. If the talk is of travel, he insists on reporting regretfully that he himself has not traveled or on describing the travels he has made. If the other person has had an accident, he quickly takes stock of accidents he has been in or of his prudence in avoiding accidents. He will even advertise his infirmities if he can give them a tragic touch.

An adolescent may have burdensome competitive tendencies even though he does not seem to be competitive. His competitiveness may be so strong that he dares not to take the chance of losing. He may have a driving competitive bent even though he remains on the side lines, carefully avoids even being around when there might be open competition for a grade or a place on a team or for a girl. It may be so desperately important for him to make a good showing that he will not risk the possibility of making a poor showing. When he fails to speak up in class, it may be because he shrinks from saying anything that is not the best and most perfect thing that might be said. In his fantasies after school he may be angry at himself for not speaking and angry at those who did speak.

When a person is driven by competition even his moments of great triumph have a melancholy flavor. If the motives that won for him were ulterior and devious, he actually has not won a struggle to overcome his difficulties. Even he may dimly perceive that his triumph is a symptom of weakness and not a sign of strength.

So, in seeking to understand an adolescent by noting the ways and the areas of life in which he competes, it is well to remember that while competition may, on the one hand, greatly enrich his life and enhance his value to the social group, it may, on the other hand, be a form of suffering and a sign of defeat.

Conformity

Conformity and competition have much in common, for both the one who conforms and the one who competes judge their conduct according to the pace and standards set by others.

The pressure to conform exercises a powerful influence on the behavior of young persons at the high school and college levels. A desire to conform is closely linked with a desire to be accepted and liked. In polls of teen-age attitudes and opinions conducted during a period of seventeen years, Remmers and his associates note that American teen-agers show substantial class differences "but in their desire for popularity and their conformist attitude they are as one: low-income or high-income, their highest concern is to be liked. . . . This is the most striking and consistent fact that has emerged from our polls through the seventeen years" (Remmers and Radler, 1958).

In their urge to conform many teen-agers do things which they claim they actually disapprove of, such as drinking or smoking. Remmers and Radler say that the whole matter is summed up in the comment of a teen-age girl: "It's hard for a teen-ager to say, 'I don't care to' when all the rest of the gang say 'Ah, come on.' "

Conforming behavior may extend through the entire community of adolescents—as when practically everyone dresses according to the current fad. Or it may be restricted to a segment of the community—as when a teen-ager conforms to the conduct of the crowd he is "running around" with or acts according to the standards of a certain gang. A youngster who does things generally viewed as bad in order to be regarded as a "good guy" by members of his gang is a conformist according to the mores of his group, even though, in the eyes of others, he is a nonconformist.[7]

Conformity is not, of course, limited to adolescents—it pervades adult society as well. A great deal of conformity among the young, notably in the intellectual sphere, is fostered by the school. Only about one-fourth of the young persons who took part in the survey by Remmers and Radler (1958) claimed that they often disagreed with the prevailing opinion in the group to which they belonged. We should expect that there would be more nonconformists than this if schools were succeeding in getting students "to think for themselves." However, as noted in Chapter 6, there is evidence that schools not only encourage but practically demand thinking of a conformist sort.

If an adolescent is to "find himself" and come into his own birthright as a separate self, it is essential for him not merely to conform. To realize his potentialities he must be a person, not just a part—a human being, not just a cog in an impersonal social machine.[8]

[7] Remmers and Radler (1958) state that probably one of the most important factors leading to delinquency is a need to be accepted by the gang.

[8] Kierkegaard (translated edition, 1949) has dealt with this issue, and Tillich (1952) considers it in his discussion of *The Courage to Be*.

Social Interests and Activities

Most of adolescents' leisure-time interests and occupations are shared with others. They are undertaken not only for their own sake but as a basis for companionship. Even homework is often done jointly with some-one else, or is the subject of long telephone conversations.

Among the most common leisure-time activities adolescents frequently share with others are "hanging around" or loafing with friends; going to the movies; playing or watching games, or participating in sports; attend-ing club meetings; going to parties (Olds, 1949). Reading is usually a solitary occupation. However, many young people do not seem to pur-sue this very passionately. In a survey by Gallup and Hill (1961), one-third of high school and college students said they had not read a book in the four months preceding the time when the survey was made.[9] Hobbies also are sometimes solitary undertakings, but a hobbyist fre-quently joins a club, or at least now and then exhibits his hobby to others.

Before television sets were available in a majority of homes, a large proportion of youngsters visited friends who had a set. Even now that TV sets are common, persons usually prefer to watch with a companion.[10]

"YOUTHESE"

Each generation of adolescents has a special lingo, a favored set of expres-sions with which they spice their conversation. This lingo constitutes only a small part of their total vocabulary. In a discussion of this "tribal tongue" Gallup and Hill (1961) note that often it is imaginative and sometimes obscene. It changes frequently and is quickly out of date; and

---

[9] This presumably refers to leisure-time reading, for more persons than this must have done some required reading at school.

[10] According to a study conducted some years ago (Battin, 1954), boys and girls of high school age reported that they spent an average of about nineteen hours a week watching television. This was less time than youngsters in the late elementary and junior high school grades devoted to TV, but it still represented one of the most universal and time-consuming adolescent leisure-time activities. Many young-sters will sit alone for long periods of time at the TV set, but often this seems to be from lack of opportunity to do something else or lack of an available companion. Scott (1953) found that 85 per cent of a group of children reported that they watched television for an average of over two hours a day, but a smaller proportion (59 per cent) named television as their first choice as a leisure-time activity.

older adolescents abandon expressions when younger ones take them up. Recently this dialect of youth included expressions such as Big Daddy (an older person); ankle-biter (a child); wazoo (the human posterior); back-seat bingo (attempting to pet in an automobile); "Shoot low, they're riding Shetlands" ("Be careful"); "Who rattled your cage?" ("Who asked for your opinion?"). Some expressions seem to be more durable than others, especially when taken over by adults (for example, the old expression "Beat it!" seems to have outlasted the "cheese-it" and the more recent, but outdated "Take off!" and "Drop dead!"). Some expressions are vivid but, according to Gallup and Hill, are difficult to translate precisely (such as, "Kill it, Dad, before it spreads").

ADOLESCENTS AND ALCOHOL

According to the survey by Gallup and Hill (1961), American youth approve of "moderate" or "social" drinking. Almost half the college students reported that their companions drank "a lot"; similar reports were made by more than 20 per cent of high school seniors and 10 per cent of high school sophomores.[11]

Drinking by adolescents is an especially serious problem when they combine it with driving a car. The precept "alcohol and gasoline don't mix" is a requiem when adolescents, who have taken more than they should, have bad automobile accidents.

One motive for drinking among younger adolescents is to appear grown-up. Another motive is to be "one of the crowd." An adolescent teetotaler is likely to be under heavy pressure to take a drink when others at a party are drinking. The pressure is especially strong on a girl at a party whom others would like to see tipsy and less self-controlled.

ADOLESCENTS AND AUTOMOBILES

A great amount of adolescent social activity centers around the use of automobiles. Driving a car serves many motives and purposes. It greatly increases the young person's range of action. The neighboring town, and

[11] According to the poll, 19 and 13 per cent, respectively, of high school sophomore boys and girls reported they did some drinking; the corresponding percentages at the high school senior level were 35 and 21, and, at the college upperclassman level, 63 and 56.

even the neighboring state, is just next door. Driving a car gives the beginner one of the most impressive and thrilling experiences of being grown-up enough to do what adults do. A car is also a form of self-display. A boy can use it not only to visit his girl friend but also to impress her and others. Cars also provide a place for love-making. They are a source of endless conversation and activity when hot-rodders get together.

According to some claims, the car has a deep significance in connection with an adolescent's strivings and conflicts. For a boy, the power he has under his control may bolster his feelings of masculinity and potency. For a girl, driving a car may be an important symbol of independence. It has also been suggested that the automobile serves as a sexual symbol and as a means of facing sexual conflicts or vicariously satisfying sexual desires. When a car does all this, in addition to serving as a means of transportation, the advertisers are almost guilty of understatement in claiming that a certain auto is an "all-purpose" car. It is no wonder that young people are so eager for a car and so many actually have one.

In the Gallup-Hill poll cited above, about one-third of the senior high school boys, 55 per cent of college men, and 78 per cent of the males who had left school to go to work had automobiles. Slightly less than one-fifth of the girls had cars.

Speeding in a car is often prompted by a desire to impress others or to share a thrill with others (although these are not the only motives). Largely as a consequence of speeding, a large proportion of youth have been in auto accidents. The proportion of accidents among drivers is much higher among boys than girls.[12] However, the fact that girls have fewer accidents than boys while driving a car themselves does not spare the girls from a high accident rate while riding in automobiles as passengers.[13]

During the teens, speeding often seems to afflict youngsters as a contagious disease. Some boys even seem to be proud of getting a ticket for speeding, even though they thereby risk the loss of their driver's license, and many do have their licenses suspended or revoked.

One sign that a youngster has grown in "social maturity" (much to

---

[12] In the poll mentioned above, 29 per cent of male high school seniors and 12 per cent of girl seniors, as drivers, had one or more accidents; among upperclassmen in college, the corresponding percentages were 51 and 25 per cent; and among working youth, 52 and 21 per cent.

[13] The percentage of boys and girls who had been in accidents as passengers was about the same for boys and girls among high school seniors (38 and 35 per cent) and among college upperclass boys and girls (43 and 41 per cent).

the relief of his parents) is that he no longer drives at a furious teen-ager pace. Some persons never seem to achieve this maturity, for a large proportion of adults are speeders. But evidence that many do slow down as they enter and move through the twenties is that the accident rates decline (and automobile insurance rates, for boys, are sharply reduced).

Chapter 13

Heterosexual Development

Dating

Dating provides one of the most thrilling pastimes in adolescence, and some of the most outstanding memories of adolescence in later years of life. As is to be expected, many youngsters embark on their first "real date" with some apprehension and shyness (Christensen, 1952), but usually this wears off in time. Some also begin to date in order to conform to group expectations, rather than from an impelling personal desire (Crist, 1953), but more adolescents date because they want to than because they think they ought to.

Dating includes a vast range of activities beyond formal arrangements for "calling" or "going out" to the movies or a party or dance. Some youngsters "date" by means of long private telephone conversations long before they start to "go together" in public. Often by prior understanding or an unspoken arrangement, boys and girls meet or seemingly "just happen" to meet in the halls or library at school, on the street, at a soda fountain, a community fair, a church supper, or elsewhere. Such meetings, whether by prearrangement or chance usually do not require that the youngsters must request permission from their parents to have a date. Neither do they commonly require that the boy is obligated to get the girl or take her home or spend money to entertain her. Through rendezvous of this sort many young persons actually are "dating" even though they are not "going together" or dating in the usual meaning of the term.

A large proportion of adolescents, particularly girls, would like to start dating before their parents wish them to do so. In a study published in 1924, G. F. Smith found that girls reported they were first interested in "going out with boys" sometime in the age range from ten to eighteen years; the median age was fourteen years. However, it was not until the typical girl reached sixteen [1] that she received permission from her parents to keep company with boys. In a survey conducted in 1950, W. M. Smith (1952) found that about 50 per cent of college men reported that they had started to date at age fourteen or younger; 5 per cent said they had started to date before they were twelve years old. Over 50 per cent of the girls had started to date at age fourteen or younger; and 7 per cent had started before they were twelve years old. From ordinary observation one gets the impression that more pre–teen-agers are dating now than was true even ten or fifteen years ago.

In a study of girls in several Iowa communities, Burchinal (1959b) found that the age at first dating was about fourteen for girls who married before they finished high school and closer to fourteen-and-a-half or fifteen for girls who did not marry before finishing high school.

DATING BEHAVIOR

Some adolescents (and some postadolescents) have one date after another which involve no more than companionable talk and going to a place of entertainment, to the beach, or the like; but such behavior is exceptional. Eventually (or immediately) the daters begin to woo and court one another. Boys usually take the initiative in this, as custom requires.

The writer knows of no study which reports exactly what occurs when young or middle teen-agers date. (Many adolescents would probably feel that this was their own business.) In a study at the college level,

---

[1] For studies dealing with dating and courtship, see G. F. Smith (1924), Punke (1944), Christensen (1952), Crist (1953), and W. M. Smith (1952).

Ehrmann (1952) classified behavior on dates on a scale of love-making ranging from no physical contact or only holding hands to sexual intercourse. Less than 5 per cent of the men and women who described their conduct while on dates confined themselves to hand-holding. About 31 per cent of the men and about 60 per cent of the women went on to the next stage, but no further, described as kissing and hugging or the boy fondling the girl's breasts with his hands outside her clothing, or both. At the time of the study 39 per cent of the men and 9 per cent of the women were going to the final stage of actually having intercourse. (The difference is accounted for in part by the fact that a large proportion of the boys' dates were with girls who were not attending college.) [2]

Most dates eventually involve necking or petting or spooning. This has been common among young people for many generations. In a study in 1924, Smith found that 92 per cent of the girls she questioned had petted or spooned. They reported beginning the practice at a median age of between sixteen and seventeen years. A contemporary study would probably show that the practice begins at an earlier average age today. Petting appears to have increased considerably in recent years, according to a review of findings by Reevy (1961). He reports that almost all of today's youth is experiencing it. Reevy (p. 58) also states that "more elaborate techniques of petting have been and are being generated by present-day adolescents."

GOING STEADY

One custom that is considerably more frequent among adolescents now than some years ago is "going steady." Going steady may, for some adolescents, be almost as serious as being engaged, while for others it means little more than a temporary understanding that the boy or girl will not date anyone else as long as the period of going steady lasts. The period may range from only a few days to several months or longer. In a study by Burchinal (1959b), referred to earlier, girls who married before completing high school had their first "steady" at an average age of 14.9, and those in a control group (girls who did not marry while in high school) at an average age of 15.47. The average number of steadies in the group that married was about three and in the control group less than two.

[2] Findings regarding the incidence of premarital sex relationships are reviewed in Chapter 4.

DIFFERENCES IN ATTITUDES OF BOYS
AND GIRLS REGARDING DATING
AND POPULARITY

On a number of visits to high school classes in which students were discussing boy-girl relationships the author noted that more girls than boys spoke up in favor of the practice of going steady and seemed to feel more deeply about it. The reasons girls gave for wanting to go steady seemed to indicate a desire for "security." There are many indications that dating, going steady, and other forms of boy-girl relationship have a deeper personal meaning for girls than for boys.

From many studies and discussions it appears that girls view dating, going steady, courtship, and prospective marriage in a more purposeful and mature way than boys. They give relatively more emphasis than boys to the prospect of having a happy home and family, while boys give relatively more emphasis to sex relationships (see, *e.g.,* Lantagne, 1958). On the other hand, girls apparently depend more heavily than boys on their popularity with the opposite sex as a means of bolstering their own self-regard. The importance girls attach to being popular with men appears in a study by Jameson (1941). He found that "unhappy states of mind" due to inability to be popular with men was reported by a large proportion of college girls and by a larger proportion of girls who were juniors (66.4 per cent) than by members of the same class when they were freshmen (29.5 per cent).

In a discussion of the conflicts relating to sex that girls encounter in college, Binger (1961) speaks of the dilemmas the girls face due to their need to be approved by men. If they are stand-offish on a date the boys may not try to see them again, but if they take the first step in accepting the boy's advances "the boy takes over, unless he himself is very timid. He tries to impose his standards and rationalizations on her." Binger speaks of the relationship between the sexes at the college age as being in an experimental phase, motivated partly by idealism, partly by a spirit of rebellion against parents or others in authority, partly by a desire young people have to find out about themselves, partly by loneliness, partly by a new conventionality and a wish not to miss anything "but above all, for the girls, by the feeling of approbation which the steady attention of one boy gives them" (p. 43).

Binger emphasizes the need for giving young people an opportunity to express their perplexities, to cultivate their gift for understanding themselves and others and to find some ethical and aesthetic pattern for their lives. According to Binger, many students "are distressed by the formless chaos that surrounds them" (p. 44).

COURTSHIP IDEALS

In naming the qualities they regard as most desirable in a prospective mate, adolescents usually emphasize character traits more than intelligence or physical appearance. Good looks receive a higher rating by boys as desirable in a girl than by girls as something desirable in a boy Girls give more emphasis than boys to such traits as considerateness, dependability, ambition, and similarity of backgrounds. Boys give relatively more emphasis than girls to youthfulness, attractiveness, and popularity.[3]

Love Between the Sexes, Falling in Love, Being in Love

During adolescence most young persons in our culture become ripe for the experience of "falling in love." Many of them, before reaching adolescence, show romantic attachments to persons of the opposite sex. At the elementary school age and even before, many youngsters are tenderly devoted to a boy or girl friend and go through acts of courtship, such as bearing gifts or walking together to and from school. About two-fifths of the men and women who took part in a study by Hamilton (1929) reported that they had had their first "love affairs" between the ages of six and eleven. Such attachments may have a deep emotional intensity, but they are not likely to have the erotic intensity of ventures in love that occur during adolescence and later years.

In our language we have a large array of terms to describe the amorous endeavors of adolescence and preadolescence. Some of these terms have a condescending touch, as when we speak of "calf love" or "puppy love." Actually, such labels do not do justice to the young person. His passion, as far as he is concerned, is real, even though it may be short-lived and even though it may strike others as a bit awkward. Another

[3] For studies dealing with this subject, see Mather (1934) and Christensen (1947, 1952). Christensen reports traits boys and girls consider desirable and undesirable in young people with whom they have dates.

term is "infatuation," which suggests feelings that are at fever heat but not likely to last. Somewhat in the same class is the "crush," which suggests a violent romantic attachment that may or may not last.

More honored in everyday usage is the state of "falling in love" or "being in love." The experience of being in love seems to differ so much in different persons that it would be difficult to present a typical picture of what the experience involves. Even the same person will have different experiences as he or she falls in love now with one person and now with another.

FREQUENCY OF LOVING

In the usual course of events it seems rarely to happen that two adolescents meet and then love each other (and no one else before or after) with equal intensity and go on to live happily ever after. Matters do not usually progress with such comfort, equality, speed, and finality.

The average young person falls in love not once but several times during early and late adolescent years. In a study of 153 women aged fifteen to thirty-five years, judged to be normal, 109 of whom were single and 44 married, Landis, Landis and Bolles (1940), found that over a third reported having been in love three to five times, and almost half said they had had six or more love affairs. These reports do not reveal how intense, absorbing, or prolonged each episode may have been. But they do suggest that it is unlikely that the first love will be lasting.

While the evidence indicates that the average girl (there is not a comparable amount of evidence concerning boys) is likely to be intensely attracted by several males before the end of the teens, it appears also that the information she gives regarding her love life will be influenced by the phrasing of the questions asked.

In a questionnaire study of college girls, Ellis (1949a, 1949b) made a distinction between infatuation and falling in love. The median girl in his study reported that she first became infatuated with a male when she was twelve years old and first fell in love when she was seventeen years old. Twenty-two per cent of the girls reported that they had been in love three or more times between their twelfth and eighteenth years. The largest percentage of infatuations occurred during the eleventh and twelfth years, while the peak percentage of love attachments, according to the girls, occurred during the seventeenth and eighteenth years.

The median girl among those who responded to the questionnaire re-

ported that she became infatuated five different times between the twelfth
and eighteenth years but fell in love only once during this period. Infatuations were described as briefer than love attachments, and recovery from
infatuation (as indicated, for example, by becoming infatuated with
someone else) was considerably quicker. However, Ellis points out that
the girls tended to interpret their past experiences as "infatuations" and
their present or recent experiences as "being in love."

According to Ellis' findings, it is not exceptional for girls to be infatuated with two males at the same time. At the time of his study a large
percentage of the girls (who at the time of filling out the questionnaire
had a median age of twenty years) reported that they had been infatuated
with two men at the same time at least once during their lives, and 25 per
cent reported that they had been in love at least once in their lives with
two men at the same time. In commenting on these figures, Ellis points
out that they are "probably minimal," and he adds that since these girls
were still relatively young, many of them presumably would become
infatuated or fall in love several more times as they grew older. Ellis
states that "the monogamic ideal of a girl's falling in love and remaining
in love with one man during her entire lifetime is being scouted by the
vast majority" of the women who took part in his study.

Falling in love several times apparently is a normal thing (in the sense
of being typical or characteristic of the average). Perhaps from a developmental point of view it is also a good thing. Young persons can learn
from the experience, grow in understanding of themselves and of the
opposite sex, and cultivate their ability to relate themselves to others.
However, findings regarding the value of falling in love several times are
meager and indecisive.[4]

EMOTIONAL ELEMENTS OF "BEING IN LOVE"

To "be in love" or to "fall in love" may have strikingly different meanings in the lives of different persons, and different meanings also at differ-

[4] As noted earlier, Burchinal (1959b) found that girls who married in their
teens had more "steadies" and said they were in love with more of their "steadies"
than girls who were unmarried when they left high school. This finding, combined
with findings from other studies that show more early than later marriages end in
divorce, suggests that a person who has been in love several times is not better prepared to establish a stable marriage relationship. But there are many factors other
than frequency of having been in love that influence the permanence or breakdown
of early marriages.

ent times within the life of one person. There are differences in the intensity of feeling, in the depth of involvement, and in the strength and tenacity of purpose. It is conceivable that one person who is often in love has a great capacity for loving, while another might fall in love often because he or she has relatively little capacity for becoming deeply attached to any one person. Again, one person might run from one love affair to another as though desperately seeking to stifle a doubt or resolve a difficulty in his own life, while another person, with more inner poise and self-assurance, might not love so hectically or so often.

The experience of being in love is a compound of many impulses and many emotions. It may include heights of ecstasy and depths of pain. To varying degrees, varying with the circumstances, it can involve a play of all the human emotions, ranging from overwhelming tenderness to bitter anger, from joy to oppressive fears and deep sorrow. Every resource in man's emotional make-up is brought into play when two persons on a high tide of feeling are carried into a relationship which, when consummated, leads to emotional intimacy, mating, and the begetting and rearing of children in an atmosphere of love.

While the mature person who is in love will have an open or hidden desire for sexual contact with the one he loves, the erotic element varies greatly in different love relationships. A boy may be attracted to a girl, or a girl to a boy, seeking to be near one another, speaking admiring words, desiring to gaze upon each other and to share tender confessions, without having any clear sexual intention. In a study cited above, Hamilton (1929) found grounds for believing that the first experience of amorous attachment in a child is not necessarily combined with sex. In a review of literature dealing with this topic, Grant (1948) cites the work of Moll (translated edition, 1924), Bühler (1931), and several other investigators, who indicate that there can be amorous attraction between children without any obvious erotic desire.

In contrast to these observations there is the view that love consists primarily of a refinement of the sexual impulse. One version of this is the view that a person "in love" is one in whom sexual desire is inhibited so that instead of appearing directly, in its physical form, it is expressed through tenderness and other sentiments. Another version is that the person in love actually is suffering from sexual frustration, which expresses itself through an idealization of the loved object and endows the loved one with great glamour and desirability.

In commenting on this issue, Grant notes that emotional aspects of sexual behavior have been persistently neglected in scientific psychological studies. Accordingly, while it is easy to cite opinions, it is difficult to come to any precise conclusion.

At any rate, the person who is in love has many experiences and impulses that cannot be explained by sexual desire alone. The very fact that love is centered on this person rather than another indicates that many complex factors other than sex alone are involved. If sex were the only consideration, practically anyone of the opposite sex, with the usual biological equipment, would do. But love does not work that way among persons who are in love, or who are seeking someone to love.

One thing that is conspicuous in the behavior of the person who is in love is that he or she desires, almost desperately, to be with the loved person rather than with any other member of the opposite sex. The lovers seek one another's company as something of supreme value.

The one who loves has feelings of tenderness, an impulse to cherish, comfort, and protect, a desire to do things that will bring joy to the other person. In these sentiments there is a large amount of other-centeredness. They are what distinguish what is known as "true love" from an infatuation consisting primarily of physical appetite. These sentiments give the state of being in love an aspect of unselfishness. The gratification that comes through the exercise of tenderness comes through the medium of having taken thought of someone else. It involves a disposition to *give* emotionally, rather than simply to take.

The expression of these tender sentiments takes many forms, ranging from bounties involving considerable sacrifice to thoughtful little acts or gifts. The value of these expressions does not depend on the magnitude of what is done or given but in the feelings they convey. Frequently they are most eloquent if offered with seeming inadvertence, or if they compress within a small token a large amount of meaning. The girl maneuvers in various ways, for example, to make things easier for the boy who does not have much spending money. The boy has perhaps overheard or observed that the girl is fond of a certain flower or that she has lost her umbrella, and then when he brings a flower or an umbrella as a gift it becomes a special expression of thoughtfulness.

Unless the sentiments of the persons who are in love are mixed with a desire to inflict hurt or a need to overcome feelings of inadequacy, the one who happens to be brighter, or more handsome, or wealthier, or of more prominent family background, or socially more popular will not play up such matters in a manner that might, by unspoken comparison, belittle the other person.

Many other currents of feeling may come into play when an adolescent is in love. There will be a vast amount of joy when love is reciprocated. It is overwhelmingly gratifying to feel warmly accepted by the one who counts for most. In discussing this phase of the experience of love, Wenkart (1949) states that the adolescent's desire to have someone acknowledge, accept, and appreciate his uniqueness as a separate self prepares the way for his first love. When an adolescent finds one of the opposite sex who thus accepts him, he is "confronted with an inner wealth which he never knew he had." This feeling gives the first love experience "the element of revelation."

Unfortunately, persons who are in love may be so overwhelmed by their feelings that they become blind to faults or conditions that in time might create unhappiness. The person who is in love may overlook bad habits, weaknesses of character, symptoms of emotional immaturity, that to a disinterested onlooker do not bode well for the future. Similarly overlooked may be differences in background, age, station in life, ideals, religious affiliation, and other social and cultural conditions which, in time, may require very difficult and perhaps insurmountable practical and psychological adjustments.

HEALTHY AND UNHEALTHY ASPECTS OF BEING IN LOVE

Loving and remaining in love is one of life's greatest fulfillments. But being in love may have roots in attitudes that are not particularly healthy. The difference between what might be regarded as "healthy" and "unhealthy" love is not easy to define, but by being somewhat arbitrary it is possible, at least in broad outline, to note some distinguishing features.

An unhealthy condition prevails when the love a person professes is not a spontaneous giving and sharing of affection. For example, there is an unhealthy element if a person with deep-seated attitudes of inferiority seeks blindly to combat his lack of self-regard by going through the motions of being in love and of getting someone to fall in love with him. Such a person is using the one he loves as a means of dealing with his own maladjustment. If being in love and being loved would free him from his affliction, it probably would be a good thing. But there is no guarantee that such a cure will occur.

There is an unhealthy attitude if a person with a long-standing grievance uses one love affair after another as a means of making conquests that inflict hurt on other persons.

An unhealthy element also exists if a person who is dependent to a childish degree uses the maneuver of being in love and having others fall in love with him in order to continue his dependency, and to avoid the labor of growing up, or, on the other hand, seeks to dominate another as his parents perhaps once dominated him. Similarly, there is an unhealthy element if a male goes from one love affair to another, driven by a continuing doubt concerning his manliness, and if a woman does the same because she is driven by doubts about her ability to fulfill a feminine role.

In these examples it is not assumed that a love relationship must be completely pure and untouched by any human frailty in order to be called "healthy." Such perfection is beyond human possibility. But we do assume that something unhealthy is afoot when a person seeks, through the glamour and excitement of being in love, a kind of relief from problems within himself which he will have to resolve before being able wholeheartedly to love another person, or to love himself.

We might ask, what are some of the characteristics of "healthy" love between the sexes? Several writers have expressed views on this subject. Macmurray (1937) mentions, for example, the kind of love in which there is *mutual self-discovery*. Horney (1946) speaks of "friendship at its best" as being the essence of love. Love, according to Horney, affords an opportunity for sharing—sharing responsibility, joy, and important undertakings, and it requires emotional sincerity. According to Horney, love also involves accepting the loved one as he or she is, which is not possible unless one can accept oneself. This acceptance is not achieved simply by being blind to the other person's shortcomings, nor by unwillingness to look at weaknesses that might be remedied. Where there is such acceptance, the person who loves is better able to see the loved one as he really is, without having to endow him with a glamour he does not possess or to delude himself into seeing in this loved person an ideal of perfection he has never been able to realize within himself.

On the subject of the role of a realistic acceptance of self and others in a love relationship there is a difference of emphasis between the writers mentioned above and a theory about love set forth in 1944 by Reik. Reik maintained that when a person falls in love it means that he has become emotionally attached to a person on whom he has projected his "ego ideal," an idealized image of himself that he cannot in reality fulfill within himself. Horney and others emphasize, on the contrary, the concept that healthy love involves self-fulfillment and a striving to grow rather than an endeavor to escape into an illusion. The healthy adolescent, according to this position, does not depend on love for another as a substitute or consolation for shortcomings in his own development.

In a discussion of "love in healthy people," Maslow (1953) mentions qualities he regards as characteristic of the love of persons who are "actualizing" themselves. The discussion does not center on young adolescents, and it deals with a degree of self-acceptance that is probably beyond the reach of many, yet it is instructive in describing a kind of maturity some persons probably become capable of achieving in late adolescence.

In addition to noting features commonly regarded as associated with loving, such as tenderness, a desire for nearness, feelings of generosity, a desire to share secrets, and the like, Maslow names other features that, in some ways, are more rugged and profound. According to him, persons who love one another in a healthy way can allow themselves to be honest; they can "let their hair down"; they can drop their defenses; and they do not continually have to conceal or impress or pretend. They can accept variations in their moods and in the intensity of their feelings. And they can allow themselves considerable freedom in the roles they play without being bound by stereotyped notions of what a supposedly manly man or womanly woman should be and do. They can be active or passive in lovemaking, take aggressive or unaggressive roles, accept the role of being the weaker or the stronger. Maslow mentions, among other characteristics, that those who love in a healthy way accept one another's individuality. They tend to be less concerned with appearances or with obvious economic or educational shortcomings than with attributes belonging to the character and the inner life.

Maslow states that in observing several "relatively healthy" young college men and women he has noted that the more mature they become, the less attracted they are by such characteristics as "handsome," "good-looking," "good dancer," "nice breasts," "physically strong," "tall," "good necker," and the more they speak of compatibility, goodness, decency, companionship, considerateness. Maslow expresses the belief that the tendency to give greater weight to character than to physical appearance is probably characteristic of increasing *health* rather than increasing *age*.

Adolescence and Marriage

During the past few decades, the age of first marriage has declined. Glick and Landau (1950) cite census data indicating that the estimated median age of the first marriage for men at the time of the 1890 census was 26.1 years; it dropped to 24.3 years in 1940, and to 22.7 years in 1949. For women the corresponding figures were 22 years in 1890; 21.6 years in 1940, and 20.3 years in 1949.

Many adolescents marry soon after high school and many marry while they are still in high school. Marriages among young people who are still in college are far more common than some generations ago. Estimates in 1957 by the Bureau of Census indicate that 2.4 per cent of boys and 14.6 per cent of girls between the ages of 14 and 19 were married. It has been estimated that 22 per cent of students in state universities and 12 per cent of those in private colleges are married (Burchinal, 1959b).

At the high school age, marriages by girls far outnumber marriages by boys. In one sampling the girls outnumbered boys seven to one (Cavan and Beiling, 1958). In this sampling, 38.9 per cent of the boys and 65.8 per cent of the girls dropped out of school at the time of marriage.

When adolescents marry they are expected to accept each other for better or for worse. They probably hope to live happily ever afterward. Many marriages are permanent, and many report they are happy in their marriages. But some are not happy. Many who hoped to find happiness later conclude they would be happier if the marriage had never taken place.

In recent years, according to estimates published by the Bureau of the Census (1955), the number of divorces in the United States has been about a fourth of the total number of marriages. The divorce rate is higher among those who marry before the age of twenty. The divorce rate also varies considerably in different sections of the country.

Apart from divorces, there are many incompatible persons who are separated (see, Waller, 1951, and Davis, 1952). And among those who are living together, there are many who do not regard their marriages as being particularly happy. As might be expected, marriage, like many other human institutions, has its tensions, and the married relationship, like any human relationship, has its stresses and strains.

CHARACTERISTICS OF THOSE WHO MARRY EARLY

Girls who married before completing high school were compared with a control group of girls who remained unmarried while in high school in a study by Burchinal (1959b). These girls (sixty in each group) had been students in eleven high schools in nine Iowa communities. Members of the married group were matched as closely as possible with those in the control group with respect to school attended, grade in school, urban or rural residence, age, level of father's occupation, parents' educational level, religious affiliation, etc.

Data concerning whether or not the married girls were pregnant prior to marriage were obtainable in the case of fifty-eight girls. Of these, twenty-three, or about 40 per cent, were premaritally pregnant. As noted in an earlier context, the ones who married dated at an earlier average age, had their first "steady" at an earlier average age, had a larger number of steadies and said they had been in love with a larger number of their steadies.

Marriages prior to completion of high school occurred more often among girls of lower socioeconomic backgrounds; and the highest grade in school completed by their mothers was lower than in the unmarried group.

Among the reasons that have been advanced to explain early marriage are dissatisfaction with home life, a broken home, rebellion against parents, a need for affection that was not gratified at home, loneliness, unfair discipline, improper exercise of authority by the father or the mother. However, Burchinal's study did not support the view that strained parent-adolescent relationships play a significant role in influencing girls to marry before they have completed high school. Almost half of the girls reported that although their folks had been "against their marriages," and "tried to talk them out of it," or "wanted them to wait," most of their folks had accepted the marriage once it was consummated. Burchinal points out that if strained parent-adolescent relationships actually did exist prior to marriage such relationships apparently, from the girls' points of view, improved rapidly soon after they were married.

As measured by a personality test, similarities between the married and unmarried girls were more conspicuous than differences. Moreover, almost an equal number of girls came from homes in which both parents were living together (80 per cent of the married and 82.2 per cent of the unmarried). Burchinal points out that if the theory of strained parent-adolescent relationships is correct, it would require more rigorous methods of investigation than the tests he applied.[5]

[5] He used the Edwards Personal Preference Schedule as a measure of a number of personality variables. He refers to preliminary results in a study by Moss and Gingles (1958) in which it was found that married girls were less well adjusted, as measured by the Emotionality Scale of the Minnesota Personality Scale.

High School Policies Regarding Student Marriages

In a study which included a number of high schools in Illinois, Cavan and Beiling (1958) observed that many high schools did not have a policy for dealing with married students and when policies did exist they varied greatly from school to school. In the Cavan and Beiling survey it was found that marriages had occurred in sixty of the eighty-four student bodies during the 1956–1957 academic year. In these schools 1.4 per cent of the sophomore girls had married, 1.8 per cent of the juniors, and 4.1 per cent of the seniors (the corresponding percentages for boys were 0.1, 2.0, and 0.7). Although these percentages are small, they would represent a very large aggregate of young persons if projected in terms of the total youth population. According to current studies it is more likely that the number is on the increase than on the wane.

Usually high school marriages were frowned upon. In a group of eighty-four schools there were about one-third in which students who marry were made to leave school even though the law dic. not require it. Only a small number of schools viewed teen-age marriages as presenting a situation in which the school had the responsibility to help the student make a success both of marriage and schooling. Cavan and Beiling describe one school in which the dean of girls tried to help the students. If a girl in the school became pregnant she was encouraged to remain in school during the first few months of her pregnancy and then allowed to continue her studies at home.

An effort was especially made to help girls who were thinking of getting married as a means of resolving a personal problem (such as difficulty at home or a desire to escape loneliness) to find ways of resolving their problems rather than, in a sense, escaping from them by taking refuge in marriage. This effort also involved an endeavor to bring parents into the situation.

In view of the great load of responsibilities high schools already carry, it is likely that many will resist the idea that one function of the high school should be to dissuade young people from marrying or to help those students who do marry to make a go of it while still continuing their education. However, marriages at the high school level often involve a poignant human situation. Such marriages cannot be brushed aside as though they meant little more than foolish behavior on the part of a few willful persons. The decision to marry or the necessity for marriage because of pregnancy springs from the total social context in which young people live. To that extent they represent a social responsibility and in many communities there probably is no institution that can deal with this problem more effectively than thoughtful and humane members of a high school faculty.

Actually, if high schools provided students with help in understanding themselves and in dealing with their personal problems—as many persons think high schools should—they would automatically provide help and counsel for those who are seeking through marriage to escape from their personal problems. In other words, the schools would not be taking on a new responsibility for dealing with young people who are thinking of getting married, but they would minister to these people in the process of meeting their responsibility for the emotional welfare of the total student body.[6]

[6] From a humanitarian point of view it should be remembered that helping young persons who are planning a marriage that might end in failure does not simply mean helping these young persons only; it means helping thousands of babies who each year are the innocent victims of teen-age divorce.

Chapter 14

Group
Affinities
and Cleavages

An adolescent's knowledge of his family's social status is a significant element in his awareness of his own identity. When youngsters reach the eighth grade their understanding of the meanings of symbols of social class is similar to that of adults, according to a study by Stendler (1949a). Stendler used a set of pictures showing the homes of the wealthy and the working class, a private summer camp, a public wading pool, persons in various occupations, such as a doctor and a filling station attendant. She found that children in the eighth grade not only recognized these symbols but were also beginning to note that there might be a difference between a person's place in society and his income.

Influence of Socioeconomic Status on Adolescent Behavior

A young person's socioeconomic status has a bearing on his social contacts, plans for the future, and outlook on life. Investigators have differed,

288]

however, in their judgment of the extent to which a child's socioeconomic background influences his mode of life and future prospects.

FIXED AND SHIFTING
CLASS MEMBERSHIP

One of the problems in dealing with levels of socioeconomic status, from the "lower" through the "upper," is that of adequately defining and describing what these levels mean not only from the point of view of obvious sociological characteristics (which are relatively easy to ascertain [1]) but from the point of view of historical antecedents and the total community context in which a given "class" is located. Until quite recently, many adolescents were the first generation of American-born children of foreign-born parents ("foreigners") living in a community-within-a-community of "Americans." Although such "foreigners" might not have a high social standing in the community as a whole they had a prestige-system of their own and, to them, being a big frog in their small pond may have been more important than being a big frog in the "pond" of the community at large. The ratings which foreign "outsiders" receive in the larger community from one generation to the next change considerably when the offspring are no longer classed as "foreigners" but as "Americans."

The total social setting in which persons of a given social class or socioeconomic level are located is also important. In many communities, families who stand high and low in the class structure live within close distance, send their children to the same schools, and attend the same churches. The star of the high school football team may be a "lower-class boy" and in the high school play an "upper-class" hero may make love to a "lower-class" heroine. On the other hand, in a large city a certain lower-class group may inhabit a large geographical area, set off from other areas. Children in such a group may seldom venture outside their area or seldom mingle with persons of another class.

One study dealing with the impact of social class membership on young people of high school age was conducted in a midwestern community (called "Elmtown") by Hollingshead (1949). Fifty per cent of the young people in this study identified themselves as "Americans"; the

---

[1] Hollingshead (1949) discusses various methods of determining various strata within the social structure of a community.

other half reported that their families came originally from one of several European countries (Germany, Ireland, Norway, Poland). These persons were known as Elmtown's foreign element. Factors that influenced the social structure of this community included not only the economic and educational status of the parents of the adolescents, but also national background, religious background, and residence in town or outside the town limits.

Many differences in social behavior and social affiliation were observed in this particular community. Members of different social groups tended to remain apart at student dances and parties. Youngsters from the "upper" groups had more than their proportionate share of representatives on the student council, yet "lower"-class boys and girls, while resenting the dominance of "upper" students in school affairs, voted them into office.

In the high school there were many cliques, and it was observed that the adolescent's ideas concerning their own importance was influenced by membership in these cliques. From 49 to 70 per cent of clique ties were with persons belonging to the same social class. Dating occurred largely according to class membership. Sixty-one per cent of all daters belonged to the same social class, 35 per cent belonged to an adjacent class, and only 4 per cent were separated by one intervening class. No dates occurred between youngsters from the highest social class represented in the school and those in the lowest class.

In the Elmtown community there were several church groups with varying prestige according to denomination and national origin. (The same situation might not prevail today in view of recent church mergers that have combined groups of varying national origins into larger synods.)

An investigation by Sargent (1953) indicates that communities may differ markedly from one another in the extent to which social class cleavages prevail. The people in a commercial and industrial California community studied by Sargent did not seem to be very class-conscious, and they were not aware of strong class distinctions in their community. The data Sargent obtained from a direct study of the people supported the opinions expressed by individuals, namely, that they were not as class-conscious as many of the other communities that have been investigated.

Findings such as this, coupled with observations a person can make in communities he happens to know, suggest that while in some communities "social class" lines determine social affiliation there are other communities in which there is much intermingling of the various elements of the population.

DIFFERENCES BETWEEN SOCIAL GROUPS
IN CHILD-REARING PRACTICES

On the basis of studies conducted some decades ago, some investigators laid great emphasis on differences between members of various socioeconomic groups in methods of child-rearing, standards of conduct, and goals for success in school and in adult life which parents impressed upon their children. A great deal was written about teachers who were trying to impose "middle-class standards on reluctant and uncomprehending "lower-class" students. Recent studies cast doubt on some of the conclusions regarding differences between standards in the middle and lower classes in communities consisting of various intermingling social groups. In a great many respects, the groups are more similar than earlier studies indicated.

It is difficult to give a precise evaluation of conflicting findings in this area. There is reason to believe, however, that *time* has a leveling effect. In recent years all segments of society have been exposed to similar ideas about child-rearing and models of behavior through the mass communication media. With the passage of time, likewise, as we have noted, cleavages due to national origins become weakened. Persons who might earlier have remained apart in separate communities are now being thrown together on the same jobs and in the same housing projects. Moreover, the power of collective bargaining by labor unions has produced shifts in economic status (college professors today, for example, have relatively far less economic advantage, if any, over skilled labor groups than they did some decades ago).

Several earlier studies have reported that typical "middle"-class families place more emphasis on cleanliness than the typical lower-class family, and that they were more rigid in "habit-training," more intolerant of aggressiveness, more prudish about sex, more inclined to restrain children from roaming freely about in the community. However, studies by Sears and his associates (1957), and by Maccoby and Gibbs (1954) and Markley (1958) do not confirm the view that lower-class or working-class parents are, on the whole, more lenient and more tolerant in dealing with these aspects of their children's behavior.

Findings regarding attitudes toward school and schooling in various socioeconomic groups have also varied. In "Elmtown," according to Hollingshead (1949), parents in the "lower" classes did not emphasize the importance of school as much as parents in the upper classes. Children in the lower classes were under less pressure, according to Hollingshead, to do their best in school. In the study by Sears and his associates (1957) it did not appear that middle-class parents put more pressure on their children for achievement in the elementary school than did working-class parents. However, there was one difference which is especially significant for the psychology of adolescence: educated middle-class parents took it more for granted that their children would go to college.

SOCIOECONOMIC STATUS AND MENTAL ABILITY

Many studies have shown that there are differences in the average scores that persons of different social classes earn on tests of mental ability, with the upper groups showing higher and the lower groups showing lower average scores (Goodenough, 1928; Terman, 1921; Havighurst and Breese, 1947; Eels, 1951). There are probably many overlapping reasons for these differences.

One explanation is that those who are endowed with above-average intelligence will gravitate toward positions that are regarded as higher in socioeconomic status, while those who are not so well endowed will tend to find their way into or remain in the "lower" classes. There is strong evidence that mental abilities such as are required by "higher" occupations are influenced to a substantial degree by genetic factors, and a person's occupation is one of the important factors that determine his socioeconomic level. Obviously, however, a genetic theory alone does not explain the matter, for differences in attitudes toward intellectual work, differences in opportunities for schooling, and differences in the cultural environment also are important factors.

SOCIOECONOMIC STATUS IN RELATION TO MORAL ATTITUDES OF PERSONALITY DEVELOPMENT

The bearing socioeconomic circumstances might have on an adolescent's habits, moral concepts, and personality traits raises interesting questions. With respect to morals, there is considerable evidence in studies conducted in the 1930's and 1940's that children from homes in the lower socioeconomic brackets were more authoritarian in their attitudes. They recommended punishments as a remedy for wrongdoing more frequently than children of higher socioeconomic status do (Harrower, 1934; Dolger and Ginandes, 1946). It was also found that children of lower socioeconomic status viewed things more from the standpoint of *right* and *wrong* (cheating is bad because it is morally wrong) while children of higher socioeconomic levels tended to judge acts in terms of their practical outcomes (cheating is bad because the outcome is not useful—one cannot learn if one does not find the answer for oneself).

Children in some lower socioeconomic groups were less permissive and more condemning in their attitudes toward various forms of behavior, such as whispering in class, talking back to parents, or stealing another child's marbles, while the youngsters in the "higher" groups were more inclined to understand and to try to find ways other than punishment for solving problems of the one who wants to whisper and the one who wants to steal (Dolger and Ginandes, 1946). The findings in many studies show a curious anomaly. Persons in lower socioeconomic groups have been found to be least tolerant of some of the practices which are presumably most prevalent in the lower groups.

Other differences between lower and higher socioeconomic groups have been noted. Kinsey (1948) found that those in the less-educated groups (which overlap the lower socioeconomic groups to a degree) had more premarital heterosexual "outlets" than those in the higher educational brackets. Whatever may be the reason, young people in the middle class tend to defer their desire for the gratification of heterosexual desires (or did, at least, when Kinsey made his study) more than do young people in some of the lower socioeconomic groups.

Middle-class adolescents show more of a tendency than those of lower status to accept "deferred gratification" as a way of life (see, *e.g.,* Schneider and Lysgaard, 1953, and Remmers *et al.,* 1952). The concept of "deferred gratification" covers a variety of ways in which a person, at a given time in his life, chooses to postpone present satisfactions so that he may, at some future time, achieve a goal he regards as more important than the gratification of the moment. A person who defers gratification will, for example, give up an opportunity to take a low-paying job that would make him economically independent so that he might continue his education and gain a better-paying job in the future. Again, he may save his money for future use instead of having dates or buying a secondhand car. A deferring of sexual gratification is also part of this pattern.

To "defer" gratification a young person must have a conviction that it is worthwhile, a measure of confidence and hope that his investment in the future will pay off. This would require a considerable amount of self-confidence in a lower-class young person, for he would have to count on attaining goals which members of his own social group have not been able to attain.[2]

VARYING PRESSURES AND OPPORTUNITIES

Some writers have suggested that the social class system in America may set up such strong barriers to social interaction as actually to prevent the majority of children of the working classes or of the slums from learning any culture but that of their own group. Klineberg (1953), in reviewing findings and opinions bearing upon this issue, takes the position, however, that to speak of "mutually exclusive cultures" caused by barriers between social classes is an exaggeration. Klineberg points out that even where differences between groups prevail there is also a considerable amount of overlapping in the child-rearing practices of members of different class groups. In addition, there is a good deal of "contact of cultures" between class groups through the influence of mass media—newspapers, radio, and television—and also by virtue of the fact that lower-class children are usually taught by middle-class teachers.

Although the psychological consequences of being born in a certain social group are not determined simply by sociological conditions, it is obvious that the odds are heavily stacked against adolescents who have been reared at the lowest socioeconomic levels, in virtual isolation from other segments of society. The obstacles are especially formidable for those who face not only the disadvantages of low socio-economic status but might also bear the added burden of racial discrimination.[3]

Persons whose lives have been molded by such an environment have little to encourage them to hope or strive for what are viewed as "the better things of life" as defined by middle-class standards. At the lowest levels, family life is usually not conducive to healthy psychological development. The illegitimacy rate is high. In many homes there is no father

[2] The role of delayed gratification is discussed in a later chapter on vocational development. As Dr. Nicholas points out, persons who seem, in the eyes of others, to postpone momentary satisfactions to gain a larger, more distant goal, may not see themselves as making a sacrifice.

[3] A large proportion of Negro families are consigned to the lowest of the lower-class levels (Hill, 1957). Factors operating in a lower-class delinquency area as described by Miller (1958) are discussed in the next chapter.

to offer financial support and to help in the child's upbringing. In other homes there may be an uncertain succession of fathers. There is no tradition of encouraging young people to aspire to continue their schooling beyond the elementary grades. The educational level is low. There may be no models and incentives for learning which are provided in an average, well-situated home and which contribute greatly to a growing person's mental growth, his intellectual curiosity, his speech, his vocabulary, his idea that it is important to read and to use his mind. Unemployment is higher than in the more privileged segments of society. There is little to encourage the young person's vocational ambitions or plans.

Crowding and physical discomforts are added to the ordinary frustrations of daily living, and such frustrations, added to a frequently high incidence of corporal punishment and an awareness of being regarded as inferior by more fortunate members of society, nourish aggressiveness, hostility, and antisocial attitudes.

It is more difficult for a youngster reared under such conditions than for one reared in more favorable circumstances to acquire healthy self-esteem, to view his family or himself with pride, to entertain lively hopes for the future.

When individuals feel caught in a web of misfortune they may be driven to adopt attitudes and standards which perpetuate their condition and which make them, in a sense, even more firmly caught. This may occur in two ways. First, they may use the actual misfortunes of their lives to rationalize their discouragement. They do this when they adopt a "what's-the-use" attitude, convincing themselves that it is futile to struggle, hopeless even to try to better their lot. They do this also when they use the hardships from which they have suffered not simply to justify anything they might have to do in self-defense but to justify antisocial behavior.

A second means whereby individuals in underprivileged circumstances perpetuate their condition is through adapting attitudes and standards to preserve their status, as though it were a freely chosen way of life (Miller, 1958).

INDIVIDUAL DIFFERENCES IN RESPONSE TO SOCIAL CLASS PRESSURES

Within groups in which families are very similar in socioeconomic status there will be great differences of emotional climate of families wthin the same socioeconomic group. This has been noted, for example, in a study of adolescents by Zucker (1943a, 1943b).

An interesting account of the way individuals within a socioeconomic group differ in behavior is given by Kinsey *et al.* (1948). While, as noted above, more heterosexual premarital "outlets" were reported among those of lower educational status, it was observed that boys who ultimately, as adults, became members of a higher socioeconomic group frequently, while they were young, did not adopt the sex habits of the group *they were moving out of,* but adopted, instead, the sex habits of the group *toward which they were moving.* Kinsey and his associates point out that it is as though the bigger the gap between the boy's parental class and the class toward which he aims, the stricter he is in bringing his sex conduct into conformity with the pattern of the group into which he is moving. They consider it "remarkable" to find these patterns established at an early age, when the boys probably are not consciously aware of the sexual habits of the members of the social group to which they will eventually belong.

Kinsey's findings regarding variations in behavior within a given group are matched by other corresponding observations. Although delinquency is common in certain lower-class neighborhoods, many of the boys do not become delinquent. Although overt aggressiveness is more frequent in the lower than in middle socioeconomic groups, many lower-group members are not particularly aggressive. Some persons in a lower-class community remain there; others move out. But the question as to why some persons move out of adverse socioeconomic conditions, while others remain in them, and others still, who once were better situated, migrate into them, is largely untold.[4]

A similar question arises in socioeconomically more heterogeneous communities, where there are no large slum districts but where the "middle"- and "lower"-class families are neighbors, and send their children to the same schools. In such neighborhoods one can sometimes see a

---

[4] In a conversation about this, my colleague, Dr. Sloan Wayland, offered several opinions to account for our lack of knowledge of these individual variations. One reason seems to be that sociologists have, on the whole, paid more attention to the "dominant" rather than the "deviant" mode of behavior in a given culture. To understand what is deviant it is necessary to study individuals, and not just groups, to examine dynamic forces in a culture as distinguished from its static structure. A thorough inquiry into the behavior of deviates (such as adolescents who are in a delinquency area but do not become delinquents, and others with a nondelinquency background who do become delinquents) would require a more penetrating inquiry into environmental and genetic factors.

"psychological migration" of adolescents (while still living at home) similar, in some respects, to the physical migrations in and out of lower-class communities in a larger city. With many persons among whom to choose, one youngster from a middle-class home aligns himself with "lower-class" youngsters—adopts their interests, their ungrammatical speech, their sexual mores, their values and conduct. Another adolescent aligns himself with the "middle class"; he avoids gangs; he is interested in schoolwork rather than in being a hot-rodder; he aims at college, not at leaving school and getting a job. Moreover, in the same community one can see "working-class" adolescents who do not fall in with the customs of their group, but strive for the status and achievement of a higher "class." What makes the difference?

The stock answer is that the parents are responsible for such "migrations." But this answer is too pat. It does not—without further enlightenment—explain the "downwardly mobile" son of a father who himself had left the ranks of the "lower class," or the fact that one adolescent in the same family is heading "down" and another "up" in the class structure.

The conditions that dispose one individual person to seek the society of a "lower class" or that impel others out of the "lower" levels have not been explored at all adequately, but there are some obvious social and economic circumstances that play an important role. The odds are heavily loaded against particular persons who are victims of racial or religious or other forms of discrimination. Yet even in the groups who suffer from the most severe prejudice there are great variations: some better their lot, some remain stationary, some deteriorate.

"Upward-" and "Downward-Mobile" Adolescents

An interesting description of characteristics of "upward" and "downward" mobile and "stable" adolescent boys has been offered in a study by Douvan and Adelson (1958). The middle teen-age boys in the study were asked what kind of work they would prefer to do as adults. The boys who sought a position generally regarded as having more social prestige than that occupied by their fathers were classed as upwardly mobile and the boys who mentioned a position generally regarded as having a "lower" place in the social scale than that occupied by their fathers were classed as downwardly mobile.

According to the data obtained from the adolescents, those whose aspirations were "upward" were lively and energetic, while those whose aspirations were "downward" were more apathetic. For example, the "upward" ones belonged to more organized groups, expressed an interest in more leisure-time activities, and did more diversified and more demanding kinds of reading.

The "upward" ones were more concerned about getting into "interesting" work and less concerned about "security." In describing their plans for the future they more often named goals they could realize only in a distant future, while the downward ones more often mentioned goals within the reach of persons of teen-age years.

The "upward," as compared with the "downward" group, less often mentioned peer acceptance as a source of self-esteem. They expressed more reliance on their own ideas as contrasted with seeking advice from others. They emphasized more "internalized" rules and controls, while the "downward" group showed a tendency to externalize rules and standards, and to express rebellion against these external pressures. The "upward" group showed more self-acceptance and self-assurance, and more realistic self-criticism.

A far-larger proportion of the "downward" than the "upward" aspiring boys reported that they had received corporal punishment from their parents, and, in response to projective tests, the "downward" group more often portrayed parents as harsh and suspicious. The "upwards" mentioned more sharing of leisure-time activity with their parents.

When asked to choose an adult ideal the "upward" ones more often chose a model outside the family or described a composite of characteristics of several people. The downward more often said there was no adult they cared to be like, but when they did name an adult ideal many chose models from within their families, particularly grandfathers and uncles.

The "downward mobile" boys in the Douvan and Adelson study showed several characteristics corresponding to the "focal concerns" of lower-class boys noted in a review in Chapter 15 of a study by Miller (1958). They showed dependence on the opinions of others as a source of self-esteem; a greater dependence on external authority and controls (while covertly rebelling against external authority); considerable concern about attainment of immediate rather than future goals.

The findings in the Douvan and Adelson study of boys with "upward" and "downward" aspirations offer a potential answer—or at least one approach to finding an answer or two—to questions raised earlier in this section, even though a more exacting, longer-term study would be required to answer these questions conclusively.

As noted, the boys were young (aged fourteen to sixteen); they were *asserting* aspirations without having had time to demonstrate how solid these aspirations might be. Moreover, the information they gave about their past relations with their families represents their claims or perceptions rather than data obtained from a firsthand study of interactions between them and their parents.

If we accept at face value the information they supplied, it appears that the youngster who is heading upward has somehow acquired more autonomy than the "downward" boy, more confidence in his capacity to manage his own affairs, a more accepting and more realistic perception of himself and his parents, and a more hopeful view of the future.

It is reasonable to expect that such a boy will have more freedom to *choose,* to *venture.*[5] A person with such freedom is not bound by self-constricting attitudes such as those Douvan and Adelson mention.

An adolescent who is not bound by self-constricting attitudes has, in a psychological sense, removed himself from the confines of his class culture, even though physically and sociologically he still resides in, and is a member of, his class group.

While the account by Douvan and Adelson of "upward" and "downward" mobile boys throws light on the psychological factors associated with class affiliation, it leaves many questions unanswered. It is more convincing in indicating how the boys describe what they aspire to be than in telling why one youngster has perceptions and acquires attitudes toward himself and others that impel him "upward" while another has perceptions and attitudes that impel him to "stay put" or to head "downward."

SIMILARITIES AND DISCREPANCIES BETWEEN SOCIOLOGICAL AND PSYCHOLOGICAL INFLUENCES

It is good to be reminded of a line of thought that already has been suggested, namely, that what happens in the *psychological* dimension of a person's life may be quite different from what seems to be happening in the sociological dimension. A child may, for example, live in a home that is favored with wealth and high social position and meet with a good deal of rejection. A child may be one of many children in a sociologically infe-

---

[5] The author came upon the above studies of social class, and those cited in the chapter on anxiety, by different routes and with a different mental set. Yet he is struck by the points which similarly arise in a psychological inquiry into class structure and an inquiry into the "intrapsychic" aspects of anxiety, notably as presented by Kierkegaard.

rior home, yet feel that everyone shares and shares alike, while another child in an upper-class home may feel that one of his brothers or sisters is getting a much larger share of things or a larger share of love and attention than he.

Psychologically, the child in a relatively poor home, who shares equally with others, may be much better off than a child in a wealthier home who feels that he is being discriminated against and unfairly treated. Similarly, even if the portion of the child in a wealthy home is very large, it is likely to have a bitter taste if he feels abused.

The fact that the sociological and the psychological dimensions may be at variance sometimes comes out strikingly when persons of different backgrounds reveal intimate features of their lives in group discussions or in group therapy. The physical and cultural circumstances of life described by one person who happens to come from the most privileged home and another person who comes from an underprivileged home may be vastly different, yet it can happen that these two have more in common, psychologically, than any other two in a group of eight or ten or more. Both may carry with them into late adolescence or adult life the effects of feeling rejected, or the effects of never having been able to cope with an older or younger sibling.

When individuals enter into a relationship in which the usual symbols of status or prestige no longer count so much—when the trappings of wealth, home surroundings, family name, education, rank, and the like are for the moment set aside—it can soon be discovered that the most important elements of human existence are not arranged according to the boundary lines of social class or economic status. Fear in the rich child is as painful as fear in the life of the one who is poor. Rejection has as bitter a taste for the child who lives on the wrong side of the tracks as for the child who lives on the right side of the tracks. Anger and love, hope and despair, grief and joy, have the same poignancy in the house that is high on a hill as they have in a home that is deep in the slums.

Prejudice

Adolescents have had many experiences that influence their attitudes toward persons in various groups in the society in which they live. In the ordinary course of his development the adolescent is likely to acquire a stronger feeling of "belonging" to the group in which he has been reared than to other groups. He will feel a closer kinship with those who have the same background as he. When he thus feels more at home with members of a group which he regards as his own he is, to a degree, placing a distance between himself and persons from other groups. Simply by showing a preference he may at times act as though he were prejudiced against persons who are not members of his group even though he feels no active ill will toward them. A "prejudice" of this sort, if we may call it prejudice, can create hardship for persons who perceive that they are regarded as outsiders. But this kind of attitude, which makes a person feel closer to his own group than to other groups, is not likely to be severe or to have a generally disturbing effect unless something more is added. Prejudice is a more active and serious matter when it includes a strong element of distaste, dislike, hostility, or fear.

There is prejudice when a person has a feeling against others because they belong to a certain group and not because of any direct personal reason for objecting to this or that individual in the group. A person is prejudiced when he has attitudes leading him to *prejudge* individuals by virtue of the group to which they belong.

When a full-blown prejudice exists, it usually includes at least three psychological elements: There is an emotional element such as the feeling of hostility or distaste, which we have just noted. The emotional element may range from cold indifference to bitter and violent hate. Secondly, a prejudice usually includes certain intellectual (or rationalized pseudo-intellectual) elements in the form of beliefs or views concerning those against whom the prejudice is directed. These views may be in the nature of stereotyped notions to the effect that persons in a certain group are quick-tempered or immoral or dirty or shiftless or sharp in their practices, and the like. Thirdly, connected with prejudice there usually is a notion as to the line of conduct one should follow in dealing with those against whom there is a prejudice, and this line of conduct may range from active persecution to efforts to avoid, ignore, or exclude them.[6]

Many adolescents have prejudices that they acquired at an early age. Ammons (1950) found evidence of prejudice as early as age four. It has been noted in some studies that by the age of eleven or twelve many individuals seem to have strongly stabilized attitudes toward various ethnic groups. In studies by Zeligs (1938, 1948) and Zeligs and Hendrickson (1933, 1934) of the attitudes of children at various age levels it was found that the order of preference shown by eleven-year-old chil-

[6] For discussions of prejudice, its psychological components, and reviews of studies of prejudice, see Allport (1950b), Morse and Allport (1952), Harding *et al.* (1954), Hirsch (1955), and Simpson *et al.* (1958).

dren was about the same as the order of preference shown by adults. This does not mean, of courses, that no shifts in preference will take place.

Prejudiced attitudes are acquired and thrive among persons who have no direct personal excuse for having attitudes that might lead members of one group to view members of another with dislike, envy, fear, suspicion, or hostility. Radke-Yarrow and Miller (1949) studied children's and adolescents' attitudes toward Negroes and Jews in a small midwestern town which contained no Negroes and only one childless Jewish family. The youngsters wrote answers in response to the questions: What do you think Americans are like? What do you think Jews (Negroes) are like? [7] At most grade levels, the youngsters made more favorable statements about "Americans" than about the other two groups. Derogatory statements about the minority groups were relatively more frequent at the high school than at the grade school level. At the upper high school level a larger percentage of those who made adverse statements about one of the two minority groups also made adverse statements about the other.

CLEAVAGES AND PREJUDICES RELATED TO ETHNIC ORIGINS

The social cleavages that prevail among adults are more likely to appear in the social behavior of adolescents than in the behavior of younger children. At the elementary level there is likely to be freer association between children of different ethnic and religious groups who happen to reside in the same community and to attend the same schools than will be true at the high school level. A study by Criswell (1939) illustrates this.[8] The children in Criswell's study were in public schools with varying percentages of Negroes and whites and, within the white group, there were several different nationalities. Criswell found that Negro and white children chose each other as seat-mates considerably more in the first three grades of the elementary school than in later grades, although even in the earliest grades white children showed a greater preference for whites. At Grade V the two groups rather consistently drew apart from each other.

[7] The method here used was perhaps prejudicial, for the questions might imply for some children that Jews and Negroes are not "Americans."

[8] It is possible that findings in a similar study conducted today might differ in some respects and that findings in a study conducted some years hence would differ even more.

In expressing their preferences, many children in the earliest grades not only chose children of a different race when naming persons of the same sex but also in naming preferred persons of the opposite sex. By Grade VIII choices of the opposite sex had almost completely ceased to cross racial lines.

Criswell concluded that attitudes related to race cleavage are initiated by the community and are assimilated by the children as they grow older. These attitudes appeared to be assimilated more fully by the white children than by the Negro children in her study, since whites tended to confine their choices to whites to a greater extent than Negroes tended to confine their choices to Negroes. Koch (1944) also found that white children showed more of a tendency than Negro children toward bias favorable to their own group.

SPECIFIC AND GENERALIZED PREJUDICES

A prejudice may be specific as, for example, if the Danes in a certain community take a dim view of the Swedes, but have no unfavorable attitude toward any other group in the world at large. It is likely, however, according to several investigations, that when there is prejudice it will have wider ramifications. Many of those who are strongly prejudiced against one minority group are also prejudiced against other minority groups (see, *e.g.*, Murphy and Likert, 1938, and Adorno *et al.*, 1950).

One study (Hartley, 1946) of attitudes of "social distance" used an alphabetical list of ethnic groups which included the names of three groups that actually did not exist. There was a high correlation between attitudes of social distance expressed toward existing ethnic groups and toward the three fictitious groups. Apparently, if a person has the kind of emotional make-up that disposes him to feel hostile or out of sympathy with a certain segment of the human race, such hostility is likely to be directed against other groups as well.

PREJUDICE AND GUILT

It is hard to conceive that persons with a moderate degree of insight can nourish a prejudice without feeling guilty about it. Prejudice goes counter to practically every precept in the canons of morality. Prejudice is notably a violation of moral principles when it is entertained by persons who openly proclaim their adherence to moral convictions. One ironic aspect of human nature is that some persons who are very prejudiced also profess to be religious.[9] In such persons, prejudice against fellow men exists side by side with a professed belief in the brotherhood of man. Another ironic touch is that many persons who have intense and active [10] prejudices fervently profess the political (and moral) doctrine that all men are created free and equal.

PREJUDICE AS DISPLACED HOSTILITY

Prejudice is often a form of displaced hostility, such as occurs when a person is angered by something or someone and centers his hostility on someone or something else. When such displacement occurs, the prejudiced person is taking out his anger on people who serve as scapegoats. Conditions that increase the frustrations of persons in a majority group may intensify their unfavorable attitudes toward a scapegoat minority group (see, *e.g.,* Cowan *et al.,* 1958).

Prejudice involving displacement of hostility is especially intense and irrational when a person resents others because they represent something he despises in himself. Ichheiser (1947) has applied the label "mote-beam mechanism" to the situation in which a person, by condemning others, draws his attention away from his own shortcomings. This happens, for example, when a student who is aggressively "on the make," but unwilling to admit it to himself, expresses bitter hostility toward

---

[9] The relationship between prejudice and training in religion has been studied by Allport (1946) who notes that tolerance may grow from certain types of religious training, but not from mere exposure to religion in the home or at church. Wilson (1960) found that persons who scored high on a scale covering the more external, institutional, or utilitarian aspects of religious practice and belief expressed more anti-Semitism than those who scored low (1960).

[10] The author uses the modifier "intense and active" here in contradistinction to what might be regarded as prejudice that is relatively mild and not actively expressed. Some such distinction, although not at all precise, must be made in speaking of prejudice because a thorough inquiry would probably show that practically everyone is prejudiced against someone or something to a greater or lesser degree, whether or not the individual recognizes it or is willing to admit it. Prejudice is so widespread, so deeply ingrained in the culture, that it is hard to conceive that anyone could escape some taint of it. When we deplore other people's prejudices we are like the proverbial dweller in a glass house, throwing stones. But prejudice exists with varying degrees of virulence. Although no person can discuss it without being guilty of a certain amount of self-righteousness, it is justifiable to say that some have houses that are glassier and some throw stones harder than others.

members of a minority group on the ground that they are overly ambitious "operators" and "apple-polishers."

TRAITS ASSOCIATED WITH PREJUDICE

A person with marked prejudices is likely to have had unfortunate childhood experiences and to show other unfavorable attitudes toward himself and others. Adorno *et al.* (1950) notes that many persons with intense prejudice have a history of rigid painful discipline. A person who has been treated harshly at home is likely to become hostile, yet he is also likely to be afraid of openly showing his hostility toward his parents. Such hostility may then be displaced to minority groups.

Also according to Adorno *et al.,* persons who express strong prejudices are more likely to be more concerned with problems of status and with an external set of values than those who are less markedly prejudiced.

Other studies have likewise indicated that persons who are anxious, or who harbor concealed hostility, or who are emotionally insecure, or have an exaggerated need to live up to conventional standards are more likely to be prejudiced than those who do not labor under these difficulties (see, *e.g.,* Gough *et al.,* 1950; Adorno *et al.,* 1950; Harris *et al.,* 1950; Ammons, 1950; and Frenkel-Brunswik, 1951).

PREJUDICE AGAINST OTHERS AS RELATED TO ATTITUDES TOWARD SELF

The foregoing observations are in keeping with the principle that there is likely to be an interweaving of the attitudes a person harbors within himself and the attitudes he holds toward others. When a person is sharply prejudiced against a certain group, he is suffering from a kind of alienation in his social relationships, but the one who is thus alienated from others is probably also, to a large degree, alienated from himself.

The fact that a person's attitudes toward others are linked to attitudes toward self is indicated in a study by Trent (1953). Working with Negro children, Trent applied tests to measure the children's attitudes toward themselves and others. The Negro children who were most self-accepting according to his tests also showed more positive attitudes toward others. Persons who were most rejecting in their attitudes toward white people also tended to be rejecting in their attitudes toward Negro children and toward themselves.

Trent observed that more of the Negro children who showed a low degree of acceptance of themselves when responding to a self-description inventory also said they wished they were white than did children who showed a higher degree of self-acceptance. In its broadest terms, the principle here is that a person who hates himself will probably also hate others; and if a person hates others, as revealed by bitter prejudice against this or that group, we can surmise that he probably hates himself.

This principle that attitudes toward self and attitudes toward others are interwoven has implications for what might be done to reduce or relieve prejudice. There have been many studies (see a review by Harding *et al.*, 1954) touching on the extent to which prejudice can be combated by giving members of various groups an opportunity to know one another better through personal contact or by studying the history and background and contributions various groups have made. It appears that an educational program, under some circumstances and with some persons, will produce some change in attitude.

However, the studies have not uniformly shown that an effort to "educate" a person out of his prejudices will be successful. We can understand why this should be true when we consider the fact that attitudes toward the others are likely to be related to attitudes toward self. An educational program often deals largely with the *objective* situation—as though it were enough for the prejudiced person to know the facts about *others*, to be told that his stereotyped notions are wrong, and so forth. Actually, such an appeal may have some effect. But as long as education is centered upon the *other* person or the *other* group it may not even begin to touch the *subjective* situation within the prejudiced person himself that impels him to feel hostile toward others. To be really effective, therefore, an educational program for combating prejudice should stress not simply understanding of other persons but should also stress understanding of oneself.[11]

When education to counteract prejudice is entirely other-centered it is, to some extent, duplicating the process by which prejudice may have arisen in the first place, namely, as a means of diverting attention from self by centering attention on others. If a prejudiced person is trying to escape the impact of an unrecognized feeling of how bad he is by thinking how bad others are, he is not likely to be cured simply by having someone tell him how good the others are, still less by having someone tell

[11] Implications of this point of view are discussed by Noble (1956).

him how bad he is. Such an appeal may simply make him feel more defensive or belligerent or guilty without touching on the central problem, that is, his need to gain a deeper and more compassionate insight into his own attitudes.

The need for self-examination in dealing with prejudice becomes doubly important when we consider that prejudice breeds more prejudice. The victims of prejudice are themselves likely to become prejudiced. It is impossible for members of a group that is the target of prejudice to avoid resenting those who are prejudiced against them. Moreover, members of one minority group against which there is a prejudice may have strong prejudices against other minority groups. And, by an unfortunate psychological twist, members of a group against which there is a prejudice may become prejudiced against segments of their own group. Thus, in the United States, some second-generation Danes are anti-Danish, some Irish are anti-Irish, some Jews are anti-Semitic, and some Negroes are anti-Negro.

Where there is a vicious circle of discrimination and recrimination it is not likely that general preachments about the duties of good citizenship will change things much. It would be more effective if these persons could come to grips with their own attitudes and get help in gaining insight into their own motivations.

Chapter 15

The Delinquent Adolescent

Almost all adolescent boys, and a large proportion of adolescent girls, have at some time committed offenses which, by strict legal interpretation, are delinquent acts. However, only a small proportion of delinquent acts are officially recorded. Records kept by social work agencies in a large city revealed that almost one-third of the children who were committing acts for which they could be charged as delinquent were entirely unknown to the police (Kvaraceus, 1954). This was also noted in a study in which two groups of problem boys were observed closely over a period of years (Murphy, Shirley, and Witmer, 1946). One group received guidance and counseling from a professional staff. Through their contacts with the problem boys the staff members learned of several thousand violations of law committed by the boys; but the community took official legal action in only a small number of these violations.

Moreover, when young persons commit offenses that actually receive attention the police may or may not take action that will result in a court record. If the young person comes from a "good" middle-class home, parents, teachers, clergymen, and others are likely to intercede for him. A lower-class youngster from a broken home is less likely to be protected in this way.

In the narrowest legal sense, a "delinquent" is a young person (usually eighteen years or younger) who has committed an offense which, if committed by an adult, would be punishable. But more is needed before an adolescent officially is a delinquent. He must be caught or apprehended; have an accuser—the one who has been offended, or the police or some other person or persons; and he must appear in court.

Incidence of Delinquency

Only a small proportion of adolescents belong to "the delinquent" group, as officially defined. However, even though the group is small proportionately, it is distressingly large in actual numbers. Moreover, in recent years the rate of juvenile delinquency has increased much more rapidly than the rate of population increase. At present, about 2 per cent of children in the age range from seven to seventeen or eighteen years are brought into court each year. Boy delinquents outnumber girl about five to one. If present trends continue, according to Kvaraceus (1958), it is likely that one boy in five will have a delinquency record by the time he reaches draft age.

The fact that many young persons violate the law without being discovered, or, if discovered, without being prosecuted, means that statistics regarding the actual incidence of delinquent conduct are very incomplete. Those who officially fall in "the delinquent" category represent only a fraction of those who would be labeled as delinquent if all law violations were known and officially recorded. This means that findings regarding the characteristics of delinquents, or the "causes" of delinquency, are based mainly on a limited sampling of persons who commit delinquent acts. Even so, it is instructive to examine what these findings reveal.

Characteristics of Officially Recorded Delinquents

As compared with "normal" or nondelinquent children (or as compared with siblings in the same family who do not become delinquent), the delinquents, as a group, make an unfavorable showing on almost every measure that has been applied.[1]

[1] For studies of the characteristics of delinquents, see Healy and Bronner (1936), Kvaraceus (1945, 1954), Wattenberg (1947), Merrill (1947), and Glueck and Glueck (1950).

As a group, delinquents compared with nondelinquents have lower average intelligence. More of them have a record of difficulty in early childhood (such as difficulty in toilet training, severe illnesses, or accidents). As children, more of them were impulsive, lacking in self-control, and extremely restless. More of them have a history of being less submissive and more socially assertive, more suspicious, defiant, hostile, and destructive. More of them have a history of being adventurous, extroverted, and stubborn. Many of them also are more suggestible than nondelinquents.

In the sphere of activities that are or come close to delinquent conduct, the delinquents far surpass the nondelinquents in the number who have a record of stealing rides or truck-hopping, keeping late hours, smoking at an early age, sneaking into theatres, destroying property, running away from home, gambling, setting fires. They have much more frequently sought places outside the home for play and recreation (such as street corners and distant neighborhoods). They have more often sought their companions among gangs, delinquents, and persons older than themselves.

Although these and other group differences between delinquents and nondelinquents are impressive, they tell very little about the individual delinquent or how he came to be a delinquent. Practically every description of delinquents as a group (with the exception of the fact that they are known to have committed delinquent acts) has a *but* connected with it. Delinquents are below average in intelligence, but many have good minds and the majority of below-average intelligence children do not officially become delinquent. Most delinquents have a history of difficulties in early childhood, but many do not; and many children who have a difficult childhood do not become delinquent. Even in traits which show conspicuous differences, such as aggressiveness and impulsiveness, delinquents and nondelinquents as groups are more alike than unlike.

Another limitation in most of the general information about delinquents is that this information has been obtained *after* the youngsters are in trouble. As we have noted in an earlier chapter, information about the earlier life history of a person who is presently in trouble is likely to be colored. The young person himself, his parents, teachers, and others are likely to single out happenings which seem to explain, excuse, or confirm the fact that the youngster was heading for trouble; similar happenings in an inquiry into the history of a nondelinquent may be unnoticed or be explained away.

A history that is reconstructed in retrospect cannot adequately reveal the experiences in the past which had a critical or crucial bearing on an individual's present condition. Similarly, an inventory of the delinquent's earlier unfavorable characteristics does not reveal which of these, if any, had an important influence on his delinquent tendencies. Neither does such information reveal how this or that personality or character trait came into being. For example, from a later case history which records that a particular delinquent had a more violent temper than his non-delinquent neighbors or siblings we cannot tell whether from the time of birth he had a predisposition toward reacting violently or whether he began life as a serene child and then was goaded into violence by a harsh environment. Further, we cannot retrace the steps through which this particular disposition had an increasingly important role in the young-ster's life as he grew older, "feeding itself," so to speak, when the child's anger provoked anger in others, and their response reinforced and ag-gravated his tendency to retaliate.

To get authentic information about the genesis of delinquent behavior and how it differs from the genesis of nondelinquent behavior it is neces-sary to study a group of children from the time of birth (with as much information as possible about their parents' genetic background, person-ality traits, attitudes and values) and then, at a later time, when some have become delinquent and others have not, to examine the earlier developmental history for clues that might explain or predict what later transpired. The examination of the record of earlier development (up to the time of the first court appearance) should preferably be made by one who does not know who the delinquents and nondelinquents are. If a research person knows in advance who is a delinquent and who is not he can easily apply the wisdom of hindsight to find all sorts of reasons to "explain" why one child became a serious and persistent law-breaker, while another became, on the whole, a law-abiding person.

Environmental, Genetic, and Existential Factors

Delinquent conduct is obviously influenced by the environment and is a response to it. An adolescent would not become a thief if the environment did not provide something for him to steal, and strong enticements to do so. However, the explanation as to why one adolescent steals and another does not is less obvious. Environmental pressures and social disapproval vary in different segments of society; but even in subcultures, where attitudes toward misconduct are rather tolerant, youngsters differ in the seriousness of the crimes they commit. And many avoid a delinquent career. Moreover, many youngsters who do not live in a "delinquency subculture" do become delinquent.

The question as to what predisposes one person, and not another, to juvenile crime is least clear when we consider youngsters who go "bad" even though they have what seems to be a favorable environment.

At present most writers place their emphasis on environmental causes of delinquency, with little or no mention of heredity. This contrasts with some earlier speculations to the effect that criminal tendencies are inherited—the criminal springs from "bad seed." Actually, no delinquent has a gene—or set of genes—that produced in him a tendency to steal a horse or a car.

But an adequate approach to understanding the problem of delinquency (or any other human condition) requires an appreciation of the fact that human beings are not just putty in the hands of the environment. The infant, the child, the older youngster, are not just oysters, drifting with the tides in Chesapeake Bay. Their way of life is shaped by their interaction with the environment.

GANG DELINQUENCY AS A CULTURAL PHENOMENON

An impressive account of cultural forces that are at work in a lower-class community which is a "generating milieu of gang delinquency" has been offered by Miller (1958).[2] According to Miller, the "gang" delinquency of adolescent street-corner groups in lower-class communities differs from the "delinquent subculture" which has arisen in areas where there is a conflict between middle-class and lower-class cultures and where the lower-class members deliberately violate middle-class norms. The "gang-delinquency" culture he speaks of (p. 5) is a lower-class community with "a long-established, distinctively patterned tradition with an integrity of its own." According to him, the traditions, attitudes and values of this culture are "designed to support and maintain the basic features of the lower-class way of life" (p. 19).

In the lower-class culture which Miller describes, one "focal concern" is about "trouble" as related to law-abiding or nonlaw-abiding behavior.

[2] Miller is speaking of what he calls the "hard-core" lower-class group, which, in his estimate, comprises about 15 per cent of the population or "about twenty-five million." According to Miller (p. 6), systematic research would probably reveal "at least four to six major subtypes of lower-class culture."

In certain situations, getting into trouble is recognized as a source of prestige.

In this culture, according to Miller, there is also an emphasis on "toughness." "The model for the 'tough guy'—hard, fearless, undemonstrative, skilled in physical combat—is represented by the movie gangster of the thirties, the 'private eye' and the movie cowboy."

Another quality that is emphasized is "smartness"—the ability to outsmart, outthink, outfox others and to avoid being outwitted, "taken" or duped oneself.

Yet another feature of this culture is the search for excitement, a thrill, through such means as using alcohol, gambling, playing the numbers.

According to Miller, another focal concern is with *fate*, fortune or luck. Many lower-class individuals feel that their lives are subject to a set of forces over which they have relatively little control. This is sometimes associated with the view that it is futile to work toward a goal—if luck is with you, things come your way; if luck is against you, it doesn't pay to try.

In this culture, as described by Miller, there is a discrepancy between overt and covert attitudes toward autonomy and authority. While expressing resentment against external authority, many lower-class people, do not desire to be autonomous. Some even seek environments in which they are subject to a great amount of external control—such as the armed forces or correctional institutions.

Persons in this culture have a great desire to "belong." They also attach great importance to status, mainly the status of seeming to be an adult. The status that is sought is not that of a responsible adult but what can be found through external symbols, such as having a car, ready cash, freedom to drink and smoke. According to Miller, action designed to gain status is more concerned with status itself than with questions as to whether it is achieved by legal or illegal, moral or immoral means.

Miller points out that there are large variations in the ways in which individuals respond to these standards. The one who adopts them does not seek to better his lot but to perpetuate it; he does not seek to be free but to be governed by external authority; he does not seek to attain self-direction, freedom of action, responsibility for himself.

Miller does not answer the question as to what coerces or impels some individuals to get into such a society while others find something quite different. But from his account, it is easy to see that a person who has once moved into it, or has been born into it, would have difficulty in getting out.

DELINQUENCY AS A PERSONAL PROBLEM

In contrast to the delinquency which is generated by a given subculture, much delinquency is an outgrowth of individual predicaments which might arise in any culture. Delinquency may be a form of problem-solving behavior, a symptom of emotional maladjustment, or a response to cumulative frustrations.

DELINQUENCY AS A FORM OF PROBLEM SOLVING

Seen from the delinquent's point of view, delinquent acts are a means of meeting a need or solving a problem. The need may range from a momentary desire—such as a desire to take an apple from a fruit stand—through a need to "fit in with his group" to a persisting, irresistible urge to act out hostile impulses. The underlying motive may be to gain favor in the eyes of a gang, to show off, or to take revenge. The means of expressing the underlying motive may be quite incidental: it may be through stealing or vandalism or a physical attack on another person or sex misconduct or placing a nail-studded board on a highway. Similar delinquent acts may spring from different motives, and similar motives may lead to differing forms of delinquent behavior. For this reason, it usually is less significant to ask what a delinquent did than to inquire why he did it.

Through his acts the delinquent usually imposes a problem or hardship on others. If the delinquent is caught in the act it creates problems for him. If he is punished, his problem—such as a desire to inflict harm on others—is likely to become more acute, and he may then use the punishment he has received as a further excuse for taking revenge.

DELINQUENCY AND EMOTIONAL MALADJUSTMENT

Many delinquents are emotionally disturbed or have personality disorders (Glueck and Glueck, 1940) which would make life a burden to them and to others even if they did not violate the law. However, some delinquents who are emotionally disturbed may be regarded as more "healthy" than some other emotionally disturbed children. They are, so to speak, "doing something" about their distress (even though it brings distress to others). They are openly expressing their aggressive impulses. In this respect they have more of a vital spark, they are more venturesome than disturbed youngsters who are entirely withdrawn and eventually are classed as mentally ill. Many delinquents seem to work out their problems sufficiently well to settle down as law-abiding citizens in later years.

Many youngsters who are emotionally disturbed are not delinquent, and, according to some writers, a youngster may be delinquent without being emotionally disturbed. Miller (Kvaraceus, Miller *et al.,* 1959), states that the middle-class offender is more likely to be an emotionally disturbed person than the lower-class offender. Many young people in lower-class groups commit acts which are delinquent from a legal point of view (such as truanting and stealing) but which are not condemned by the lower-class group to which they belong. When his social group tolerates or condones delinquent actions, the young person has less reason for feeling anxious or guilty than when these actions are condemned. In a middle-class group, where the standards are more rigorous and where a youngster faces severe disapproval for acts which are not condemned in a lower-class group, misconduct represents a more severe defiance of the social norm and therefore is more likely to involve emotional turmoil.

DELINQUENCY AS A RESPONSE TO CUMULATIVE FRUSTRATION

Delinquent acts frequently are aggressive acts springing from frustrations. All children, however, meet innumerable frustrations, and most manage to cope with frustrations without officially becoming delinquents. Therefore we face a puzzling question as to why some youngsters respond to frustration by becoming delinquent and some do not.

From an early age, children differ greatly in their tolerance of frustration (such as a delay in feeding or having their movements restrained) and in their tendency to accept it passively or to cry out or resist. Parents who happen to have one adolescent who reacts aggressively to frustration by open rebellion, and another who displays little overt aggressiveness, will often report that the difference appeared early in childhood, but this does not solve the riddle as to what was responsible for the difference.

Whatever a youngster's tolerance for frustration might be, it is likely that his aggressiveness will be affected by the severity of his frustrations. Many delinquents not only live in an environment that is frustrating (overcrowded, uncomfortable, retaliative, filled with reminders of their inferior status, etc.), but also have a long history of severe frustration, notably at school.

Frustrations at school that lead to aggressive behavior often have a "snowballing" effect: the aggressive youngster is disapproved, punished, belittled, and such experiences add to his frustrations and his impulse to respond aggressively.

Delinquents who are below average in intelligence, especially in the kind of verbal intelligence that is important for academic success, are especially a target of animosity in the school. The youngster who is backward in his school subjects is waging a losing battle. He is reminded by others, and is aware himself, of his failures. His self-esteem, which may or may not have been low at the beginning, is constantly under assault. When punished by being kept after school hours in a "detention room" he feels resentful. He is also thrown in with peers who are being punished for the same reason. Now the youngster is caught in a tragic chain of circumstances. As time passes, his resentment mounts. According to Kvaraceus (1958), a delinquent's attitude toward school is commonly "charged with hate and hostility." Moreover, he and his fellow failures share their resentments. When he and peers like himself show their resentments at school they are, in effect, making a counterattack against assaults that have been heaped on them as a consequence of their own shortcomings. In so doing they incur the further displeasure of their teachers.

These youngsters incur not only the wrath of their teachers but also the disfavor of their more respectable classmates. They have no feeling of belonging. In this inhospitable atmosphere, they not only feel ostracized but ostracize themselves. In several studies it has been noted that delinquents take little part in extracurricular school activities. One reason for this probably is that they feel unwelcome. Another reason may be that resentments generated in the regular work of the school are directed against teachers who are in charge of extracurricular activities. This happens, for example, when a youngster with a fine voice quits the glee club at a time when his resentment against school is reaching a boiling point.

Public Response to Delinquents

Delinquent acts inflict innumerable hardships upon those against whom they are directed—anger, fear, grief, loss of property, and loss of life. When a person meets such hardship *directly*—as when juveniles have entered his home and stolen his things—he feels outraged, angry, and he also has an uneasy feeling, a feeling that his home has been violated and is not a safe place. If he did not feel angry he would be less than human. Likewise, a driver whose fenders have been wrinkled by a speeding juvenile is bound to feel anger mixed with fear. It is difficult also for a teacher not to feel annoyed, or even helplessly angry, when a delinquent pupil obviously hates the school and the teacher even if the teacher is just a convenient target for resentments aroused by other persons and conditions.

There is little in a delinquent's conduct, especially when it is aggressive, that appeals to sentiments of kindness and sympathy—unless the aggrieved person can look beyond the delinquent's manifest ill-will and sense his hidden hurts, anxiety, and desperation. However, it seems that attitudes toward delinquents are sometimes more severe among those who have not been victims of delinquent acts than among those who have. In the population at large, including parents, teachers, jurists, there are many persons who want delinquents to be treated harshly, while others who have actually suffered from acts of delinquents feel compassion for the delinquents.

According to Kvaraceus (1958), there is considerable evidence that the public, and even some professional workers, are less interested in attacking the problem of delinquency than in attacking the delinquent himself. Prescriptions for dealing with delinquency often seem to be designed more for revenge than for prevention or reform.

Moreover, the press and public opinion, when not attacking the delinquent himself, sometimes turn their spite against his parents and even against professional workers who are hired to help the offender. Kvaraceus calls attention to "a rash of anti-parent legislation enacted in many states" and " 'get tough with parents' attitudes visible in most communities." A punitive attitude toward the delinquent as a person, as distinguished from an effort to combat delinquency as a problem, appears also in "periodic waves of criticism leveled against 'soft' courts, 'muddle-headed psychiatrists,' and 'egg-head researchers' " who undertake to study and work with the non-conforming child (1958, p. 5).

Exploitation of Delinquents and Delinquency

Delinquents are often exploited by adults. Exploitation which is most obvious, and which arouses the greatest public indignation, occurs when vicious adults use teen-agers for criminal purposes, such as prostitution and other forms of traffic in sex, for the sale of dope, or as accomplices in burglary, pickpocketing, shoplifting and other forms of theft. However, it is not just criminals who exploit delinquents and delinquency. The exploiters may be respectable members of society who use delinquents to satisfy "psychic needs" (Kvaraceus, Miller et al., 1959).

DELINQUENTS AS SCAPEGOATS

The practice of "finding a scapegoat" is a common one in our society and apparently in most societies. The scapegoat is frequently an institutionalized target of suppressed hostility. According to Miller (Kvaraceus, Miller et al., 1959, p. 26), the delinquent "serves today to syphon off much of the aggression inevitable in any complex society such as our own." In the past, ethnic and racial groups have served as scapegoats, and they still serve this purpose (as we noted in our discussion of prejudice). However, according to Miller, it is no longer fashionable in certain groups to display hostility toward ethnic and religious groups. As these "traditional and established hostility targets have lost their utility" many people, according to Miller, have sought other more "respectable" scapegoat groups. Delinquents provide one such group. One can "really hate them with gratifying vengeance."

COMMERCIAL EXPLOITATION OF DELINQUENTS

The delinquent often is a "best-seller" in popular fiction, and the main attraction in movies. He is often depicted as a heartless, sex-crazy, rapacious, conscienceless, and monstrous character. His (or preferably her) lurid picture on the cover helps to sell paperbacks. Thus portrayed, he has great sales value as a means by which the viewer or reader can find a vicarious outlet for aggressive impulses and sexual desires. The delinquent who is portrayed enables the viewer or reader to be a voyeur without risk of being caught, to participate in all kinds of sordid adventures without staining his clothes or besmirching his public morals.

Miller states that the portrayal of the delinquent in the mass media is frequently an inaccurate and exaggerated fabrication. It is often as superficial and phoney as the portrayal of criminals in the old "crime doesn't pay" radio programs. But even though manufactured as commercial entertainment, this fabrication may also have sinister effects. According to Kvaraceus, Miller *et al.* (1959, p. 29), the "distorted picture begins to actualize itself" when youngsters begin to act out what they have seen. When parents, teachers, and other adults accept and perpetuate the fictional image of "the delinquent," they "actually help to bring into being the very situation which they so sanctimoniously condemn."

Temporary and Persisting Law-Violating Behavior

Many persons who were delinquent in their early teens go from bad to worse while many others cease their criminal behavior in their late teens and twenties. This appears in a follow-up study by Glueck and Glueck (1940) of 1,000 boy delinquents who had been brought into the Boston Juvenile court at an average age of thirteen and a half years. When 846 of these had reached an average age of twenty-nine,[3] records of the intervening years showed that as the years had gone by, there had been a steady decrease in the number who continued to be offenders. Almost 40 per cent had ceased to be criminals.

Moreover, among those who continued to commit crimes there was a drop in serious offenses. During the period intervening between the time of the first contact with the delinquents included in the study and a follow-up fifteen years later, the proportion of serious offenders, among those who still were committing crimes, dropped from 75.6 to 47.8 per cent. There was a marked decrease in arrests for "property crimes" (stealing). Although there was an increase in crimes against persons (assault and battery) crimes of this sort constituted a small proportion of causes for arrest (6.9 per cent) in the older group.

One of the sharpest increases occurred in arrests for drunkenness

[3] In the meantime, some had died and it was not possible to get complete information about some of the others.

(none at all in the earlier years, and 43 per cent of all arrests in the third five-year period of the follow-up study). This high incidence of arrests for drunkenness indicates that many persons who, when young, directed aggressive acts against others, commit self-destructive acts when they are older (an alcoholic often inflicts dangers and hardships on others, but he invariably also inflicts damage upon himself).

From the evidence in this follow-up study and in other research, Glueck and Glueck (p. 264) advance the theory that "the physical and mental changes that comprise the natural process of maturation offer the chief explanation of this improvement in conduct with the passing of the years." They note that through the process of maturation, "the development and integration of a person's physical and mental powers," a person who has reached adulthood has more capacity for "self-control, foresight, and planfulness"; he is better able to postpone immediate desires for later ones and to profit by experience. They note (p. 269) also that with the passage of time, "the human being loses some of his energy and aggressiveness; he tends to slow down and become less venturesome." [4]

Glueck and Glueck point out that there are marked individual differences in the pattern and rate of maturation. They found that, in later years, delinquents or former delinquents resemble each other more in their conduct when compared in terms of the number of years that have elapsed since the onset of their delinquency than when compared according to chronological age (*e.g.,* persons who became delinquent at twelve and persons whose delinquency began at age fifteen are more alike five years later, at the respective ages of seventeen and twenty, than when the conduct of the latter group at age seventeen is compared with the conduct of the former group at age seventeen). They found a "marked resemblance" in conduct "at a point equidistant from the time of onset of delinquency" among youngsters living in different communities and subjected to many and varied kinds and qualities of correctional treatment. This suggests that "delinquent tendencies, at least in young persons, are inclined to run a course that is not too readily modifiable by present methods of treatment" (p. 265).

[4] This theory that changes occur in the human organism, in the process of maturation, which are not due to learning or conditioning alone is in keeping with findings from many studies of children (several studies on this subject, including some of his own research, have been reviewed by the writer 1960). However, while naming maturation as an important factor in accounting for less rambunctious and impulsive behavior in young adults, the Gluecks also point out that there is need for more systematic study to examine in detail what is involved in the process of maturation as a person advances through the teens and into early adult years.

In this study, Glueck and Glueck (p. 265) also found that the delinquents who had reformed after fifteen years "were endowed with a better
heredity and enjoyed a more wholesome early environment" than those
who continued to commit crimes (p. 265). The process of maturation
was "apparently facilitated by the better equipment of certain offenders
and retarded or blocked by the poorer resources of others" (p. 265).

Although it is encouraging to find that many young offenders mend
their ways as they grow older, it is disturbing to note that over half of
them continue to commit crimes or to run afoul of the law.

Hostility Toward Those Who Desire to Help

One of the severest obstacles in efforts to help delinquents is their hostility.
Most of them have felt the lash of punishment, disapproval, and rejection.
Even when not physically punished they sense the anger directed against
them. The fact that their own conduct has provoked anger in others
does not lessen their anger.

Moreover, juvenile delinquents (as well as nondelinquents) often
face an unequal struggle with hostile adults. This happens, for example,
when spiteful policemen are "out to get" juveniles who may or may not
be offenders. The author has records of many instances in which adolescents who drive a car within the speed limit have, on suspicion, been
stopped by police, who then proceeded to empty the trunk and the glove
compartment, and then take off, leaving the contents strewn about.
Moreover, the writer frequently has heard police use foul and abusive
language with teen-agers. (If the teen-agers had responded in kind they
would be liable to arrest.)

Whatever his own role in provoking the hostility of others might be,
the juvenile delinquent is likely to encounter many situations where he
feels helpless rage. This rage is likely to be expressed one way or another.
It is often directed against persons who are eager to help the delinquent.
This means that teachers,[5] social workers, and others who try to befriend
a delinquent frequently get nothing but a sullen response. One of the
most demanding aspects of working with delinquents is to appreciate the
hurt and tragedy that often lie hidden beneath the sullen mask.

[5] One way to vent rage on teachers is to damage school property. According to
Kvaraceus (1954), as many as 265,000 school window panes have been broken by
vandals in a single year in New York City.

part six | Education and Vocation

Chapter 16

The Adolescent
at School

In this chapter we will first discuss the adolescent in high school, then give a brief account of college youth. This will be followed by a discussion of issues that are important from a personal and educational point of view at both the secondary and college levels.

High School Youth

The high school has—or might have—a powerful influence in shaping adolescents' concepts of what they are and what they might be. It impinges on most facets of young persons' lives in their transition from childhood to adulthood. It is a way station toward the larger world into which the young persons are moving. When youngsters succeed in high school, their future remains open. When they fail and leave school, it usually means that many doors to the future have been closed.

In many respects the high school is in a more strategic position than the home to influence the lives of adolescents. The school has more access to and can exercise more authority over the peer group. Also, high school teachers and counselors are freer than parents to view adolescents (other than their own children) objectively. Teachers are not as emotionally involved with the adolescent as are his parents. If he or she confides an aspiration, or has a problem, or confesses a weakness, the high school teacher has less reason than the parent to feel personally responsible for the adolescent's state of mind. This should, or could, enable the high school teacher to counsel other parents' adolescents with more freedom than he possesses in counseling his own adolescent son or daughter.

What adolescents bring to their high school experience will have an important influence on what they get from it. With the exception of those few whose lives have been blighted almost beyond repair, each adolescent student is still teachable and malleable. Each is still in a condition to be inspired, or restored, or impaired.

ATTITUDES TOWARD HIGH SCHOOL

There are far more high school students who say they like school than say they do not like it. In a poll taken in 1953, Remmers and Radler (1957) found that even though most students like school in general they find much to complain about in particular. They also found that a majority of teen-agers do not place a high value on academic studies. Only 14 per cent of those who took part in a poll rated academic competence ("skill in basic subjects like English and mathematics") as "the most important thing young people should get out of high school.

Coleman (1959), in a study of approximately eight thousand high school boys and girls, found that there was nonchalance and even a negative attitude toward academic matters. According to Coleman (p. 330) "there is coming to be more and more an independent 'society of adolescents,' an adolescent culture which shows little interest in education and focuses the attention of teenagers" on matters unrelated to school, such as cars, dates, sports, popular music (Coleman questions whether this is a "natural" or inevitable state of affairs.)

In the Remmers-Radler poll a "sense of discipline and responsibility" received the highest rating as the most important goal of a high school education (named by 38 per cent), and the second highest rating was given to "knowing how to get along with other people" (35 per cent). Sixty per cent of the high school students said they would like more help than they were getting in planning their education or in making a choice of their job.

When asked directly about their liking for school or their attitudes toward their teachers, high school students give a more favorable response than when questioned indirectly.

In a Remmers and Radler poll, taken in 1948, 50 per cent of those questioned said they thought their teachers were friendly and sympathetic (40 per cent said they were not; 10 per cent answered "undecided"). A less cheerful account appeared in a study by Symonds (1949), cited in an earlier chapter. In responding to a picture projection test, most adolescents spoke of punishment and the threat of failure when they told stories about school.

An interesting confirmation of this appears in a study of high school seniors by Johnson (1958), who used a projective technique consisting of written accounts of "ambiguous" situations connected with school. One of the sketches described a classroom situation as it might be seen by an interested outside observer. In giving their interpretations of this sketch, 52 per cent of the students viewed the situation as involving a serious discipline problem rather than interpreting it as a pleasant, or at least a neutrally toned situation. In another little sketch, which told that a teacher had requested a conference with parents, 81 per cent interpreted this to mean that there was trouble, of either a disciplinary or an academic sort. Only one student in about two hundred interpreted this request to mean that the teacher simply wanted to become better acquainted with the parents.

In evaluating the academic program a large proportion of students, according to a Gallup poll (1961), said they wished the requirements were stiffer. Many said the courses are "too easy." This should be taken with a grain of salt, however. If the students did not feel they were getting enough intellectual nourishment at school there was nothing to prevent them from supplementing it with a little reading and study of their own. However, according to the same poll, young people spent relatively little time reading, and only a small proportion of their reading was of a serious nature.

When students say they want harder assignments it is likely that some of them actually would prefer to be required to learn more than they do. But it is also likely that some say this because of an uneasy conscience about what they are doing at school. In many instances, there is a lack of "closure" in what they learn. This happens, for example, when a student memorizes his assignments in geometry but actually does not grasp the underlying principles. It happens also when a student has learned the assignments in a course in French or Spanish but cannot use the language well enough to order a meal in a French restaurant or must rely on sign language when he makes purchases in a Spanish grocery store. A moderately bright student cannot help but feel that he is a dabbler when he learns enough to pass the examinations in a number of subjects but has no real mastery of any of them.

A majority of students in the study by Johnson (1958) said they liked high school better than elementary school, but the reasons they gave for liking high school did not touch primarily on the academic program. Many youngsters, for example, liked high school better because there were more activities, more privileges, an opportunity to meet more friends. Relatively small percentages of pupils spoke of high school courses as being more interesting or as inspiring an interest in learning.

Several studies indicate that as young people advance into and through high school a large number show a decreased interest in the academic program.[1]

In a study by the writer and Tasch (1949) the evidence indicates that as the youngsters move up through the grades many of them become less eager about things that definitely belong to school, more inclined to complain, relatively more interested in recess periods, in social activities connected with school, and in games and sports than in schoolwork as such (see Table 16.1). (However, although there is this decline in interest in the academic program, a substantial proportion of students retain an interest in it. In Grades I–VI, 81.4 per cent of the pupils mentioned academic subjects, or information gained from academic subjects, as what they "liked best" in school. At the VII–XII grade levels, 52.8 per cent mentioned items in this category.) The high school youth, more often than the younger children, expressed dislike of teachers, the school program, discipline, and rules and regulations. Almost 10 per cent of junior high school students (as compared with less than 1 per cent of those in the elementary grades) mentioned relief from school duties or the last day of school when describing the "happiest day" of their lives.

There are many reasons for a decline of interest in school during adolescence. For one thing, the adolescent has many interests the school cannot readily satisfy. Moreover, many young people are more critical as adolescents than they were when they were younger concerning circumstances in their lives, both in and out of school. Another reason may be

[1] For studies bearing on this see Symonds (1949), Jersild and Tasch (1949), Jersild (1952), Coleman (1959), Allen (1960), and Demos (1960).

TABLE 16.1

PERCENTAGE OF STUDENTS GIVING RESPONSES IN SELECTED CATEGORIES
WHEN REPORTING WHAT THEY LIKED BEST AND DISLIKED MOST
AT SCHOOL *

Grade	Like Best I–VI	Dislike Most I–VI	Like Best VII–XII	Dislike Most VII–XII
Age	6–12	6–12	12–18	12–18
Number of Students	996	996	602	602
Games, Sports, Gym, Recess, etc.	5.1	5.4	31.9	2.8
Academic Subjects and Information	81.4	42.7	52.8	46.2
Art	11.5	4.8	10.5	3.2
People	4.0	4.6	5.3	15.1
Students	*1.0*	*4.1*	*4.0*	*7.0*
Teachers	*3.1*	*.2*	*.7*	*8.0*
Others	*0*	*.2*	*.7*	*.8*

* Adapted, by permission, from A. T. Jersild and R. Tasch, *Children's Interests.*
New York: Teachers College, Columbia University, 1949.

that the high school demands more homework than did the earlier grades. In addition, it reminds some young people of unpleasant realities of which they were not so pointedly reminded before, such as shortcomings accumulated in earlier grades, lacks in academic skills, and poor work habits. For these and many other reasons we might expect a larger number of older students to feel lukewarm about school.

However, many of the students who express a dislike of what they have to learn at school mention serious topics when they tell what they *would* like to learn more about. In a study by the writer and Tasch (1949) 27 per cent of the students mentioned matters under the general heading of self-improvement, self-understanding, and preparation for a job when asked what they would like to learn more about. In this investigation the social studies, including history, civics, and local and world affairs, were consistently mentioned as "liked least" more often than they were mentioned as "liked best." Yet when the students named things they would like to learn more about, many of them mentioned topics in the area of the social studies. From discussions with the students it appeared that social studies are often taught in an academic way, with little personal meaning.

TEACHERS' AND PUPILS' PERCEPTIONS
OF CAUSES OF FAILURE

Students and teachers differ considerably in their ideas about what causes high school students to fail. Such differences are shown in Table 16.2, from a study by Gilbert (1931) briefly referred to in an earlier chapter.

TABLE 16.2

RANK ORDER, FROM 1 (MOST IMPORTANT) TO 9 (LEAST IMPORTANT) OF VARIOUS REASONS FOR STUDENTS' FAILURE IN HIGH SCHOOL SUBJECTS AS JUDGED BY 830 STUDENTS AND 50 TEACHERS *

	Boys	Girls	Boys and Girls	Teachers
Lack of Brains	9	8	8	1
Laziness	1	1	1	2
Dislike for Subject	2	3	2	6
Dislike for Teacher	8	7	8	9
Hard to Study at Home	4	4	4	3
Clubs and Teams	5	9	9	8
Shows and Parties	7	5	5	4
Dates	6	6	6	7
Sickness	3	2	3	5

* Adapted from H. H. Gilbert, "High-School Students' Opinions on Reasons for Failure in High-School Subjects," *Journal of Educational Research* (1931), 23, 46–49. Reproduced by permission. The original table gives separate findings for Freshmen, Sophomores, Juniors, and Seniors.

Teachers regarded lack of intellectual ability as the most important reason for failure in high school subjects, but students placed lack of such ability as among the least important reasons. The students gave greatest emphasis to lack of motivation rather than lack of ability. They gave laziness and dislike of the subject as two of the most important reasons for failure. Many of the other reasons listed in the table also indicate some lack of motivation, stressing the point that students are more interested in diversions outside the classroom than in some of the things that are taught at school.

It cannot be ascertained from Table 16.2 whether the teachers or the students were more nearly correct in the reasons they gave for failure. When the teachers ascribed difficulty in school to lack of ability more often than did the students, the teachers were perhaps in one way more realistic than the students. However, the table also suggests that the teachers were not as realistic as they might have been. They gave a rather low rating to "dislike for subject" as a reason for students' failure. Yet any teacher need only reflect on courses he has taken, or if he is honest with himself, perhaps courses he has given, to realize that many courses are uninspiring.

The fact that sickness was ranked rather high by the students as a reason for failure is interesting, since sickness is a good excuse for staying home from school and for falling behind in the work at school. Undoubtedly sickness does make it difficult for some students to complete their assignments at school, but sickness can also be used as an excuse for not attending class (or for not studying at home) when the real reason is a lack of interest.

QUALITIES ADOLESCENTS LIKE AND DISLIKE IN THEIR TEACHERS

Each "good" teacher has his own unique qualities. Moreover, the "goodness" of a teacher does not depend on himself alone; it depends also upon the characteristics and motives of those he teaches. A highly motivated student will, for example, warmly approve a teacher who "knows his stuff and puts it across" even though, in an out-of-class situation, he might not like this teacher as a person.[2]

Some of the characteristics students single out for special mention when they describe teachers whom they like best or dislike most are shown in Table 16.3. One fact stands out in this table, namely, that the students emphasize the teacher's qualities as a human being and the emotional qualities that he brings into his personal relationships with his students far more than his academic competence. Similar findings have emerged from other studies (see, e.g., Hart, 1934). The two categories that included mention of the teacher's kindness and friendliness as a person and his tendency to be considerate and thoughtful of the learner when he acts in his role as a disciplinarian include considerably more responses than the category pertaining to the teacher's performance as an instructor and a source of information. Even in this latter category there were subcate-

[2] For studies dealing with qualities students like and dislike in their teachers, see Rostker (1940), Jersild (1940), Bousfield (1940), Moore (1940), Steckle (1941), Dodge (1943), Doll (1947), Weber (1953), and Ryans (1953).

TABLE 16.3

RELATIVE FREQUENCY OF MENTION OF VARIOUS CHARACTERISTICS
IN DESCRIPTIONS BY STUDENTS OF TEACHERS WHOM THEY
"LIKED BEST" AND "LIKED LEAST OR DISLIKED MOST" *

Teachers Liked Best

	IV–VI	VII–XII
Grade Level		
Number of persons reporting	303	298
Number of characteristics named	370	604
	Per Cent	*Per Cent*
Human qualities as a person: kind, sympathetic, companionable, "she likes us," cheerful, etc.	22	28
Qualities as director of class and as disciplinarian: fair, impartial, has no pets, discipline strict but firm and fair, does not treat failure to learn as moral wrong, etc.	24	26
Performance as a teacher, teaching: makes things interesting, knows a lot, explains well, helps individuals with their lessons, permits students to express opinions	27	32
Participation in students' games, activities	6	3
Physical appearance, dress, grooming, voice	7	5
Other	14	6

Teachers Disliked Most

	IV–VI	VII–XII
Number of persons reporting	99	265
Number of characteristics named	170	459
	Per Cent	*Per Cent*
Human qualities as a person: harsh, unkind, sarcastic, ridicules, "makes fun of you," sour, glum, cross, nervous, "queer," etc.	21	32
Qualities as director of class and disciplinarian: unfair, has pets, punishes too much, rigid, too strict, constant scold, treats failure to learn as moral wrong, preachy, etc.	43	35
Performance as teacher, teaching: dull, dry, poor at making assignments, doesn't know much, no help for individual pupils, too much homework, etc.	17	18
Participation in students' interests and activities	1	1
Physical appearance, grooming, voice, etc.	8	7
Other	10	7

* Adapted from A. T. Jersild, "Characteristics of Teachers Who Are 'Liked Best' and 'Disliked Most,'" *Journal of Experimental Education* (1940), 9, 139–151. Reproduced by permission.

gories (not here reproduced) that deal with the human side of the teacher, such as his willingness to let students express their opinions and have a voice in the affairs of the class.

ADOLESCENTS WHO DROP OUT OF SCHOOL

Many students who enter high school do not graduate. This still leaves a decidedly larger number of young persons who now graduate from high school than did so a few decades ago. According to a biennial survey conducted in 1950–1952 by the United States Department of Health, Education and Welfare, 77.3 per cent of persons aged fourteen to seventeen attended school in the early fifties, as contrasted with 11.4 per cent at the beginning of the century. However, drop-outs represent a very serious problem, both from an educational and a human point of view. Dillon (1949) cites figures compiled by the U. S. Office of Education which indicated that of 1,000 children who were in the fifth grade in 1933, 792 entered high school, and 462 of these graduated from high school in 1941. According to Gragg (1949) only about 50 per cent of boys and girls who entered high school in the late 1940's could be expected to graduate.

Even though some persons question whether we should expect a majority of young people to go to high school or to finish high school, the fact remains that a high school diploma is a valuable possession. Given two young persons with similar ability, the one who has a diploma has a better chance in life than the one who does not. The lack of a diploma bars many young people from opportunities that might otherwise be open to them. They are left out when announcements of job openings read, "only high school graduates should apply." According to a survey by the Bureau of Labor Statistics (1962), the rate of unemployment among drop-outs in the "civilian labor force" in 1961 (persons who either had jobs or were looking for them) was 27 per cent as compared with a rate of 18 per cent among high school graduates.

Moreover, the advantage of a diploma does not consist simply in a better chance for employment. The person who has a diploma will glean pride and personal satisfaction, even though he might have been a marginal student who just managed to slip through. The person who does not have a diploma is considered by many as a personal failure.

As might be expected, many adolescent drop-outs have lower intelligence quotients than the average of those who finish school (Dillon,

1949). But intelligence is not the only factor, and in many instances it is not the deciding factor (see, *e.g.,* Smith, 1944; Penty, 1956).

Among students who drop out, some give as the reason that they cannot afford the expense of going to school or that they need the money they could earn by getting a job. Undoubtedly one reason for leaving school is often financial, but as C. B. Smith points out (1944), the reasons students advance frequently are not the real ones.

Many students who drop out of school have lived through a long succession of failures (Hecker, 1953). Often, in the records of drop-outs, there is also evidence of lack of encouragement at home (see, *e.g.,* Ekstrom, 1946; Penty, 1956). Many of the early school-leavers come from homes low in the socioeconomic scale where schooling beyond the elementary grades is not in the family tradition.

Among those who leave school before graduation there are many who did not participate freely in the total life of the school. Hecker (1953) noted, for example, that many who left school early failed to take part in the school's extracurricular activities or lacked opportunity to take part.

The relation of poor reading ability to early school leaving has been studied by Penty (1956). Penty's population included almost six hundred tenth-grade students who were in the lowest fourth of their class in a reading test. Of these, almost half dropped out of school, but about half remained to graduate. Penty's population also included about six hundred students who were in the highest quarter of the class in reading performance. Most of them remained to graduate, but not all; about 15 per cent dropped out. Penty found that the difference between the intelligence quotients of the poor readers who dropped out of school and the poor readers who graduated was not significant from the standpoint of educability.

One difficulty connected with being a poor reader at the high school (or college) level is that a poor reader looks like a misfit and is probably regarded as such by some of his teachers. Usually we assume that a child will learn to read in the first two or three grades, and if he has not done so, we tend almost to assume that there is something perverse or morally bad about him. Yet in spite of this discouraging handicap it is possible for nonreaders or poor readers at the high school level to make substantial progress in reading if they are given help, even though they have labored under their handicap for many years (see, *e.g.,* Witty, 1947; Ephron, 1953; Fisher, 1953; and Penty, 1956).

In Penty's study it was found that the median grade level growth between the ninth and the twelfth grades of 106 poor readers who had received only incidental help in reading was from 5.9 to 8.3.

The poor readers who dropped out in Penty's study showed evidence of much less acceptance of self as a characteristic associated with their reading difficulties than those who graduated. Many more of the drop-outs than of the graduates felt inferior, were ashamed in class, felt disgusted with themselves, or wanted to leave school because of their handicap. Feelings of this sort were reported by 73 per cent of the drop-outs and by only 28 per cent of those who stayed on to graduate.

The reasons given by the graduates for staying in school until graduation, even though they had experienced some difficulty in reading, included strong personal desire to graduate, encouragement from the family, family expectations, interest in specific subjects, interest in sports and in other activities, desire for a better job, help of counselors and teachers, and liking to be with other young people.

Family attitudes had an important influence on those who remained in school to graduate even though their reading performance in the tenth grade was poor. More of the family members of those who graduated had finished high school. There was evidence, also, that the families of those who remained were more stable, were financially more secure, and were in a position to give the students encouragement and moral support.

Very important in determining the fate of poor readers, according to Penty, is the influence of an understanding classroom teacher who is accepting of young people as they are and who will help them to face their weaknesses and develop their potentialities. The assurance of the friendship of the teacher and of fellow students was a crucial factor in the lives of many of the adolescents who persevered in spite of their serious shortcomings.

Youth in College

Most beginning college students are adolescents in the sense that they are still continuing the process of "ripening" and maturing. They are still growing in intellectual power. Many of them are still working on tasks which confronted them earlier in the adolescent period, such as "finding themselves" and striving for independence and self-direction. A large proportion are still undecided about their vocational careers. In a group of 241 college students (171 men and 170 women) studied by Webb (1949), including a large number of juniors and seniors, 55 per cent had chosen no vocation or were uncertain as to the appropriateness of their choice.

THE COLLEGE POPULATION

The present-day college enrollment, compared with some years ago, includes a larger percentage of the total youth population (Wise, 1958); a larger proportion of persons aged twenty-five or over; a larger representation of students from lower socioeconomic levels; a substantial number of married students (in 1957, 29 per cent of the men students and 10 per cent of the women students); a larger proportion of students earning part or all of their college expenses (71 per cent). The consensus of many observers is that present-day college students are willing to work harder than in years past.

Although the drop-out rate has not changed greatly, it is somewhat smaller than it was some decades ago. In a compilation of drop-out statistics, Wise (1958) reports that slightly over a third of the freshmen in 1931 did not continue beyond the first year in the college in which they were first enrolled; in 1950 the percentage was slightly above 27. Less than 40 per cent of freshmen graduated in the institution in which they first enrolled in 1931, and less than 50 per cent of those who entered in 1950 graduated after four years.[3]

OUTCOMES OF COLLEGE

Due to the diversity among college students and large differences in the entrance requirements and scholastic standards of various colleges, it is difficult to generalize about "the college student" or about what is meant by a "college education." However, students and colleges do have many characteristics in common. Liberal arts colleges, for example, are designed to provide a "liberal" education. Liberal education has been variously defined, but most college faculty members would probably agree that it aims to provide intellectual nurture and discipline, to promote knowledge and enlightenment, to encourage a disposition to take a thoughtful view of things, to inquire into the logic and facts underlying an issue instead of resorting to emotional bias or intellectual preconceptions, and to culti-

[3] It is difficult to determine just how many persons who enter college stay to finish the job, for some who drop out from the institution they first entered later enroll elsewhere.

vate an appreciation of the arts, the humanities, and all branches of learning.

When a student goes to college, a feast for the intellect is laid out before him. The library is a storehouse of the wisdom of the past. In the laboratory he can use equipment that has been wrought by the minds of great scientists and engineers. Members of the faculty are ready to bequeath to him the fruits of their scholarly labors. He is, in large measure, an "heir of all the ages." In addition, he has an opportunity to share with his fellow students. And, with proper encouragement, he can not only enjoy what other scholars offer him but he can also begin to make original scholarly contributions of his own.

What does the student derive from all this during his four years at college? The most obvious outcomes appear in the practical sphere when students use the four-year period to acquire information and skills which they can apply when they leave college. It seems that the typical student places a high value on a college education, but not mainly for intellectual reasons. He places a higher value on the prestige of being a college graduate, on vocational opportunities that are opened for him, and on friendships that will be helpful to him.

In many of the studies that have been made of the outcomes of college education, it is apparent that the investigators have assumed that the college should have an influence on the student's personal philosophy and his outlook on life. This is perhaps a dubious assumption, for many colleges do not claim that it is their aim to influence the student's philosophy of life and make little or no systematic effort to do so. Moreover, judging by their own statements, it seems that many students who go to college are not consciously seeking to examine their personal values or to formulate a more mature philosophy. Therefore, it probably should not be regarded as surprising if we find that many persons who have gone to college do not change their outlook on life to a great degree.

In recent years several studies have been made of what college education does to or for the student as a person—his values, his philosophy of life, his intellectual pursuits after college, his convictions, his attitudes toward social and civic issues, and his ways of dealing with the affairs of his own personal life.

One of the most extensive studies of the impact of college has been reported by Jacob (1957), who used a variety of standardized tests designed to measure the values and opinions of several thousand college students in a number of institutions. According to Jacob's findings, some colleges seem to have a "peculiar potency" in providing an institutional atmosphere, a "climate of values" in which students are "decisively influenced." But according to the tests Jacob applied, something less than this usually occurs.

The average student in a majority of colleges shows some changes in thought and outlook, although not to what might be called a decisive degree. The typical student, as he moves from the freshman through the senior year, becomes somewhat more tolerant, more concerned about civil liberties, and better able to apply "critical thinking in social science," resulting in an increased tendency to reach judgments by reasoned thought.

The drift toward a greater tolerance and interest in civil liberties does not, however, in the typical student, seem to result in an active concern about social issues or a zeal for participation in civic affairs.

Jacob also found, according to the measures he used, that one trend in the thinking of students as they continued in college was toward uniformity: the seniors in his study were, on the average, more similar than freshmen in their values and beliefs. Many students moved toward the norm, giving up extreme views which would set them apart from others.

The trend toward intellectual uniformity described by Jacob has also been observed by others. Sanford (1958) notes that in the peer culture in college "the accent is on moderation and leveling." Students should be "open-minded and non-controversial." In making an ethical decision, "the proper course is to see what others think" and the decision "will then be very likely to accord with the morality that prevails in our culture as a whole."

However, the trend toward uniformity in dealing with controversial ideas and ethical issues (as indicated by professed abstract moral values in response to a paper-and-pencil test) does not necessarily mean that students in all colleges increasingly adopt similar formulas in dealing with personal issues in their own lives. In a long-term study of students in a women's college Sanford (1957) noted that the senior girls were, on the average, more self-critical, more uncertain of themselves than they were as freshmen. The seniors in Sanford's study showed "greater breadth of consciousness, more self-insight, more familiarity with their inner life." They had more capacity for discrimination, were more aware of their inner impulses. Sanford regards this increase in self-scrutiny as a sign of increased maturity and believes that the college had a considerable influence in bringing it about. He also notes that the average senior in his study was less complacent and more "upset" than she was in her freshman year. She had learned to question her earlier values but had not yet fully established a new and firm set of values of her own. Moreover, many of the seniors in this group were also troubled by the fact that the life that awaited some when they left college differed from their mode of life while in college.[4]

The changes that occurred in the college population Jacob studied seemed (with a few exceptions) to be unrelated to the particular course of study pursued by students in college and (with some exceptions) seemed to be relatively independent of the quality of instruction offered by individual teachers. Values expressed by students who were most interested in the social sciences differed little from those of students majoring in engineering, business administration, natural science, and agriculture. The social science students "ran with the pack" in most of their expressed interests and values.

In a study by Pace (1941) information was obtained from 1,600 students ten or fifteen years after they had left college. A fourth of the men and women who were interviewed said they had fairly often discussed problems in philosophy, morals, and religion, but many of them apparently had not arrived at firm convictions or judgments. "In their philosophies, their reactions to difficulties, their interests in religion and philosophy, and their emotional maturity there were no differences between the average graduate and non-graduate" (p. 78).

Half the men and two-thirds of the women in Pace's study reported that they had experienced some major crisis in their personal lives. In describing their way of dealing with personal difficulties their major solutions were (1) to think that things will turn out all right in the end (62 per cent of the men and 60 per cent of the women); (2) to realize that other people are worse off (59 and 64 per cent); (3) to buckle down and work harder (50 and 41 per cent); (4) to be glad you still have the love and respect of your family (38 and 40 per cent); (5) to pray for strength and guidance (34 and 45 per cent). These solutions by persons who had attended college probably do not differ significantly from solutions that might be proposed by persons who have not been to college.

According to Pace, the college graduates showed many inconsistencies in their attitudes and ideas and many discrepancies between their activi-

[4] It is not clear whether the college women in Sanford's study were an exceptional group as compared with the majority of students in Jacob's population or whether the differences in the findings of the two studies were due to differences in the methods that were used and the kind of information the women were asked to give.

ties, interests, and attitudes. Their ideas were "fragmented"; they did not appear to be aware of interrelationships that might enable them better to "see their own lives and their contemporary world as parts of an integrated whole." According to Pace, there was a similar fragmentation in the college education they received—a lack of coherence and unity.

One favorable finding about college students indicates that they take a more humane and thoughtful view of human foibles than younger persons do. Although it is not clear from the evidence whether this is a result of growing older or of going to college, the evidence on this score, in a study by Porter (1959), is impressive. Porter compared a number of groups with regard to their attitudes toward a list of child behavior problems. High school seniors to a far greater degree than college seniors advocated punishment as a means of dealing with a child who had problems (38.4 per cent of the responses at the senior high school level were punitive as compared with 10.7 per cent at the senior college level). On the other hand, college seniors considerably more often advocated an effort to study the child to find the cause of his behavior (19.2 per cent of the college and 5.9 per cent of the high school seniors' responses included this recommendation). College seniors also relatively more often advocated such steps as talking to the problem child, praising and encouraging him, and making an adjustment in the work he was required to do.

Academic, Utilitarian, and Personal Aspects of Secondary and Higher Education

In many studies that have been made of high school and college students, it appears that the aims and hoped-for outcomes of education, as viewed by instructors, differ from the aims and hoped-for outcomes of the students. Instructors usually aim to promote intellectual competence and scholarly interests but the students' main motives for going to high school and college seem to be to conform to what others do, and to "get ahead," rather than to become absorbed in scholarship. Students name occupational advantage as a main reason for planning to go to college (Slocum, 1958), and this, presumably, is their main reason for taking courses in high school that will enable them to apply for entrance to college. After they enter college, students continue to name socioeconomic advantage as the main goal of a college education (Jervis and Congdon, 1958).

A marked discrepancy also often exists between instructors' academic preoccupations and the student's personal concerns. In a study which included college and high school girls, Frank and his associates (1953) drew a sharp contrast between the impersonal intellectual content of what the students were required to study and the highly charged emotional concerns that prevailed in their own lives. When thus beset by personal problems, the student must manage, as best he can, to live in two worlds: the academic world and the world of his own personal preoccupations.[5]

Additional evidence of a difference between the preoccupations of instructors and students appears in statistics regarding high school and college drop-outs. As noted earlier, a large proportion of students drop out of high school. The proportion of drop-outs in college is also large. From Pace's study, cited above, and a review of findings by Wise (1958), it appears that approximately half of the students who enter college do not remain to graduate. Although among those who drop out there are many who are below average in ability as compared with the rest of the student body, many who are well below average in intelligence remain to graduate. On the other hand, many in the highest levels of ability drop out (Wise, 1958).

When students drop out, it usually is taken to mean that *they* have failed. At the college level, a great deal of attention has been given to the question: what can we learn about those who have failed in the past that will enable us in the future to reject similar persons when they apply for admission?

Less often is it assumed that perhaps in some way the school has failed. Less systematic attention has been given to the question: what might the institution do to prevent failure, to help remedy shortcomings within the college and within the individual student that produce failure?

At any rate, it is clear that what high schools and colleges offer and require very frequently differs from what the students want or are able to deliver.

Although several studies indicate that there is a discrepancy between the goals college students and their instructors regard as most important, it is interesting to note that college students have a high respect for the integrity of their teachers. In a study by Reynolds (1958), students in twenty institutions were presented with this proposition:

[5] Jervis and Congdon (1958) found that while instructors and students differed in defining the most important goal of education they agreed in giving second rank to experiences that might promote self-understanding and third rank to experiences that might produce self-acceptance. Students reported, however, that the goal of self-understanding was least adequately realized.

It has been said that ideals are nice if you can afford them, and that life consists of a series of compromises. Listed below are a number of fields of work. In which do you think you would have to "conform" the least and make the fewest concessions with your personal beliefs?

In response to this, college teaching topped the list (with an average rank of 1.8). College instructors were regarded as more true to their personal beliefs than doctors (medicine had an average rank of 4.5). And college teachers were almost in a world apart from persons in government service (with a rank of 10.1); and persons in labor organizations were next to the bottom in ranking on personal integrity (with an average rank of 11.8). The sharpest difference was between persons in college teaching and persons in politics. The highest rank for college teaching (1.8) contrasted with the lowest rank (12.5) for persons in politics. (This finding should be taken with some grains of salt, for it is safer for a college teacher, once established in his job, with tenure, to be uncompromising in his ideas than it is for an elected official. However, it still is interesting to note that the teachers rate so high.)

THE PROBLEM OF PERSONAL MEANING

In discussions of the aims of education there has been much controversy as to whether education should be concerned with the student's emotional welfare. Many have claimed that education designed to help students to use their minds effectively should center exclusively on cultivating intellectual competence and academic knowledge of an impersonal sort. According to this view, education should not be concerned with personal problems or what sometimes has been called "personal adjustment." It should aim at mental excellence, not at mental health.

In the writer's opinion, such a view negates the idea that education should help students to use their minds effectively. One of the most profound ways in which a person can employ his mind is to inquire into the properties of the mind and the conditions within himself that influence his mental life. Such an inquiry inevitably will touch upon personal concerns and problems. In the writer's opinion the view that education should not be concerned with what is sometimes spoken of as "personal adjustment" is unfortunate from a social point of view and untenable from an intellectual point of view.

There are reasons for believing that the lack of interest in the academic program shown by many students is not just due entirely to their own shortcomings or to poor teaching in earlier grades or to competing interests in the outside world but is due in part to shortcomings inherent in the program itself. To be interested in what is taught it is important that the student find something of *meaning* and *value* for him in what is being taught. One of the most frequent reasons given by college students for loss of interest in high school subjects was a failure to see the need for the subject (Shuttleworth, 1938).

If a student is compliant, ambitious, and fairly bright, he can manage to learn even the most meaningless things. But if a student has a little spunk or is not ambitious to learn something just because someone else thinks he ought to, the road is not so smooth. Where there is no personal involvement, it is hard to find anything meaningful. Moreover, this is not a problem facing students alone. Many teachers report that they can see little or no meaning in much of what they have to learn and what they have to teach (Jersild, 1955).

The problem of personal meaning has two major facets. First, where there is meaning the student is intellectually absorbed. His mind is active in learning things that really count for him. Learning for him is a *living* thing rather than a mechanical exercise of memorizing something that someone else requires. What the student is learning helps him in satisfying ways to realize and appreciate his capacity for using his mind. Through his learning he is pressing into a widening world of knowledge and experience. He is finding himself, realizing his potentialities, exercising his curiosity, and getting a sense of achievement.

The other facet is that what is meaningful is not only a challenge to the intellect but is also significant from the point of view of concerns and issues in the student's personal life. He is able to relate what he learns to himself. He is as one who not only enjoys the rising sun, but also as one for whom the rays of the sun illuminate something within himself, throw light on his intimate concerns and reach into the depths of his own existence. In the writer's opinion, education that is really meaningful will inevitably touch upon personal issues and concerns, including personal problems. Elsewhere we have noted many of these concerns and problems: those connected with vocational choice; the struggle for identity and for autonomy; concerns connected with sex, with the young person's need for relating himself intimately to others; the need for coming to grips with all the forces in the outer and the inner world which produce conflict, anxiety, loneliness, grief, and resentment.

When learning has a personal meaning for a student it helps him to gain insight into the conditions in his private life that affect his emotional welfare. It also increases his ability to accept the joys of living and learning and his ability to cope with life's adversities.

EDUCATION FOR SELF-UNDERSTANDING

According to the views set forth above, one important aim in the education of adolescents is to help them to understand themselves. The idea that the pursuit of knowledge should embrace self-knowledge is an ancient one. It was expressed by Socrates over two thousand years ago when he repeated the admonition "Know thyself," which had been brought down to him from earlier times. Education currently, and for generations, has required young people to study almost every subject except the most important subject—the young people themselves. But although the idea of self-knowledge has, to a large extent, been ignored in practice, it is widely accepted, in theory, as representing one of the most important goals in education.[6]

RESOURCES FOR PROMOTING KNOWLEDGE OF SELF

Every subject and skill in the course of study offers an opportunity for helping students to understand themselves. Every current of feeling that is openly expressed provides a point of departure for inquiry into human motives and emotions. There are countless opportunities also to explore feelings that usually are hidden or disguised. Such feelings can be explored directly if the instructor and students mutually are able to create an atmosphere in which individuals are free to reveal their feelings. But they can also be explored obliquely or by indirection.

Many areas of scholarship are really meaningful *only if* the students

[6] In one of a series of investigations by the writer (1955), eleven groups of teachers and graduate students in education, totaling a thousand persons, were asked to give their reactions to the idea that schools should promote self-understanding. Over 90 per cent responded that in their judgment the idea was promising and worthwhile. In the various groups, from one-half to two-thirds of the persons expressed the view that the promotion of knowledge of self is or might be "the most significant" aspect of education.

At the college level, both students and instructors in a study by Jervis and Congdon (1958), cited earlier, mentioned self-fulfillment and self-understanding as the second and third most important benefits that higher education might provide.

can relate what they learn to themselves—can experience the implications of what they are studying in terms of what is happening in their own lives.

Previously established attitudes and preconceptions are likely to influence, to a greater or lesser degree, a student's response to practically every subject he takes in college. This means that when an instructor presents ideas to a student he must not only ask students to examine these ideas, as though they existed in a world apart, but must also, as far as he is able, ask students to examine the ideas in the light of their own personal attitudes.[7] For example, in a course in literature, students read the works of great authors. The language of great works of literature is a universal language: it dwells upon experiences that are timeless and common to all mankind. It makes articulate many things which the reader clearly or dimly can perceive as belonging to his own existence. To appreciate what an author has said, students have to relate it to their own personal experience. Under the leadership of an instructor, who himself has the courage and freedom to explore, a discussion of a work of literature will move far into personal meanings. In such a discussion, Hamlet is not just a remote prince nor Lady Macbeth a vicious queen set off in a literary frame. The characters come alive. What they say, think, feel, and do strike a resonant chord in the reader's own existence. If, through exploring and perceiving their kinship with an author or his characters or their aversion to them, students become aware of conditions in their own inner lives which they previously had not perceived, they have made an advance in understanding themselves. If, in such a discussion, a student acknowledges (publicly, or privately to himself) a facet of his mental life which previously he had tried to conceal from others or from himself, he is now appraising himself more realistically than before.

A course in history, like a course in literature, provides an almost inexhaustible source of human "case material" that can be used for self-examination. The heroes and villains of history were impelled by overt and covert motives such as exist to some degree in every person who studies history. With proper encouragement, this or that student, or all

[7] Some college subjects touch more directly than others on issues in this or that student's personal life. Ruff (1951) and Cogan (1961) have discussed ways in which physical education can be employed to help students to understand themselves. Bantel (1956) has described feelings and attitudes revealed by students in a course designed to provide opportunities for understanding of self and others. Orton (1959) has given a detailed account of the concerns college instructors must face in their own personal lives when they teach "emotionally loaded" subject matter in areas such as family life and psychology of personal adjustment. Orton briefly reviews earlier studies dealing with teaching in the areas of psychology and mental hygiene.

members of the class, may discover within themselves the attributes of Cleopatra or King Henry VIII or Napoleon and perhaps attributes of all three. In exploring the personal meaning of history they may discover in themselves some of the malevolence of a Hitler and some of the benevolence of a Lincoln. They may find that one of the issues over which the Civil War was fought still prevails right within their own classroom or within themselves, in the form of prejudice.

Other subjects likewise provide rich opportunities for self-examination and self-discovery. Biology could offer such opportunities through inquiry, for example, into sex and genetics. Courses in physical education could touch upon a large range of personal issues; among them are all the psychological meanings and problems connected with physical development that were discussed earlier in this book. The social studies offer opportunities for self-exploration, too. It would be difficult to find a subject more *social* and at the same time more personal and worthy of study than dating and boy–girl relationships or the open and hidden delinquency that prevails in most communities.

In the writer's judgment, an effort to delve into the personal meanings of standard academic subjects enriches the scholarly content of these courses. The author believes that an effort to capture personal meanings represents a higher order of scholarship than a policy of evading these meanings. In addition to the resources for promoting self-knowledge that are inherent in the formal academic subjects, there is an almost endless supply of raw material in the life of the school and in the private experiences of the students. Every issue that prevails within the inner lives of adolescents, every problem that besets them, is present at school. Each classroom is populated with aspirations, hopes, and ambitions; currents of loyalty and tenderness, fears, resentments, disappointments, and sorrows. If students are being taught how to use their minds effectively it is not just proper, but essential, to try to deal with these issues and problems.

As we have noted, attention to some of these personal concerns can be incorporated to an important degree into the teaching of standard subjects. However, it may not always be feasible to do so, due to the varying interests and abilities of the teachers of the regular subject matter courses. There could also be special courses for dealing with personal concerns, staffed by interested teachers who are especially qualified by training and temperament to offer such courses.[8]

[8] In advocating that teaching should aim to promote self-discovery, whether in regular courses or in special courses, the author does not imply that such teaching can take the place of special services for disturbed youngsters. He recognizes also

This is a controversial subject. The writer has had the privilege of working in classrooms with a number of teachers in such special courses and, in so doing, has observed that there usually is some opposition to these courses within the faculty and in the community at large. Many educators do not regard courses of this kind as academically respectable. Some parents may object to having their youngsters discuss personal concerns (although, in the writer's experience, such parents have been a small minority). Some parents and students (and faculty members) object because such courses do not help students to pass college entrance requirements.[9]

PREMISES UNDERLYING EDUCATION FOR KNOWLEDGE OF SELF

Before proceeding further it will be useful to review and supplement the premises and assumptions underlying the idea that education should promote knowledge of self.

1. Most persons move from childhood and adolescence into adulthood with a burden of unresolved personal problems. Many of these are linked with the inevitable adversities of human existence. But an education designed to help young people to use their minds effectively should aim to help students to take a thoughtful view of their personal concerns.

2. Strictly from a scholarly point of view, the full meaning and value of many academic subjects (such as literature, history, biology, health, and physical education) can be achieved only if the student can relate what is taught to his own personal experience.

3. It is possible, in education, to offer adolescents something more meaningful to them, as persons, than the usual impersonal academic

---

that teachers differ greatly in their aptitude and training for dealing with personal concerns and that some are able to inspire a zeal for learning (and thus promote their students' self-realization) even though they are not interested in their students' personal problems.

[9] For discussions and findings dealing with the promotion of self-understanding at the high school and college levels, and the teaching of psychology to high school students, and problems connected with such teaching, see: Jung (1933); Evans (1950); Engle (1947, 1950, 1952a, 1952b, 1955, 1956, and 1957); Spranger (1952); Jersild (1952, 1955); Helfant (1952); Jersild and Helfant (1953); Levitt and Ojemann (1953); Boodish (1953); Ojemann et al. (1955); Ojemann (1961); Kubie (1954a, 1954b); Wolf and Schwartz (1955); Patti (1956); Engle and Bunch (1956); Bryant (1957); Coffield and Engle (1960); Harris and Liba (eds.) (1960); Morse and Dressel (eds.) (1960); Jersild, Lazar, and Brodkin (1962).

routine. This, in the writer's judgment, can make an important difference in their lives even though the teacher who tries to provide such instruction does not offer, or pretend to provide, the more intensive kind of self-scrutiny which psychotherapists try to provide.

4. Self-examination is more profitable when a person is in the process of making crucial decisions than after such decisions have been made.

5. Adolescents have more desire, and capacity, for self-inquiry than has been recognized in the kind of education they usually receive.

When adolescents have an opportunity to work with teachers who open the door to self-inquiry many of them eagerly respond as though they were hungry for help, although others hold back, at least for a time, as though they were resisting or had no problems to share (for statements regarding responses of students see, for example, the earlier-mentioned studies by Evans, 1950; Jersild, 1952; and Patti, 1956). In a study dealing with this matter, the writer has pointed out (1952) that as soon as teachers take even a little step in the direction of dealing with personal problems, it is likely that a great number of problems will be revealed.

SELF-UNDERSTANDING IN RELATION TO HELPING OTHERS UNDERSTAND THEMSELVES

Earlier we cited findings which indicated that a large proportion of teachers regard the promotion of self-understanding as an important goal in education. The persons who took part in a study by the writer (1955) were also questioned about the kind of help they thought they would need to put this idea into practice. About half to over four fifths of persons in the eleven groups indicated a need for a kind of education that might help them to deal with emotional issues in their own lives (as distinguished from abstract and professional or academic issues).[10]

In voicing a need for this kind of preparation, these teachers underscored the idea that to help others to obtain self-knowledge it is essential for the teachers to seek to understand themselves. This idea was emphasized also in a study by Barker (1946). Barker's findings, based on a com-

[10] Between one fifth and one half of the members of the various groups expressed a need for help such as might be obtained through group therapy. We cannot assume that all who expressed a favorable attitude to the idea of therapy would take steps to procure it, although in some communities the percentage of teachers who have sought and received professional psychological help is quite large.

bination of methods, including interviews, ratings, and case studies, led her to conclude that a philosophy of life and knowledge enabling teachers to deal more competently with problems in their own lives are fundamental if teachers are to help students to face their problems.

When a teacher believes that knowledge of himself is essential for understanding or helping his students how does he go about achieving such knowledge? At the present time, the most systematic means of seeking self-understanding is to undergo intensive psychotherapy. (In recent years, an increasing number of teachers have sought help through this channel.) However, there are other resources. Everything that transpires between a teacher and his students might help the teacher to learn something about himself, as well as something about the students.

If teachers have the desire and courage to examine themselves in the light of their experiences with students, they will have an opportunity again and again to inquire into the meaning of their own likes and dislikes, their prejudices, their anxieties, their attitudes toward persons in authority, their attitudes toward sex, their tendency to expect too little or too much of themselves or of others, their need to dominate others or to placate them, their desire to face or their need to evade reminders of their own hopes, disappointments, wishes, and fears. A person can learn something about himself by seeing a motion picture of himself and his students during a class period or by hearing a recording of his voice.

In many courses, teachers and students can jointly seek self-knowledge by reading books written by compassionate persons who have struggled to know themselves.

One important means through which a teacher can acquire self-knowledge is comparing his perceptions of his students with the perceptions other teachers report. For example, he and others independently record what they hear, see, and feel while listening to a class discussion. Then he and the others compare the record of their impressions. Differences between what he and others noticed or did not notice, differences in the feelings that were aroused, the assumptions that were made, the conclusions that were drawn, provide a starting point for self-examination. Through a comparison of observations of this sort a teacher may discover that he was projecting feelings of his own in ways he did not at the time suspect. What he perceives "objectively" may be, to a large degree, a revelation of his own subjective state and thus tell more about himself than about those whom he observes.

Feelings might be aired in a revealing and growth-producing way if individuals could help one another to learn to be free to come out from behind the curtain that commonly conceals their emotions from others and from themselves. The writer believes that future developments of vast importance in education will come from plowing this fertile field.

The teacher's and student's efforts to grow in self-understanding are more likely to take place through many little glimpses than through dramatic flashes of illumination. Now and then a certain individual faces an insight so brilliant that it almost blinds him for the moment and continues, thereafter, to pour new light into his life. But oftener the light is more like a flicker than a flame. Frequently the one who gains an insight does so almost as though it were an afterthought, a way of underlining a truth he had already accepted but had not clinched in his thoughts.

Knowledge of self is not something that is acquired once and for all, like mastery of the multiplication table. Even those who are quite blind to themselves have a little of it and a capacity to acquire more. And one of the outstanding marks of those who have achieved the deepest knowledge of self is that they are still seeking. No one procedure alone will give the answer, since the search for selfhood, when genuine, is pursued through all channels of experience as long as a person lives.

Chapter 17

Vocational
Development

By Phoebe Overstreet Nicholas*

One difference between the adult and the child in our culture is that the adult spends a large part of his time in economically productive work, while the child does not. In this respect, the adolescent is "in between." He may engage in part-time paid work or may work full time during vacations, but the role of worker is not one that he is as yet required to fill. As he moves on from the early adolescent years to later in his teens, however, the time for going to work or preparing more specifically for an occupation comes closer. Many young people become more actively concerned about their future vocational or educational plans.

Choices that have vocational implications are required at certain points, usually beginning in adolescence, and failure to make a choice at such a time is itself a decision by default. When he is ready for high school, the young person has to make some and perhaps all of the following important decisions: whether to attend high school; whether to go to a school that offers an academic, business, technical, or trade program; what curriculum to take; which electives to select. Other decisions are required later: to stay in school or drop out; to remain in the curriculum selected or change to another; to study or to loaf; to take part in this or

* I am indebted to Dr. Phoebe Overstreet Nicholas for preparing this chapter. A. T. J.

that extracurricular activity or in none. All such choices may influence the adolescent's vocational future, even though he may not realize this when he makes them. Choice-making continues during the high school years until the adolescent leaves school by graduation or by dropping out. Toward the end of the high school period other important decisions must be made: whether to get a job or take further training, and what kind of job or training to select. Girls may have to decide about marriage: whether now or later, whether in addition to or instead of more education or paid employment.

As time passes, each decision reduces a little the possibility of taking a different course of action. A decision can be changed, of course, as when a student shifts from one curriculum to another or when an adult quits a job to take a different one, but some inconvenience is always involved and often some loss. The longer a particular course of action is followed, the harder it usually is to make a change. Even when one is young and may not realize it, time is a precious possession, and the loss of time caused by a change in educational or vocational plans may be painful and costly. (Nevertheless, it is probably less painful than clinging to a plan that is unsuitable.)

To make vocationally relevant decisions is not an easy task for the adolescent in our complex society. Mentally, he must project his partially known and not completely understood self into only partially known or unknown future activities. Much of what goes on in the world of work cannot be directly observed by the young person. He may see people pass in or out of factory gates or office buildings, but he ordinarily does not see them at their work. Of the many different occupations in which workers engage, the adolescent may have direct knowledge of only a few. Yet he must ready himself to take a place in the unfamiliar adult world beyond the home, the playground, and the school.

The Process of Making Choices

Although decisions that are relevant for occupational choice and/or eventual vocational adjustment are required at certain culturally determined choice points, making occupational choices and achieving vocational adjustment are processes which take place over a period of time. They may, therefore, be termed processes of vocational development (Super, 1953; Beilin, 1955). During much of adolescence, matters of occupational choice are more salient aspects of vocational development than matters of vocational adjustment. Accordingly, choice is emphasized in this chapter.

There is still much to be learned and to be understood about making vocational choices and adjusting to work. In an effort to synthesize what is now known and to provide a focus for further research, several theories about vocational choice and adjustment have been proposed.[1] Highlights of some of these formulations and a few of the relevant research findings will be discussed. Such a brief overview cannot do justice to the authors' ideas, however, and the interested reader is referred to the original publications for further information.[2]

Ginzberg, Ginsburg, Axelrad, and Herma (1951) formulated an approach to a theory of occupational choice which was based on an exploratory study of a limited number of subjects. Their study focused on the question of how vocational decisions are made. Eight subjects at each of eight educational levels were interviewed about occupational choice. Males of superior intellectual capacity and above average socioeconomic status were studied. They were drawn from Grades VI, VIII, X, and XII, the freshman and senior years of college, and graduate school; the age range was from eleven to twenty-four. In addition to the basic group of sixty-four subjects, seventeen boys of lower socioeconomic status and ten college girls were studied, as well as a number of persons seen in preliminary or supplementary interviews.

On the basis of their findings, Ginzberg and his colleagues concluded that occupational choice ". . . is a process; the process is largely irreversible; compromise is an essential aspect of every choice" (Ginzberg *et al.*, 1951, p. 186). They identified three periods in the process, distinguished by the characteristics of the choices that are made. A period of fantasy choices coincided in general with the latency period of development (from about six to eleven years of age). Tentative choices were characteristic of adolescence, while realistic choices usually began in early adulthood. Early in the period of tentative choices, from about ages eleven to twelve, the young person bases his choices largely on his interests; then he begins to pay more attention to his capacities and shows an awareness of such matters as different training requirements for different occupations; somewhat later, he tries to assess and synthesize many

---

[1] In most instances, the proposals have been termed by their authors frameworks for research or elements of theories rather than theories. For convenience in designation, the various points of view to be discussed in this section will all be called theories, with the recognition that their proponents might not so term them.

[2] In addition to the theories discussed here, see: Roe (1957); Super and Bachrach (1957, Chapter 6); Holland (1959); and Tyler (1959).

factors and evaluate them in terms of his values and goals, which he is also in the process of formulating. At about the age of seventeen, the adolescent enters a period of transition from the more subjective considerations he has emphasized in the past toward the more realistic considerations he will emphasize in the future (Ginzberg *et al.*, pp. 73–95).

Super has proposed a theory of vocational development which he is testing in the Career Pattern Study (Super, 1953; Super *et al.*, 1957; Super and Overstreet, 1960). Although vocational development is a continuous process, stages of growth, exploration, establishment, maintenance, and decline may be distinguished, each characterized by appropriate developmental tasks.[3]

The adolescent is most likely to be in the exploratory life stage, although some older adolescents may have moved on into the establishment stage. Super (Super *et al.*, in press) suggests that crystallization of a vocational preference is a developmental task of early and middle adolescence, from about age fourteen to age eighteen; specification of a vocational preference ordinarily follows in middle and late adolescence, ages eighteen to twenty-one; and implementation of a preference generally occurs in late adolescence and early adulthood, ages eighteen to twenty-five. Stabilization in a vocation is seen as a task of late adolescence and early adulthood, from twenty-one to thirty or later. In other words, the usual sequence would be as follows: the young person formulates general ideas about appropriate fields and levels of work, then makes a specific choice, which is acted upon by entering training or finding a job; eventually he settles down in his chosen occupation.

Three kinds of factors are suggested as being especially important in the development of vocational behavior: factors of self and role, personal factors such as intelligence and interests, and situational factors such as socioeconomic status. Concept of self is formed through identification, role-playing, and varied life experiences. In making vocational choices, the individual attempts to translate his self concept into occupational terms.

Super and his associates are studying vocational development in a group of young men who are being followed up periodically over a

---

[3] Developmental task has been defined by Havighurst (1953, p. 2) as ". . . a task which arises at or about a certain period in the life of the individual, successful achievement of which leads to his happiness and to success with later tasks, while failure leads to unhappiness in the individual, disapproval by the society, and difficulty with later tasks."

twenty-year period.[4] The subjects were studied initially when in the eighth or ninth grade. Analysis of data from 105 of the ninth-graders, who had been studied in 1951–1952, suggested that vocational maturity in this group consisted primarily in preparation for vocational choice (Super and Overstreet, 1960). Super concluded that it is often premature to require the making of specific vocational choices at the ninth-grade level. Education in the ninth grade should make available experiences which foster planfulness and orient adolescents to the choices they will have to make and to factors that should be considered in the process. Guidance in this grade should help students make the preliminary choices that are required "in ways which keep as many doors open as possible for as long a time as possible" (Super and Overstreet, 1960, p. 158).

Tiedeman and his associates (Tiedeman, O'Hara, and Matthews, 1958; Tiedeman, 1961; Tiedeman and O'Hara, 1962) have been writing and conducting research studies on career development [5] for a number of years. A few salient points from his conceptualization of the process are mentioned in the following paragraphs.[6] Tiedeman's point of view is in some respects similar to Super's, and in some respects similar to that of Blau and associates (which we shall presently discuss), while independent of either.

In the course of growth and life experiences, the individual evolves an "ego identity," a meaning which he has for himself and which has been learned in interpersonal experiences throughout life. Work also has meanings, and the person's internal frame of reference toward himself, toward work in general, and toward the specific position he holds or wishes to

[4] In the Career Pattern Study, an attempt is being made to evaluate vocational behavior in terms of maturity and outcomes, to trace career patterns, and to determine factors associated with vocational maturity. According to Super's theory, maturity of vocational behavior may be assessed by determining whether an individual is coping with the vocational developmental tasks of his age group or by comparing his handling of developmental tasks with that of others dealing with the same tasks. Evaluation of vocational behavior in terms of its outcomes is essentially assessment of vocational adjustment, which includes satisfaction and success.

[5] "Career development . . . is self development viewed in relation with choice, entry, and progress in educational and vocational pursuits. It is an evolving conception of self-in-situation which is occurring over *time* in man who is capable of anticipation, experience, evaluation, and memory" (Tiedeman and O'Hara, 1962, p. 78).

[6] Tiedeman feels that career development in men and women is sufficiently different so that a separate theory is needed for each; he is concentrating on a theory for men, and one of his students (Matthews) is studying career development in women.

obtain in the world of work must be understood in order adequately to predict his career. The young person entering the world of work for the first time meets with a major change in his environment. How he makes the necessary adjustments is most important for his developing sense of ego identity. Although ego identity includes unconscious and nonrational elements, it is the conscious and rational aspects which Tiedeman emphasizes.

Not all people have careers (consecutive, continued progress is involved in a career); to have a career, a person must think about it. Problems relevant to one's career occur not once but several and perhaps many times. To solve such problems, decisions are required. One goes through a similar process each time one makes a rational decision. Tiedeman's paradigm for the process is, in brief, as follows. A period of anticipation or preoccupation with the problem precedes making a decision or choice. During this period, a phase of exploration may occur, when a number of different possible alternatives or goals may be considered. The individual can imagine himself in various situations; in doing so, he probably thinks about his interests, his aspirations, his ability, and other considerations before making a decision. Alternative goals may be ordered by a valuing process. Eventually crystallization takes place—the situation becomes defined, and a choice is made. The choice is clarified and the individual is ready to act upon his decision: to enter training, to look for a job, to change from one job to another.

When a choice has been made and action has been taken on the decision, the individual enters a period of implementation or adjustment. Induction into training or into a new position places the individual in a social situation, where his reactions tend initially to be responsive and later, when he feels he has been accepted in the new situation, more assertive. At length, integration occurs; the individual and the group are in a state of dynamic equilibrium with each other.

Among the published research by Tiedeman and his students is a study of 1,021 boys in the freshman through senior classes of a parochial high school (O'Hara and Tiedeman, 1959). Congruence between self estimates and test estimates of interests, aptitudes, values, and social class was determined for each grade level. As in Ginzberg's study, the research design was cross-sectional, which creates some difficulty in evaluating the findings from a developmental frame of reference. Results were interpreted as indicative of increasing clarification of self concepts (except in the area of social class) from Grades IX through XII.

A group of social scientists from the fields of economics, psychology, and sociology, Blau, Gustad, Jessor, Parnes, and Wilcock (1956) have proposed a conceptual framework for occupational choice. Consistent with much of the current thinking about the subject, they see choice as a process taking place over a period of time. Earlier decisions affect later ones; a progressive narrowing down of alternatives is effected by the consequences of actions taken on the basis of prior decisions. Occupational entry is controlled by a selection process as well as by a choice process. The young person may choose to attend a particular college or to work for a certain company, but he has to be chosen as well as choose. If a selector decides against him, his own choice is accordingly modified.

According to the point of view of Blau and his colleagues, in making an occupational decision an individual considers the rewards different alternatives may offer and his chances of realizing each alternative.[7] His decision will be a compromise between preferences and expectations. If he has very little expectation of obtaining his first preference, he will probably not select it for his goal.

As choice implies a decision between alternatives, it follows that the chooser must be aware of alternatives in order to make a choice. Lack of information about existing opportunities thus restricts choice. However, the choice process does not necessarily include a conscious weighing of alternatives.

The immediate determinants of entry into an occupation, according to Blau and his associates, are four factors in the individual (occupational information possessed, technical qualifications, social role characteristics, and his value hierarchy of rewards) and four factors of the occupation (job opportunities, demand for workers; functional requirements such as requisite technical qualifications; nonfunctional requirements such as appearance; and amount and type of rewards offered). Although other variables influence careers, it is hypothesized that their effects can be traced through these immediate determinants.

Relevant Factors

It is beyond the scope of this chapter to discuss the many variables that may have some effect on vocational development. Those which are considered in the following pages should not, therefore, be considered a

[7] The selector considers his own ideal standards and estimates chances of finding a better qualified candidate within a reasonable period of time, when he decides about an applicant.

definitive listing of all relevant variables. It should also be noted that, although they are discussed separately, they may interact in varying ways in the process of vocational development.

SEX DIFFERENCES

Vocational development differs in boys and girls because of differences in their social roles. The culture strongly supports one vocational role over others for females: that of wife and mother. Males have no such traditionally favored vocational role. Instead, theirs is the more general role of principal economic support of the family, which may be expressed in many different occupations. The adolescent boy is, therefore, faced with a greater variety of potential kinds of work from which to choose a vocation, but he usually does not have to decide whether or not eventually to seek employment. That decision the culture has made for him. He is expected to work during most of his adult life, and his worth as a person, in his own opinion as well as in the opinion of others, may be to a considerable extent measured by his occupation.

For girls, the situation is more ambiguous. It is generally expected that they will find employment after leaving school and until marriage. Although such employment is often considered a temporary arrangement, the young woman cannot be sure how temporary it actually will be. She may not marry, or she may continue working after marriage. If she does leave paid employment when she marries, she may want to, or have to, re-enter the labor market later. Yet the married woman who is employed is not expected to make a career of her job outside the home. To the adolescent girl, then, matters of vocational preparation and selection may seem less important than to the adolescent boy. Her vocational decisions may be more important than she had anticipated, however. As a consequence of the trend for girls to marry young, women will be freed from major child-care responsibilities at an age when they will still have many years ahead of them. A number of these women will re-enter the labor force and spend a substantial amount of time in paid employment.[8] Young women would, therefore, be wise to consider occupations which will be rewarding to them from a long-range as well as from a short-range point of view.

In some ways, it is easier for the adolescent girl to learn her traditional

[8] For further discussion of this topic, see National Manpower Council (1957); Garfinckle (1958).

role than it is for the boy. The mother provides a model for the girl who is herself going to become a homemaker some day. It is possible for the girl, from an early age, to begin to participate in some of the functions of the adult female homemaker role. The boy's role is not so clearly demonstrated. In the urban middle class the father typically does not work at home, so his son cannot observe his work or participate in it, and sometimes it is difficult for him to get a clear idea of what his father is doing (Parsons, 1942). There are exceptions to this situation, as in the rural setting where the potential farmer works side by side with his father, or in a family-owned small business, where the son helps out in the afternoons and over week-ends.

Yet the girl's role is not as clearly defined as it once was, with resultant confusion and uncertainty for some.[9] Achievement for most women once meant a successful marriage, a fine family of children, and a pleasant home. Now, varied kinds of achievement for women are more generally possible (though outer space has not yet been domesticated!), some of which are not easily combined with having a home and a family.

INTELLIGENCE AND SPECIAL ABILITIES

Intelligence is influential in vocational development in several ways. Since it is related to academic success and attainment, it is an important factor in determining how much education a person will be able to complete. Amount of education affects entry into many occupations, especially the professions. Intelligence is also related in a general way to the occupational level at which a person will have the best chance to compete. It has been demonstrated that the average intelligence of members of different occupational groups varies in such a way that occupations may be arranged in a hierarchy according to these averages. However, it has also been shown that there is considerable variation around the averages, with the result that there is much overlapping in the range of scores between different occupational groups (Fryer, 1922; Stewart, 1947).

Some occupations require special abilities in addition to a certain level of general intelligence. The importance of special talent in music or art is obvious. Specialized abilities and aptitudes of different kinds also play a part in vocational adjustment in other fields; for example, speed and

[9] Sanford (1956) has noted that women college seniors frequently experience an "identity crisis," which may result in a flight into marriage, sometimes with unfavorable results.

accuracy of perception are helpful in clerical work; ability to comprehend mechanical relationships is important in skilled mechanical work;
fine manual dexterity is an advantage in some occupations, and good
eye–hand coordination and satisfactory hand–arm dexterity are important
in others. In jobs where extremely high degrees of skill are not required,
special aptitudes may be more important during the initial learning
period than later. Those who can learn to do the work fairly readily will
be less likely to become discouraged and quit, and they run less risk of
being fired for inefficiency during the learning period than do employees
who are not as adept.[10]

VOCATIONAL INTERESTS

Certain occupational groups have distinctive measured interests (Strong,
1943). However, neither expressed nor measured interests agree perfectly
with occupations actually entered, because interests are not the only determinants of choice or of occupation engaged in.[11]

The exact age at which genuine vocational interests begin to appear is
not known. It is logical to assume that there is individual variation in
this respect. Likes and dislikes are, of course, displayed from a very early
age.[12] Children can and do express interests and state choices in answer
to questions about what they want to do when they grow up. Among
many children, however, such expressed preferences are easily changeable.
Children take vocational roles in some of their play, though the roles may
seem unrealistic to an adult observer. Little boys play cowboys, policemen,
and firemen; little girls play mother, teacher, and nurse.

Sometimes meaningful vocational preferences as reflected in later
occupational choice are expressed in childhood. This may frequently be
the result of a special talent which becomes apparent early and is of such
a kind that its vocational implications are readily discernible. Potential
musical virtuosi, ballet dancers, perhaps some artists and writers, may
show appropriate abilities and preferences at an early age.

[10] For more information about intelligence and special abilities, see Super and
Crites (1962).

[11] *Expressed interest* refers to the verbal profession of interest, while *measured
interest* refers to the assessment of interest by standardized inventories.

[12] Sex differences in interests have been demonstrated at the first grade level,
and such differences seem well established by age ten (Tyler, 1951, 1955). By the
middle adolescent years, organized patterns of measured interests are apparent,
although changes do occur thereafter (Carter, 1940, 1944a; Taylor, 1942).

Early-appearing interests that had implications for future vocations have been identified in certain studies of special groups. In a longitudinal study of a group of intellectually gifted individuals, 58 per cent of those who in childhood had expressed a preference for engineering actually became engineers later (Terman, 1954, p. 10). Ten of twenty biologists in a study of eminent scientists (Roe, 1952) showed interest in natural history as children; the other ten did not recollect any particular interests before high school, when several began to display scientific interests. Many of the physical scientists recalled marked early interest in mechanical gadgets of various kinds. The most frequent early interests of the social scientists were literature and the classics, not apparently related to a future career in the social sciences, yet dealing with human situations such as are considered in a different way by the social scientist.

Norton (1953a, 1953b) has studied the development of expressed interests in vocations through interviews with teachers and factory workers. There was typically no *one* interest, but a waxing and waning of various interests over the years. That interest development was still continuing in adulthood, though on a reduced scale, was indicated by an upswing in interests reported in the late twenties and by the fact that vocational goals other than present occupations were reported.[13]

PERSONALITY

The relationship between personality and vocational development, although assumed to be important, is not well understood. Research studies have not as yet found relationships between personality characteristics and occupational group membership on a sufficiently wide scale to allow broad generalizations, although some such relationships have been found.[14]

Attempts to investigate the significance of personality traits in occupational choice or vocational adjustment are complicated by the fact that a given occupation may provide an opportunity for many kinds of activity (Berg, 1953). For example, in medicine the work may be very impersonal, as in medical research, or it may be highly personal, as in general

---

[13] For additional information about vocational interests, see: Bordin (1943); Berdie (1944); Carter (1944b); Darley and Hagenah (1955); and Super and Crites (1962).

[14] See Roe (1952, 1953); Terman (1954); and Super and Crites (1962, pp. 514–586).

practice. Furthermore, people may have different motives for entering a given occupation. It is quite possible that, within limits that are more or less wide depending upon the individual as well as the occupation, different needs may be met by the same occupation and the same needs may be met by different occupations.

Roe (1957) has hypothesized that the pattern of satisfaction or frustration of basic needs in infancy and childhood is related to eventual vocational choice and to motivation for accomplishment. In brief, if there is insufficient satisfaction of needs or if their satisfaction is delayed, such needs may become largely unconscious motivators, or they may be expunged. Need satisfaction in the early years of life is to a large extent dependent upon parents. Roe suggested possible relationships between parental attitude toward the child and the development of major orientations toward persons or nonpersons. She also suggested broad occupational groupings whose members tend to be characterized by one or the other of these orientations. Orientation toward persons would be found in most of those who select occupations in service, business contact, and arts and entertainment fields. Orientation toward nonpersons would be more typical among those who choose technological, outdoor, and scientific occupations.

Roe's interesting theory has stimulated several research studies (see, for example, Grigg, 1959; Hagen, 1960; Switzer, Grigg, Miller, and Young, 1962; and Utton, 1962). However, the findings have not, in general, tended to substantiate the theory. Two other studies, not designed to test Roe's theory but in a somewhat similar vein, offer some support for a need theory of vocational choice (Nachmann, 1960; Segal, 1961).

Small (1953) explored the effects of differences in ego strength on realism of vocational choice. (Realism was defined as having vocational goals that were in accord with personal qualifications.) His subjects were adolescent boys ranging in age from fifteen to nineteen, including a psychologically disturbed group and a group of better-adjusted boys, all of whom had come for vocational counseling. He found that the better-adjusted boys made more realistic vocational choices than the disturbed boys did. Among the better-adjusted boys reality played a greater part in the first choice of an occupation and fantasy in the second choice, while the reverse was true among the disturbed boys. In the better-adjusted group, the needs shown in the fantasy content of the choices were of a kind that would make for involvement with the environment, whereas the needs shown by the disturbed group suggested withdrawal from the environment.

Small's study shows how psychological adjustment may affect vocational choice. That psychological adjustment also affects vocational adjustment is suggested by the Terman and Oden (1952) study of intellectually gifted persons. When the most successful and the least successful men in the group (success being defined as the extent to which they had made use of their intelligence) were compared, it was found that the two groups had differed in emotional stability and in social adjustment in childhood, and these differences were shown even more clearly when they were adults. Friend and Haggard (1948) found that persons who were better adjusted to work and those who were less well adjusted to work differed more markedly in their attitudes, feelings, and ideas than in their aptitudes.

FAMILY BACKGROUND AND SOCIOECONOMIC STATUS

The adolescent's family background affects his vocational development by its influence on his becoming the kind of person he is, and by the effects of the general socioeconomic milieu of the family on the young person's attitudes, values, opportunities, and the reactions of others toward him. From his parents comes his heredity, including the genetically based aspects of intelligence, of special abilities, and, possibly, of temperament. The developing individual's environment during his preschool years is almost entirely that of the home and immediate neighborhood. When he enters school, he is exposed to a broader, more heterogeneous environment, but he comes equipped with reaction tendencies he has already learned. These may be modified, of course, by new experiences, but from the learnings of infancy and early childhood they probably develop certain needs and motivations and a basic core of personality.

We have already considered intelligence, special abilities, and personality in preceding sections. The effects of socioeconomic status will be briefly discussed in the following paragraphs.

Family socioeconomic status affects the young person's social status in the community and may influence his interpersonal relationships (see, for example, Hollingshead, 1949). The financial situation of the family determines to some extent how far the individual will go in school. Many children from poor homes do not complete high school, sometimes because of economic necessity and sometimes for other reasons, such as lack of encouragement or lack of interest.

The father's occupation often has a direct influence upon the occupation his son selects. Rogoff (1953) found that, although the majority of sons do not enter the same occupation as their fathers, they are more likely to enter their father's occupation than any other. Findings from another study (Jenson and Kirchner, 1955) indicate that sons tend to follow the general type of occupation that their fathers have engaged in; when they do not, sons tend in general to enter an occupation at a higher socioeconomic level.

It would seem that there are some differences in values at different socioeconomic levels.[15] Persons at the higher socioeconomic levels tend to derive satisfaction from their work itself, while at lower socioeconomic levels concomitants of work, such as economic rewards and financial security, tend to be more highly valued. (It should be noted that the nature of the work offers more opportunity for intrinsic satisfaction in some occupations than in others.) Furthermore, socioeconomic groups may differ to some extent in their orientation toward the present or the future, with members of the working class tending to emphasize the present and members of the middle class more strongly oriented toward the future. Such differences may reflect differences in willingness to postpone gratification (Ginzberg, 1948).

Findings by Beilin (1952, 1956) suggest that what the observer interprets as postponement of gratification may not seem so to the individual concerned. He studied boys of lower socioeconomic status and above-average intelligence, some of whom planned to attend college and some of whom did not. Presumably, the college-going group was potentially upward-mobile. It was conjectured that the boys planning on college would have to postpone certain gratifications in order to realize their plans, while those who went to work directly after high school would not. Beilin found that the college-bound group did not feel deprived of satisfaction by their plans for college. Instead, the prospect of pursuing these plans was satisfying. Results tentatively suggested the existence of two different patterns within the same socioeconomic group: that of the apparently upward-mobile individuals and that of the less mobile.

[15] Pertinent references are: Centers (1949); Beilin (1952); Friedmann and Havighurst (1954); Singer and Stefflre (1954); Darley and Hagenah (1955); and Lyman (1955).

Realism and Stability

We have summarized several theories about the processes of occupational choice and vocational adjustment and have considered some of the factors that may be important in choice or adjustment. What about the choices adolescents make? How realistic are they? Are such choices likely to remain stable over the period of time that may elapse between the expression of the choice and readiness to prepare for or enter an occupation? What happens when youth try to implement their choices?

REALISM OF CHOICE

Vocational choices named by young people in questionnaire surveys are often unrealistic.[16] Data about the amount of realism of expressed vocational choices are inconsistent, however; in some studies such choices have been found to be more realistic than in others (see, for example, Stephenson, 1957; Lockwood, 1958). Some of these inconsistencies probably occur because *choice* has a variety of meanings. Depending on the way questions are phrased and the points of view from which answers are given, the occupation an adolescent names when asked about his choice may be one he expects to enter, or one he would like in his fantasies to enter. Talks with students who seemingly had made unrealistic choices led a high school counselor (Dresden, 1948) to surmise that adolescents are actually much more realistic in their plans than some questionnaire data suggest. Some apparently misunderstand the meanings of words; others respond in a self-protecting way by giving answers they think are expected.

When lack of realism in vocational choice has been found, it frequently involves aspiration for occupations at the higher socioeconomic levels. It is evidenced in the discrepancy between the number desiring occupations at the upper levels (typically professional and managerial) and the opportunities that will probably be available, as judged from census data. It is shown, too, when adolescents select occupations requiring substantially higher levels of intelligence than they possess.

[16] Studies dealing with realism of choice include: Lehman and Witty (1934); Kroger and Louttit (1935); Byrns (1939); Myers (1947); Carp (1949); and Moser (1949).

The preference for occupations at the upper socioeconomic levels displayed by a number of young persons is understandable, because such occupations are often better paid than those at other levels and entail a way of life that appeals to many. Such occupations enjoy considerable prestige in our culture. When individuals have been asked to rank occupations according to their social standing (Counts, 1925; Deeg and Paterson, 1947), professional and "higher" business groups are commonly ranked high; skilled trades are placed in an intermediate position; semiskilled and unskilled groups usually receive low rankings.

In a study of perception of occupations, Grunes (1956, 1957) found considerable agreement among high school students, but she also found that the higher-status students were able to make finer differentiations within the higher-level occupations than the lower-status students did. On the other hand, the students from lower-status homes tended to make finer differentiations among lower-level occupations, although the evidence for this tendency was not as clear. Grunes also found that many of the adolescents she studied had an unrealistic dream goal which was different from their stated action goal, and in many instances the expected job was even unlike the action goal.

Intelligent children tend to report what would appear to be more appropriate preferences, but this may reflect the fact that the tendency to prefer higher-level occupations fits better with their potential than with that of less-able children. However, the measured interests of the more intelligent tend to agree better with their expressed interests than do those of the less intelligent (Carter, 1944b; Super, 1947). It seems reasonable to assume, therefore, that the more intelligent have more accurate understanding of their vocational possibilities at an earlier age (or that it is easier to recognize pleasant than unpleasant things about oneself).

STABILITY

Stability of choice and of plans is, at least to some extent, dependent upon their realism. Among young persons who have chosen unsuitable occupations a number may be expected to change their plans (see Holden, 1961). These are more realistic, although less consistent, than others who continue to pursue unsuitable goals.

Porter (1954) found that about 86 per cent of a group of boys contacted six months after high school graduation were following the vocational plans they had stated shortly before graduation, or ones on a comparable prestige level. These results indicate substantial stability over a short time-span. Less "follow through" of plans was evidenced among boys in another study (Rothney, 1958), about 53 per cent of whom showed consistency between plans and subsequent activities over a comparable length of time. The boys in Porter's group were of predominantly upper-middle-class background, which may have facilitated the carrying-out of their plans.

The Wisconsin Counseling Study (Rothney, 1958) has other interesting information on stability of vocational choices during adolescence and early adulthood. Among a group of boys and girls who were counseled in the tenth, eleventh, and twelfth grades, nearly two-thirds changed their vocational choices at least once during the three-year period; slightly over one-third retained the same choice all three years (Schmidt and Rothney, 1955). Of the total group in Rothney's study (about half received counseling and half did not), 11 per cent were completely consistent in their choices and subsequent vocational activities over five points in time, covering a period of eight years: [17] in the tenth grade, one month before graduation, and six months, two and one-half years, and five years after graduation. (When broad occupational categories were used to classify the data, instead of specific occupations, a greater degree of consistency was indicated.) Five years after high school graduation about one-third of the group was engaged in, or preparing for, occupational areas which they had designated, shortly before high school graduation, as their choices for five years later. Sufficient shifting around was evidenced, however, for the investigator to conclude that "Variability rather than consistency was the rule in the making of vocational choices and in carrying them through into action" (Rothney, 1958, p. 481).

In view of the many factors that may affect entrance into an occupation, it is not surprising to find some amount of change in plans and activities over a time span. Even if a young person's choice remained stable, implementation of the choice could be blocked by failure to be admitted to requisite training,[18] inability to get a job in the chosen occupation, or any one of a number of fortuitous circumstances. Changes for the better also occur, as when a young person who had not planned

[17] The Korean War took place during part of this time span.

[18] Initial turn-down for training does not necessarily constitute a permanent block to goal attainment. For example, of a group of premedical students who had not been admitted to a university school of medicine on first application, two-thirds were eventually admitted to some medical school; 80 per cent went into medicine or related occupations (Stephenson, 1961).

on college is enabled by a scholarship to attend, or when someone finds he is happier in a job he took out of necessity than he was in a previous line of work.

During the early post-high-school years, a number of young persons show a considerable amount of job change (Davidson and Anderson, 1937; Hollingshead, 1949; Miller and Form, 1951). This may represent healthy, self-confident exploration of the newly entered adult world, or it may indicate trial and error.[19] Difficulty in becoming established vocationally is shown by the fact that although young people constitute less than 10 per cent of the labor force, they constitute 20 per cent of the unemployed. Their inexperience and, frequently, their lack of skills make it hard for them to compete in getting jobs (see Cohen, 1962).

Shifting about in the occupational world is undoubtedly affected by economic conditions. (For example, persons who begin their careers in the midst of an economic depression may be retarded in their vocational progress compared to those who enter the labor market at a time of full employment.) It probably also reflects the young worker's efforts to find the "right job" for himself. Particularly for those who have no clear idea of what they want to do, or for those who have unrealistic expectations, trial and error in the process of occupational adjustment is to be expected. Members of occupations requiring extensive training, such as the skilled trades or the professions, may not flounder as much in the process of settling down vocationally as others do. To a certain extent, they have had their tryout experience through their specialized training. Furthermore, they have a greater personal stake in sticking to an occupation in preparation for which they have already invested a considerable amount of time.

In a study of adults engaged in manual occupations (Reynolds and Shister, 1949), it was found that most of the workers took the first job they could get and did not shop around to compare it with other job possibilities. About half the workers said they had had no plans at all while still in school, and in most instances the parents' plans for their children had been vague. Less than a quarter of the group reported that their first job coincided with plans made while in school.[20] Most of the

[19] Changes in training or in employment for valid reasons make sense. Remaining over-long in unsuitable training or in an inappropriate job is not indicative of good vocational adjustment, but neither is aimless shifting about with no clear idea of what one wants to do.

[20] In another study (Ledvina, 1954), approximately 63 per cent of recent graduates of a small high school in a predominantly agricultural area reported they had chosen their present occupation after high school graduation.

first jobs were blind alleys. It is not surprising that floundering occurs under such circumstances.

Whether consistency in vocational choices and activities during high school and post-high-school training and during the early working years is desirable or undesirable is a matter of value judgment. Purposeful exploration does, however, seem preferable to more or less aimless trial and error, both from the point of view of the individual and that of society.

Guidance Needs and Programs

Not all adolescents have a difficult time in making vocational decisions and in adjusting to the world of work. To some, these decisions and adjustments are a stimulating challenge and a rewarding adventure; such young persons are able to make appropriate plans and to implement them without special assistance. But not all adolescents have an easy time of it. Insufficient self-understanding and insufficient knowledge of the world of work are problems for some and perhaps many adolescents. Such problems in understanding interfere with the adequacy of vocational choices and occupational adjustment. Some of the difficulty is rooted in cultural attitudes, which are usually slow to change. Some of the difficulty is due to economic conditions that are beyond the control of the individual. Yet self-understanding can be increased and a more accurate and comprehensive knowledge of the occupational world can be provided. Schools, government agencies, and other institutions in our society are helping through counseling and related services.

Many schools have established guidance programs at the junior high and high school levels in an effort to assist adolescents with their educational and vocational planning. Information about occupational opportunities and requirements may be given in courses organized for the purpose or as a part of other courses. Some schools have occupational information materials in the school library. Some arrange tryout work experiences for their students. Standardized psychological tests of abilities, achievement, and interests may be given. Group discussions and/or individual interviews with the guidance counselor are used to help students understand the educational and vocational implications of differences in abilities and interests, and to help them clarify their planning.

However, many schools do not offer any of these services, and among those that do, the services are not always adequate. Understaffing of guidance programs, with consequent over-heavy case loads, restricts the amount of individual counseling and of group guidance that can be done. This is a serious problem. Growth in self-understanding cannot be produced mechanically by the interpretation of test results. Much interview time is needed by those who have unclear or inaccurate pictures of themselves, but the necessary time may not be available. Another handicap to adequate guidance services is the fact that in some school systems the persons who have been assigned guidance responsibilities may lack sufficient professional training in this field. Gradually this problem is being faced by the establishment of specific certification requirements for guidance workers and by an increasing supply of trained personnel. A good beginning has been made by many school systems in introducing guidance services, but much remains to be done.[21]

Counseling services and related activities are also available through other sources than our public schools. Assistance for the young man or woman who is about to enter the labor market is available at the local branch of the State Employment Service; some have staff members who specialize in working with young people. Provision for aid, when appropriate, to youths of sixteen and above is included in the Manpower Development and Training Act. State Divisions of Vocational Rehabilitation, under the leadership of the Office of Vocational Rehabilitation of the Department of Health, Education, and Welfare, help the physically, mentally, and emotionally handicapped who are fourteen years of age and older.

Largely under the stimulus of the Veterans Administration during and after the second World War, many colleges and universities established counseling services for veterans. Such services were often extended to nonveterans. Although some of these counseling centers were later closed, many institutions continued the service, and others have established centers. A number of college and university centers provide service to nonstudents as well as to students, but often on a fee basis for nonstudents. The Veterans Administration still offers counseling to those who are eligible, under different arrangements from those just mentioned. A number of adolescents are eligible for counseling and assistance in education and training through the Veterans Administration under the War Orphans Educational Assistance Act.

Some social agencies or other community agencies, especially those

21 The National Defense Education Act of 1958 includes provisions to extend and to improve the guidance services in our schools. See Carlson and Williams (1959) for details about NDEA.

concerned with rehabilitation of the handicapped, provide vocational and educational counseling services. Guidance services are also offered by some reputable private agencies, but private agencies are generally located in large communities and their fees may be higher than those of nonprofit organizations.

Concluding Statement

Some of the material that we have considered in this chapter may give the impression that the process of making occupational choices is to a considerable extent a matter of explicit verbal reasoning, in which the individual inventories his assets and liabilities, relates them to opportunities, and makes the most satisfactory compromise he can between his wishes and reality considerations. How accurately this describes vocational decision-making in most adolescents is not clear. As we have pointed out, there is much that we do not yet know or understand about vocational development.[22]

From what is known and from theory, we can recognize that vocational development is a complex process, and that it is affected by a number of factors, some within the individual and some environmental. Some can be anticipated and some cannot. The young person may be clearly aware of certain influences, only vaguely cognizant of others, and not at all aware of still others. If he has a broad understanding both of himself and of his environment, the adolescent should be able to make vocational decisions more adequately. The purpose of counseling and guidance is to help the young person achieve such understanding.

Some of those who need help may be extremely reluctant to accept it, or may altogether refuse help. Counseling is not likely to be effective if it is forced on people or if it is passively received. It requires active participation by the counselee. Ideally, it also requires a counselor who not only has knowledge concerning vocations and individual interests and aptitudes, but also has insight into human motives, including his own, who understands his "self," and who can help the adolescent toward self-

[22] Further knowledge is to be expected from research programs such as Super's Career Pattern Study, the work of Tiedeman and his students on career development, and a more recent program which we have not discussed: Project TALENT. Project TALENT (Dailey and Shaycoft, 1961; Flanagan et al., 1962) is a large-scale study of high school youth, of the schools they attend, and of their guidance programs. At the time of this writing, detailed information about the project's findings was not available, but such material should soon be forthcoming.

understanding. But the adolescent is after all human and limited, no matter what his potential, and so is the counselor, no matter what his competence or desire to help. Thus, there are limits to the amount of self-understanding that can be achieved, to the information that can be absorbed, to the knowledge upon which action is based. Counselors and counselees have to live with limitations as well as assets, to accept the fact that they do not and cannot always know the solutions to problems, while at the same time striving to learn more and to understand more fully.

Certain choices must be made as youth progress through school, and even if adolescents avoid or postpone decision-making as long as they can, action of one sort or another, with or without an explicit, verbalized decision, is eventually required by circumstances. It makes sense, then, to prepare boys and girls to make their decisions. The idea that work of one sort or another must eventually be undertaken can, in the writer's opinion, be understood and accepted even before early vocational decisions need be made. Positive but realistic attitudes toward work are a good preparation for making vocational choices and for eventual vocational adjustment. Not all occupations offer intrinsic satisfactions to the worker, but the possibilities for personal growth and mature satisfaction in the knowledge that one is a productively functioning member of society are very great. Adolescents, like adults, benefit from feeling and being useful and needed in their homes and communities. Such feelings can be fostered by the provision of opportunities for young persons to work, in a volunteer capacity, as a part of recreational programs, in well-supervised work-study programs in the schools, and (when the legal working age is reached) in part-time or summer employment while still in school.

In the junior high school and high school years, pressure for specific vocational choices should be minimized in favor of general planning, with decisions about possible future occupational level being made first, decisions about occupational fields being made later, and the more restrictive decisions concerning specific occupations being made last (Super and Overstreet, 1960, pp. 150–158). This does not mean the postponement of decision-making, but the making of decisions, insofar as possible, in a sequence from the broader, more inclusive ones to the narrower, more specific ones, as the individual matures, acquires more experience and, hopefully, more understanding of self and of society.

Chapter 18

Religion
and Morals

The Role of Religion

An adolescent's religious background, and the teachings of his religion regarding the nature and destiny of man, play an important role in determining his conception of who and what he is, and what he should aspire to be.

Religion, as we meet it in everyday life, consists of a system of professed beliefs, attitudes, and practices, commonly centered around a place of worship. The religion of one who is firmly committed is the most intimate and inclusive set of beliefs on which his ideas and attitudes concerning the meaning of his life are grounded.

From the personal point of view of a religious person, religion is that which is of ultimate concern. It is for many an answer to man's hunger for certainty, for assurance, for a faith to which he can cling, and for a sustaining hope. This hunger remains when all the desires of the flesh have been fulfilled.

From a social point of view, a person seeks through his religion to enter into meaningful relationships with others, reaching for a commit-

[373

ment he can share with others and seeking to join with others in common devotion to it. Although, as we will note later, religion frequently seems to be more a formal profession than a passionate personal concern, it is for many the keystone to a philosophy of life. Allport *et al.* (1948) found, for example, that 68 per cent of Harvard students and 82 per cent of Radcliffe students answered *Yes* to the question: "Do you feel that you require some form of religious orientation or belief in order to achieve a fully mature philosophy of life?"

Adolescence and Religious Expectations

In many religious denominations adolescence is regarded as an especially important period. Some religious groups have regarded adolescence as the time of "awakening," the time when a borrowed faith becomes a personal possession. In some religious groups it has been assumed that adolescence is a time when the young person is ripe for religious conversion or is ready to plunge into religion with more passionate certainty than he showed as a child. The rites of Confirmation, Bar Mitzvah and Bas Mitzvah, and other forms of introduction into adult religious privileges and practices and obligations, represent, for many persons, the most impressive acknowledgments of a young person's transition from childhood to responsible youthful adulthood.

Prevalence of Religious Beliefs and Practices

The typical adolescent of high school and early college age is "religious," at least to the extent of assenting to a number of religious beliefs and taking part in religious observances. A large proportion of young people profess a religious faith and a belief in the necessity of religion in life.[1]

The percentage of young people expressing belief in God has been found to vary somewhat in different populations, yet the percentage is almost invariably high. In several samplings about 90 per cent or more have expressed some kind of belief in God.[2] Such expressions of belief do

[1] Nelson (1940), Beekman 1947), Pixley and Beekman (1949), Dudycha (1950), Ross (1950), Myers (1951), Remmers, Myers, and Bennett (1951).
[2] Dudycha (1933, 1950), Kuhlen and Arnold (1944), Nelson (1950), Myers (1951), Gilliland (1940).

not, however, tell what the young person's religious convictions really are or how deeply he realizes his religion as a significant personal experience.

Religious beliefs and attitudes professed by persons at the high school and college level persist, in the case of most individuals, into later years. Nelson (1956), in 1950, applied several scales for the measurement of religious attitudes to about 900 persons who had responded as college students to the same scales in 1936. Eighty-six per cent of the persons showed either little or no shift in attitude, or a shift toward more favorable attitudes; only 14 per cent shifted toward less-favorable attitudes. As measured by these scales, the former college students were more religious, on the average, in 1950 than in 1936.

In several studies college women have described themselves as having stronger religious convictions and sentiments than men. Women also more often attend church and say daily prayers (see, *e.g.,* Allport *et al.,* 1948, and Nelson, 1940, 1956). Nelson (1956) found, however, that men and women were more similar in their religious attitudes after they had been out of college fourteen years than while they were still in college.

The religious beliefs professed by adolescents conform closely to what is found when persons in the adult population at large are questioned. In a Gallup poll (1954a) one question that was asked of the adults was: "Do you yourself believe in God?" Ninety-six per cent answered *Yes,* 1 per cent answered *No,* and 3 per cent replied that they did not know. At all age levels from twenty-one to fifty and over, over 90 per cent of those questioned answered that they believed in God. Moreover, at least 90 per cent of those at three educational levels in the sampling (college, high school, and grade school) expressed a belief in God.

Polls of high school and college students, and of the general population indicate that for the vast majority of persons an accepting attitude toward religion is a "must"—either as a matter of sincere conviction or of conformity. The percentages fall off sharply when more specific questions are asked pertaining to the faith they profess.

In another Gallup poll (1954b), it was noted, for example, that only 34 per cent of adults in a sampling knew the answer to the question, "Who delivered the Sermon on the Mount?" Only 21 per cent responded correctly when asked: "Can you name one of the prophets named in the Old Testament of the Bible?" On the other hand, 95 per cent correctly answered the question, "Who was the Mother of Jesus?" and 49 per cent were able to name the first book of the Bible.

Influence of Childhood Experiences
on Religious Attitudes in Adolescence

In the religious sphere, as in others, we can expect that a young person's developing convictions and attitudes must build upon what he has already learned and accepted. The young person's total personality and his upbringing until the time he reaches adolescence will have a significant bearing on his religious orientation during adolescent and later years (Roberts, 1950).

To realize the meaning of love, as emphasized in religion, the young person must draw upon his own experience with loving people. To realize what the concept of faith might mean, the young person likewise must build upon the foundations of faith and trust that have already been established in his earlier development and upbringing. All people have faith of some sort, whether formulated in religious terms or not. But it is difficult for an adolescent to find meaning in the religious faith he is taught if religion has been presented to him only in the form of doctrines and creeds and confessionals, which he had to memorize, like the names of the states of the Union.

The same principle applies to other aspects of religion.

Most religions emphasize common devotion that binds people together, giving the individual communion with something in which he is deeply involved and which also deeply involves him with others. To achieve such a state of devotion, the young person must draw upon experiences of relatedness to others in his own life.

Religions emphasize an inner state as being an important condition of religious faith and devotion when they stress a close and intimate relationship between the believer and the God in whom he believes. Presumably, if he is a real believer, his whole mind and his full heart will be involved in this relationship. To many persons, according to the religion they profess, this relationship means that they, the finite ones, are in communion with the infinite; that they who live within the boundaries of time and who reside in a temporal sphere are, through their religious beliefs, brought into touch with the eternal. The meaning of such a professed relationship must also build upon a young person's capacities for relatedness that have developed in the process of his own rearing and growth.

According to Roberts (1950), a person, as he moves toward adolescence and adulthood, may show two types of reaction if he has been brought up in a situation in which there is a contrast between the religious precepts that are taught and the actual example of religious living that is shown him. He may cling to a formal acceptance of ideals and religious convictions in a desperate attempt to assure himself that the universe is a secure place and that life is worthwhile despite the unsatisfactoriness of his actual experiences. He may make a desperate effort to maintain the semblance of faith as a means of escape from the reality of an existence that holds little meaning or faith. Obviously, this is not a joyful religion. As such a person nears adult years, it may occur to him now and then to take stock. But the prospect of facing the grim dislocation between what he professes and what he realizes, may be so frightening that he quickly pushes the issue aside.

Another reaction by a person who has been brought up in a home where there is inconsistency between attitudes that are displayed and standards that are professed is to become cynical and to reject ideals and religious beliefs altogether. He may treat them as "bunk" because of the gulf between what these ideals and beliefs are supposed to stand for and the emptiness he, as a child, encountered in his life with those who taught these ideals and beliefs. (On the other hand, when the parents' religious ideals are grounded in a capacity to give and to receive love, the child will be more likely gradually to appropriate a workable set of religious beliefs.)

It is not in the home alone, of course, but also in the religious instruction he receives outside the home that the child and adolescent meet individuals who may help them to integrate religious principles into their own lives, or make it difficult for them to do so. If surveys were made of the attitudes young people have toward religious teachers and clergymen, the findings probably would parallel those obtained from similar studies of attitudes toward teachers in secular schools (such findings are reviewed in an earlier chapter). The qualities of kindness, considerateness, and other "human" traits of the religious person would probably be stressed more than his religious views, just as the adolescents emphasize the human qualities of high school teachers more than their academic skills.

One of the problems connected with a young person's religious upbringing is that those who profess a religion—like persons in the secular field—may use their profession as a means of acting out unresolved personal problems. Examples are given by Overstreet (1953) of what might happen when an "unloving personality" enters actively into religious work. Overstreet describes character traits that many adults and older adolescents who have been associated with religious institutions will recognize. When a person who has been unable to relate himself to others in his daily life, or to accept others, or to win acceptance, affiliates himself with a church, he may remain basically as hostile and moved by anxious self-concern as he was before. He may be a pillar of the church, one who attends faithfully and works ardently; and yet his religious activities may take an unbending, dogmatic, and disapproving turn, colored by intolerance and a lack of forgiveness.

When one overhears adolescents (or adults) express bitterness when they speak of religion, the explanation may be that their religious upbringing was marred by personalities of this unloving type. Such bitterness is understandable. The hostility of the people who provoked such bitterness in the adolescent is perhaps not so easy to understand or to forgive, yet their condition, of course, springs from hurts in their own lives. It must be remembered that it is not only in the church, nor even primarily in the church, that one meets anxious and unloving persons who project their troubles upon others.

Developmental Changes in Expressed Attitudes and Beliefs

There are many trends in the development of the adolescent that might bring about a change in the way he thinks and feels about religion as he moves from the early teens into the early twenties. When development proceeds in a healthy way, the young person, as he moves along in years, has a greater capacity to examine the meanings of beliefs and ideas which earlier he took for granted and accepted secondhand from his parents and teachers. Such self-examination is a sign of healthy growth. The more thoughtful the adolescent is concerning his convictions, the more he will be able to test them. The more his convictions mean to him, the more courage he will have to explore their meaning.

As an adolescent grows in his ability to understand the meaning of life about him, he also, potentially, becomes capable of a deeper understanding of the meaning of religion. As he moves on in school, he will have an opportunity also to see his religious views in a widened perspective. When he meets persons who differ from him in religion, he may find it necessary to look a little more closely at his own beliefs. If he takes courses in science, literature, and philosophy, he will observe how human beings have striven to find and to phrase the truth, and how various are the answers they have found. If he keeps an open mind, he may realize, as never before, that what to him is a matter of belief is to others a matter of doubt. As he studies the cultural subjects in high school and college, he is likely to meet viewpoints and come upon theories and facts that touch upon his particular religious views and throw some doubt on the way he has formulated them. He will read about gods that seem strange to him and yet realize that at some time, in another place, there were persons like himself who believed in these gods and worshipped them, perhaps even more devoutly than he worships his own God. He will, if he allows his imagination free play, hear strange prayers ascending to these strange gods, and he will realize out of his own yearnings and needs why these prayers were said, and perhaps wonder whether they were heard.

Young people become more capable, as they reach adolescence, to think in terms of abstract ideas. In keeping with this development, we might expect that they would acquire a more profound understanding of the meaning of their religion.

Some changes in religious orientation appeared in a study conducted by Dawson (1900) in New England many years ago. This study dealt with the interest young people from about the age of eight to twenty showed in various parts of the Bible. Older children showed a lessened interest in the historical aspects of the Scriptures and an increased interest in the poetic parts of the Bible and in the Gospels. The shift was not impressively large, but it suggests that as children move into adolescence, the symbolism of their religion appears somewhat less in the form of images of certain external happenings (such as Daniel in the lion's den) and more in terms of beliefs and feelings. The younger person, in reading the story of Job, for example, would be impressed by the fact that Job was a man who was rich and good and owned 7,000 sheep and 3,000 camels and who remained a good man even though he had trouble and ended by being more richly blessed than ever, with 14,000 sheep and 6,000 camels. A more mature person, on the other hand, would be less impressed by Job's wealth and more impressed by the moral struggle and the soul-searching Job went through after he had lost his children and his possessions and was smitten with boils and given a rugged test of his faith. However, we cannot infer from Dawson's study how many adolescents might look at Job's inner struggle rather than the facts concerning his livestock.

Many observations indicate that young people take a less literal view of things as they grow older (Allport et al., 1948; Dudycha, 1933c; Jones,

1943). The older person is probably better able than the younger one to conceive, for example, of the six days of creation not as representing six twenty-four-hour days but as representing long periods of time.

One interesting finding in a study by Franzblau (1934) was that while still attending a religious school, the older children tended to question teachings they had accepted at the age of twelve. The mere fact of getting older and having continued contact with a religious institution did not mean that the young people grew more confirmed in their acceptance of religious beliefs. Many of them rejected religious dogmas as they matured, even though they attended religious school faithfully. Neither did they seem to gain steadily in intellectual understanding of the meaning of religious teachings as they grew older and continued their education. In this study, as in studies dealing with children belonging to many religious denominations, it was found that there was no close relationship between knowledge of religious history or ceremonies, on the one hand, and growth of character or personality, on the other.

One study indicates that a person of university age is less likely than a child to ask for specific things in prayer and that he uses prayer as a means of expressing or communicating his own attitude toward the situation and as a means of seeking peace of mind (Pixley and Beekman, 1949).

A study by Kuhlen and Arnold (1944), dealing with changes in religious beliefs in the age range from twelve to eighteen, shows some shifts, but the similarities between twelve- and eighteen-year-olds are generally more striking than the differences. For example, questions concerning heaven and hell are mentioned as being problems at all three age levels (twelve, fifteen, and eighteen) by over half the young people. More of the eighteen-year-olds than of the twelve-year-olds stated that they had problems due to conflicts between science and religion. Yet even in connection with this problem, which presumably should be more of an issue for the older than the younger person, the differences between the three age levels were not outstanding (42 per cent of the twelve-year-olds, 50 per cent of the fifteen-year-olds, and 57 per cent of the eighteen-year-olds mentioned problems on this score).

In a study comparing college underclassmen with upperclassmen, Katz and Allport (1931) found that a majority of college students in their group maintained substantially the same beliefs near the end of their college careers that they had on entering college, even though there were some shifts. The upperclassmen showed slightly less belief in a personal God and in prayer, and tended more to believe in an impersonal God than did the underclassmen. According to their own estimates, the students showed a tendency, during their college years, to shift toward a less orthodox position in religion. The trend toward unorthodoxy was consistent but moderate and was not in the nature of a revolution of thought and feeling.

While there are indications of changes in thinking such as those illustrated above, there are indications also that some young people do not change very much in their religious thinking as they move into the teens. Dimock (1937), for example, reports that the boys of sixteen in his study were just as likely as boys of thirteen to think of God as a person sitting on a golden throne, punishing the bad and answering prayers for material things.

Other findings suggest that while some young people, during the teens, go through a period of questioning some of their religious beliefs, they later return to them. Some persons, in their twenties or early thirties, when they become parents, take up religious practices which, for a time, they had neglected (see, *e.g.*, Bossard and Boll, 1943). Many others, also according to Pace (1941), expect to send their children to Sunday school even though they do not attend church themselves.

Emotional Aspects of Religious Doubt

From biographies and autobiographies we can see that religious experiences in adolescence may in some individuals be deeply charged with feeling, ranging from ecstatic joy to despair and despondency.

If a young person seriously sets out to examine the religious beliefs he has been taught, and raises doubts about them, the process of doubting is likely to be painful. It is disquieting at any time of life to question what one has been taught by those one respects and loves. It is disturbing if one feels that one must reject what one has believed and taken for granted over a period of several years. To question one's religion is equivalent to questioning an important foundation of one's approach to life. When a young person questions his religious beliefs, it is not just a doctrine or a theory that he is questioning. He is, in a sense, calling into question his own capacity for understanding as well as the relationship with those who have taught him and in whom he has placed his trust. Moreover, if his beliefs have been more than lip service, he is, in a sense, questioning the image of God he has formed and the conception of ultimate truth on which he had built his faith.

The fact that doubt may be very uncomfortable perhaps accounts in part for the fact that a large proportion of adolescents do not doubt very seriously. In the religious sphere young people show resistance to the idea of self-examination as they do in other areas of their lives.

An indication of the fact that in the religious sphere, as in other spheres, young people are not encouraged by others, or eager themselves, to use their ability to think and inquire into the position they profess to have taken appears in an interesting study by Watson (1929). Ratings were obtained from several hundred older boys who participated in religious services of various types. Among the services there was one consisting mainly of music; one that brought in passages of poetry and music; one, entitled "Silence," extolling by poetry and by pauses and prayers, the concept of being silent in the presence of the universe and the Almighty; and one called "A Quest," prepared on the assumption that the boys might, in connection with their worship, wish a more adequate concept of God. The "Quest" received the lowest ratings.

One consequence of lack of serious inquiry into the meaning and implications of religious beliefs is that some beliefs are inconsistent with each other. An interesting sidelight on religious beliefs appears in a study by Dudycha (1933), in which 74 per cent of the college students expressed a belief in immortality. Fifty-one per cent expressed a belief in a final day of judgment but only 39 per cent expressed a belief in the existence of hell. The author is not suggesting that young people *should* believe there is a hell, but, as a matter of consistency, if one believes literally that there will be a final day of judgment, the logic of this belief would imply that the judgment might be unfavorable. Allport *et al.* (1948) also noted inconsistencies. For example, a large number of persons, while professing some type of belief in God also maintained that religion should rule out the supernatural.

Discrepancy Between Formal Profession and Personal Commitment

The fact that many young people, while saying they accept religious beliefs, are merely giving passive assent to the idea of religion, is indicated in a study by Ross (1950). About two thousand persons, representing the constituency of a number of Y.M.C.A. groups, took part. A large percentage of young people appeared to lack a clear understanding of the concepts and symbols in which they said they believed, and these concepts and symbols frequently did not seem to be related to their lives in any significant way. About three-fourths of those questioned stated that they adhered to orthodox ideas of God, Jesus, and the Bible. But, according to Ross (p. 158), only about 16 per cent of the total number possessed "that combination of firm belief, zest for life, and sense of security" which he regarded as being characteristic of a religious person. The findings indicated that for a large number of young people religion is a "vague body of inherited or acquired ideas" which they have not, to any substantial degree, experienced or understood.

There were some differences between members of various faiths in the extent to which those who professed religious beliefs also regularly undertook religious practices, such as church attendance, prayer, Bible reading, and the like. But in all denominations, according to this study, a sizable proportion of those professing religion do not realize to any degree of depth the religious beliefs they profess. The evidence indicates that those who professed religious beliefs did not, on the whole, show a more kindly attitude toward their fellow men. They did not, for example, show a greater practical application of the concept of the brotherhood of man.

In a foreword comment, Allport (1950) speaks of a "central paradox" in Ross's findings. He points out that nearly everyone professes belief in God; prayer is a widespread practice; there is a friendly estimate of the church and a widely expressed conviction that mankind needs religion. At the same time, according to Allport, there seems to be a "ghostly quality" about these attitudes.

In his study of Elmtown's youth, Hollingshead (1949) similarly indicates that while the young people in the community he studied accepted religion by way of formal assent and seemed to assume that Christianity was the one right and true religion, it appeared that for many of these young people religion consisted to a large extent in an amorphous body of beliefs symbolized by a number of awesome words.[3]

Science, Reason, and Religion

Some adolescents have difficulty reconciling science and religion as though there were an irreconcilable conflict between the two. Others never give the issue a second thought.

A conflict is likely to arise, especially among some thoughtful young

[3] This matter of giving lip service to professed beliefs is not, however, limited to religion. It appears also in connection with academic aspects of life at school.

people as they move into late adolescence, if they have the view that they must choose religion or reason, or religion or science, but cannot choose both. It would help such an adolescent if he could be led to examine the viewpoint that science and religion, instead of being essentially in conflict, might support and supplement each other. At any rate, it probably would be helpful for the adolescent to realize that the more truly scientific a person is, or the more profoundly religious he is, the more he is a seeker of the truth and the more he will hesitate to cast scorn on others who also appear to be sincere seekers.

Macmurray (1937) has pointed out that it is the immature scientist, like the immature religious person, who is cocksure. According to Macmurray, the mature scientist is humble and tentative. He realizes the immensity of his ignorance. The profoundly religious person, likewise, is humble; he will hesitate to quarrel with the scientist, and he will hesitate to be dogmatic in dealing with his co-religionists.

As an adolescent matures and seeks to fathom the meaning of life he will have many opportunities to observe that scientists who delve deeply into the secrets of nature have much in common with theologians who try to interpret the meaning of life from a religious point of view. The closer a scientist comes to the boundary of the known, the more aware he becomes of the vastness and mystery of the unknown. And even in contemplating the known, he will at times have a feeling of awe, perhaps a feeling of reverence. He cannot help wondering what might be the meaning of what he knows and what answers might ultimately emerge as men's minds penetrate farther and farther into space and more and more deeply into the essence of matter. When the scientist thus begins to speculate about meanings, he is involved in a search not unlike that of a religious person who raises questions about ultimate meaning.

Some Overlapping Emphases in Psychological and Religious Approaches to Self-Fulfillment

Those adolescents who, as they move toward adult years, are examining themselves from a psychological point of view and are examining their religious beliefs, can discover many parallels between the psychology of self-realization and religion.[4]

[4] For discussions of some of the common elements in a psychological and a religious approach, see, for example, Fromm (1950), Roberts (1950), Bruder (1952), Silverman (1952), de Laszio (1953), Katz (1953), and Overstreet (1953).

One common emphasis is on the concept of love. When religion stresses loving one's neighbor as oneself it invokes the psychological principle that healthy love of self and love of others are intertwined.

Both a psychological and a religious approach emphasize the common humanity a person shares with others. The great religious faiths look upon human creatures as precious, regardless of differences in age, talent, or social status. In psychology, likewise, the further an adolescent goes toward finding himself and realizing himself, especially in the emotional sphere, the more he realizes that he has a kinship with others that cuts across the boundaries of age, sex, social class, or ethnic origin.

There is an acceptance of emotion both in religion and psychology. In the process of finding himself from a psychological point of view a person encounters love, pity, jealousy, anger, fear, terror, sorrow, grief, and lamentation. These emotions also flow through religious literature. The Psalmist weeps. He becomes weary of his groaning, and he waters his couch with his tears. But he also asks the people of all lands to make a joyful noise unto the Lord, to serve Him with gladness and to come before His presence with singing. In the New Testament there likewise is a strong stream of feeling. Jesus wept. He flared with anger. He showed compassion. He promised joy which no man can take away. The disciples cried out in terror. They went on their way rejoicing.

Both psychology and religion focus on the "inner life" rather than on outward appearance. The religious person recognizes this when he believes that the kingdom of God is within. He believes it would not profit a man if he gained the whole world and lost his soul. The Talmud recognizes the inner content rather than the outer form or possession when it inquires, "Who is rich?" and answers, "He who rejoices in his portion." These statements are from religion. Yet with a slight change of words they express attitudes that are emphasized in a psychology of self-fulfillment.

Another parallel between a religious and a psychological approach to life is that both involve an attitude of humility. In the religious and psychological sense this does not mean subservience, weakness, or self-abasement. Nor is it the opposite of being proud, for a person can be humble and still quietly take pride in his own integrity. Neither is humility the same as melancholy. It is rather a kind of "humble cheerfulness," a kind of dignity that makes it unnecessary for a person to pretend to be what he is not.

Kubie (1950) speaks of humility and a willingness to change, a willingness to become different, as something a person seeks when he goes for psychological help and also as something that sometimes occurs in the process of religious conversion.

In both the religious sphere and the psychological sphere there is an acceptance of the concept that the person who is trying to live according to his convictions will meet with trying times. He will face sorrow. He is likely to experience the hurt of being rejected because of his integrity.

The concept of guilt appears also commonly both in the psychological and in the religious conception of the human personality. There are differences between psychologists and scholars in religion (as well as within both of these groups) concerning the nature and origin of guilt and the means whereby this condition might be relieved. In both approaches, however, a distinction is made between healthy and unhealthy experiences of guilt. The language of religion calls for *true repentance*. This implies that repentance is different from false self-accusation. In psychology, similarly, a distinction is made between a healthy kind of remorse and an unhealthy kind of guilt feeling.

Guilt of an irrational sort is not health-inducing, either in a psychological or a religious sense. From a psychological point of view, such guilt represents a kind of sickness within the self. From a religious point of view, it denotes a lack of faith.

IMPLICATIONS FOR ADOLESCENCE

Parallels between psychology and religion, such as those described above, do not imply that psychology and religion are the same. It is implied, however, that when we seek to understand the adolescent, whether to guide him or to appreciate the nature of his existence, we face issues concerning the nature of human experience and questions of meaning and value that go beyond this or that fact or finding about adolescent development. Many of these issues and questions of meaning and value are much the same, whether one seeks to understand adolescence from the standpoint of an adolescent or a parent, or from the standpoint of psychology, education, or religion.

Moral Development

COGNITIVE ASPECTS

As young persons approach and enter the adolescent years they become increasingly able to *generalize* and *conceptualize* moral rules and principles. With the ability to understand general moral concepts, the adolescent is able to move beyond a morality based on specific rules to a morality based on principles that cover a wide variety of concrete situations. The concept of honesty, for example, covers a number of conditions such as being truthful, obeying rules against cheating, being scrupulous about others' possessions.

The process of generalizing is likely to be very uneven, however. A youngster who would not steal personal property, such as a schoolmate's flashlight, may not recognize that it is dishonest to steal public property, such as a lantern left on the road by highway repairmen. He may apply the principle of honesty by literally telling the truth, but not recognize that he is dishonest when he pretends to be friendly in order to take advantage of others. He may carefully apply principles of fair play in games, without appreciating that he is violating these principles when he gossips behind another person's back.

In his studies of the development of moral judgment, Piaget (1932) makes several distinctions between less mature and more mature moral ideas. According to Piaget there is a transition from *heteronomous* to *autonomous* moral judgment—from a morality based on laws laid down by others, toward a morality based on the individual's own judgment and convictions.

There is also a shift from *moral realism* to *moral relativism*. The "moral realist" makes a literal interpretation. He follows the letter of the law. He judges the seriousness of an act by its practical consequences: the person who stumbles and breaks a dozen eggs is morally more at fault than the one who deliberately smashes one egg. The moral realist also judges seriousness by the severity of the punishment that follows: a youngster who is flogged for stealing an apple has committed a greater offense than one who is mildly scolded for cheating on a test.

The "moral relativist," on the other hand, takes account of intentions as well as practical consequences: a youngster who deliberately spills a drop of ink of another's handkerchief is a more serious offender than one who accidentally spills a bottle of ink of another's clothes. The relativist also makes allowances: a hungry boy who steals a pie is morally less culpable than a well-fed boy who snitches a doughnut and throws it away.

In studies of moral judgments of adolescents it has been found that the average young person of adolescent age (and even prior to adolescence) is likely to subscribe to ideas of right and wrong that come close to the ideas held by adults. Lockhard (1930) found that the ideas of elementary school children as to the seriousness of various forms of wrongdoing and concerning the conditions under which it would be defensible to break a law correspond closely to the ideas of adults.

MORAL JUDGMENTS AS RELATED TO EMOTIONAL ADJUSTMENT

While intellectual understanding has an important role in the development and application of moral concepts, motives and emotions also play an important role. Youngsters who rate higher than average in emotional adjustment are likely to make more mature moral judgments than persons, with similar intelligence, who are emotionally disturbed (Shumsky, 1956). Those with superior emotional adjustment are better able to take account of intentions and circumstances in judging the moral seriousness of various acts. Those who are emotionally maladjusted tend to be more punitive than those with more favorable adjustment, and tend also to base their moral judgments on a concept of absolute authority.[5]

Moral Attitudes and Values

The findings in various studies suggest that in formulating their moral standards many adolescents emphasize conformity to rules of conduct more than loyalty and fellow-feeling. In all the grades from six to twelve in a study by Thompson (1949), the young people rated being honest as more praiseworthy than being kind. In a study by Mitchell (1943) high school seniors, in rating the importance of various virtues, gave the highest rank to *honesty*. *Kindness* and *charity* were both ranked as less important than such virtues as *honesty* or *sportsmanship*.

[5] For a fuller discussion of moral values and attitudes see Allport and Vernon (1931), Grace and Grace (1952), Taba (1953), V. Jones (1954), Anderson and Anderson (1954), and Peck and Havighurst *et al.* (1960). Moral attitudes as related to socioeconomic status have been discussed in Chapter 14.

In a discussion of the moral beliefs of sixteen-year-old adolescents, Taba (1953) similarly points out that they tend to accept familiar stereotypes in expressing their moral values, without inquiring very deeply into what they might mean. The young people in Taba's study were unanimous, for example, in expressing the feeling that one must defend people against gossip, but they showed doubt and apprehension about taking a stand that would arouse the displeasure of someone in authority or jeopardize their popularity with their peers. The sixteen-year-olds were reluctant to face squarely a conflict of moral values, tending instead to attempt to compromise or to adopt slogans. In a conflict between his own interests and the demands of the school, an adolescent might, for example, come forth with the idea that it is necessary to obey school rules, as though this were one of the verities of life, and yet the same adolescent might show many exceptions and inconsistencies in applying this idea in specific situations without asking whether he really believed that the rules laid down by the school were infallible, or whether he was really convinced concerning his own rights in the matter.

Studies of the moral values adolescents claim to embrace indicate that young people, like many of their elders, often follow the rule of what is most expedient and what they think others will regard as most expedient. As a result, in a specific situation (whether to cheat or not to cheat, whether to defend a classmate who is the victim of bias or unfair attack) there may be a wide discrepancy between the moral principle a person claims to accept and his actual conduct.[6]

In a study of thirty-four children from their tenth to their seventeenth year, Peck and Havighurst *et al.* (1960) classified moral character according to five "types."

One was the "amoral type," representing the most infantile, impulsive, and irresponsible kind of character, without internalized moral principles and without regard for the consequences of behavior. Next in the scale was the "expedient type": a person described as primarily self-centered, one who considers other people's welfare only to gain his own ends, and behaves morally only so long as it suits his purpose—to get what he wants and to avoid disapproval. Third was the "conforming type," whose main moral principle was to do what others do and what they say he *should do*. Such a person, as described by the investigators,

---

[6] Among the writers who have emphasized the way in which moral issues have psychological implications from the standpoint of mental health are Jung (1933), Fromm (1947), and Tillich (1952). Murphy (1947) has discussed the way in which a person who is insecure in his own self-regard tends to bolster himself by rigid and authoritarian moral standards.

in conforming to his group and seeking to avoid disapproval, follows literal rules specific for each occasion instead of having generalized moral principles. Fourth was the "rational conscientious type": this person is described as one who has his own internal standard of right and wrong by which he judges his acts, but he is rigid in applying his moral principles. He regards an act as good or bad because he defines it as such and not out of consideration for the good or ill effects his conduct might have on others.

The fifth type described by Peck and Havighurst *et al.* is the "rational altruistic type": this type, according to the classification scheme used by the authors, represents "the highest level of moral maturity." He has a stable set of moral principles by which he is guided; he tries realistically to appraise the results of a given act and assesses it in terms of whether or not it serves others as well as himself. He is rational in his assessment of his conduct in the light of his principles, and he is altruistic in showing a concern about the welfare of others as well as himself.

Each of the subjects in the study was assigned to a "type group" according to the "predominant configuration" of his character profile, even though none of the persons was a "pure" type.

At age sixteen there were youngsters belonging to each of these five types. Five of the thirty-four children were classed as having an "amoral" type of character. Four seemed unmistakably to belong to the "rational altruist" group; and an additional five were classed as being "near" to this type. The remaining youngsters were distributed among the other types, with the largest single group (eight in number) classed as belonging to the "conforming" type.

These investigators found that there was a marked tendency for children to show the same level of morality at ages thirteen and sixteen as they had shown at the age of ten.

As can be seen, only a minority of the persons in this study reached what the authors regarded as the most mature type of moral development. It appears from this study that morals that are established by the age of ten persist into later years. After the age of ten moral character was relatively unaffected by experiences at school or children's relationships with peers and other persons outside the home.[7]

---

[7] The investigators attribute a youngster's character type almost exclusively to what he has learned under the influence of his parents, although they note that their data do not prove whether factors that affect character development might somehow be genetically inherited through transmission of similarities from one generation to the next.

part seven | Toward the Future

Chapter 19

Personality
Development
and Self-Fulfillment

This final chapter will summarize some of the main currents in the life of the adolescent as he takes his place in adult society, facing the future on the foundation he has built in the past. While this, in part, will be a review of lines of thought presented in earlier chapters, new material is also included.

The Meaning of Personality

An adolescent's personality is the sum of his attributes and qualities as a person as well as the way these are integrated into the total way of his life. The adolescent's personality includes all of his measurable traits and abilities, his temperament, and his disposition. It includes all the emotional tendencies and behavior patterns that mark him as a well-adjusted or maladjusted person as measured by the standards of the society in which he lives. It includes his strengths and his weaknesses. It includes the obvious and the hidden motives that govern his way of life. The "center" of his personality, from his own point of view, consists in all the ideas and attitudes that are embodied in his conception of himself.

Stability and Change in Personality Development

In the process of development from birth to adulthood there usually is a high degree of stability or sameness in an individual's personality traits from year to year, but there also are many changes. The changes that occur often consist of a modification, with age, in the overt way in which a certain trait is revealed or expressed (as, for example, when a youngster who was crudely aggressive as a little child is more subtly aggressive as a young adult).

Changes also occur when a youngster, at a certain stage of growth, discovers or realizes resources which were not so important or apparent before but which are now important to him. For example, qualities that make a person attractive to the opposite sex are more significant in middle and late adolescence than in early childhood.

Changes may also occur when a person must deal with stresses and strains for which he is not prepared. (This happens when a person who was protected in earlier childhood "breaks down" under the challenges of adolescence.)

In the readily measurable attributes of an adolescent's personality, consistency and constancy are more conspicuous than change. There is a high correspondence from year to year, during the period of physical growth, in the young person's height and weight. The adolescent's mental ability, as measured by intelligence tests, usually remains very stable. His "social personality"—as judged by his peers, and as measured by sociometric tests—although less "constant" than the I.Q., shows a high correlation from year to year, at least through the high school period. And in the sphere of character development, there likewise is considerable consistency when the same criteria for judging character are applied over a period of years (Peck and Havighurst et al., 1960).

There are many factors that produce both stability and change in the adolescent.

Interaction Between Genetic and Environmental Factors

The adolescent's genetic endowment, which he received at the time of his conception, remains relatively unchanged during his lifetime. But this genetic endowment produces both stability and change in his manifest characteristics in the course of his growth.

As noted in Chapter 3, many physical characteristics that are influenced by heredity (such as, early or late sexual maturing, the timing and extent of the growth spurt, and the distribution of fatty tissue) are not apparent until the adolescent years. These physical characteristics have an important bearing on the adolescent's view of himself and his relationships with others. As noted also in Chapter 3, an inherited predisposition to mental illness may not manifest itself until the adolescent years or later.

On the other hand, temperamental qualities, which are apparent from the time of birth, and which are rooted in genetically-determined biochemical properties of the organism, have the effect of producing stability in the adolescent's personality. The adolescent's inborn temperamental qualities influence not only the way he responds to his environment but also determine to an important degree the nature and structure of his environment through the effects they have on others.

SELF-PERPETUATING ASPECTS OF PERSONALITY DEVELOPMENT

Many personal characteristics, when once established, tend to become firmly established as times goes on. This may be due to the effect a person's characteristics have on others, or to the way the person himself rationalizes or justifies his characteristics, or to a combination of both of these factors.

Social Reinforcement of Personality Traits

In several earlier sections of this book it has been noted that a youngster's characteristics are nourished by the response they evoke in others. For example, an aggressive individual is likely to arouse counteraggression, and this adds fuel to his own aggressiveness. Similarly, a youngster who is socially "outgoing" is more likely than not to create a friendly atmosphere: he invites others to be friendly, and when they respond in kind they support his own friendly tendencies.

Reinforcement Through a Striving for Self-Consistency

A youngster's characteristics are often perpetuated through his own endeavor to maintain a consistent view of himself. The concept of self-consistency has been explored more thoroughly in theoretical studies than in studies tracing the development of children from year to year. But this concept helps to account for much in the adolescent that otherwise would be hard to fathom. The theory that an individual has a strong motive to maintain a consistent view of himself has been set forth by Lecky (1945). The same idea runs through many other writings dealing with the development of the self. In earlier chapters of this book there are many illustrations of the need a person has for building what seems to be a reasonable interpretation of himself. An individual tries to construct what to him seems a logical and internally coherent accounting of his feelings and conduct even when in doing so he creates difficulty for himself.

In his striving for self-consistency, a person will perceive and interpret what happens to him in the light of his preconceptions. He will seek experiences that are in keeping with the conception he has of himself. What he chooses to hear and see, or not to hear and see, will be influenced by his desire to maintain beliefs and attitudes he already has formed. Even his memory will abet him, in that he is more likely to remember happenings in his past that accord with a particular view he has of himself. When his memories are not easy to manipulate, he is likely, in what he recalls, to give greatest weight to those which support ideas and attitudes concerning himself that he would like to maintain.

There is something durable, something that persists through time, within each unique personality. When we deal with an adolescent it is important to remember that his personal characteristics, habits, and attitudes have been a long time in the making. They are likely to be tenacious and not easily changed. It is especially important to bear this fact in mind when we deal with adolescents who are in trouble. If we do not, we are likely to demand too much of the adolescent, or to blame him or his parents, or to blame ourselves, when our efforts to help him seem to have little effect.

Capacity for Change

But there is a paradox here. Even though there is a high degree of consistency in the adolescent's personality, and a considerable degree of resistance to change, the typical adolescent also has a capacity for flexibility and great potentiality for changing. Even an adolescent who is severely disturbed emotionally has a capacity for growth and self-repair.

Moreover, some changes occur in the process of maturing. In an earlier chapter we noted that many persons who are delinquents in their teens became less aggressive and settle down as law-abiding citizens some years later.

In addition, changes in the life situation may also bring a change in the manifest aspects of an individual's personality. In a long-term study of a group of young persons, Anderson, Harris *et al.* (1959) found that some children who were rated low in adjustment improved and achieved satisfactory adjustment when they were "on their own and freed from home and school."

Personality Problems

All adolescents have "problems." They cannot live without encountering difficulties and predicaments that are linked with human existence. The adolescent who ventures must accept the risk as well as the promise that goes with each of his ventures. The adolescent who strives to realize his potentialities is bound to meet disappointments and frustrations. The more enterprising he is, the more likely he is to face choices pertaining to the present and the future that involve conflict between contending motives within himself. Such problems are part of the business of living. They are problems neither the "well-adjusted" nor the "maladjusted" can side-step. The only way to avoid them would be to retreat and withdraw from life; but to do that would be to create other problems, for unless the adolescent has been beaten and discouraged to the point of apathy and despair, his urge to live and to do and to venture will be strong.

In addition to the problems that every creature must face as something inseparable from the living of a life, there are some problems that place an additional burden upon the individual adolescent. Such problems prevail when he is not simply laboring with concerns of the present, or struggling with uncertainties about the future, but is still fighting a rear-guard action with his past.

IRRATIONAL HOSTILITY

Adolescents who stand out publicly as seriously disturbed comprise only a small number of those who struggle with unresolved personal problems. In Chapter 9 we noted, for example, the way in which attitudes of hostility make it necessary for the adolescent to refight old battles, as though those who had hurt him in the past had taken lodging in the persons he is dealing with in the present.

When an adolescent attaches old grievances to new persons and to new circumstances, he is not facing the tasks of life in a realistic way. He uses his energy to fight fruitless battles. He may create an enemy where he might have found a friend. The result is that the one who is punished most severely by the adolescent who harbors unresolved attitudes of hostility is the adolescent himself.

ANXIETY

Another condition that has a prominent place among the personality problems of adolescents is anxiety (which was discussed at length in Chapter 10). Probably all adolescents are anxious to some degree. Anxiety may prevail as an inevitable, and even a constructive, response to the predicaments of human existence. But it may also be, and often is, a form of needless suffering and self-defeat.

It is impossible, on the basis of present evidence, to assess how widely self-defeating anxiety prevails in the total adolescent population, for often anxiety is hidden, both from the eyes of the anxious one and from others; it may even appear in the disguise of a virtue. An assessment of the more obvious symptoms of anxiety, known in the literature as "manifest anxiety," indicates that the typical person has many such symptoms.[1]

OTHER PROBLEMS

The typical adolescent is, in many ways, a troubled person. As noted in earlier chapters, and especially Chapter 10, he suffers from a variety of personal problems—such as, currents of self-rejection, worries about the present and the future, and difficulties in his relationships with others.

Although these difficulties place a burden on the typical adolescent's life, they are not so severe that he is unable eventually to assume the normal responsibilities of adult life.

[1] As noted in Chapter 10, in tests of about two thousand college students with a manifest anxiety scale which contained fifty items, Taylor (1953) found that the average score was fifteen.

Reaching for Maturity

Adolescence is a process of maturing, and, if all goes well, the individual will be more "mature" when he enters young adulthood than when he entered the adolescent phase of growth. However, the concept of maturity as related to adolescents should not be regarded as denoting a fixed state or an end point in the process of development. Maturity is a relative term, denoting the degree to which, at any juncture of his life, a person has discovered and is able to employ the resources that become available to him in the process of growth.

Maturity is, in part, a biological product: it is linked with the maturation of the organism. Maturity is also a product of learning: it is only through training, discipline and experience that a person's psychological potentials can be put to use. Maturity is, in addition, a cultural concept, for when we assess a person's maturity we do so, in large measure, in terms of standards and values of the culture in which we live.

In assessing maturity in this or that sphere of life (mental, social, moral, and emotional), it is essential to take account of the level attained by the normal or typical person and also to consider the condition of exceptional persons: those who do not measure up to normal standards and those who exceed these standards. When an adolescent is "immature" (for example, is more dependent than most persons of his own age or has "childish" moral standards) one question we face (among others) is how he came to be that way: is it because of inherent limitations or because of unfortunate upbringing or both? When an adolescent far exceeds normal standards, he provides a model of what a person with a superior endowment or with an optimum environment within a given culture, or a combination of these, can achieve. This model is a valuable one, for in defining the goals and desirable outcomes of adolescent development it is important to know not only what is *probable* under ordinary circumstances but also what is *possible* under the best circumstances.

INTELLECTUAL MATURING

As noted in Chapter 6, one aspect of maturing in the intellectual sphere appears in an increase, with age, in the abilities that are measured by intelligence tests. This increase normally continues through the teens and probably into the twenties. In the college group, seniors are likely to earn higher average mental test scores than they earned as freshmen (Shuey, 1948; Owens, 1953). During the teens and twenties and for several years thereafter, if all goes well, there also is likely to be a continuing increase in knowledge gained from experience, an increase in judgment, common sense, and what we refer to as "horse sense."

Another aspect of intellectual maturity consists of ability to deal with generalizations and to apply abstract principles, to master logical principles and to learn to apply them to specific cases, at least in some areas.

The capacity for creative thinking apparently continues to increase well beyond the twenties, as measured by the age at which persons who have gained distinction in science, literature, the arts and other fields, made their first contributions (Lehman, 1953). Since it takes time and opportunity to complete a creative task, it is possible that the underlying creative abilities reached their peak well in advance of the time when these persons first gained distinction. In some areas a few noteworthy creative persons made their first contribution before the age of twenty. But in practically all areas far more made their first noteworthy contribution in their twenties, thirties, forties or beyond.

PHYSICAL MATURING

Although adolescents differ considerably in the timing of various physical developments such as the growth spurt and the onset of the menarche, most of them have reached the major developments leading to physical maturity by the time they reach the age of twenty.

MORAL MATURING

According to available findings, the typical adolescent does not appear to show a steadily increasing degree of "moral maturity" during the teen-age years, or even while attending college.

Ideally, from the point of view of a moral philosopher, the growing person would move toward "moral autonomy," with an internalized set of moral standards, convictions, and commitments. He would apply his moral principles in a rational way, with due regard for his social responsibilities. Also, ideally, a "morally mature" young person would be able, in passing judgment on others, to take account of their motives and intentions and the extenuating circumstances.

Actually as we have noted in Chapter 18, many of the moral decisions made in late adolescence are based on conformity and expediency. There is no reason to believe, however, that in this respect adolescents differ from the typical adult.

MATURING OF SELF-INSIGHT

There are some indications that young persons, during the course of adolescence, acquire an increasing insight into themselves. But the evidence on this score is very fragmentary. We do not know what the typical adolescent actually achieves by way of insight or what he potentially might achieve.

Here and there in earlier chapters we have noted that during the course of adolescence, or soon thereafter, many persons assume a more "mature" view of themselves. In the chapter on vocational development, Dr. Nicholas pointed out that many young persons in the late teens are more realistic in their thinking about their vocational plans than they were at an earlier age. In Chapter 16 we noted that a study by Sanford (1957) indicated that seniors in a woman's college were more inclined to examine their values and had more insight into themselves than they displayed as freshmen.

In this earlier chapter we also noted that students who took part in an investigation by Jervis and Congdon (1958) named growth in self-understanding as one of the most important objectives in college education; but the investigators report that "the only objective the students felt was being inadequately met was self-understanding." Apparently these students regarded a gain in self-understanding as something that potentially *could* be achieved even though they were disappointed in what they actually did gain.

Steps Toward Emotional Maturing

Much of what is said in this concluding statement discusses a kind of emotional maturity toward which the adolescent is moving if he is realizing his possibilities.

SOME CULTURAL ASPECTS OF EMOTIONAL MATURITY

From a cultural point of view an adolescent is emotionally mature if he conforms to the stereotype of maturity prevailing in the culture in which he lives.

In one of the pioneer efforts to define emotional maturity as related to adolescence, Hollingworth (1928) notes that many of the tests of fitness for manhood and womanhood in ancient pubic ceremonies were tests of the capacity to suffer. The assumption underlying them seems to have been that one who has fortitude and who can endure pain silently and without protest is a mature person.

The "mature" lad in Sparta would be one who could suffer intense pain without flinching or crying for help. But in another culture such a person might be regarded as having a childish notion of what it means to be mature.

In one cultural group a "mature" man has many wives and perhaps is looking for more, while in another cultural group it is a sign of immaturity when a man, once he has got a woman, keeps chasing after others.

According to one set of standards, the person who is most rigorously competitive, and who is best able to sustain both the defeats and the triumphs of competition, is the most mature, while in another group it is not the one who is most competitive but the one who is most cooperative who is the most mature.

PSYCHOLOGICAL MEANINGS OF MATURITY

In naming what she regarded as mature behavior, Hollingworth (1928) stated that the emotionally mature person is (1) *capable of gradations or degrees of emotional response.* He does not respond in all-or-none fashion but is moderate and keeps within bounds. He is also able (2) *to delay his responses;* he does not act impulsively as a young child would. He shows his maturity also in (3) *his handling of self-pity;* he does not show unrestrained pity for himself but feels no sorrier for himself than others would feel for him.

Other earlier accounts of the meaning of emotional maturity have stressed the ability to bear tension, outgrowing of adolescent moodiness and sentimentality, and an indifference toward certain kinds of happenings that would arouse the emotions of a child or an adolescent but should not arouse an adult.

These accounts describe some aspects of self-control which, in our culture, we more or less take for granted as characteristics of a mature person. However, maturing emotionally does not mean simply to control emotion or to keep a lid on feeling. Maturing emotionally also means an ability to use emotional resources to get satisfaction from enjoyable things; to love and to accept love; to experience anger when faced with thwartings that would arouse the temper of any reasonable person; to accept and to realize the meaning of the fear that arises when one faces frightening things, without needing to put on a false mask of courage; to reach out and to seek what life might offer, even though to do so means to face the possibility of gain and of loss, of enjoyment and of grief.[2]

CAPACITY FOR GIVING AS WELL AS TAKING

When all goes well, persons who are biologically able to beget children are also emotionally able to devote themselves to the care of children. There are, of course, young people who have the biological capacity for becoming fathers or mothers without possessing a psychological capacity for fatherly or motherly feeling. By contrast, a person may be capable of intense motherly or fatherly feeling even though he or she does not happen to have fathered or mothered a son or a daughter. Deutsch (1944–1945) has pointed out that a woman, for example, can be a "psychological mother" even though, being childless, she is not a "biological mother."

The development of the capacity to give makes it possible for a father or mother to watch over a child in spite of fatigue and discomfort. It is this development that makes it possible for teachers to be *psychological* mothers or fathers and to devote themselves wholeheartedly to their students. It is a development that will help the adolescents as they move into adulthood to be devoted to each other as husbands and wives in spite of the difficulties and frictions that occur in every marriage.

If this aspect of emotional development has not taken place during childhood, adolescence, and early adulthood, the job of being a parent or of assuming the role of a substitute parent (a role teachers and many

[2] For other accounts of the meanings of maturity see Saul (1947), Cole (1959), and Allport (1961).

others occupy) will be a burden, and the task of having relations with people in the world at large will be filled with countless grievances and frustrations.

INCREASING REALISM IN APPRAISING PEOPLE

One aspect of emotional maturing is an increasing ability to see people as real persons, to perceive and appreciate the humanity of others, not to expect the good person to be a perfect saint nor the bad person to be an all-out sinner.

With allowance for many lapses, the adolescent as he matures may be able to perceive, without becoming cynical, that even the teacher he likes best is a human being who has weaknesses. He will realize that the pastor in his church, who urges his flock to be charitable, has his own uncharitable moments. He will recognize that the school psychologist, who helps others to cope with their anxieties, also has anxieties of his own. He will suspect (if he gets around, is astute in his observations) that the marriage counselor, after a hard day's work, sometimes goes home and quarrels with his wife, and the psychiatrist (if the town can afford one) at times shows rejection of a son or daughter. He may even suspect that the nutritionist at school now and then has a hot fudge sundae with whipped cream when she should be eating spinach.

An immature person might respond to such signs of human frailty as something to blame and he might take the line that, when others thus are less than perfect, he has a moral right to be a great deal less than perfect.

REVIEWING OF HOPES AND ASPIRATIONS

During the period of adolescence young people face the task of bringing their hopes into line with the realities of life. If all goes well a process of selecting and discarding takes place, and while hopes run high in some youngsters, others are called upon to make the kind of emotional adjustment that is required when plans that are visionary must be abandoned or reduced to a humbler scale. The process of trimming hopes and expectations is, of course, not limited to adolescence. For many persons it continues far into the years of adult life, and for some it begins much earlier in life.

TOLERANCE OF ALONENESS

As adolescents mature, many of them must be able to tolerate a feeling of being alone when they reach for independence, or what they regard as their independence. Some, in pursuing their own interests and working for goals they consider important, run the risk of being thought "queer," and queer people often are lonely people. For some, to be lonely is a condition which, although uncomfortable, is less painful, as they see it, than to follow the crowd on its own terms. Younger children, too, know what it is to be lonely, but they have more freedom to seek comfort from others.

INCREASED CAPACITY FOR COMPASSION

Much of what has been said in this and earlier chapters suggests that compassion is the ultimate and most meaningful embodiment of emotional maturity. It is through compassion that a person achieves the highest peak and deepest reach in his search for self-fulfillment.[3]

Compassion means fellowship of feeling. It denotes a capability of entering the feelings involved in emotional experiences—joy or sorrow, anger or fear, pride or shame, hope or despair. To be compassionate means to be able to appreciate some of the personal meanings and the subjective reality of emotion—another's emotion, one's own emotion. To be compassionate a person must be able to enter into his own feelings, absorb them, and draw upon them. Only to the extent that he has the strength and freedom to experience the quality of his own feelings and to be at home with them can he respond with feeling to what someone else is experiencing.

To be compassionate, a person must be able to bear the brunt of an emotion, to feel its sharp edge, to taste its bitterness or sweetness, and then tolerate it, sustain it, and harbor it long enough to accept its meaning and to enter into a fellowship of feeling with the one who is moved by the emotion. This is the heroic feature of compassion: to be able to face the ravage of rage, the impact of fear, the tender promptings of love, and then to encompass these in a larger context that involves an accept-

[3] This section is built largely on some of the author's earlier efforts to explore the meaning of emotional maturity (1954, 1955).

ance of these feelings and an appreciation of what they mean to the one who experiences them.

To be compassionate means to partake in passion, to participate in feeling rather than viewing it as a spectator might. Compassion has a greater sweep than anger, love, or fear, since it incorporates these emotions in a larger context of feeling.

To be compassionate is not simply to be sympathetic, tender, or thin-skinned. To be compassionate a person has to be tough. The thin-skinned person turns anxiously away when confronted with pain, sorrow, or anxiety of another. Or he hastily tells the other "Don't cry," "Keep a stiff upper lip," "Don't take it so hard," not because this will help the other person but because the other's tears are threatening to him and because he cannot endure seeing someone else tremble with fear or give way to anger. To be compassionatae, one must have enough ruggedness to endure these emotions. Compassion is not the emotion of the weak but the hard-gotten property of the strong.

But compassion is not all toughness. A compassionate person responds to joy as well as to anger or fear. Moreover, he has a certain delicacy of response which enables him, at least sometimes and with some persons, to detect feeling even though it is not violently expressed.

A central and essential feature of compassion can perhaps best be expressed by the idea of *acceptance*. The compassionate person accepts emotion as a condition that prevails in himself and in others. He does not take the attitude, in advance, that some emotions (such as anger or fear) are bad and should be rooted out, and that some emotions (such as cheerfulness) are good and should be encouraged. He accepts the fact of emotion in himself and others without having an immediate and over-ruling impulse to defend, to attack, to excuse, to blame or condone. He accepts himself as a person who gets angry and accepts this fact for what it is worth, without having an instantaneous impulse to snuff out his anger or to feel guilty about it. Acceptance of emotion means accepting oneself and others as having a capacity for tender feelings, erotic feelings, feelings tied to a desire for recognition, and so on.

The concept of acceptance, as used here, does not refer to self-pity or smugness or license to give way to any and all kinds of emotional outbursts. To accept oneself as one who has the right to be angry or afraid does not mean that every time one is angry one will automatically conclude that the anger is justified or the fear well grounded.

The one who is free to experience his feelings does not necessarily allow himself unlimited freedom in the expression of feeling. He does not go about openly spilling his emotions all over the place. While free to feel, he is also able to think and to plan and to perceive what is fitting. Freedom to feel is not to be confused with irresponsibility. This point is emphasized here because, in discussing the concept of emotional maturity with adolescents and adults, the writer has found that many persons have been so conditioned to the idea that emotions should be "controlled" that they seem to feel that it is unwise and even dangerous to question the idea that control in itself is a virtue.

In trying to act in a responsible way, a person does not suppress a show of emotion simply because he considers such suppression in itself a worthy thing. He will realize that there are times when to show fear might be frightening to others and so, if he is able to conceal his fear he will do so. But he will also realize that there are times when to show fear is heartening to others who are frightened.

In another connection the writer (1955) has used anger to illustrate what is meant by compassion. To be compassionate with one who is angry means that one allows oneself to enter in the meaning of this anger. It does not mean that at the moment of compassion one becomes as angry as the angry person (if one did, rage, not compassion, would be the primary emotion). It does not mean that one feels sorry for the angry one (one might feel sorry, but that is not the essence of compassion); nor that one deplores the anger (although one might rightly, as a separate consideration, feel that the anger is deplorable); nor that one feels that the angry person would be justified in feeling far more angry than he actually is (one might, as a matter of independent judgment, have this impression, but that is not the same as compassion).

To be compassionate with one who is angry means to know, in an emotional way, the nature of anger and the meaning it has for the one who is angry. To feel compassion for one who is lonely or hungry or jealous or sad or sexually aroused means that one has drawn upon one's own resources for experiencing what these emotions, moods, and appetites mean.

Sharp differences in this ability to perceive the feelings of others can sometimes be observed when we associate with adolescents. Almost any young person can perceive distress when he comes upon a child who is weeping or a crippled beggar who piteously asks for help. But one who can draw upon a capacity for compassion does not need to meet distress in so naked a form to perceive it. He may be able to perceive it in a person who is silent and expressionless, who is not pointedly displaying the fact that he is lonely or anxious or beaten down by rejection at home or by failure at school. He may even be able to perceive that when the feelings of such a troubled person do burst forth they may look and sound more like anger than pain. He may be able to perceive, further, that this "anger" may be directed not against a tormentor, but against a friendly person.

The ability to pierce the disguises of feeling, to detect a vein of anxiety or grief beneath what seems to be angry or "fresh" and impudent behavior, and to feel moved by the hurt that is concealed is one of the most hard-won properties of compassion.

How capable, we might ask, are young people of achieving compassion? We have few scientific data bearing on this question. We do not know what the "norm" is. But now and then one can observe an adolescent who can see the distress that is concealed under the camouflage of bitterness, spitefulness, bullying, sarcasm, and cruelty in the behavior of their elders and peers.

This matter of compassion is something that adolescents cannot learn from books. One does not mature emotionally at second hand. In this respect there is a difference between intellectual and emotional development. In the intellectual sphere, one can, to a large degree, appropriate to oneself what others have experienced and put into words. One can have a pretty thorough knowledge of ancient Rome without having been there; one can have an intellectual picture of ancient Greece without having seen it. In mathematics, chemistry, and all other sciences, if one has enough brain power, one can grasp and incorporate as one's own the meanings others have found in painstaking discoveries. One learns that the earth is round and does not have to go through the struggle, still less the persecution, of those who proved the earth was not flat.

But there are no such short-cuts in the emotional sphere. Each generation can, if it will, pick up the intellectual legacies of the past; but in the emotional sphere each generation must, in a sense, start from the beginning.

In his emotional development each child is a pioneer. He can, as he grows older, absorb to some extent from the poets some of the feeling that has gone into the building of the world up until his time; he can catch certain overtones and undertones of anguish and hope, joy and sorrow, anger and fear, in the great literature and the great paintings that have been bequeathed to the young people of his generation. But to realize the meaning of emotion, he must experience it at first hand. He can never know what it is to *feel* simply by reading. He cannot know pain and suffering simply by seeing the expression of pain in a great painting.

Love will forever be a colorless thing to him until he has a chance to experience it directly.

The emotional maturity we speak of here as compassion is hard won. No wealth can buy it. One can go to the best schools and miss it. One cannot send a proxy into the struggle and gain it through him. It is something distinctly intimate and personal. It is had only through direct personal involvement. There are elements of compassion one can possess only at the price of pain. There are other elements that one can possess only through having known the meaning of joy. But the full tide of compassion comes from all the streams of feeling that flow through human existence.

Bibliography

Abernethy, E. M., 1925. "Correlations in Physical and Mental Growth," *Journal of Educational Psychology,* **16,** 458–466, 539–546.

———, 1936. *Relationships Between Mental and Physical Growth,* Monographs of the Society for Research in Child Development, **I,** No. 7. Washington, D.C.: National Research Council.

Abraham, W., 1957. "A Hundred Gifted Children," *Understanding the Child,* **6,** 116–120.

Abt, L. E., and L. Bellak, 1950. *Projective Psychology.* New York: Knopf.

Adler, A., 1929. *Understanding Human Nature.* Garden City, L.I.: Garden City.

Adorno, T. W., E. Frenkel-Brunswik, D. J. Levinson, and R. N. Sanford, 1950. *The Authoritarian Personality.* New York: Harper.

Allen, E. A., 1960. "Attitudes of Children and Adolescents in School," *Educational Research,* **3,** 65–80.

Allport, G. W., 1950a. "Foreword," in M. G. Ross, *Religious Beliefs of Youth.* New York: Association Press.

———, 1950b. "Prejudice: A Problem in Psychological and Social Causation," *Journal of Social Issues,* Supplementary Series, No. 4.

———, 1961. *Pattern and Growth in Personality.* New York: Holt, Rinehart and Winston.

————, J. M. Gillespie, and J. Young, 1948. "The Religion of the Postwar College Student," *Journal of Psychology,* 25, 3–33.

————, and B. M. Kramer, 1946. "Some Roots of Prejudice," *Journal of Psychology,* 22, 9–39.

————, and P. E. Vernon, 1931. *A Study of Values.* Boston: Houghton Mifflin.

Almy, M., 1962. "Intellectual Mastery and Mental Health," *Teachers College Record,* 63, No. 6, 468–478.

Alschuler, R. H., and L. A. Hattwick, 1943. "Easel Painting as an Index of Personality in Preschool Children," *American Journal of Orthopsychiatry,* 13, 616–626.

Amatora, Sister Mary, 1957. "Developmental Trends in Pre-adolescence and in Early Adolescence," *Journal of Genetic Psychology,* 91, 89–97.

Ames, L. B., J. Learned, R. W. Metraux, and R. N. Walker, 1952. *Child Rorschach Responses: Developmental Trends from Two to Ten Years.* New York: Paul B. Hoeber.

Ammons, R. B., 1950. "Reactions in a Projective Doll-Play Interview of White Males Two to Six Years of Age to Differences in Skin Color and Facial Features," *Journal of Genetic Psychology,* 76, 323–341.

Anastasi, A., N. Cohen, and D. Spatz, 1948. "A Study of Fear and Anger in College Students Through the Controlled Diary Method," *Journal of Genetic Psychology,* 73, 243–249.

Anderson, H. H., and G. L. Anderson (eds.), 1951. *An Introduction to Projective Techniques and Other Devices for Understanding the Dynamics of Human Behavior.* Englewood Cliffs, N.J.: Prentice-Hall.

————, 1954. "Social Development," Chapter 19, pp. 1162–1215 in *Manual of Child Psychology,* 2nd edition, L. Carmichael (ed.). New York: John Wiley.

Anderson, J. E., 1939. "The Limitations of Infant and Preschool Tests in Measurement of Intelligence," *Journal of Psychology,* 8, 351–379.

————, and D. B. Harris, *et al.,* 1959. *A Survey of Children's Adjustment Over Time.* Institute of Child Development and Welfare: University of Minnesota.

Angelino, H., J. Dollins, and E. Mech, 1956. "Trends in the Fears and Worries of School Children as Related to Socio-economic Status and Age," *Journal of Genetic Psychology,* 89, 263–276.

Antrobus, J. S., 1962. "Patterns of Dreaming and Dream Recall," Doctor of Philosophy dissertation (in progress), Teachers College, Columbia University.

Aserinsky, E., and N. Kleitman, 1953. "Regularly Occurring Periods of Eye Motility, and Concomitant Phenomena, During Sleep," *Science,* 118, 273–274.

Ausubel, D. P., 1958. *Theory and Problems of Child Development.* New York: Grune and Stratton.

————, E. E. Balthazar, I. Rosenthal, L. S. Blackman, S. H. Schpoont, and J. Welkowitz, 1954. "Perceived Parent Attitudes as Determinants of Children's Ego Structure," *Child Development,* 25, 173–183.

Baker, H. V., 1942. *Children's Contributions in Elementary School General Discussions*. Child Development Monographs, No. 29. New York: Teachers College, Columbia University.

Baldwin, A. L., J. Kalhorn, and F. H. Breese, 1945. *Patterns of Parent Behavior*. Psychological Monographs, **58,** No. 3. Evanston, Ill.: American Psychological Association.

Bantel, E., 1956. "Attitudes Revealed by Students Participating in a College Course Designed to Provide Opportunities for Understanding of Self and Others," unpublished Doctor of Education dissertation, Teachers College, Columbia University.

Barker, M. E., 1946. *Personality Adjustments of Teachers Related to Efficiency in Teaching*. New York: Bureau of Publications, Teachers College, Columbia University.

Bartlett, F., 1959. *Thinking*. New York: Basic Books, Inc.

Bath, J. A., and E. C. Lewis, 1962. "Attitudes of Young Female Adults Toward Some Areas of Parent-Adolescent Conflict," *Journal of Genetic Psychology,* **100,** 241–253.

Battin, T. C., 1954. *TV and Youth,* National Association of Radio and Television Broadcasters.

Bayley, N., 1933. *Mental Growth During the First Three Years: A Developmental Study of Sixty-One Children by Repeated Tests,* Genetic Psychology Monographs, **14,** No. 1.

———, 1940. "Mental Growth in Children," *Yearbook of the National Society for the Study of Education,* **39,** 11–47.

———, 1941. "Body Build in Adolescents Studied in Relation to Rates of Anatomical Maturing with Implications for Social Adjustment," *Psychological Bulletin* (Abstract), **38,** 378.

———, 1943. "Skeletal Maturing in Adolescence as a Basis for Determining Percentage of Completed Growth," *Child Development,* **14,** 1–46.

———, 1949. "Consistency and Variability in the Growth of Intelligence from Birth to Eighteen Years," *Journal of Genetic Psychology,* **75,** 165–196.

———, 1954. "Some Increasing Parent-Child Similarities During the Growth of Children," *Journal of Educational Psychology,* **45,** 1–21.

———, 1956. "Individual Patterns of Development," *Child Development,* **27,** 45–74.

———, and M. C. Jones, 1941. "Some Personality Characteristics of Boys with Retarded Skeletal Maturity," *Psychological Bulletin* (Abstract), **38,** 603.

———, and M. H. Oden, 1955. "The Maintenance of Intellectual Ability in Gifted Adults," *Journal of Gerontology,* **10,** 71–107.

Beck, S. J., 1937. *Introduction to the Rorschach Method: A Manual of Personality Study*. Research Monograph of the American Orthopsychiatric Association No. 1. Menasha, Wis.: American Orthopsychiatric Association.

Beekman, E., 1947. "What High School Seniors Think of Religion," *Religious Education,* **42,** 333–337.

Beier, E. G., and F. Ratzeburg, 1953. "The Parental Identification of Male and Female College Students," *Journal of Abnormal Social Psychology,* 48, 569–572.

Beilin, H., 1952. "Factors Affecting Occupational Choice in a Lower Socio-economic Group," unpublished Doctor of Philosophy dissertation, Teachers College, Columbia University.

———, 1955. "The Application of General Developmental Principles to the Vocational Area," *Journal of Counseling Psychology,* 2, 53–57.

———, 1956. "The Pattern of Postponability and its Relation to Social Class Mobility," *Journal of Social Psychology,* 44, 33–48.

Bender, L., and J. Frosch, 1942. "Children's Reactions to the War," *American Journal of Orthopsychiatry,* 12, 571–586.

Berdie, R. F., 1944. "Factors Related to Vocational Interests," *Psychological Bulletin,* 41, 137–157.

Berezin, D., 1959. "An Inquiry into the Temperamental Differences of Infants Noted by Their Boarding Mothers in Adoption Studies," unpublished Doctor of Education dissertation, Teachers College, Columbia University.

Berg, I. A., 1953. "Personality Structure and Occupational Choice," *Personnel and Guidance Journal,* 32, 151–154.

Berger, E. M., 1952. "The Relation Between Expressed Acceptance of Self and Expressed Acceptance of Others," *Journal of Abnormal Social Psychology,* 47, 778–782.

Bilhuber, G., 1927. "Functional Periodicity and Motor Ability in Sports," *American Physical Education Review,* 32, 22–25.

Bills, R. E., E. L. Vance, and O. S. McLean, 1951. "An Index of Adjustment and Values," *Journal of Consulting Psychology,* 15, 257–261.

Binger, C., 1961. "The Pressures on College Girls Today," *Atlantic Monthly,* 207, No. 2, 40–44.

Birns, B., 1962. "Constancy of Response to External Stimuli in the Neonate," Doctor of Philosophy dissertation (in progress), Teachers College, Columbia University.

Bjerre, P., 1925. "The Way to and From Freud," *Psychoanalytic Review.* 12, 39–66.

———, 1936. *Das Traumen als Heilungsweg der Selle.* Zurich: Rascher.

Blatz, W. E., and D. A. Millichamp, 1937. "The Mental Growth of the Dionne Quintuplets," University of Toronto Studies, Child Development Series, No. 12, in W. E. Blatz *et al., Collected Studies of the Dionne Quintuplets.* Toronto, Canada: University of Toronto Press.

Blau, P. M., J. W. Gustad, R. Jessor, H. S. Parnes, and R. C. Wilcock, 1956. "Occupational Choice: A Conceptual Framework," *Industrial and Labor Relations Review,* 9, 531–543.

Block, V. L., 1937. "Conflicts of Adolescents with Their Mothers," *Journal of Abnormal and Social Psychology,* 32, 193–206.

Blum, L. H., H. H. Davidson, and N. D. Fieldsteel, 1954. *A Rorschach Workbook.* New York: International Universities Press.

Boas, F., 1932. "Studies in Growth," *Human Biology,* 4, 307–350.

Bonar, H. S., 1942. "High School Pupils List Their Anxieties," *School Review*, 50, 512–515.

Bond, A., 1961. "Grandmothers' Attitudes and Mothers' Concerns," unpublished Doctor of Philosophy dissertation, Teachers College, Columbia University.

Bond, H. M., 1960. "Wasted Talent," pp. 116–137 in *The Nation's Children, Vol. 2, Development and Education,* E. Ginzberg (ed.). New York, Columbia University Press.

Bonney, M. E., 1943a. "The Constancy of Sociometric Scores and Their Relationship to Teacher Judgments of Social Success and to Personality Ratings," *Sociometry,* 6, 409–424.

———, 1943b. "The Relative Stability of Social, Intellectual, and Academic Status in Grades II to IV, and the Interrelationships Between These Various Forms of Growth," *Journal of Educational Psychology,* 34, 88–102.

———, 1943c. "Personality Traits of Socially Successful and Socially Unsuccessful Children," *Journal of Educational Psychology,* 34, 449–472.

———, 1946. "A Sociometric Study of Some Factors to Mutual Friendships on the Elementary, Secondary, and College Levels," *Sociometry,* 9, 21–47.

———, 1947. "Sociometric Study of Agreement Between Teacher Judgments and Student Choices; in Regard to the Number of Friends Possessed by High School Students," *Sociometry,* 10, 133–146.

Bonsall, M. R., and B. Stellfre, 1955. "The Temperament of Gifted Children," *California Journal of Educational Research,* 6, No. 4, 162–165.

Boodish, H. A., 1953. "Educating the Whole Child," *Social Studies,* 44, 187–189.

Bordin, E. S., 1943. "A Theory of Vocational Interests as Dynamic Phenomena," *Educational and Psychological Measurement,* 3, 49–65.

Bossard, J. H. S., and E. S. Boll, 1943. *Family Situations.* Philadelphia: University of Pennsylvania Press.

Bousfield, W. A., 1940. "Students' Ratings of Qualities Considered Desirable in College Professors," *School and Society,* 51, 253–256.

Boyd, W. C., 1953. *Genetics and the Races of Man.* Boston: Little, Brown.

Bradley, N. C., 1947. "The Growth of the Knowledge of Time in Children of School-Age," *British Journal of Psychology,* 38, 67–78.

Bradway, K. P., 1944. "IQ Constancy on the Revised Stanford-Binet from the Preschool to the Junior High School Level," *Journal of Genetic Psychology,* 65, 197–217.

Brandt, R. M., 1958. *The Accuracy of Self Estimate: A Measure of Self-Concept Reality.* Genetic Psychology Monographs, 58, 55–99.

Bretsch, H. S., 1952. "Social Skills and Activities of Socially Accepted and Unaccepted Adolescents," *Journal of Educational Psychology,* 43, 449–458.

Briggs, V., and L. R. Schulz, 1955. "Parental Response to Concepts of Parent-Adolescent Relationships," *Child Development,* 26, 279–284.

Bromley, D. D., and F. H. Britten, 1938. *Youth and Sex: A Study of 1300 College Students.* New York: Harper.

Bruch, H., 1940. "Obesity in Childhood. III. Physiologic and Psychologic Aspects of the Food Intake of Obese Children," *American Journal of Disturbed Children,* **59,** 739.

———, 1947. "Physiological Aspects of Obesity," *Psychiatry,* **10,** 373.

Bruder, E. E., 1952. "Psychotherapy and Some of Its Theological Implications," *Journal of Pastoral Care,* **6,** 28.

Bryant, L. W., 1957. "Exploratory Psychology Course for Teen-Agers," *National Association of Secondary School Principals Bulletin,* **41,** 75–79.

Buhler, C., 1931. "Zum Probleme der sexuellen Entwicklung," *Z. Kinderheilkunst,* **51,** 612–642.

———, 1952. "The Diagnostic Problem in Childhood Schizophrenia," *Nervous Child,* **10,** 60–62.

Burchinal, L. G., 1959a. "Adolescent Role Deprivation and High School Marriage," *Marriage and Family Living,* **21,** 378–384.

———, 1959b. "Does Early Dating Lead to School-Age Marriages?" *Iowa Farm Science,* **13,** No. 8, 11–12.

———, 1959c. "How Successful Are School-Age Marriages?" *Iowa Farm Science,* **13,** No. 9, 7–10.

———, 1960a. "Research on Young Marriage: Implications for Family Life Education," *The Family Life Coordinator,* **IX** (1–2, September–December), 6–24.

———, 1960b. "School Policies and School-Age Marriages," *The Family Life Coordinator,* **VIII,** No. 3, 43–47.

———, and L. Chancellor, 1958. "What About School-Age Marriages?" *Iowa Farm Science,* **12,** No. 12, 12–14.

Burks, B. S., D. W. Jensen, L. M. Terman *et al.,* 1930. *The Promise of Youth: Follow-Up Studies of One Thousand Gifted Children. Genetic Studies of Genius,* Vol. III. Stanford, Calif.: Stanford University Press.

Busemann, A., 1926. *Die Jugend im eigenen Urteil.* Langensalza.

Byrns, R., 1939. "Relation of Vocational Choice to Mental Ability and Occupational Opportunity," *School Review,* **47,** 101–109.

Cannon, K. L., 1958. "Stability of Sociometric Scores of High School Students," *Journal of Educational Research,* **52,** 43–48.

Carlson, T. E., and C. P. Williams, 1959. *Guide to the National Defense Education Act of 1958* (revised edition). U. S. Department of Health, Education, and Welfare. Washington, D.C.: U. S. Government Printing Office.

Carp, F. M., 1949. "High School Boys Are Realistic About Occupations," *Occupations,* **28,** 97–101.

Carter, H. D., 1940. "The Development of Vocational Attitudes," *Journal of Consulting Psychology,* **4,** 185–191.

———, 1944a. *Vocational Interests and Job Orientation.* Stanford, Calif.: Stanford University Press. (Published for American Association for Applied Psychology.)

———, 1944b. "The Development of Interest in Vocations," pp. 255–276 in *43d Yearbook of the National Society for the Study of Education,* Part I, *Adolescence,* N. B. Henry (ed.). Chicago: University of Chicago Press.

Casler, L., 1961. *Maternal Deprivation: A Critical Review of the Literature.* Monographs of the Society for Research in Child Development, 26 (2), Serial No. 80.

Cavan, R. S., and G. Beiling, 1958. "A Study of High School Marriages," *Marriage and Family Living,* 20, 293–295.

Centers, R., 1949. *The Psychology of Social Classes.* Princeton, N.J.: Prince ton University Press.

Chess, S., and A. Thomas, 1959. "The Importance of Nonmotivational Behavior Patterns in Psychiatric Diagnosis and Treatment," *Psychiatric Quarterly,* 33, 326–334.

———, A. Thomas, and H. B. Birch, 1959. "Characteristics of the Individual Child's Behavorial Responses to the Environment," *American Journal of Orthopsychiatry,* 29, 791–802.

Christensen, H. T., 1947. "Student Views on Mate Selection," *Marriage and Family Living,* 9, 85–88.

———, 1952. "Dating Behavior as Evaluated by High-School Students," *American Journal of Sociology,* 57, 580–586.

Clay, H. M., 1954. "Changes of Performance With Age on Similar Tasks of Varying Complexity," *British Journal of Psychology,* 45, 7–13.

Coffield, K. E., and T. L. Engle, 1960. "High School Psychology: A History and Some Observations," *American Psychologist,* 15, 350–352.

Cogan, M., 1961. "Self-Understanding Through College Programs of Physical Education for Men," unpublished Doctor of Education dissertation, Teachers College, Columbia University.

Cohen, E. E., 1962. "The Employment Needs of Urban Youth," *The Vocational Guidance Quarterly,* 10, 85–89.

Cole, L., 1959. *Psychology of Adolescence,* 5th edition. New York: Rinehart and Co.

Coleman, J. S., 1959. "Academic Achievement and the Structure of Competition," *Harvard Educational Review,* 29, 330–351.

Collignon, M., 1960. "Conquête de L'Autonomie et Taille D'Après les Appréciations de Garçons et de Filles de 12 à 15 Ans" (Conquest of Autonomy and Height According to the Judgments of Boys and Girls 12 to 15 Years of Age), *Enfance,* No. 3, 291–319.

Conn, J. H., 1940. "Children's Reactions to the Discovery of Genital Differ ences," *American Journal of Orthopsychiatry,* 10, 747–755.

Connolly, P. C., 1945. *The Unquiet Grave.* New York: Harper.

Connor, R., T. B. Johannis, Jr., and J. Walters, 1954. "Parent-Adolescent Relationships. I. Parent-Adolescent Conflicts: Current and Retrospect," *Journal of Home Economics,* 46, 183–186.

Corsini, R. J., and K. K. Fassett, 1953. "Intelligence and Aging," *Journal of Genetic Psychology,* 83, 249–264.

Counts, G. S., 1925. "The Social Status of Occupations: A Problem in Vocational Guidance," *School Review,* 33, 16–27.

Cowell, C. C., 1935. "An Abstract of a Study of Differentials in Junior High School Boys Based on the Observation of Physical Education Activities, A Study of 'Fringers' vs. 'Actives,' " *Research Quarterly,* VI, No. 4, 129–136.

Cowen, E. L., J. Landes, and D. E. Schaet, 1958. "The Effects of Mild Frustration on the Expression of Prejudiced Attitudes," *Journal of Abnormal and Social Psychology,* 58, 33–38.

Cox, C. M., 1946. "Gifted Children," pp. 886–953 in *Manual of Child Psychology,* L. Carmichael (ed.). New York: Wiley.

Crampton, C. W., 1908. "Physiological Age—a Fundamental Principle, I," *American Physical Education Review,* 13, 141, 154.

Crespi, L. P., and A. E. Stanley, 1948–49. "Youth Looks at the Kinsey Report," *Public Opinion Quarterly,* 12, 687–696.

Crist, J. R., 1953. "High School Dating as a Behavior System," *Marriage and Family Living,* 15, 23–28.

Criswell, J. H., 1939. *A Sociometric Study of Race Cleavage in the Classroom.* Archives of Psychology, No. 235.

Cruickshank, W. M., and G. O. Johnson (eds.), 1958. *Education of Exceptional Children and Youth.* Englewood Cliffs, N.J.: Prentice-Hall.

Cureton, T. K., 1943. "The Unfitness of Young Men in Motor Fitness," *Journal of the American Medical Association,* 123, 69–74.

Curry, E. T., 1946. "Voice Changes in Male Adolescents," *Laryngoscope,* 56, 795–805.

Dailey, J. T., and M. F. Shaycoft, 1961. *Types of Tests in Project Talent.* U. S. Department of Health, Education and Welfare, Cooperative Research Monograph No. 9. Washington, D.C.: U. S. Government Printing Office.

Darley, J. G., and T. Hagenah, 1955. *Vocational Interest Measurement Theory and Practice.* Minneapolis: University of Minnesota Press.

Davenport, C. B., 1923. *Body-Build and Its Inheritance.* Washington, D.C.: Carnegie Institution.

Davidson, P. E., and H. D. Anderson, 1937. *Occupational Mobility in an American Community.* Stanford, Calif.: Stanford University Press.

Davis, A., and R. J. Havighurst, 1952. "Social Class and Color Differences in Child-Rearing," in *Readings in Social Psychology* (rev. ed.), G. E. Swanson, T. M. Newcomb, and E. L. Hartley (eds.). New York: Holt.

Davis, K., 1952. "Divorce," Chapter XII in *Readings in Marriage and the Family,* J. T. Landis and M. G. Landis (eds.). Englewood Cliffs, N.J.: Prentice-Hall.

Dawson, G. E., 1900. "Children's Interest in the Bible," *Pedagogical Seminary,* 7, 151–178.

Deeg, M. E., and D. G. Paterson, 1947. "Changes in Social Status of Occupations," *Occupations,* 25, 205–208.

de Laszio, V., 1953. "The Goal in Jungian Psychotherapy," *British Journal of Medical Psychology,* 26, 3–14.

Dement, W., 1960. "The Effect of Dream Deprivation," *Science,* 131, No. 3415, 1705–1707.

———, and N. Kleitman, 1957a. "Cyclic Variations in EEG During Sleep and Their Relation to Eye Movements, Body Motility, and Dreaming," *Electroencephalography and Clinical Neurophysiology,* 9, 673–690.

———, 1957b. "The Relation of Eye Movements During Sleep to Dream Activity: An Objective Method for the Study of Dreaming," *Journal of Experimental Psychology,* 53, 339–346.

———, and E. A. Wolpert, 1958a. "Relationships to the Manifest Content of Dreams Occurring on the Same Night," *Journal of Nervous and Mental Disease,* 126, No. 6, 568–578.

———, 1958b, "The Relation of Eye Movements, Body Motility, and External Stimuli to Dream Content," *Journal of Experimental Psychology,* 55, No. 6, 543–553.

Demos, G. D., 1960. "Attitudes of Student Ethnic Groups on Issues Related to Education," *California Journal of Educational Research,* 11, 204–206.

Dennis, W., 1960. "Causes of Retardation Among Institutional Children: Iran," *Journal of Genetic Psychology,* 96, 47–59.

Deutsch, H., 1944–45. *The Psychology of Women,* 2 vols. New York: Grune and Stratton.

Dillon, H. J., 1949. *Early School Leavers.* New York: National Child Labor Committee. Publication No. 401.

Dillon, M. S., 1934. "Attitudes of Children Toward Their Own Bodies and Those of Other Children," *Child Development,* 5, 165–176.

Dimock, H. S., 1937. *Rediscovering the Adolescent.* New York: Association Press.

Dodge, A. F., 1943. "What Are the Personality Traits of the Successful Teacher?" *Journal of Applied Psychology,* 27, 325–337.

Dolger, L., and J. Ginandes, 1946. "Children's Attitudes Toward Discipline as Related to Socioeconomic Status," *Journal of Experimental Education,* 15, 161–165.

Doll, R. C., 1947. "High-School Pupils' Attitudes Toward Teaching Procedures," *School Review,* 55, 222–227.

Dorfman, R. I., W. W. Greulich, and C. I. Solomon, 1937. "The Excretion of Androgenic and Estrogenic Substances in the Urine of Children," *Endocrinology,* 21, 741–743.

Douvan, E., and J. Adelson, 1958. "The Psychodynamics of Social Mobility in Adolescent Boys," *Journal of Abnormal and Social Psychology,* 56, 31–44.

Dresden, K. W., 1948. "Vocational Choices of Secondary Pupils," *Occupations,* 27, 104–106.

Drews, E. M., 1957. "A Four-Year Study of 150 Gifted Adolescents." A report presented to the American Psychological Association, December, 1957 (mimeographed).

———, 1961. "A Critical Evaluation of Approaches to the Identification of

Gifted Students," Chapter 9 in *Measurement and Research in Today's School,* A. E. Traxler (ed.). Washington, D.C.: American Council on Education.

Dudycha, G. J., 1933. "The Religious Beliefs of College Students," *Journal of Applied Psychology,* **17,** 585–603.

———, 1950. "The Religious Beliefs of College Freshmen in 1930 and 1949," *Religious Education,* **45,** 165–169.

———, and M. M. Dudycha, 1933a. "Some Factors and Characteristics in Childhood Memories," *Child Development,* **4,** 265–278.

———, 1933b. "Adolescents' Memories of Preschool Experiences," *Journal of Genetic Psychology,* **42,** 468–480.

Dunlap, J. M., 1958. "The Education of Children with High Mental Ability," pp. 147–188 in *Education of Exceptional Children and Youth,* W. M. Cruickshank and G. O. Johnson (eds.). Englewood Cliffs, N.J.: Prentice-Hall.

Ebert, E., and K. Simmons, 1943. *The Brush Foundation Study of Child Growth and Development: I. Psychometric Tests.* Monographs of the Society for Research in Child Development, **8,** No. 2.

Eckstrom, R. B., 1959. *Experimental Studies of Homogeneous Grouping.* Princeton, N.J.: Educational Testing Service (April).

Eels, K. W., 1951. *Intelligence and Cultural Differences.* Chicago: University of Chicago Press.

Ehrmann, W., 1952. "Dating Behavior of College Students," *Marriage and Family Living,* **14,** 322–326.

———, 1959. *Premarital Dating Behavior.* New York: Henry Holt.

Eichorn, D. H., 1959. "Two-Generation Similarities in Weight, Height and Weight/Height During the First Five Years." Reported at the Twenty-fifth Anniversary Meeting, Society for Research in Child Development, National Institutes of Health, Bethesda, Md., March 10, 1959.

Ekstrom, G. F., 1946. "Why Farm Children Leave School," *School Review,* **54,** 231–237.

Elder, R. A., 1949. "Traditional and Developmental Conceptions of Fatherhood," *Marriage and Family Living,* **11,** 98–100, 106.

Elias, L. J., 1949. *High School Youth Look at Their Problems.* Pullman, Wash.: State College of Washington.

Ellis, A., 1949a. "A Study of Human Love Relationships," *Journal of Genetic Psychology,* **75,** 61–71.

———, 1949b. "Some Significant Correlates of Love and Family Attitudes and Behavior," *Journal of Social Psychology,* **30,** 3–16.

———, 1953. "From the First to the Second Kinsey Report, 2," *International Journal of Sexology,* **3,** 64–72.

Engel, M., 1959. "Stability of the Self-Concept in Adolescence," *Journal of Abnormal and Social Psychology,* **58,** 211–215.

Engle, T. L., 1947. "Psychology: Pupils in Six High Schools Compare the Value of the Subject with that of Six Other Fields," *Clearing House,* **21,** 469–473.

————, 1950. "An Analysis of High School Textbooks in Psychology," *School Review,* **58,** 343–347.

————, 1951. "A National Survey of the Teaching of Psychology in High Schools," *School Review,* **59,** 464–471.

————, 1952a. "Teaching of Psychology in High Schools," *American Psychologist,* **7,** 31–35.

————,1952b. "Attitude of Teachers and Pupils Toward a High School Course in Psychology," *National Association of Secondary School Principals Bulletin,* **36,** 145–151.

————, 1955. "Psychology as a High-School Science," *Science Teacher,* **22,** 235–237.

————, 1956. "High School Psychology," *Contemporary Psychology,* **1,** 140–143.

————, 1957. "High-School Psychology Courses as Related to University Psychology Courses," *National Association of Secondary School Principals Bulletin,* **41,** 38–42.

————, and M. E. Bunch, 1956. "The Teaching of Psychology in High School," *American Psychologist,* **11,** 188–193.

Ephron, B. K., 1953. *Emotional Difficulties in Reading: A Psychological Approach to Study Problems.* New York: Julian Press.

Espenschade, A., 1940. *Motor Performance in Adolescence.* Monographs of the Society for Research in Child Development, 5, No. 1.

Evans, H. M., *et al.,* 1950. "Cooperative Research and Curriculum Improvement," *Teachers College Record,* **51,** 410–474.

Fauquier, W., 1940. "The Attitudes of Aggressive and Submissive Boys Toward Athletics," *Child Development,* **11,** 115–125.

————, and J. Gilchrist, 1942. "Some Aspects of Leadership in an Institution," *Child Development,* **13,** 55–64.

Feinberg, M. R., 1953. "Relation of Background Experience to Social Acceptance," *Journal of Abnormal and Social Psychology,* **48,** 206–214.

————, M. Smith, and R. Schmidt, 1958. "An Analysis of Expressions Used by Adolescents at Varying Economic Levels to Describe Accepted and Rejected Peers," *Journal of Genetic Psychology,* **93,** 133–148.

Fey, W. C., 1955. "Acceptance by Others and Its Relation to Acceptance of Self and Others: a Revaluation," *Journal of Abnormal Social Psychology,* **50,** 274–276.

Finger, F. N., 1947. "Sex Beliefs and Practices Among Male College Students," *Journal of Abnormal Social Psychology,* **42,** 57–67.

Fisher, B., 1953. "Group Therapy with Retarded Readers," *Journal of Educational Psychology,* **44,** 354–360.

Flanagan, J. C., J. T. Dailey, M. F. Shaycoft, W. A. Borham, D. B. Orr, and I. Goldberg, 1962. *Design for a Study of American Youth.* Boston: Houghton Mifflin

Fleege, U. H., 1945. *Self-Revelations of the Adolescent Boy.* Milwaukee, Wis.: Bruce.

Flory, C. D., 1936a. *Osseous Development in the Hand as an Index of Skele-tal Development.* Monographs of the Society for Research in Child Development, **I**, No. 3.

————, 1936b. *The Physical Growth of Mentally Deficient Boys.* Mono-graphs of the Society for Research in Child Development, **I**, No. 6.

Ford, C. S., and F. A. Beach, 1951. *Patterns of Sexual Behavior.* New York: Harper.

Foshay, A. W., 1951. "The Teacher and Children's Social Attitudes," *Teachers College Record,* **52**, 287–296.

Frank, L. K., 1949. "Projective Methods for the Study of Personality," *Journal of Psychology,* **8**, 389–413.

————, R. Harrison, E. Hellersberg, K. Machover, and M. Steiner, 1953. *Personality Development in Adolescent Girls.* Monographs of the Society for Research in Child Development, **XVI**, No. 53, 1951.

Franzblau, A. N., 1934. *Religious Belief and Character Among Jewish Adolescents.* Contributions to Education, No. 634. New York: Bureau of Publications, Teachers College, Columbia University.

Freeman, F. A., and C. D. Flory, 1937. *Growth in Intellectual Ability as Measured by Repeated Tests.* Monographs of the Society for Research in Child Development, **II**, No. 2.

Frenkel-Brunswik, E., 1951. "Patterns of Social and Cognitive Outlook in Children and Parents," *American Journal of Orthopsychiatry,* **21**, 543–558.

Freud, A., 1937. *The Ego and the Mechanisms of Defense.* London: Hogarth Press.

————, 1955. "Safeguarding the Emotional Health of Our Children—An Inquiry into the Concept of the Rejecting Mother," *Child Welfare,* **34**, 1–4.

————, and S. Dann, 1951. "An Experiment in Group Upbringing," *The Psychoanalytic Study of the Child,* Vol. 6, pp. 127–168. New York: In-ternational Universities Press.

Freud, S., 1936. *The Problem of Anxiety.* New York: Norton.

————, 1950. *The Interpretation of Dreams.* (Translated by A. A. Brill.) New York: Modern Library.

————, 1953. *Collected Papers.* (Translated under supervision of Joan Riviere.) London: Hogarth Press.

Friedman, K. C., 1944a. "Time Concepts of Elementary School Children," *Elementary School Journal,* **44**, 337, 342.

————, 1944b. "Time Concepts of Junior and Senior High School Pupils and of Adults," *School Review,* **52**, 233–238.

Friedmann, E. A., and R. J. Havighurst, 1954. *The Meaning of Work and Retirement.* Chicago: University of Chicago Press.

Friend, J. G., and E. A. Haggard, 1948. *Work Adjustment in Relation to Family Background.* Applied Psychology Monographs, No. 16. Stanford, Calif.: Stanford University Press. (Published for American Psychological Association.)

Fromm, E., 1947. *Man for Himself.* New York: Rinehart.

———, 1950. *Psychoanalysis and Religion.* New Haven, Conn.: Yale University Press.

———, 1951. *The Forgotten Language.* New York: Rinehart.

Fryer, D., 1922. "Occupational Intelligence Standards," *School and Society,* **16,** 273–277.

Fuller, J. L., and W. R. Thompson, 1960. *Behavior Genetics.* New York: Wiley.

Gallup, G., 1954a. " 'Americans Express Almost Universal Belief in God'; 'What's Behind the Revival of Religious Interest in America? II,' " December 18, 1954. Princeton, N.J.: American Institute of Public Opinion.

———, 1954b. " 'How Well Do You Know the Bible?' 'What's Behind the Revival of Religious Interest in America? III,' " December 19, 1954. Princeton, N.J.: American Institute of Public Opinion.

———, and E. Hill, 1961. "Youth: the Cool Generation," *Saturday Evening Post,* December 22–30, pp. 63–80.

Garfinkle, S. H., 1958. "Marriage and Careers for Girls," *The Vocational Guidance Quarterly,* **6,** 146–148.

Garn, S. M., 1960. "Growth and Development," pp. 24–42 in *The Nation's Children, Vol. 2, Development and Education,* E. Ginzberg (ed.). New York: Columbia University Press.

Gates, G. S., 1926. "An Observational Study of Anger," *Journal of Experimental Psychology,* **9,** 325, 336.

Gesell, A., 1928. *Infancy and Human Growth.* New York: Macmillan.

Getzels, J. W., and P. W. Jackson, 1960. "The Study of Giftedness: A Multidimensional Approach," *The Gifted Student,* Cooperative Research Monographs, No. 2, U. S. Office of Education, Washington, D.C., pp. 1–18.

Gilbert, H. H., 1931. "High-School Students' Opinions on Reasons for Failure in High-School Subjects," *Journal of Educational Research,* **23,** 46–49.

Gilbert, J. C., 1941. "Memory Loss in Senescence," *Journal of Abnormal and Social Psychology,* **36,** 73–86.

Gilliland, A. R., 1940. "The Attitude of College Students Toward God and the Church," *Journal of Social Psychology,* **11,** 11–18.

Ginzberg, E., 1948. "Sex and Class Behavior," pp. 131–145 in *About the Kinsey Report,* D. P. Geddes and E. Curie (eds.). New York: New American Library of World Literature.

———, S. W. Ginsburg, S. Axelrad, and J. L. Herma, 1951. *Occupational Choice, an Approach to a General Theory.* New York: Columbia University Press.

Gips, C., 1956. "How Illness Experiences Are Interpreted by Hospitalized Children," unpublished Doctor of Education dissertation, Teachers College, Columbia University.

Glick, P. C., and E. Landau, 1950. "Age as a Factor in Marriage," *American Sociological Review,* **15,** 517–529.

Glueck, S., and E. Glueck, 1940. *Juvenile Delinquents Grown Up*. New York: The Commonwealth Fund.

――――, 1950. *Unraveling Juvenile Delinquency*. Cambridge, Mass.: Harvard University Press.

Goldberg, M., 1959. "A Three Year Experimental Program at De Witt Clinton High School to Help Bright Underachievers," *High Points*, Board of Education of the City of New York (January), pp. 5–35.

――――, 1962. "Research on the Gifted." Mimeographed report, Horace Mann–Lincoln Institute of School Experimentation, Teachers College, Columbia University, March, 1962.

――――, L. G. Gotkin, and A. J. Tannenbaum, 1959. "Cultural, Social and Personal Factors Influencing Talent Fruition." Mimeographed report, Horace Mann–Lincoln Institute of School Experimentation, Teachers College, Columbia University.

Goldberg, M., and A. H. Passow, 1961. "The Effects of Ability Grouping" (First Draft), Talented Youth Project, *Interim Reports*, Horace Mann–Lincoln Institute of School Experimentation, Teachers College, Columbia University.

Goldfarb, W., 1943. "The Effects of Early Institutional Care on Adolescent Personality," *Journal of Experimental Education*, 12, No. 2, 106–129.

Goldstein, K., and M. Scheerer, 1941. *Abstract and Concrete Behavior: An Experimental Study with Special Tests*. Psychological Monographs, 53, No. 2.

Goodenough, D., A. Shapiro, M. Holden, and L. Steinschriber, 1959. "A Comparison of 'Dreamers' and 'Nondreamers': Eye Movements, Electroencephalograms, and the Recall of Dreams," *Journal of Abnormal and Social Psychology*, 59, 295–302.

Goodenough, F. L., 1928. "The Relation of the Intelligence of Preschool Children to the Occupations of Their Fathers," *American Journal of Psychology*, 40, 284–294.

――――, and M. M. Maurer, 1942. *The Mental Growth of Children from Two to Fourteen*. Minneapolis: University of Minnesota Press.

Gottesman, I. I., 1962. "Differential Inheritance of Psychoneuroses." Paper read at annual meeting of the American Institute of Biological Sciences, Corvallis, Oregon, August 30, 1962.

Gough, H. G., D. B. Harris, W. E. Martin, and M. Edwards, 1950. "Children's Ethnic Attitudes: I. Relationship to Certain Personality Factors," *Child Development*, 21, 83–91.

Gowan, J. C., 1955. "The Underachieving Gifted Child, A Problem for Everyone," *Journal of Exceptional Children*, 21, 247–249.

Grace, G. L., and H. A. Grace, 1952. "The Relationship Between Verbal Behavioral Measures of Values," *Journal of Educational Research*, 46, 123–131.

Gragg, W. L., 1949. "Some Factors Which Distinguish Drop-outs from High School Graduates," *Occupations*, 27, 457–459.

Grant, V. W., 1948. "A Major Problem of Human Sexuality," *Journal of Social Psychology*, 28, 79–101.

Greulich, W. W., *et al.*, 1938. *A Handbook of Methods for the Study of Adolescent Children*. Monographs of the Society for Research in Child Development, **III,** No. 2.

——, 1942. *Somatic and Endocrine Studies of Puberal and Adolescent Boys*. Monographs of the Society for Research in Child Development, **VII,** No. 3.

Grigg, A. E., 1959. "Childhood Experience with Parental Attitudes: A Test of Roe's Hypothesis," *Journal of Counseling Psychology,* **6,** 153–155.

Gronlund, N. E., 1953. "Relationships Between the Sociometric Status of Pupils' and Teachers' Preferences for or Against Having Them in Class," *Sociometry,* **16,** 142–150.

——, and L. Anderson, 1957. "Personality Characteristics of Socially Accepted, Socially Neglected, and Socially Rejected Junior High School Pupils," *Educational Administration and Supervision,* **43,** 329–339.

——, and W. S. Holmlund, 1958. "The Value of Elementary School Sociometric Status Scores for Predicting Pupils' Adjustment in High School," *Educational Administration and Supervision,* **44,** 255–260.

Grunes, W. F., 1956. "On Perception of Occupations," *Personnel and Guidance Journal,* **34,** 276–279.

——, 1957. "Looking at Occupations," *Journal of Abnormal and Social Psychology,* **54,** 86–92.

Guilford, J. P., 1950. "Creativity," *American Psychologist,* **5,** 444–454.

——, 1959. "Three Faces of Intellect," *American Psychologist,* **14,** 469–479.

——, and P. R. Merrifield, 1960. *The Structure of Intellect Model: Its Uses and Implications (Rep. Psychol. Lab., No. 24)*. Los Angeles: University of Southern California.

——, R. C. Wilson, and P. R. Christensen, 1952. *A Factor-Analytic Study of Creative Thinking. II. Administration of Tests and Analysis of Results (Rep. Psychol. Lab., No. 8)*. Los Angeles: University of Southern California.

——, and D. J. Lewis, 1951. *A Factor-Analytic Study of Creative Thinking. I. Hypotheses and Description of Tests*. Los Angeles: University of Southern California.

Gurin, G. J., J. Veroff, and S. Feld, 1960. *Americans View Their Mental Health: A Nationwide Interview Survey*. Joint Commission on Mental Illness and Health, Monograph Series, No. 4. New York: Basic Books.

Gutheil, E. A., 1951. *The Handbook of Dream Analysis*. New York: Liveright.

Habbe, S., 1935. "Nicknames of Adolescent Boys," *American Journal of Orthopsychiatry,* **7,** 371–377.

Hadfield, J. A., 1954. *Dreams and Nightmares*. London: Penguin Books.

Hagen, D., 1960. "Careers and Family Atmosphere: An Empirical Test of Roe's Theory," *Journal of Counseling Psychology,* **7,** 251–256.

Hall, C., 1953. *The Meaning of Dreams*. New York: Dell.

Halverson, H. M., 1940. "Genital and Sphincter Behavior of the Male Infant," *Journal of Genetic Psychology*, **56**, 95–136.

Hamilton, G. V., 1929. *A Research in Marriage*. New York: A. and C. Boni.

Harding, J., B. Kutner, H. Proshansky, and I. Chein, 1954. "Prejudice and Ethnic Relations," Chapter 27 in *Handbook of Social Psychology*, Vol. II, G. Lindzey (ed.). Cambridge, Mass.: Addison-Wesley.

Harlow, H. F., 1958. "The Nature of Love," *American Psychologist*, **13**, 673–685.

———, 1962. "The Heterosexual Affectional System in Monkeys," *American Psychologist*, **17**, 1–9.

Harris, C. W., and M. R. Liba (eds.), 1960. *Encyclopaedia of Educational Research*, 3rd edition. New York: Macmillan.

Harris, D. B., 1959. "Sex Differences in the Life Problems and Interests of Adolescents, 1935 and 1957," *Child Development*, **30**, 453–459.

———, H. G. Gough, and W. E. Martin, 1950. "Children's Ethnic Attitudes: II. Relationship to Parental Beliefs Concerning Child Training," *Child Development*, **21**, 169–181.

Harrower, M. R., 1934. "Social Status and the Moral Development of the Child," *British Journal of Educational Psychology*, **1**, 75–95.

Hart, F. W., 1934. *Teachers and Teaching*. New York: Macmillan.

Hartley, E. L., 1946. *Problems in Prejudice*. New York: King's Crown Press.

Havighurst, R. J., 1953. *Human Development and Education*. New York: Longmans, Green.

———, and F. H. Breese, 1947. "Relation Between Ability and Social Status in a Mid-western Community. III, Primary Mental Abilities," *Journal of Educational Psychology*, **38**, 241–247.

———, M. Z. Robinson, and M. Dorr, 1946. "The Development of the Ideal Self in Childhood and Adolescence," *Journal of Educational Research*, **40**, 241–257.

———, and H. Taba, 1949. *Adolescent Character and Personality*. New York: John Witty.

Healy, W., and A. F. Bronner, 1936. *New Light on Delinquency and Its Treatment*. New Haven, Conn.: Yale University Press.

Heath, C. W., and L. W. Gregory, 1946. "Problems of Normal College Students and Their Families," *School and Society*, **63**, 355–358.

Hecker, S. E., 1953. "Early School Leavers in Kentucky," *Bulletin of the Bureau of School Services*, College of Education, University of Kentucky, **25** (4), 1–74.

Helfant, K., 1952. "The Teaching of Psychology in High Schools: A Review of the Literature," *School Review*, **60**, 467–473.

Helper, M. M., 1958. "Parental Evaluations of Children and Children's Self-Evaluations," *Journal of Abnormal Social Psychology*, **56**, 190–194.

Hertzman, J., 1948. "High School Mental Hygiene Survey," *American Journal of Orthopsychiatry*, **18**, 238–256.

Hess, R. D., and I. Goldblatt, 1957. "The Status of Adolescents in American Society: A Problem in Social Identity," *Child Development*, **28**, 459–468.

Hetzer, H., 1959. "Der Körper in der Selbstdarstellung von Kinder im Jahre 1926 und im Jahre 1957 (The Body in Self-Descriptions of Children in 1926 and 1957), *Zeitschrift für Experimentale und Angewandte Psychology*, **6**, 15–21.

Hicks, J. A., and M. Hayes, 1938. "Study of the Characteristics of 250 Junior High School Children," *Child Development*, **9**, 219–242.

Hill, D. S., 1930. "Personification of Ideals by Urban Children," *Journal of Social Psychology*, **1**, 379–392.

Hill, M. C., 1957. "Research on the Negro Family," *Marriage and Family Living*, **19**, 25–31.

Hirsch, S. G., 1955. *The Fears Men Live By*. New York: Harper.

Hoch, P., and J. Zubin (eds.), 1950. *Anxiety*. New York: Grune and Stratton.

Holden, G. S., 1961. "Scholastic Aptitude and the Relative Persistence of Vocational Choice," *Personnel and Guidance Journal*, **40**, 36–41.

Holland, J. L., 1959. "A Theory of Vocational Choice," *Journal of Counseling Psychology*, **6**, 35–44.

Hollingshead, A., 1949. *Elmtown's Youth*. New York: John Wiley.

Hollingworth, L. S., 1914. *Functional Periodicity, an Experimental Study of the Mental and Motor Abilities of Women During Menstruation*. Contributions to Education, No. 69. New York: Teachers College, Columbia University.

———, 1926. *Gifted Children: Their Nature and Nurture*. New York: Macmillan.

———, 1928. *Psychology of the Adolescent*. New York: D. Appleton-Century.

———, 1939. "What We Know About the Early Selection and Training of Leaders," *Teachers College Record*, **40**, 575–592.

———, 1942. *Children Above 180 IQ: Origin and Development*, H. L. Hollingworth (ed.). Yonkers, N.Y.: World Book Company.

Honzik, M. P., 1938. "The Constancy of Mental Test Performance During the Preschool Period," *Journal of Genetic Psychology*, **52**, 285–302.

———, 1957. "Developmental Studies of Parent-Child Resemblance in Intelligence," *Child Development*, **28**, 215–228.

Horney, K., 1939. *New Ways in Psychoanalysis*. New York: Norton.

———, 1945. *Our Inner Conflicts*. New York: Norton.

———, 1946. *Growth Through Love and Sex*. New York: Auxiliary Council to the Association for the Advancement of Psychoanalysis.

———, 1950. *Neurosis and Human Growth*. New York: Norton.

Horrocks, J. E., and B. A. Wear, 1953. "An Analysis of Interpersonal Choice Relationships of College Students," *Journal of Social Psychology*, **38**, 87–98.

Ichheiser, G., 1947. "Projection and the Mote-Beam Mechanism," *Journal of Abnormal and Social Psychology*, **42**, 131–133.

Inhelder, B., and J. Piaget, 1958. *The Growth of Logical Thinking from Childhood to Adolescence*. New York: Basic Books.

Isaacs, S., 1933. *Social Development in Young Children*. New York: Harcourt.

Jacob, P. E., 1957. *Changing Values in College: An Exploratory Study of the Impact of College Teaching*. New York: Harper.

James, Wm., 1910. *Psychology, Briefer Course*. New York: Henry Holt.

Jameson, S. H., 1941. "Adjustment Problems of University Girls Arising From the Urge for Recognition and New Experience," *Journal of Social Psychology*, **144**, 129–144.

Jennings, H. H., 1937. "Structure of Leadership," *Sociometry*, **1**, 99–143.

——, 1947. "Leadership and Sociometric Choice," *Sociometry*, **10**, 32–49.

Jenson, P. G., and W. K. Kirchner, 1955. "A National Answer to the Question, 'Do Sons Follow Their Fathers' Occupations?'" *Journal of Applied Psychology*, **39**, 419–421.

Jersild, A. T., 1940. "Characteristics of Teachers Who Are 'Liked Best' and 'Disliked Most,'" *Journal of Experimental Education*, **9**, No. 2, 139–151.

——, 1951. "Self-Understanding in Childhood and Adolescence," *American Psychologist*, **6**, 122–126.

——, 1952. *In Search of Self*. New York: Bureau of Publications, Teachers College, Columbia University.

——, 1954. "Emotional Development," Chapter 14 in *Manual of Child Psychology*, 2nd edition, L. Carmichael (ed.). New York: Wiley.

——, 1955. *When Teachers Face Themselves*. New York: Bureau of Publications, Teachers College, Columbia University.

——, 1960. *Child Psychology*, 5th edition. Englewood Cliffs, N.J.: Prentice-Hall.

——, and S. F. Bienstock, 1934. "A Study of the Development of Children's Ability to Sing," *Journal of Educational Psychology*, **25**, 481–503.

——, and K. Helfant, 1953. *Education for Self-Understanding*. New York: Bureau of Publications, Teachers College, Columbia University.

——, and F. B. Holmes, 1935. *Children's Fears*. New York: Bureau of Publications, Teachers College, Columbia University.

——, E. Lazar, and A. Brodkin, 1962. *The Meaning of Psychotherapy in the Teacher's Life and Work*. New York: Bureau of Publications, Teachers College, Columbia University.

——, F. V. Markey, and C. L. Jersild, 1933. *Children's Fears, Dreams, Wishes, Daydreams, Likes and Dislikes, Pleasant and Unpleasant Memories*. Child Development Monographs, No. 12. New York: Teachers College, Columbia University.

——, and M. F. Meigs, 1943. "Children at War," *Psychological Bulletin*, **40**, No. 8, 541–573.

——, and R. J. Tasch, 1949. *Children's Interests*. New York: Bureau of Publications, Teachers College, Columbia University.

——, E. S. Woodyard, and C. del Solar, 1949. *Joys and Problems of Child Rearing*. New York: Bureau of Publications, Teachers College, Columbia University.

Jervis, F., 1954. "Self Description Inventory," Counseling Service University of New Hampshire, Durham, New Hampshire.

————, 1958. "The Meaning of a Positive Self-Concept," unpublished Doctor of Philosophy dissertation, Teachers College, Columbia University.

Jervis, F. M., and R. G. Congdon, 1958. "Student and Faculty Perceptions of Educational Values," *American Psychologist,* 13, 464–466.

Johnson, A. H., 1958. "The Responses of High School Seniors to a Set of Structured Situations Concerning Teaching as a Career," *Journal of Experimental Education,* 26, 263–314.

Jones, H. E., 1943. *Development in Adolescence.* New York: Appleton-Century.

————, 1949a. *Motor Performance and Growth.* Berkeley, Calif.: University of California Press.

————, 1949b. "Adolescence in Our Society" from "Anniversary Papers of the Community Service Society of New York," pp. 70–82 in *The Family in a Democratic Society.* New York: Columbia University Press.

————, 1959. "Intelligence and Problem-solving," Chapter 20, pp. 700–738 in *Handbook of Aging and the Individual,* J. M. Birren (ed.). Chicago: University of Chicago Press.

————, and H. S. Conrad, 1933. *The Growth and Decline of Intelligence: A Study of Homogeneous Group Between the Ages of Ten and Sixty.* Genetic Psychology Monographs, 13, No. 3.

Jones, M. C., 1960. "A Comparison of the Attitudes and Interests of Ninth-grade Students over Two Decades," *Journal of Educational Psychology,* 51, 175–186.

————, and N. Bayley, 1950. "Physical Maturing Among Boys as Related to Behavior," *Journal of Educational Psychology,* 41, 129–148.

————, and P. H. Mussen, 1958. "Self-Conceptions, Motivations, and Interpersonal Attitudes of Early- and Late-Maturing Girls," *Child Development,* 29, 491–501.

Jones, V., 1954. "Character Development in Children—An Objective Approach," Chapter 13 in *Manual of Child Psychology,* 2nd edition, L. Carmichael (ed.). New York: John Wiley.

Jourard, S. M., and R. M. Remy, 1955. "Perceived Parental Attitudes, the Self and Security," *Journal of Consulting Psychology,* 19, 364–366.

Jung, C. G., 1933. *Modern Man in Search of a Soul.* New York: Harcourt.

————, 1953. *Collected Works. Volume 12. Psychology and Alchemy.* New York: Pantheon Press.

Kahl, J. A., 1953. "Educational Aspirations of 'Common Man' Boys," *Harvard Educational Review,* 23, 186–203.

Kallman, F. J., 1953. *Heredity in Health and Mental Disorder.* New York: Norton.

Kaplan, D. M., and W. Goodrich, 1957. "A Formulation for Interpersonal Anger," *American Journal of Orthopsychiatry,* 27, 387–395.

Katz, D., and F. H. Allport, 1931. *Students' Attitudes: A Report of the*

Syracuse University Reaction to Study. Syracuse, N.Y.: The Craftsman Press.

Katz, R. L., 1953. "Aspects of Pastoral Psychology and the Rabbinate," *Jewish Social Service Quarterly,* 29, 367–373.

Kay, H., 1955. "Some Experiments on Adult Learning," pp. 259–267 in *Old Age in the Modern World.* London: E. and S. Livingstone.

Kierkegaard, S., 1940. *Stages on Life's Way.* Translated by W. Lowrie. Princeton, N.J.: Princeton University Press.

————, 1941. *Sickness Unto Death.* Translated by W. Lowrie. Princeton, N.J.: Yale University Press.

————, 1944. *The Concept of Dread.* Translated by W. Lowrie. Princeton, N.J.: Yale University Press.

————, 1949. *Either/Or.* Translated by W. Lowrie. Princeton, N.J.: Princeton University Press.

Kimball, B., 1953. "Case Studies in Educational Failure During Adolescence," *American Journal of Orthopsychiatry,* 23, 405–415.

Kimmins, C. W., 1915–16a. "The Interests of London Children in the War at Different Ages," *Journal of Experimental Pedagogy,* 3, 145–152.

————, 1915–16b. "The Interests of London Children at Different Ages in Air Raids," *Journal of Experimental Pedagogy,* 3, 225–236.

Kinsey, A. C., W. B. Pomeroy, and C. E. Martin, 1948. *Sexual Behavior in the Human Male.* Philadelphia: W. B. Saunders.

————, 1953. *Sexual Behavior in the Human Female.* Philadelphia: W. B. Saunders.

Klineberg, O., 1935. *Negro Intelligence and Selective Migration.* New York: Columbia University Press.

————, 1938. "The Intelligence of Migrants," *American Sociological Review,* 3, 218–224.

————, 1953. "Cultural Factors in Personality Adjustment of Children," *American Journal of Orthopsychiatry,* 23, 465–471.

Klopfer, B., 1937. "The Technique of the Rorschach Performance," *Rorschach Research Exchange,* 2, 1–14.

————, *et al.,* 1956. *Developments in the Rorschach Technique.* Yonkers, N.Y.: World Book Company.

————, and D. McG. Kelley, 1946. *The Rorschach Technique.* Yonkers, N.Y.: World Book Company.

Koch, H. L., 1935. "An Analysis of Certain Forms of So-Called 'Nervous Habits' in Young Children," *Journal of Genetic Psychology,* 46, 139–170.

————, 1944. "A Study of Some Factors Conditioning the Social Distance Between the Sexes," *Journal of Social Psychology,* 20, 79–107.

Komarovsky, M., 1946. "Cultural Contradictions and Sex Roles," *American Journal of Sociology,* 52, 184–189.

Kroger, R., and C. M. Louttit, 1935. "The Influence of Father's Occupation on the Vocational Choices of High School Boys," *Journal of Applied Psychology,* 19, 203–212.

Krogman, W. W., 1962. "How Your Children Grow," *Saturday Evening Post,* July 14–21, pp. 50–53.

Krugman, M., 1940. "Out of the Inkwell: The Rorschach Method," *Character and Personality,* 9, 91–110.

Kubie, L. S., 1950. *Practical and Theoretical Aspects of Psychoanalysis.* New York: International Universities Press.

———, 1954a. "The Forgotten Man of Education," *The Goddard Bulletin,* 19, No. 2.

———, 1954b. "Some Unresolved Problems of the Scientific Career," *American Scientist,* 42, 104–112.

Kuhlen, R. G., and M. Arnold, 1944. "Age Differences in Religious Beliefs and Problems During Adolescence," *Journal of Genetic Psychology,* 65, 291–300.

———, and H. S. Bretsch, 1947. "Sociometric Status and Personal Problems of Adolescents," *Sociometry,* 10, 122–132.

———, and B. J. Lee, 1943. "Personality Characteristics and Social Acceptability in Adolescence," *Journal of Educational Psychology,* 34, 321–340.

Kvaraceus, W. C., 1945. *Juvenile Delinquency and the School.* Yonkers, N.Y.: World Book Company.

———, 1954. *The Community and the Delinquent.* Yonkers, N.Y.: World Book Company.

———, 1958. *Juvenile Delinquency.* Washington, D.C.: Department of Classroom Teachers, American Educational Research Association of the National Education Association.

———, and W. B. Miller *et al.,* 1959. *Delinquent Behavior.* Washington, D.C.: National Education Association.

Lafore, G. G., 1945. *Practices of Parents in Dealing with Preschool Children.* Child Development Monographs, No. 31. New York: Teachers College, Columbia University.

La Mare, N., 1957. *Love and Fulfillment in Women.* New York: Macmillan.

Landis, C., A. T. Landis, and M. M. Bolles *et al.,* 1940. *Sex in Development.* New York: Paul B. Hoeber.

Landis, P. H., 1954. "The Ordering and Forbidding Techniques and Teen-Age Adjustment," *School and Society,* 80, 105–106.

Lantagne, J. E., 1958. "Interests of 4,000 High School Pupils in Problems of Marriage and Parenthood," *Research Quarterly of the American Association for Health, Physical Education and Recreation,* 28, 407–416.

Latham, A. J., 1951. "The Relationship Between Pubertal Status and Leadership in Junior High School Boys," *Journal of Genetic Psychology,* 78, 185–194.

Laughlin, F., 1954. *The Peer Status of Sixth and Seventh Grade Children.* New York: Bureau of Publications, Teachers College, Columbia University.

Lawrence, E. M., 1931. "An Investigation into the Relation Between Intelligence and Inheritance," *British Journal of Psychology Monograph Supplement,* 16.

Lecky, P., 1945. *Self-Consistency: A Theory of Personality*. New York: Island Press.

Ledvina, L. M., 1954. "A 100 Per Cent Follow-up," *Personnel and Guidance Journal*, 33, 90–93.

Lehman, H., 1953. *Age and Achievement*. Princeton, N.J.: Princeton University Press.

Lehman, H. C., and P. A. Witty, 1934. "Vocational Guidance: Some Basic Considerations," *Journal of Educational Sociology*, 8, 174–184.

Levitt, E. E., and R. H. Ojemann, 1953. "The Aims of Preventive Psychiatry and 'Causality' as a Personality Pattern," *Journal of Psychology*, 36, 393–400.

Levy, D. M., 1928. "Fingersucking and Accessory Movements in Early Infancy," *American Journal of Psychiatry*, 7, 881–918.

Levy, J., and R. Monroe, 1938. *The Happy Family*. New York: Knopf.

Libby, W., 1908. "The Imagination of Adolescents," *American Journal of Psychology*, 19, 249–252.

Lloyd, R. C., 1952. "Parent-Youth Conflicts of College Students," *Sociology and Social Research*, 36, 227–230.

Lockhard, E. G., 1930. "The Attitudes of Children Toward Certain Laws," *Religious Education*, 25, 144–149.

Lockwood, W. V., 1958. "Realism of Vocational Preferences," *Personnel and Guidance Journal*, 37, 98–106.

Lorge, I., 1936. "Psychometry: The Evaluation of Mental Status as a Function of the Mental Test," *Journal of Educational Psychology*, 27, 100–110.

————, 1945. "Schooling Makes a Difference," *Teachers College Record*, 46, 483–492.

Lund, F. H., 1944. "Adolescent Motivation: Sex Differences," *Journal of Genetic Psychology*, 64, 99–103.

Lunger, R., and J. D. Page, 1939. "The Worries of College Freshmen," *Journal of Genetic Psychology*, 54, 457–460.

Lyman, E. L., 1955. "Occupational Differences in the Value Attached to Work," *American Journal of Sociology*, 61, 138–144.

Lynn, D. B., 1959. "A Note on Sex Differences in the Development of Masculine and Feminine Identification," *Psychological Review*, 66, 126–135.

Maccoby, E. E., P. K. Gibbs *et al.*, 1954. "Methods of Child Rearing in Two Social Classes," pp. 380–396 in *Readings in Child Development*, W. E. Martin and C. B. Stendler (eds.). New York: Harcourt, Brace.

Machover, K., 1949. *Personality Projection in the Drawing of the Human Figure: A Method of Personality Investigation*. Springfield, Ill.: Charles C Thomas.

MacIver, R. M., 1948. "Sex and Social Attitudes," pp. 85–95 in *About the Kinsey Report*, D. P. Geddes and E. Curie (eds.). New York: New American Library.

Macmurray, J., 1937. *Reason and Emotion*. New York: D. Appleton-Century.

Manis, M., 1958. "Personal Adjustment, Assumed Similarity to Parents, and Inferred Parental Evaluations of the Self," *Journal of Consulting Psychology,* **22,** 481–485.

Markley, E. R., 1958. "Social Class Differences in Mothers' Attitudes Toward Child Rearing," unpublished Doctor of Philosophy dissertation, Teachers College, Columbia University.

Marsh, C. J., 1942. "The Worries of the College Woman," *Journal of Social Psychology,* **15,** 335–339.

Maslow, A. H., 1953. "Love in Healthy People," pp. 57–93 in *The Meaning of Love,* A. Montagu (ed.). New York: Julian Press.

Mather, W. G., 1934. "The Courtship Ideals of High-School Youth," *Sociology and Social Research,* **19,** 166–172.

May, R., 1950. *The Meaning of Anxiety.* New York: Ronald Press.

McCann, W. H., 1941. "Nostalgia: A Review of the Literature," *Psychological Bulletin,* **38,** 165–182.

———, 1943. "Nostalgia: A Descriptive and Comparative Study," *Journal of Genetic Psychology,* **62,** 97–104.

McFarlane, M., 1925. "A Study of Practical Ability," *British Journal of Psychology Monograph Supplement,* **3,** No. 8, 35–36.

McKee, J. P., and A. C. Sherriffs, 1959. "Men's and Women's Beliefs, Ideals, and Self-Concepts," *American Journal of Sociology,* **44,** 356–363.

Meek, L. H., 1940. *Personal-Social Development of Boys and Girls with Implications for Secondary Education.* New York: Committee on Workshops, Progressive Education Association.

Meltzer, H., 1933. "Students' Adjustments in Anger," *Journal of Social Psychology,* **4,** 285–309.

Merrill, M. A., 1947. *The Problems of Child Delinquency.* Boston: Houghton Mifflin.

Mill, S. R., 1953. "Personality Patterns of Sociometrically Selected and Sociometrically Rejected Male College Students," *Sociometry,* **16,** 151–167.

Miller, D. C., and W. H. Form, 1951. *Industrial Sociology.* New York: Harper.

Miller, W., 1958. "Lower Class Culture as a Generating Milieu of Gang Delinquency," *Journal of Social Issues,* **14,** 5–19.

Mills, C. A., 1939. *Climatology.* Springfield, Ill.: Charles C Thomas.

———, and C. Ogle, 1936. "Physiologic Sterility of Adolescents," *Human Biology,* **8,** 607–615.

Mitchell, C., 1943. "Do Virtues and Vices Change?" *School and Society,* **57,** 111–112.

Moll, A., 1924. *The Sexual Life of the Child.* New York: Macmillan.

Montagu, A., 1946. *Adolescent Sterility.* Springfield, Ill.: Charles C Thomas.

——— (ed.), 1953. *The Meaning of Love.* New York: Julian Press.

———, 1959. *Human Heredity.* Cleveland: World Publishing Company.

Moore, J. E., 1940. "Annoying Habits of High School Teachers," *Peabody Journal of Education,* **18,** 161–165.

Moreno, J. L., 1934. *Who Shall Survive?* Washington, D.C.: Nervous and Mental Disease Publishing Company.

————, 1946. *Psychodrama.* New York: Beacon House.

————, 1954. "Old and New Trends in Sociometry: Turning Points in Small Group Research," *International Social Science Bulletin,* 17, 179–193.

Morse, H. T., and P. L. Dressel (eds.), 1960. *General Education for Personal Maturity.* Dubuque, Iowa: Wm. C. Brown.

Morse, N. C., and F. H. Allport, 1952. "The Causation of Anti-Semitism: An Investigation of Seven Hypotheses," *Journal of Psychology,* 34, 197–233.

Moser, W. E., 1949. "Vocational Preference as Related to Mental Ability," *Occupations,* 27, 460–461.

Moss, J., and R. Gingles, 1958. "A Preliminary Report of a Longitudinal Study of Early Marriages in Nebraska." (Cited by Burchinal, 1959a. Original not seen.)

Mowrer, O. H., 1950. "Pain, Punishment, Guilt, and Anxiety," Chapter 3, pp. 27–40, in *Anxiety,* P. H. Hoch and J. Zubin (eds.). New York: Grune and Stratton.

————, 1953. "Some Philosophical Problems in Mental Disorder and Its Treatment," *Harvard Educational Review,* 23, 117–127.

Murphy, F. J., M. M. Shirley, and H. L. Witmer, 1946. "The Incidence of Hidden Delinquency," *American Journal of Orthopsychiatry,* XVI, 686–696.

Murphy, G., 1945. "The Freeing of Intelligence," *Psychological Bulletin,* 42, 1–19.

————, 1947. *Personality.* New York: Harper.

————, and R. Likert, 1938. *Public Opinion and the Individual.* New York: Harper.

Murray, H. A., 1938. *Explorations in Personality.* New York: Oxford University Press.

Mussen, P. H., and M. C. Jones, 1957. "Self-Conceptions, Motivations, and Attitudes of Late- and Early-Maturing Boys," *Child Development,* 28, 243–256.

Myers, M. S., 1951. "The Role of Certain Religious Values for High School Youth," *Studies in Higher Education,* Purdue University, 79, 79–85.

Myers, W. E., 1947. "High School Graduates Choose Vocations Unrealistically," *Occupations,* 25, 332–333.

Nachmann, B., 1960. "Childhood Experience and Vocational Choice in Law, Dentistry, and Social Work," *Journal of Counseling Psychology,* 7, 243–250.

Nathanson, I. T., L. Towne, and J. C. Aub, 1943. "Urinary Sex Hormone Studies," in R. N. Sanford, *Physique, Personality and Scholarship,* Monographs of the Society for Research in Child Development, 8, 70–81.

National Manpower Council, 1957. *Womanpower.* New York: Columbia University Press.

Neel, J. V., 1960. "The Genetic Potential," pp. 1–23 in *The Nation's Children, Vol. 2, Development and Education,* E. Ginzberg (ed.). New York: Columbia University Press.

Nelson, E., 1940. *Student Attitudes Toward Religion.* Genetic Psychology Monographs, 22, 323–423.

————, 1956. *Patterns of Religious Attitude Shifts from College to Fourteen Years Later,* Psychological Monographs, 70, No. 17.

Neugarten, B. L., 1946. "Social Class and Friendship Among School Children," *American Journal of Sociology,* 51, 305–313.

Newton, N., 1955. *Maternal Emotions.* New York: Harper.

Noble, J. L., 1956. *The Negro Woman's College Education.* New York: Bureau of Publications, Teachers College, Columbia University.

Northway, M. L., and B. T. Wigdor, 1947. "Rorschach Patterns Related to the Sociometric Status of School Children," *Sociometry,* 10, 186–199.

Norton, J. L., 1953a. "Patterns of Vocational Interest Development and Actual Job Choice," *Journal of Genetic Psychology,* 82, 235–262.

————, 1953b. "General Motives and Influences in Vocational Development," *Journal of Genetic Psychology,* 82, 263–278.

Oakden, E. C., and M. Sturt, 1922. "Development of the Knowledge of Time in Children," *British Journal of Psychology,* 12, 309–336.

O'Hara, R. P., and D. V. Tiedeman, 1959. "Vocational Self Concept in Adolescence," *Journal of Counseling Psychology,* 6, 292–301.

Ojemann, R. H., 1961. "Investigations on the Effects of Teaching and Understanding Behavior Dynamics," pp. 378–397 in *Prevention of Mental Disorders in Children,* G. Caplan (ed.). New York: Basic Books.

————, E. E. Levitt, W. H. Lylie, and M. F. Whiteside, 1955. "The Effects of a 'Causal' Teacher-Training Program and Certain Curricular Changes on Grade School Children," *Journal of Experimental Education,* 24, 95–114.

Olds, E. B., 1949. "How Do Young People Use Their Leisure Time?" *Recreation,* 42, 458–463.

Orgel, S. Z., and J. Tuckman, 1935. "Nicknames of Institutional Children," *American Journal of Orthopsychiatry,* 5, 276–285.

Orton, J., 1959. "Personal and Practical Concerns Faced by Teachers of Family Life, Psychology and Personal Adjustment Courses at the College Level," unpublished Doctor of Education dissertation, Teachers College, Columbia University.

Overstreet, B. W., 1953. "The Unloving Personality and the Religion of Love," *Pastoral Psychology,* 4, 14–20.

Owens, W. A., Jr., 1953. *Age and Mental Abilities: A Longitudinal Study.* Genetic Psychology Monographs, 48, 3–54.

Pace, R. C., 1941. *They Went to College.* Minneapolis: University of Minnesota Press.

Parsons, T., 1942. "Age and Sex in the Social Structure of the United States," *American Sociological Review,* 7, 604–616.

Passow, A. H., M. Goldberg, A. J. Tannenbaum, and W. French, 1955 *Planning for Talented Youth*. New York: Bureau of Publications, Teachers College, Columbia University.

Patti, J. B., 1956. "Elementary Psychology for Eighth Graders?" *American Psychologist*, **11**, 194–196.

Peck, R. F., R. J. Havighurst, R. Cooper, J. Lilienthal, and D. Moore, 1960. *The Psychology of Character Development*. New York: Wiley.

Penty, R. C., 1956. *Reading Ability and High School Drop-Outs*. New York: Bureau of Publications, Teachers College, Columbia University.

Phillips, E. L., 1951. "Attitudes Toward Self and Others: A Brief Questionnaire Report," *Journal of Consulting Psychology*, **15**, 79–81.

Piaget, J., 1932. *The Moral Judgment of the Child*. London: The Free Press.

Pixley, E., and E. Beekman, 1949. "The Faith of Youth as Shown by a Survey of Public Schools in Los Angeles," *Religious Education*, **44**, 336–342.

Polansky, N., R. Lippit, and F. Redl, 1950. "The Use of Near-Sociometric Data in Research on Group Treatment Processes," *Sociometry*, **13**, 39–62.

Pope, C., 1943. "Personal Problems of High School Pupils," *School and Society*, **57**, 443–448.

Porter, J. R., 1954. "Predicting Vocational Plans of High School Senior Boys," *Personnel and Guidance Journal*, **53**, 215–218.

Porter, R. M., 1959. "Student Attitudes Toward Child Behavior Problems," *Journal of Educational Research*, **52**, 349–352.

Potashin, R., 1946. "Sociometric Study of Children's Friendships," *Sociometry*, **9**, 48–70.

Powell, M. G., 1948. "Comparison of Self-Ratings, Peer Ratings, and Expert Ratings on Personality Adjustment," *Educational and Psychological Measurement*, **8**, 225–234.

Pressey, S. L., and A. W. Jones, 1955. "1923–53 and 20–60 Age Changes in Moral Codes, Anxieties, and Interests, as Shown by the 'X-O Tests,' " *Journal of Psychology*, **39**, 485–502.

———, and R. G. Kuhlen, 1957. *Psychological Development Through the Life Span*. New York: Harper.

Preston, R. C., 1942. *Children's Reactions to a Contemporary War Situation*. Child Development Monographs, 28. New York: Teachers College, Columbia University.

Pritchard, M. C., K. M. Horan, and L. S. Hollingworth, 1940. "The Course of Mental Development in Slow Learners Under an 'Experience Curriculum,' " National Society for the Study of Education. *Intelligence: Its Nature and Nurture*, Thirty-ninth Yearbook, Part II, 245–254. Bloomington, Ill.: Public School Publishing Company.

Pullias, E. V., 1937. "Masturbation as a Mental Hygiene Problem—A Study of the Reliefs of Seventy-Five Young Men," *Journal of Abnormal and Social Psychology*, **32**, 216–222.

Punke, H. H., 1944. "Dating Practices of High School Youth," *National Association of Secondary School Principals Bulletin*, **28**, 47–54.

Radke-Yarrow, M., and J. S. Miller, 1960. "Children's Concepts and Attitudes About Minority and Majority American Groups," Chapter 57, pp. 617–635 in *The Adolescent: A Book of Readings,* J. Seidman (ed.). New York: Holt, Rinehart, and Winston.

Ramsey, G. V., 1943. "The Sexual Development of Boys," *American Journal of Psychology,* 56, 217–233.

Raph (Beasley), J., and A. Tannenbaum, 1961. "Underachievement: Review of the Literature." Talented Youth Project, Horace Mann–Lincoln Institute of School Experimentation, Teachers College, Columbia University. (Revised, unpublished.)

Reevy, W. R., 1961. "Adolescent Sexuality," pp. 52–67 in *The Encyclopedia of Sexual Behavior,* A. Ellis (ed.). New York: Hawthorn.

Reik, T., 1944. *A Psychologist Looks at Love.* New York: Rinehart.

Remmers, H. H., R. E. Horton, and S. Lysgaard, 1952. "Teen-Age Personality in Our Culture; Report of Poll No. 32," *Purdue Opinion Panel,* 11 (3), 131 v.p., Rep. No. 32.

————, M. S. Myers, and E. M. Bennett, 1951. "Some Personality Aspects and Religious Values of High School Youth," *Purdue Opinion Panel,* 10 (3).

————, and D. H. Radler, 1957. *The American Teenager.* New York: Bobbs-Merrill Company.

————, 1958. "Teenage Attitudes," *Scientific American,* 198, 25–29.

Reynolds, E. L., 1951. *The Distribution of Subcutaneous Fat in Childhood and Adolescence.* Monographs of the Society for Research in Child Development, 15, No. 2.

————, and J. V. Wines, 1948. "Individual Differences in Physical Changes Associated with Adolescent Girls," *American Journal of Diseases of Children,* 75, 329–350.

Reynolds, L. G., and J. Shister, 1949. *Job Horizons.* New York: Harper.

Reynolds, N. B., 1958. "Job Ranking on an Ethics Scale," *Educational Record,* 39, 192–193.

Rheingold, H. L., and N. Bayley, 1959. "The Later Effects of an Experimental Modification of Mothering," *Child Development,* 30, 363–372.

Richardson, R. F., 1918. *The Psychology and Pedagogy of Anger.* Educational Psychology Monographs, No. 19. Baltimore: Warwick and York.

Richey, H. G., 1937. *The Relationship of Accelerated, Normal and Retarded Puberity to the Height and Weight of School Children.* Monographs of the Society for Research in Child Development, II, No. 1. Washington, D.C.: National Research Council.

Roberts, D. E., 1950. *Psychotherapy and a Christian View of Man.* New York: Scribner.

Roe, A., 1952. *The Making of a Scientist.* New York: Dodd, Mead.

————, 1953. *A Psychological Study of Eminent Psychologists and Anthropologists, and a Comparison with Biological and Physical Scientists,* Psychological Monographs, 67, No. 2, whole No. 352.

————, 1957. "Early Determinants of Vocational Choice," *Journal of Counseling Psychology,* 4, 212–217.

Roff, C., 1959. "The Self-Concept in Adolescent Girls," *Dissertation Abstracts,* **20,** 385.

Roffwarg, H. P., W. C. Dement and C. Fisher, 1962. "Observations on the Sleep-Dream Pattern in Neonates, Infants, Children and Adults." Unpublished report of investigation supported by Research Grant MY-3267 to Drs. Fisher and Dement from the National Institutes of Mental Health.

Rogers, C. R., 1942. "A Study of the Mental Health Problems in Three Representative Elementary Schools," *A Study of Health and Physical Education in Columbus Public Schools.* Monographs of the Bureau of Educational Research, No. 25. Columbus: Ohio State University Press.

————, and R. F. Dymond (eds.), 1954. *Psychotherapy and Personality Change.* Chicago: University of Chicago Press.

Rogoff, N., 1953. *Recent Trends in Occupational Mobility.* Glencoe, Ill.: The Free Press.

Rorschach, H., 1937. *Psychodiagnostik, Methodik und Ergebnisse eines wahrehmungsdiagnostischen Experiments,* 3rd edition. Berlin: Huber.

————, 1942. *Psychodiagnostics, a Diagnostic Test Based on Perception.* Translated by P. Lemkau and B. Kronenberg. New York: Grune and Stratton.

Rose, A. A., 1944. "Insecurity Feelings in Adolescent Girls," *Nervous Child,* **4,** 46–59.

————, 1947. "A Study of Homesickness in College Freshmen," *Journal of Social Psychology,* **26,** 185–202.

Ross, M. G., 1950. *Religious Beliefs of Youth.* New York: Association Press.

Rostker, L. E., 1940. "The Measurement and Prediction of Teaching Ability," *School and Society,* **51,** 30–32.

Rothney, J. W. M., 1958. *Guidance Practices and Results.* New York: Harper.

Ruff, W. K., 1951. "A Study of Some Aspects of Personal Adjustment Common to High School Boys, with Implications for Physical Education," unpublished Doctor of Education dissertation, Teachers College, Columbia University.

Ryan, F. R., and J. S. Davie, 1958. "Social Acceptance, Academic Achievement, and Aptitude Among High School Students," *Journal of Educational Research,* **52,** 101–106.

Ryans, D. G., 1953. "The Investigation of Teacher Characteristics," *Educational Record,* **34,** 371–396.

Sanders, B. S., 1934. *Environment and Growth.* Baltimore: Warwick and York.

Sanford, N., 1956. "Personality Development During the College Years," *Personnel and Guidance Journal,* **35,** 74–80.

————, 1957. "The Uncertain Senior," *Journal of the National Association of Women Deans and Counselors,* **XXI,** 9–15.

——, 1958. "The Professor Looks at the Student," pp. 3–25 in *The Two Ends of the Log,* R. M. Cooper (ed.). Minneapolis: University of Minnesota Press.

Sanford, R. N., *et al.,* 1943. *Physique, Personality and Scholarship.* Monographs of the Society for Research in Child Development, **VIII,** No. 1. Washington, D.C.: National Research Council.

Sargent, S. S., 1953. "Class and Class-counsciousness in a California Town," *Social Problems,* **1,** 23–27.

Sartre, J. P., 1956. *Being and Nothingness.* Translated by H. E. Barnes. New York: Philosophical Library.

Saul, L. J., 1947. *Emotional Maturity.* Philadelphia: J. B. Lippincott.

Schilder, P., 1935. *The Image and Appearance of the Human Body:* Studies in the Constructive Energies of the Psyche. Psyche Monographs, No. 4. London: Kegan Paul, Trench, Trubner.

Schmidt, J. L., and J. W. M. Rothney, 1955. "Variability of Vocational Choices of High School Students," *Personnel and Guidance Journal,* **34,** 142–146.

Schneider, L., and S. Lysgaard, 1953. "The Deferred Gratification Pattern: A Preliminary Study," *American Sociological Review,* **18,** 142–149.

Schonbar, R. A., 1959. "Some Manifest Characteristics of Recallers and Nonrecallers of Dreams," *Journal of Consulting Psychology,* **23,** 414–418.

Schonfeld, W. A., 1950. "Inadequate Masculine Physique as a Factor in Personality Development of Adolescent Boys," *Psychosomatic Medicine,* **12,** 49–54.

——, and G. W. Beebe, 1942. "Normal Growth and Variations in the Male Genitalia from Birth to Maturity," *Journal of Urology,* **48,** 759–777.

Scott, L. F., 1953. "A Study of Children's TV Interests," *California Journal of Educational Research,* **4,** 162–164.

Sears, R. R., E. E. Maccoby, and H. Levin, 1957. *Patterns of Child Rearing.* Evanston, Ill.: Row, Peterson.

Secord, P., and S. M. Jourard, 1953. "The Appraisal of Body-cathexis: Body-cathexis and the Self," *Journal of Consulting Psychology,* **17,** 343–347.

Segal, S. J., 1961. "A Psychoanalytic Analysis of Personality Factors in Vocational Choice," *Journal of Counseling Psychology,* **8,** 202–210.

Shaffer, L. F., 1930. *Children's Interpretation of Cartoons.* Contributions to Education, No. 429. New York: Bureau of Publications, Teachers College, Columbia University.

——, and E. J. Shoben, Jr., 1956. *The Psychology of Adjustment.* Boston: Houghton Mifflin.

Sheerer, E. T., 1949. "An Analysis of the Relationship Between Acceptance of and Respect for Self and Acceptance of and Respect for Others in Ten Counseling Cases," *Journal of Consulting Psychology,* **13,** 169–175.

Sherman, A. W., Jr., 1946. "Emancipation Status of College Students," *Journal of General Psychology,* **68,** 171–180.

Shirley, M. M., 1933. *The First Two Years: A Study of Twenty-five Babies,*

III, Personality Manifestations. Institute of Child Welfare Monographs, Series No. 8. Minneapolis: University of Minnesota Press.

Shoobs, N., 1947. "Sociometry in the Classroom," *Sociometry,* **10,** 154–164.

Shuey, A. M., 1948. "Improvement in the Scores of the American Council on Education Psychological Examination from Freshman to Senior Year," *Journal of Educational Psychology,* **39,** 417–426.

Shumsky, A., 1956. "Emotional Adjustment and Moral Reasoning in Children," unpublished Doctor of Education dissertation, Teachers College, Columbia University.

Shuttleworth, F. K., 1937. *Sexual Maturation and the Physical Growth of Girls Age Six to Nineteen.* Monographs of the Society for Research in Child Development, **II,** No. 5. Washington, D.C.: National Research Council.

————, 1938. *The Adolescent Period.* Monographs of the Society for Research in Child Development, **III,** No. 3. Washington, D.C.: National Research Council.

————, 1949. *The Adolescent Period: A Pictorial Atlas.* Monographs of the Society for Research in Child Development, **14** (Serial No. 50, published 1951). Washington, D.C.: National Research Council.

Silverman, H. L., 1952. "Some Thoughts on the Relation of Religion and Psychology," *Psychiatric Quarterly Supplement,* **26,** 261–268.

Silverman, S. S., 1945. *Clothing and Appearance: Their Psychological Implications for Teen-Age Girls.* New York: Bureau of Publications, Teachers College, Columbia University.

Simmons, K., and W. W. Greulich, 1943. "Menarcheal Age and the Height, Weight and Skeletal Age of Girls Age 7 to 17 Years," *Journal of Pediatrics,* **22,** 518–548.

Simpson, G. E., and J. M. Yinger, 1958. *Racial and Cultural Minorities: An Analysis of Prejudice and Discrimination* (rev. ed.). New York: Harper.

Singer, S. L., and B. Stefflre, 1954. "The Relationship of Job Values and Desires to Vocational Aspirations of Adolescents," *Journal of Applied Psychology,* **38,** 419–422.

Skeels, H. M.. R. Updegraff, B. L. Wellman, and H. M. Williams, 1938. "A Study of Environmental Stimulation: An Orphanage Preschool Project," *University of Iowa Studies in Child Welfare,* **1,** 56.

Skodak, M., and H. M. Skeels, 1949. "A Final Follow-up of One Hundred Adopted Children," *Journal of Genetic Psychology,* **75,** 85–125.

Slater, E., 1951. *An Investigation into Psychotic and Neurotic Twins.* London: University of London.

Slocum, W. L., 1958. "Educational Planning by High School Seniors," *Journal of Educational Research,* **51,** 583–590.

Small, L., 1953. "Personality Determinants of Vocational Choice," *Psychological Monographs,* **67,** No. 1, whole No. 351.

Smith, C. B., 1944. "A Study of Pupils Dropping Out of a Midwestern High School," *School Review,* **52,** 151–156.

Smith, G. F., 1924. "Certain Aspects of the Sex Life of the Adolescent Girl," *Journal of Applied Psychology,* 8, 347–349.

Smith, R. B., 1932. "The Development of an Inventory for the Measurement of Inferiority Feelings at the High School Level," *Archives of Psychology,* 144.

Smith, W. M., 1952. "Rating and Dating: A Re-study," *Marriage and Family Living,* 14, 312–317.

Sollenberger, R. T., 1940. "Some Relationships Between the Urinary Excretion of Male Hormones by Maturing Boys and Girls and Their Expressed Interests and Attitudes," *Journal of Psychology,* 9, 179–189.

Sorokin, P. A., and R. C. Hanson, 1953. "The Power of Creative Love," pp. 97–159 in *The Meaning of Love,* A. Montagu (ed.). New York: Julian Press.

Spitz, R. A., 1951. "The Psychogenic Diseases in Infancy: An Attempt at Their Etiologic Classification," pp. 255–275 in *Psychoanalytic Study of the Child,* Vol. 6. New York: International Universities Press.

Spivack, S., 1956. "A Study of a Method of Appraising Self-Acceptance and Self-Rejection," *Journal of Genetic Psychology,* 88, 183–202.

Spranger, O., 1952. "Psychoanalytic Pedagogy," *Psychoanalysis,* 1, 59–70.

Srole, L., T. S. Langner, S. T. Michael, M. K. Opler, and T. A. C. Rennie, 1962. *Mental Health in the Metropolis: The Midtown Manhattan Study.* Volume 1. New York: McGraw-Hill.

Staples, R., and J. W. Smith, 1954. "Attitudes of Grandmothers and Mothers Toward Child Rearing Practices," *Child Development,* 25, 91–97.

Stendler, C. B., 1949. *Children of Brasstown.* Urbana: University of Illinois Press.

Stephenson, R. M., 1957. "Realism of Vocational Choice: A Critique and an Example," *Personnel and Guidance Journal,* 8, 483–494.

Stephenson, R. R., 1961. "Occupational Choice as a Crystallized Self Concept," *Journal of Counseling Psychology,* 8, 211–216.

Stephenson, W., 1935. "Correlating Persons Instead of Tests," *Character and Personality,* 4, 17–24.

———, 1952. "Some Observations on Q-technique," *Psychological Bulletin,* 6, 483–498.

Stewart, N., 1947. "AGCT Scores of Army Personnel Grouped by Occupation," *Occupations,* 26, 5–41.

Stolz, H. R., and M. C. Jones, and J. Chaffey, 1937. "The Junior High School Age," *University High School Journal,* 15, 63–72.

———, and L. M. Stolz, 1944. "Adolescent Problems Related to Somatic Variations," Chapter 5, pp. 80–99, in *43d Yearbook of the National Society for the Study of Education.* Part I, *Adolescence,* N. B. Henry (ed.). Chicago: University of Chicago Press.

———, 1951. *Somatic Development of Adolescent Boys.* New York: Macmillan.

Stott, L. H., 1940a. "Adolescents' Dislikes Regarding Parental Behavior and Their Significance," *Journal of Genetic Psychology,* 57, 393–414.

————, 1940b. "Home Punishment of Adolescents," *Journal of Genetic Psychology,* **57,** 415–428.

Strang, R., 1956. "Gifted Adolescents' Views of Growing Up," *Exceptional Children,* **23,** 10–15.

Stratton, G. M., 1929. "Emotion and the Incidence of Disease: The Influence of the Number of the Diseases and of the Age at Which They Occur," *Psychological Review,* **36,** 242–253.

Strong, E. K., Jr., 1943. *Vocational Interests of Men and Women.* Stanford, Calif.: Stanford University Press.

Sullivan, H. S., 1947. *Conceptions of Modern Psychiatry.* Washington, D.C.: William Alanson White Psychiatric Foundation.

————, 1948. *The Meaning of Anxiety in Psychiatry and in Life.* New York: William Alanson White Institute of Psychiatry.

————, 1953. *The Interpersonal Theory of Psychiatry.* New York: Norton.

Super, D. E., 1947. "Vocational Interests and Vocational Choice: Present Knowledge and Future Research in Their Relationship," *Educational and Psychological Measurement,* **7,** 375–383.

————, 1953. "A Theory of Vocational Development," *American Psychologist,* **8,** 185–190.

————, and P. B. Bachrach, 1957. *Scientific Careers and Vocational Development Theory.* New York: Bureau of Publications, Teachers College, Columbia University.

————, and J. O. Crites, 1962. *Appraising Vocational Fitness By Means of Psychological Tests* (rev. ed.). New York: Harper.

————, R. C. Hummel, H. P. Moser, P. L. Overstreet, and C. F. Warnath, 1957. *Vocational Development, A Framework for Research.* Career Pattern Study Monograph One. New York: Bureau of Publications, Teachers College, Columbia University.

————, J. P. Jordaan, R. Starishevsky, and N. Matlin, 1962. "Essays in Vocational Development," unpublished report, Teachers College, Columbia University.

————, and P. L. Overstreet, in collaboration with C. N. Morris, W. Dubin, and M. B. Heyde, 1960. *The Vocational Maturity of Ninth-Grade Boys.* Career Pattern Study Monograph Two. New York: Bureau of Publications, Teachers College, Columbia University.

Switzer, D. K., A. E. Grigg, J. S. Miller, and R. K. Young, 1962. "Early Experiences and Occupational Choice: A Test of Roe's Hypothesis," *Journal of Counseling Psychology,* **9,** 45–48.

Symonds, P. M., 1942. *Adolescent Fantasy,* New York: Columbia University Press.

————, and A. R. Jensen, 1961. *From Adolescent to Adult.* New York: Columbia University Press.

————, and M. Sherman, 1949. "Personality Survey of a Junior High School," pp. 23–50, in *The Measurement of Student Adjustment and Achievement,* W. T. Donahue (ed.). Ann Arbor: University of Michigan Press.

Taba, H., 1953. "The Moral Beliefs of Sixteen-Year-Olds," Chapter 54, pp. 592–596, in *The Adolescent: A Book of Readings,* J. Seidman (ed.). New York: Dryden Press.

Tannenbaum, A. J., 1959. "A Study of Verbal Stereotypes Associated with Brilliant and Average Students," unpublished Doctor of Philosophy dissertation, Teachers College, Columbia University.

Tanner, J. M., 1955. *Growth at Adolescence.* Springfield, Ill.: Charles C Thomas.

Taschuk, W. A., 1957. "An Analysis of the Self-Concept of Grade Nine Students," *Alberta Journal of Educational Research,* III, No. 2, 94–103.

Taylor, J. A., 1953. "A Personality Scale of Manifest Anxiety," *Journal of Abnormal Social Psychology,* 48, 285–290.

Taylor, K., von F., 1942. "Reliability and Permanence of Vocational Interests of Adolescents," *Journal of Experimental Education,* 11, 81–87.

Terman, L. M., 1916. *The Measurement of Intelligence.* Boston: Houghton Mifflin.

———, 1954. *Scientists and Nonscientists in a Group of 800 Gifted Men,* Psychological Monographs, 68, No. 7, whole No. 378.

———, et al., 1925. *Mental and Physical Traits of a Thousand Gifted Children, Genetic Studies of Genius,* Vol. I. Stanford, Calif.: Stanford University Press.

———, and M. Oden, 1940. "Status of the California Gifted Group at the End of Sixteen Years," National Society for the Study of Education. *Intelligence: Its Nature and Nurture.* Thirty-ninth Yearbook, Part I, pp. 67–89. Bloomington, Ill.: Public School Publishing Company.

———, 1952. "The Development and Adult Status of Gifted Children," pp. 199–210, in *Psychological Studies of Human Development,* R. G. Kuhlen and G. G. Thompson (eds.). New York: Appleton-Century-Crofts.

———, 1959. *The Gifted Group at Mid-Life: Thirty-five Years' Follow-up of the Superior Child. Genetic Studies of Genius,* Vol. 5. Stanford, Calif.: Stanford University Press.

———, et al., 1947. *The Gifted Child Grows Up: Twenty-five Years' Follow-up of a Superior Group. Genetic Studies of Genius,* Vol. 4. Stanford, Calif.: Stanford University Press.

Thompson, G. G., 1949. "Age Trends in Social Values During Adolescent Years," *American Psychologist,* 4, 250.

Thorndike, R. L., 1947. "The Prediction of Intelligence at College Entrance from Earlier Test," *Journal of Educational Psychology,* 38, 129–148.

———, 1948. "Growth of Intelligence During Adolescence," *Journal of Genetic Psychology,* 72, 11–15.

———, and E. Hagen, 1961. *Measurement and Evaluation in Psychology and Education,* 2nd edition. New York: Wiley.

Tiedeman, D. V., 1961. "Decision and Vocational Development: A Paradigm and Its Implications," *Personnel and Guidance Journal,* 40, 15–21.

———, and R. P. O'Hara, 1962. *Differentiation and Integration in Career*

Development. Harvard Studies in Career Development No. 23. Graduate School of Education, Harvard University. (Mimeographed.)

———, and E. Matthews, 1958. *Position Choices and Careers: Elements of a Theory*. Harvard Studies in Career Development No. 8. Graduate School of Education, Harvard University. (Mimeographed.)

Tillich, P., 1952. *The Courage To Be*. New Haven, Conn.: Yale University Press.

Todd, T. W., 1930. *The Adolescent Lag,* Physical and Mental Adolescent Growth. Proceedings of Conference on Adolescence. Cleveland, Ohio: Brush Foundation, Western Reserve University.

———, 1937. *Atlas of Skeletal Maturation* (Hand). St. Louis: C. V. Mosby, Co.

Torrance, E. P., 1959a. "Highly Intelligent and Highly Creative Children in a Laboratory School" (Explorations in Creative Thinking in the Early School Years, No. 6), *Research Memo* BER–59–7. Minneapolis: Bureau of Educational Research, University of Minnesota.

———, 1959b. "Personality Studies of Highly Creative Children" (Explorations in Creative Thinking in the Early School Years, No. 9), *Research Memo* BER–59–12. Minneapolis: Bureau of Educational Research, University of Minnesota.

———, 1962. *Guiding Creative Talent*. Englewood Cliffs, N.J.: Prentice-Hall.

Trent, R., 1953. "The Correlates of Self-acceptance Among Negro Children," unpublished Doctor of Education dissertation, Teachers College, Columbia University.

Tryon, C. M., 1939. *Evaluation of Adolescent Personality by Adolescents*. Monographs of the Society for Research in Child Development, **4,** No. 4.

———, 1944. "The Adolescent Peer Culture," *43rd Yearbook of the National Society for the Study of Education,* Part I, pp. 217–239. University of Chicago Press.

Tyler, L. E., 1951. "The Relationship of Interests to Abilities and Reputation Among First-Grade Children," *Educational and Psychological Measurement,* **11,** 255–264.

———, 1955. "The Development of 'Vocational Interests': I. The Organization of Likes and Dislikes in Ten-Year-Old Children," *Journal of Genetic Psychology,* **86,** 33–44.

———, 1959. "Toward a Workable Psychology of Individuality," *American Psychologist,* **14,** 75–81.

Ullman, C. A., 1952. *Identification of Maladjusted School Children: A Comparison of Three Methods of Screening*. Public Health Monographs, No. 7. Washington, D.C.: Government Printing Office.

United States Bureau of Labor Statistics, 1962. Reviewed under the title "The Grim Prospects for Dropouts" in *New York Herald Tribune,* September 9, 1962.

United States Department of Commerce, Bureau of the Census, Statistical Abstracts of the United States, 1957. Washington, D.C.: the Bureau.

Utton, A. C., 1962. "Recalled Parent-Child Relations as Determinants of Vocational Choice," *Journal of Counseling Psychology*, 9, 49–53.

Waller, W., 1951. *The Family: A Dynamic Interpretation*. Revised by Reuben Hill. New York: Dryden Press.

Wallin, P., 1950. "Cultural Contradictions and Sex Roles: A Repeat Study," *American Sociological Review*, 15, 288–293.

Watson, G. B., 1929. "An Approach to the Study of Worship," *Religious Education*, 24, 849–858.

———, 1957. "Some Personality Differences in Children Related to Strict or Permissive Parental Discipline," *Journal of Psychology*, 44, 227–249.

Wattenberg, W. W., 1947. "Boy Repeaters." Mimeographed report privately distributed by the College of Education, Wayne State University.

———, 1955. *The Adolescent Years*. New York: Harcourt, Brace.

Webb, W. B., 1949. "Occupational Indecision Among College Students," *Occupations*, XVII, 331–332.

Weber, C. A., 1953. "Some Characteristics of College Teachers," *Journal of Educational Research*, 46, 685–692.

Wenkart, A., 1949. *Healthy and Neurotic Love*. New York: The Auxiliary Council to the Association for the Advancement of Psychoanalysis.

Wertheimer, R. R., 1957. "Consistency of Sociometric Status Position in Male and Female High School Students," *Journal of Educational Psychology*, 48, 385–390.

White House Conference on Child Health and Protection, Committee on the Family and Parent Education, 1934. *The Adolescent in the Family. A Study of Personality Development in the Home Environment*. Section III, Education and Training. New York: D. Appleton-Century.

Whyte, W. F., 1943. "A Slum Sex Code," *American Journal of Sociology*, 49, 24–31.

Williams, C. D., 1950. "College Students' Family Problems," *Journal of Home Economics*, 42, 179–181.

Wilson, W. C., 1960. "Extrinsic Religious Values and Prejudice," *Journal of Abnormal and Social Psychology*, 60, 286–288.

Winkler, J. B., 1949. "Age Trends and Sex Differences in the Wishes, Identifications, Activities, and Fears of Children," *Child Development*, 20, 191–200.

Wise, W. M., 1958. *They Come for the Best of Reasons: College Students Today*. Washington, D.C.: American Council on Education.

Wittenberg, R. M., and J. Berg, 1952. "The Stranger in the Group," *American Journal of Orthopsychiatry*, 22, 89–97.

Witty, P. A., 1930. "A Study of One Hundred Gifted Children," *University of Kansas Bulletin of Education*, Vol. II, No. 7. Lawrence, Kansas: Bureau of School Service and Research, University of Kansas.

———, 1947. "Reading Problems in the Secondary School," *School and Society*, 65, 113–116.

——— (ed.), 1951. *The Gifted Child*. Boston: Heath.

Wolf, A., and E. K. Schwartz, 1955. "The Psychoanalysis of Groups: Implications for Education," reprinted from *The International Journal of Social Psychiatry*, autumn, 1955.

Wylie, R. C., 1961. *The Self Concept*. Lincoln: University of Nebraska Press.

Young, P. T., 1937. "Laughing and Weeping, Cheerfulness and Depression: A Study of Moods Among College Students," *Journal of Social Psychology*, **8**, 311–384.

Zazzo, B., 1960. "L'Image de Soi Comparée à L'Image de ses Sembables Chez L'Adolescent" (The Self-concept Compared with the Conception of Peers Among Adolescents), *Enfance*, No. 2, 121–141.

Zeligs, R., 1938. "Tracing Racial Attitudes Through Adolescence," *Sociology and Social Research*, **23**, 45–54.

——, 1948. "Children's Intergroup Attitudes," *Journal of Genetic Psychology*, **72**, 101–110.

——, and G. Hendrickson, 1933. "Racial Attitudes of Two Hundred Sixth-Grade Children," *Sociology and Social Research*, **18**, 26–36.

——, 1934. "Checking the Social Distance Technique Through the Personal Interview," *Sociology and Social Research*, **18**, 420–430.

Zucker, H. J., 1943a. "Affectional Identification and Delinquency," *Archives of Psychology*, No. 286. New York: Archives of Psychology.

——, 1943b. "The Emotional Attachment of Children to Their Parents as Related to Standards of Behavior and Delinquency," *Journal of Psychology*, **15**, 31–40.

Indexes

Author
Indexes

Author Index*

Abernethy, E. M., 74, 101
Abraham, W., 135
Abt, L. E., 157
Adelson, J., *see* Douvan E.
Adler, A., 107
Adorno, T. W., 19, 303, 305
Allen, E. A., 328
Allport, F. H., *see* Katz, D.
Allport, F. H., *see* Morse, N. C.
Allport, G. W., 301, 304, 374, 375, 379,
    382, 383, 388, 403
Almy, M., 119–120
Alschuler, R. H., 157
Amatora, M., 412
Ames, L. B., 157
Ammons, R. B., 301, 305
Anastasi, A., 190, 191, 204, 243
Anderson, G. L., *see* Anderson, H. H.
Anderson, H. D., *see* Davidson, P. E.
Anderson, H. H., 19, 157, 388
Anderson, J. E., 128, 396

Anderson, L., *see* Gronlund, N. E.
Angelino, H., 204
Antrobus, J. S., 164
Arnold, M., *see* Kuhlen, R. G.
Aserinsky, E., 163
Aub, J. C., *see* Nathanson, I. T.
Ausubel, D. P., 56, 242
Axelrad, S., *see* Ginzberg, E.

Bachrach, P. B., *see* Super, D. E.
Baker, H. V., 116–117
Baldwin, A. L., 19
Balthazar, E. E., *see* Ausubel, D. P.
Bantel, E., 345
Barker, M. E., 348
Bartlett, F., 141
Bath, J. A., 230
Battin, T. C., 268
Bayley, N., 49, 50, 52, 59, 60, 128, 129,
    131
Bayley, N., *see also* Jones, M. C.

* The numbers refer to pages in the main text. The full references to authors
and their co-authors are listed on pages 411–446.

[449

Bayley, N., *see also* Rheingold, H. L.
Beach, F. A., *see* Ford, C. S.
Beck, S. J., 157
Beebe, G. W., *see* Schonfield, W. A.
Beekman, E., 374
Beekman, E., *see also* Pixley, E.
Beier, E. G., 242
Beilin, H., 352, 364
Beiling, G., *see* Cavan, R. S.
Bellak, L., *see* Abt, L. E.
Bender, L., 114
Bennett, E. M., *see* Remmers, H. H.
Berdie, R. F., 361
Berezin, D., 58
Berg, I. A., 361
Berg, J., *see* Wittenberg, R. M.
Berger, E. M., 30
Bienstock, S. F., *see* Jersild, A. T.
Bilhuber, G., 77
Bills, R. E., 30
Binger, C., 275–276
Birch, H. B., *see* Chess, S.
Birns, B., 58
Bjerre, P., 163, 169
Blackman, L. S., *see* Ausubel, D. P.
Blatz, W. E., 58
Blau, P. M., 357
Block, V. L., 190, 243, 244
Blum, L. H., 157
Boas, F., 74
Boll, E. S., *see* Bossard, J. H. S.
Bolles, M. M., *see* Landis, C.
Bonar, H. S., 203
Bond, A., 20
Bond, H. M., 134
Bonney, M. E., 258, 260, 262
Bonsall, M. R., 135
Boodish, H. A., 347
Bordin, E. S., 361
Borham, W. A., *see* Flanagan, J. C.
Bossard, J. H. S., 381
Bousfield, W. A., 331
Bower, P. A., 102
Boyd, W. C., 56
Bradley, N. C., 115
Bradway, K. P., 128
Brandt, R. M., 38
Breese, F. H., *see* Baldwin, A. L.
Breese, F. H. *see* Havighurst, R. J.
Bretsch, H. S., 258
Bretsch, H. S., *see also* Kuhlen, R. G.
Briggs, V., 20

Britten, F. H., *see* Bromley, D. D.
Brodkin, A., *see* Jersild, A. T.
Bromley, D. D., 91
Bronner, A. F., *see* Healy, W.
Bruch, H., 55
Bruder, E. E., 384
Bryant, L. W., 347
Buhler, C., 58, 279
Bunch, M. E., *see* Engle, T. L.
Burchinal, L. G., 13, 94, 273, 274, 278, 284–285
Burks, B. S., 143
Busemann, A., 13
Byrns, R., 365

Cannon, K. L., 258, 260
Carlson, T. E., 370
Carp, F. M., 365
Carter, H. D., 360, 361, 366
Casler, L., 183
Cavan, R. S., 284, 286
Centers, R., 364
Chaffey, J., *see* Stolz, H. R.
Chancellor, L., *see* Burchinal, L. G.
Chein, I., *see* Harding, J.
Chess, S., 58
Christensen, H. T., 272, 273, 276
Christensen, P. R., *see* Guilford, J. P.
Clay, H. M., 133
Coffield, K. E., 347
Cogan, M., 345
Cohen, E. E., 368
Cohen, N., *see* Anastasi, A.
Cole, L., 403
Coleman, J. S., 326–328
Collignon, M., 37
Congdon, R. G., *see* Jervis, F. M.
Conn, J. H., 89
Connolly, P. C., 54
Connor, R., 243, 244
Conrad, H. S., *see* Jones, H. E.
Cooper, R., *see* Peck, R. F.
Corsini, R. J., 131
Counts, G. S., 366
Cowell, C. C., 107
Cowen, E. L., 304
Cox, C. M., 143
Crampton, C. W., 78–79
Crespi, L. P., 93
Crist, J. R., 272, 273
Criswell, J. H., 302–303
Crites, J. O., *see* Super, D. E.

Cruickshank, W. M., 143
Cureton, T. K., 104
Curry, E. T., 84

Dailey, J. T., 418
Dailey, J. T., see also Flanagan, J. C.
Dann, S., see Freud, A.
Darley, J. G., 361, 364, 371
Davenport, C. B., 59
Davidson, H. H., see Blum, L. H.
Davidson, P. E., 368
Davie, J. S., see Ryan, F. R.
Davis, A., 418
Davis, K., 284
Dawson, G. E., 379
Deeg, M. E., 366
de Laszio, V., 384
del Solar, C., see Jersild, A. T.
Dement, W., 163, 164, 170
Dement, W. C., see also Roffwarg, H. P.
Demos, G. D., 328
Dennis, W., 183
Deutsch, H., 403
Dillon, H. J., 333–334
Dillon, M. S., 89
Dimock, H. S., 78–79, 87, 107, 381
Dodge, A. F., 331
Dolger, L., 293
Doll, R. C., 331
Dollins, J., see Angelino, H.
Dorfman, R. I., 73
Dorr, M., see Havighurst, R. J.
Douvan, E., 297–298, 299
Dresden, K. W., 365
Dressel, P. L., see Morse, H. T.
Drews, E. M., 135
Dubin, W., see Super, D. E.
Dudycha, G. J., 148, 374, 379, 382
Dudycha, M. M., see Dudycha, G. J.
Dunlap, J. M., 135
Dymond, R. F., see Rogers, C. R.

Ebert, E., 128
Eckstrom, R. B., 143
Edwards, M., see Gough, H. G.
Eels, K. W., 292
Ehrmann, W., 91, 92, 274
Eichorn, D. H., 59, 61
Ekstrom, G. F., 334
Elder, R. A., 20
Elias, L. J., 224, 225
Ellis, A., 93, 277–278

Engel, M., 37
Engle, T. L., 347
Engle, T. L., see also Coffield, K. E.
Ephron, B. K., 335
Espenschade, A., 98, 99–100
Evans, H. M., 347, 348

Fassett, K. K., see Corsini, R. J.
Fauquier, W., 107, 263
Feinberg, M. R., 258, 259, 261
Feld, S., see Gurin, G. J.
Fey, W. C., 30
Fieldsteel, N. D., see Blum, L. H.
Finger, F. N., 91
Fisher, B., 334
Fisher, C., see Roffwarg, H. P.
Flanagan, J. C., 371
Fleege, U. H., 224
Flory, C. D., 52, 101
Flory, C. D., see also Freeman, F. A.
Ford, C. S., 75
Form, W. H., see Miller, D. C.
Foshay, A. W., 258, 262
Frank, L. K., 17, 157, 222, 225, 341
Franzblau, A. N., 380
Freeman, F. N., 120–121
French, W., see Passow, A. H.
Frenkel-Brunswick, E., 305
Frenkel-Brunswick, E., see also Adorno,
    T. W.
Freud, A., 25, 184, 242
Freud, S., 25, 166, 171, 211, 219
Friedman, K. C., 115, 116
Friedmann, E. A., 364
Friend, J. G., 363
Fromm, E., 163, 384, 389
Frosch, J., see Bender, L.
Fryer, D., 359
Fuller, J. L., 124

Gallup, G., 268, 269–270, 327–328, 375
Garfinkle, S. H., 358
Garn, S. M., 54
Gates, G. S., 190, 192
Gesell, A., 58
Getzels, J. W., 141–142
Gibbs, P. K., see Maccoby, E. E.
Gilbert, H. H., 135, 330
Gilbert, J. C., 132
Gilchrist, J., see Fauquier, W.
Gillespie, J. M., see Allport, G. W.
Gilliland, A. R., 374

Ginandes, J., *see* Dolger, L.
Gingles, R., *see* Moss, J.
Ginsburg, S. W., *see* Ginzberg, E.
Ginzberg, E., 353, 356, 364
Gips, C., 61
Glick, P. C., 283–284
Glueck, E., *see* Glueck, S.
Glueck, S., 309, 314, 319–321
Goldberg, I., *see* Flanagan, J. C.
Goldberg, M., 135, 137, 139, 143
Goldberg, M., *see also* Passow, A. H.
Goldblatt, I., *see* Hess, R. D.
Goldfarb, W., 185
Goldstein, K., 185
Goodenough, D., 164
Goodenough, F. L., 128, 292
Goodrich, W., *see* Kaplan, D. M.
Gotkin, L. G., *see* Goldberg, M.
Gottesman, I. I., 60
Gough, H. G., 305
Gough, H. G., *see also* Harris, D. B.
Gowan, J. C., 138
Grace, G. L., 388
Grace, H. A., *see* Grace, G. L.
Gragg, W. L., 333
Grant, V. W., 279
Gregory, L. W., *see* Heath, C. W.
Greulich, W. W., 53, 71, 72
Greulich, W. W., *see also* Dorfman, R. I.
Greulich, W. W., *see also* Simmons, K.
Grigg, A. E., 362
Grigg, A. E., *see also* Switzer, D. K.
Gronlund, N. E., 258, 261, 263
Grunes, W. F., 366
Guilford, J. P., 139, 140–141, 142
Gurin, G. J., 225, 226
Gustad, J. W., *see* Blau, P. M.
Gutheil, E. A., 163

Habbe, S., 64
Hadfield, J. A., 163, 169, 171
Hagen, D., 362
Hagen, E., *see* Thorndike, R. L.
Hagenah, T., *see* Darley, J. G.
Haggard, E. A., *see* Friend, J. G.
Hall, C., 163, 165–166, 168
Halverson, H. M., 89,
Hamilton, G. V., 276, 279
Hanson, R. C., *see* Sorokin, P. A.
Harding, J., 301, 306
Harlow, H. F., 182–183
Harris, C. W., 347

Harris, D. B., 13
Harris, D. B., *see also* Anderson, J. E.
Harris, D. B., *see also* Gough, H. G.
Harrison, R., *see* Frank, L. K.
Harrower, M. R., 293
Hart, F. W., 331
Hartley, E. L., 303
Hattwick, L. A., *see* Alschuler, R. H.
Havighurst, R. J., 224, 234, 292, 354
Havighurst, R. J., *see also* Davis, A.
Havighurst, R. J., *see also* Friedmann, E. A.
Havighurst, R. J., *see also* Peck, R. F.
Hayes, M., *see* Hicks, J. A.
Healy, W., 188, 309
Heath, C. W., 225, 245
Hecker, S. E., 334
Helfant, K., 347
Helfant, K., *see also* Jersild, A. T.
Hellersberg, E., *see* Frank, L. K.
Helper, M. M., 242
Hendrickson, G., *see* Zeligs, R.
Herma, J. L., *see* Ginzberg, E.
Hertzman, J., 224
Hess, R. D., 37, 39
Hetzer, H., 13
Heyde, M. B., *see* Super, D. E.
Hicks, J. A., 190, 191
Hill, D. S., 234
Hill, E., *see* Gallup, G.
Hill, M. C., 294
Hirsch, S. G., 301
Hoch, P., 211
Holden, G. S., 366
Holden, M., *see* Goodenough, D.
Holland, J. L., 353
Hollingshead, A., 289–290, 291–292, 363, 368, 383
Hollingworth, L. S., 7, 76, 77, 135, 136, 143, 402
Hollingworth, L. S., *see also* Pritchard, M. C.
Holmes, F. B., *see* Jersild, A. T.
Holmlund, W. S., *see* Gronlund, N. E.
Honzik, M. P., 124, 128
Horan, K. M., *see* Pritchard, M. C.
Horney, K., 149, 211, 219–222, 282
Horrocks, J. E., 261
Horton, R. E., *see* Remmers, H. H.
Hummel, R. C., *see* Super, D. E.

Ichheiser, G., 304

Inhelder, B., 117
Isaacs, S., 89

Jackson, P. W., *see* Getzels, J. W.
Jacob, P. E., 337–338, 339
James, W., 8
Jameson, S. H., 95, 275
Jennings, H. H., 256, 258, 259
Jensen, A. R., *see* Symonds, P. M.
Jensen, D. W., *see* Burks, B. S.
Jenson, P. G., 364
Jersild, A. T., 33, 66, 67, 113, 114, 165, 177, 187, 191, 195, 203, 217, 329, 332, 347
Jersild, C. L., *see* Jersild, A. T.
Jervis, F. M., 30, 341, 344, 401
Jessor, R., *see* Blau, P. M.
Johannis, Jr., T. B., *see* Connor, R.
Johnson, A. H., 327, 328
Johnson, G. O., *see* Cruickshank, W. M.
Jones, A. W., *see* Pressey, S. L.
Jones, H. E., 75, 85, 97, 103, 105–106, 129, 130, 131, 133, 257, 258, 259, 379
Jones, M. C., 13, 86, 87
Jones, M. C., *see also* Bayley, N.
Jones, M. C., *see also* Mussen, P. H.
Jones, M. C., *see also* Stolz, H. R.
Jones, V., 388
Jordaan, J. P., *see* Super, D. E.
Jourard, S. M., 242
Jourard, S. M., *see also* Secord, P.
Jung, C. G., 163, 389

Kahl, J. A., 137
Kalhorn, J., *see* Baldwin, A. L.
Kallman, F. J., 56, 60
Kaplan, D. M., 192
Katz, D., 380
Katz, R. L., 384
Kay, H., 133
Kelley, D. McG., *see* Klopfer, B.
Kierkegaard, S., 142, 211, 213–214, 219, 266, 299
Kimball, B., 138
Kimmins, C. W., 114
Kinsey, A. C., 15, 80, 89, 90, 91, 92, 93, 94, 96, 293, 296
Kirchner, W. K., *see* Jenson, P. G.
Kleitman, N., *see* Aserinsky, E.
Kleitman, N., *see* Dement, W.
Klineberg, O., 124, 294

Klopfer, B., 157
Koch, H. L., 89, 303
Komarovsky, M., 35, 36
Kramer, B. M., *see* Allport, G. W.
Kroger, R., 365
Krogman, W. W., 60
Krugman, M., 157
Kubie, L. S., 144, 347, 385
Kuhlen, R. G., 258, 259, 374, 380
Kuhlen, R. G., *see also* Pressey, S. L.
Kutner, B., *see* Harding, J.
Kvaraceus, W. C., 308, 309, 315, 316, 317–318, 319, 321

Lafore, G. G., 241
La Mare, N., 82
Landau, E., *see* Glick, P. C.
Landes, J., *see* Cowen, E. L.
Landis, A. T., *see* Landis, C.
Landis, C. A., 19, 40, 76, 95, 277
Landis, P. H., 431
Langner, T. S., *see* Srole, L.
Lantagne, J. E., 95, 275
Latham, A. J., 86, 258
Laughlin, F., 188, 258, 260
Lawrence, E. M., 124
Lazar, E., *see* Jersild, A. T.
Learned, J., *see* Ames, L. B.
Lecky, P., 396
Ledvina, L. M., 368
Lee, B. J., *see* Kuhlen, R. G.
Lehman, H. C., 365, 400
Levin, H., *see* Sears, R. R.
Levinson, D. J., *see* Adorno, T. W.
Levitt, E. E., 347
Levitt, E. E., *see also* Ojemann, R. H.
Levy, D. M., 89
Levy, J., 234
Lewis, D. J., *see* Guilford, J. P.
Lewis, E. C., *see* Bath, J. A.
Liba, M. R., *see* Harris, C. W.
Libby, W., 154
Likert, R., *see* Murphy, G.
Lilienthal, J., *see* Peck, R. F.
Lippit, R., *see* Polansky, N.
Lloyd, R. C., 235, 243
Lockhard, E. G., 388
Lockwood, W. V., 365
Lorge, I., 125–126, 132
Louttit, C. M., *see* Kroger, R.
Lowrie, W., 213
Lund, F. H., 101

Lunger, R., 204
Lylie, W. H., *see* Ojemann, R. H.
Lyman, E. L., 364
Lynn, D. B., 35
Lysgaard, S., *see* Remmers, H. H.
Lysgaard, S., *see* Schneider, L.

Maccoby, E. E., 291
Maccoby, E. E., *see also* Sears, R. R.
Machover, K., 157
Machover, K., *see also* Frank, L. K.
MacIver, R. M., 93
Macmurray, J., 282, 384
Manis, M., 242
Markey, F. V., *see* Jersild, A. T.
Markley, E. R., 291
Marsh, C. J., 204
Mark Twain, 238
Martin, C. E., *see* Kinsey, A. C.
Martin, W. E., *see* Gough, H. G.
Martin, W. E., *see* Harris, D. B.
Maslow, A. H., 283
Mather, W. G., 276
Matlin, N., *see* Super, D. E.
Maurer, M. M., *see* Goodenough, F. L.
May, R., 211, 217–218, 242
McCann, W. H., 236
McFarlane, M., 98
McKee, J. P., 35
McLean, O. S., *see* Bills, R. E.
Mech, E., *see* Angelino, H.
Meek, L. H., 433
Meigs, M. F., *see* Jersild, A. T.
Meltzer, H., 190
Merrifield, P. R., *see* Guilford, J. P.
Merrill, M. A., 309
Metraux, R. W., *see* Ames, L. B.
Michael, S. T., *see* Srole, L.
Mill, S. R., 262
Miller, D. C., 368
Miller, J. S., *see* Radke-Yarrow, M.
Miller, J. S., *see* Switzer, D. K.
Miller, W., 294, 295, 298, 312–313, 315, 318–319
Miller, W. B., *see* Kvaraceus, W. C.
Millichamp, D. A., *see* Blatz, W. E.
Mills, C. A., 75
Mitchell, C., 433
Moll, A., 279
Monroe, R., *see* Levy, J.
Montagu, A., 56, 75
Moore, D., *see* Peck, R. F.

Moore, J. E., 331
Moreno, J. L., 157, 256
Morris, C. N., *see* Super, D. E.
Morse, H. T., 347
Morse, N. C., 301
Moser, H. P., *see* Super, D. E.
Moser, W. E., 365
Moss, J., 285
Mowrer, O. H., 218
Murphy, F. J., 308
Murphy, G., 144, 303, 389
Murray, H. A., 157
Mussen, P. H., 87
Mussen, P. H., *see also* Jones, M. C.
Myers, M. S., 374
Myers, M. S., *see also* Remmers, H. H.
Myers, W. E., 365

Nachmann, B., 362
Nathanson, I. T., 71
Neel, J. V., 134
Nelson, E., 374, 375
Neugarten, B. L., 258
Newton, N., 76
Nicholas, P. O., 294, 351–372, 401 (*see also* Overstreet, P. L.)
Noble, J. L., 306
Northway, M. L., 258, 262
Norton, J. L., 361

Oakden, E. C., 115
Oden, M. H., *see* Bayley, N.
Oden, M., *see* Terman, L. M.
Ogle, C., *see* Mills, C. A.
O'Hara, R. P., 356
O'Hara, R. P., *see also* Tiedeman, D. V.
Ojemann, R. H., 347
Ojemann, R. H., *see also* Levitt, E. E.
Olds, E. B., 268
Opler, M. K., *see* Srole, L.
Orgel, S. Z., 64
Orr, D. B., *see* Flanagan, J. C.
Orton, J., 345
Overstreet, B. W., 377, 384
Overstreet, P. L., *see* Super, D. E.
Owens, Jr., W. A., 129, 131, 400

Pace, R. C., 339, 340, 341, 381
Page, J. D., *see* Lunger, R.
Parnes, H. S., *see* Blau, P. M.
Parsons, T., 359
Passow, A. H., 143

Passow, A. H., *see also* Goldberg, M.
Paterson, D. G., *see* Deeg, M. E.
Patti, J. B., 347, 348
Peck, R. F., 388, 389–390, 394
Penty, R. C., 334–335
Phillips, E. L., 30
Piaget, J., 117, 387–388
Piaget, J., *see also* Inhelder, B.
Pixley, E., 374
Polansky, N., 258
Pomeroy, W. B., *see* Kinsey, A. C.
Pope, C., 224
Porter, J. R., 366
Porter, R. M., 340
Potashin, R., 258
Powell, M. G., 224
Pressey, S. L., 13, 18
Preston, R. C., 114
Pritchard, M. C., 125
Proshansky, H., *see* Harding, J.
Pullias, E. V., 91
Punke, H. H., 273

Radke-Yarrow, M., 302
Radler, D. H., *see* Remmers, H. H.
Ramsey, G. V., 80, 89–90
Raph (Beasley), J., 137, 138
Ratzeburg, F., *see* Beier, E. G.
Redl, F., *see* Polansky, N.
Reevy, W. R., 90, 274
Reik, T., 282
Remmers, H. H., 267, 293, 326–327, 374
Remy, R. M., *see* Jourard, S. M.
Rennie, T. A. C., *see* Srole, L.
Reynolds, E. L., 52–54, 73, 78
Reynolds, L. G., 368
Reynolds, N. B., 341–342
Rheingold, H. L., 183
Richardson, R. F., 193
Richey, H. G., 47
Roberts, D. E., 376–377, 384
Robinson, M. Z., *see* Havighurst, R. J.
Roe, A., 353, 361, 362
Roff, C., 37
Roffwarg, H. P., 164
Rogers, C. R., 30, 149, 224
Rogoff, N., 364
Rorschach, H., 157, 222
Rose, A. A., 236
Rosenthal, I., *see* Ausubel, D. P.
Ross, M. G., 374, 382–383

Rostker, L. E., 331
Rothney, J .W. M., 367
Rothney, J. W. M., *see also* Schmidt, J. L.
Ruff, W. K., 64, 345
Ryan, F. R., 258
Ryans, D. G., 331

Sanders, B. S., 105
Sanford, N., 38, 39, 338–339, 359, 401
Sanford, R. N., 154
Sanford, R. N., *see also* Adorno, T. W.
Sargent, S. S., 290
Sartre, J. P., 10
Saul, L. J., 403
Schaet, D. E., *see* Cowen, E. L.
Scheerer, M., *see* Goldstein, K.
Schilder, P., 62
Schmidt, J. L., 367
Schmidt, R., *see* Feinberg, M. R.
Schneider, L., 293
Schonbar, R. A., 163
Schonfeld, W. A., 81–82, 86–87, 88
Schpoont, S. H., *see* Ausubel, D. P.
Schulz, L. R., *see* Briggs, V.
Schwartz, E. K., *see* Wolf, A.
Scott, L. F., 268
Sears, R. R., 291
Secord, P., 64
Segal, S. J., 362
Shaffer, L. F., 115, 155–156
Shapiro, A., *see* Goodenough, D.
Shaycroft, M. F., *see* Dailey, J. T.
Shaycroft, M. F., *see* Flanagan, J. C.
Sheerer, E. T., 33
Sherman, A. W., 235
Sherman, M., *see* Symonds, P. M.
Sherriffs, A. C., *see* McKee, J. P.
Shirley, M. M., 58
Shirley, M. M., *see also* Murphy, F. J.
Shister, J., *see* Reynolds, L. G.
Shoben, E. J., Jr., *see* Shaffer, L. F.
Shoobs, N., 258
Shuey, A. M., 400
Shumsky, A., 388
Shuttleworth, F. K., 47, 48, 71, 74, 343
Silverman, H. L., 384
Silverman, S. S., 68
Simmons, K., 74
Simmons, K., *see also* Ebert, E.
Simpson, G. E., 301

Singer, S. L., 364
Skeels, H. M., 123, 124, 125
Skeels, H. M., *see also* Skodak, M.
Skodak, M., 122–124
Slater, E., 60
Slocum, W. L., 340
Small, L., 362
Smith, C. B., 334
Smith, G. F., 94, 273, 274
Smith, J. W., *see* Staples, R.
Smith, M., *see* Feinberg, M. R.
Smith, R. B., 112, 136
Smith, W. M., 13, 273
Sollenberger, R. T., 73
Solomon, C. I., *see* Dorfman, R. I.
Sorokin, P. A., 182
Spatz, D., *see* Anastasi, A.
Spitz, R. A., 183
Spivack, S., 30, 33, 37, 112, 224
Spranger, O., 347
Srole, L., 225, 226
Stanley, A. E., *see* Crespi, L. P.
Staples, R., 20
Starishevsky, R., *see* Super, D. E.
Steiner, M., *see* Frank, L. K.
Steinschriber, L., *see* Goodenough, D.
Stellfre, B., *see* Bonsall, M. R.
Stellfre, B., *see* Singer, S. L.
Stendler, C. B., 288
Stephenson, R M., 365
Stephenson, R. R., 367
Stephenson, W., 30
Stewart, N., 359
Stolz, H. R., 45, 46, 49, 53, 65, 81, 87
Stolz, L. M., *see* Stolz, H. R.
Stott, L. H., 190, 191, 243, 244–245
Strang, R., 135
Stratton, G. M., 192
Strong, E. K., Jr., 360
Sturt, M., *see* Oakden, E. C.
Sullivan, H. S., 211, 214–217, 219
Super, D. E., 352, 353, 354–355, 360, 361, 366, 371
Switzer, D. K., 362
Symonds, P. M., 154, 157, 158–162, 195, 224, 328

Taba, H., 388, 389
Taba, H., *see also* Havighurst, R. J.
Tannenbaum, A. J., 103–104
Tannenbaum, A. J., *see also* Goldberg, M.

Tannenbaum, A. J., *see also* Passow, A. H.
Tannenbaum, A., *see also* Raph (Beasley), J.
Tanner, J. M., 12, 59, 75
Tasch, R. J., *see* Jersild, A. T.
Taschuk, W. A., 38
Taylor, J. A., 222, 398
Taylor, K. von F., 360
Terman, L. M., 135, 136, 143, 292, 361, 363
Terman, L. M., *see also* Burks, B. S.
Thomas, A., *see* Chess, S.
Thompson, G. G., 388
Thompson, W. R., *see* Fuller, J. L.
Thorndike, R. L., 122, 127, 128, 135
Tiedeman, D. V., 355, 356
Tiedeman, D. V., *see also* O'Hara, R. P.
Tillich, P., 266, 389
Todd, T. W., 52
Torrance, E. P., 141, 142
Towne, L., *see* Nathanson, I. T.
Trent, R., 305–306
Tryon, C. M., 16, 249, 259–260
Tuckman, J., *see* Orgel, S. Z.
Tyler, L. E., 316

Ullman, C. A., 194, 224
United States Bureau of Census, 284
United States Bureau of Labor Statistics, 333
Updegraff, R., *see* Skeels, H. M.
Utton, A. C., 362

Vance, E. L., *see* Bills, R. E.
Vernon, P. E., *see* Allport, G. W.
Veroff, J., *see* Gurin, G. J.

Walker, R. N., *see* Ames, L. B.
Waller, W., 284
Wallin, P., 35, 36
Walters, J., *see* Connor, R.
Warnath, C. F., *see* Super, D. E.
Watson, G. B., 19, 382
Wattenberg, W. W., 53, 309
Wayland, S., 296
Wear, B. A., *see* Horrocks, J. E.
Webb, W. B., 335
Weber, C. A., 331
Welkowitz, J., *see* Ausubel, D. P.
Wellman, B. L., *see* Skeels, H. M.
Wenkart, A., 184, 281

Wertheimer, R. R., 260
White House Conference on Child Health and Protection, 248
Whiteside, M. F., see Ojemann, R. H.
Whyte, W. F., 94
Wigdor, B. T., see Northway, M. L.
Wilcock, R. C., see Blau, P. M.
Williams, C. D., 191
Williams, C. P., see Carlson, T. E.
Williams, H. M., see Skeels, H. M.
Wilson, R. C., see Guilford, J. P.
Wilson, W. C., 304
Wines, J. V., see Reynolds, E. L.
Winkler, J. B., 203
Wise, W. M., 336, 341
Witmer, H. L., see Murphy, F. J.

Wittenberg, R. M., 262
Witty, P. A., 143, 334
Witty, P. A., see also Lehman, H. C.
Wolf, A., 347
Wolpert, E. A., see Dement, W.
Woodyard, E. S., see Jersild, A. T.
Wylie, R. C., 33, 146, 242

Yinger, J. M., see Simpson, G. E.
Young, J., see Allport, G. W.
Young, P. T., 192
Young, R. K., see Switzer, D. K.

Zazzo, B., 37
Zeligs, R., 301
Zubin, J., see Hoch, P.
Zucker, H. J., 296

Subject Index

Abstract thinking, as related to religious beliefs, 379

Abstractions, ability to deal with, 114–115

Abused, feelings of being, 198–199

Academic achievement, as related to I.Q., 131

Academic studies, low popularity of, 326

Acceptance, by peers, 256 *ff.;* as related to compassion, 406

Accidents, automobile, frequency of, 270

"Actual self," 23, 30 *ff.;* discrepancy between, and "ideal self," 31, 33

Adipose tissues, 52 *ff.*

Adjustment, as related to social acceptance, 261–262; and vocational choice, 363

Adolescence, glamorized versions of, 18–19; as seen in retrospect, 17–18; scope of, 5

Adolescent-parent relationships, 229–250

Adolescents, as viewed by themselves and by adults, 39–40

Adopted children, intelligence of, 122 *ff.*

Adult attitudes toward adolescents, 3

Adult judgments regarding adolescents' acceptance and rejection of one another, 262–263

Affection, 181 *ff.;* parental, role of, 239 *ff.* (*see also* Love)

Age differences, in projections, 161–162

Aggression, in fantasies, 155 *ff.;* verbal, 194 (*see also* Anger)

Aggressive sexual behavior, 95

Aggressiveness, attitudes toward, 291

Aging, effects on intelligence test performance, 132–133

Alcohol, use of, 269

Aloneness, toleration of as aspect of maturity, 405

Altruism, as related to moral maturity, 390

Androgens, 71, 72

Anger, 189–202; as related to compassion, 407 *ff.;* homesickness, 236; at parents, 243 *ff.;* deprecation of, 40–

Anger (*Continued*)
41; in fantasies, 195; mention of in self-assessment, 201; suppression of, 180; role of in anxiety, 207 *ff.*

Annoyances, in relations with parents, 243 *ff.*

Anxiety, 207–226; as a personality problem, 398; denial of, 41; in parents, 245–246, 248

Appearance, personal, 65; interplay of physical and psychological factors in, 68 *ff.* (*see also* Body image, *and* Adipose tissues)

Aprocrine sweat glands, 83

Art, popularity of, 329

Aspirations, as related to "ideal self," 23 *ff.;* of "upward" and "downward mobile" boys, 298–299; reviewing of, as an aspect of maturity, 404

Athletic ability and popularity, 102 *ff.*

Attitudes, moral, 388 *ff.;* religious, 376; age changes in, 378 *ff.;* toward human weaknesses, 340; toward self as related to prejudice, 305–306; toward self as related to sex conduct, 95–96 (*see also* Self-acceptance, Self-rejection, Morals, *and* Prejudice)

Automobile, adolescents' interests in, 269 *ff.;* incidence of accidents with, 270

Autonomy, moral, 387

Authority, overt and covert attitudes toward, among delinquents, 313

Autobiographies, 29–30

Beliefs, fidelity to, 342; religious, age changes in, 378 *ff.*

Bible, age changes in interests in, 379

Body build as related to sexual maturation, 51

Body image, 62 *ff.*

Boredom, 188

Breasts, development of, 78; enlargement of in boys, 53

California growth study, 101

Candor, role of in self-description, 30–31

Career Pattern Study, 355, 371

Careers (*see* Vocational Development)

Cartoons, interpretation of, 115

Case histories, factors leading to distortion in, 310–311

Character, emphasis on in self-description, 33

Childhood assets and liabilities, bearing of on adolescence, 21

Childhood difficulties, as related to delinquency, 310

Childhood experiences, influence of on religious attitudes, 376

Child-rearing, as related to socioeconomic status, 291 *ff.*

Choice: as related to anxiety, 212–213; necessity of, 10–11; vocational, 351 *ff.*

Cliques, 290

Cognition, 140 (*see also* Thinking *and* Mental Growth)

Cognitive aspects of insight, 146; of moral development, 387 *ff.*

College, outcomes of, 336 *ff.*

College youth, 335 *ff.;* and religion, 375 *ff.*

Compassion, 405 *ff.*

Compensatory mechanisms, 87

Competition, 263 *ff.*

Competitiveness, as defense against anxiety, 219; as source of anxiety, 217 *ff.;* as related to low self-esteem, 264 *ff.*

Complaints, regarding school, 326–327

Compositions, as means of self-revelation, 29

Concept mastery, tests of, 131

Conceptual thinking, 113 *ff.*

Confidants, parents as, 248 *ff.*

Confidence, in self, as related to mental ability, 113

Conflict, emotional, 179; in connection with dating, 275; in worries, 204 (*see also* Anxiety)

Conflicting and confusing cultural forces, 19–20

Conflicting pressures, on parents, 247

Conformity, 40–41, 266 *ff.;* and convergent thinking, 142; intellectual, in college students, 338; morality based on, 389–390

Consistency, in personality traits, 395 *ff.;* in relative height, 49; in sociometric ratings, 260; striving for, in view of self, 32

Consistency and change in rate of mental growth, 127 *ff.*

Constancy of I.Q., 127 *ff.;* of vocational, 366–367

"Contact comfort" as source of affection, 182

Convergent thinking, 140 *ff.*

Counseling, vocational, 369–371

Courtship ideals, 276 (*see also* Dating *and* Love between the sexes)

Creative youth, characteristics of, 141–142

Creativity, 141 *ff.*

Crime (*see* Delinquency)

Crises, personal, incidence of among college graduates, 339

Crying, 193–194

Cultural aspects of emotional maturity, 402

Cultural factors, in suppression of emotions, 179 *ff.*

Cultural forces, in delinquency, 312 *ff.*

Curiosity, 119–120

Dating, 272 *ff.;* sex behavior connected with, 92

Daydreams, 150 *ff.;* themes in, 156

"Death wish," 195

Defense mechanism, 210

Defenses against anxiety, 210, 219 *ff.* (*see also* Strategies)

Deferred gratification, 364; as related to socioeconomic status, 293–294, 296

Delinquency, 308–321

Democratic practices, 20

Dependency on parents, outgrowing of, 231 *ff.*

Deprivation, effects of on mental growth, 124–125; emotional effects of, 183

Desire, realization of through fantasy, 152 *ff.*

Detachment, as defense against anxiety, 219 *ff.*

Developmental changes in religious attitudes and beliefs, 378 *ff.*

Diaries, 29–30

Digits, memory of, 133

Diploma, value of, 333

Discrepancy between personal and social adjustment, 262

Displaced anger, 196–197; and delinquency, 317 *ff.;* and prejudice, 304 *ff.*

Displacement, in dreams, 169

Divergent thinking, 140 *ff.*

Divorce, 284, 287

Dominant genes, 56–57

Double standard, 92

Doubt, religious, 381–382

"Downward mobile" adolescents, 297–298

Dreaming, 162–173; effects of deprivation of, 170; patterns of, 163 *ff.*

Dress and grooming, 68–69

Drinking, 269

Dropouts, from high school, 333 *ff.;* sociometric ratings of, 261; from college, 336, 341

Drunkenness, in later histories of delinquents, 319–320

Early environment, as related to later careers of delinquents, 321

Early marriage, as related to being in love, 278, 283–286

Economic unemployment, 14–15

Education: and adolescence, 325–372; and socioeconomic status, 295; effects on prejudice, 306; of gifted youth, 143 *ff.*

Educational implications of mental pattern, 126–127

Educational level, and intelligence, 123–125

Ego, 25–26

"Ego identity," as related to occupational choice, 355

Ego strength, and realism in vocational choice, 362

Ejaculation, 80

Electroencephalograph, as an indicator of dreaming, 164

Elmtown's Youth, 289–291

Emancipation from parents, 9, 229, 231 *ff.*

Emotion, nature and development of, 177–226; release of through daydreams, 154

Emotional adjustment: and moral judgment, 388; of intellectually gifted, 135–136; of underachievers, 137

Emotional aspects: of being in love, 278–279; of prejudice, 301 *ff.;* of religious doubt, 381–382; of sex behavior, 94–95

Emotional difficulties, ways of dealing with, 339
Emotional emancipation (*see* Emancipation from parents)
Emotional maladjustment: and delinquency, 314 *ff.* (*see also* Problems *and* Personality)
Emotional maturity, 7, 401 *ff.*; of college compared with non-college youth, 339
Emotional stability, and vocational success, 363
Endocrine glands, 71
Environment: as related to mental ability, 122 *ff.* (*see also* Socioeconomic status *and* Family background)
Environmental factors in delinquency, 311 *ff.*
Erections, 83
Estrogens, 71, 72
Ethnic groups, 301 *ff.*
Expediency, morality of, 389
Exploitation, of delinquents, 318 *ff.*
Externalization, 146; of hostility, 197–198
Eye-movements, as an indication of dreaming, 163 *ff.*

Failure: as related to anger, 193; parental feelings of, 246; persisting fears of, 205; students' and teachers' ascribed reasons for, 135, 330
Faith, 9 (*see also* Religion)
Falling in love, 276 *ff.*
Family attitudes, as related to dropping out of school, 335
Family background: and vocational development, 363; as related to underachievement, 138; effects of on religious attitudes, 376 *ff.* (*see also* Socioeconomic status)
Family relationships (*see* Adolescent-parent relationships)
Fantasies, 150–162
Fantasy vs. realism, in occupational choice, 353
Fat deposits, 52 *ff.*; psychological effects of, 53–55
Fate, as focal concern in delinquent sub-culture, 313

Fear, 202–205; as response to delinquents, 317; concealment of, 179
Feeling, 178 *ff.*; expression of among friends, 255; importance of communication of, 249; interplay with thinking, 144 *ff.*, role of in compassion, 405 *ff.*
Fels Research Institute, 73
Feminine role, as related to vocational development, 358–359
Femininity, acceptance of, 35–36
Fertility, as related to time of menarche, 73 *ff.*
"Focal concerns" in delinquent sub-culture, 312 *ff.*
Free association, as an exploratory form of thinking, 172; as means of self-revelation and self-discovery, 28–29
Freedom, and anxiety, 213–214
Freedom, nature, limits, and effects of, 4, 10–11
Freedom of choice, 299
Freudian theory, 25–27, 234 (*see also* Freud, S., in author index)
Friendships, 254 *ff.*

Gallup poll, 268–269, 326, 375
Gang codes, 94
Gang delinquency, 313 *ff.*
Genes, 55 *ff.*
Genetic background, need for knowledge of in studying delinquency, 311, 312
Genetic factors, 55 *ff.*; indirect influence of on socioeconomic status, 292; significance of, 60–62; in early and late maturing, 86
Genetic and environmental factors, interaction between, 58–60, 394–395
Genital organs, male, growth of, 81 *ff.*
Genotypes, 56 *ff.*
Gifted youth: age trends in mental growth of, 131; characteristics of, 134 *ff.*; training of, 143 *ff.*
Gifts, as source of joy, 187
Girdle fat, 53
Goals of adolescent development, 5–9
God, professed belief in, 373 *ff.*
Going steady, 274 *ff.*
Grievances, 199
Growth, course of physical, 45–108; impulse toward, 149

Guidance, in vocational decisions, 369–370

Guilt: and prejudice, 303–304; as related to fantasies, 160; parental feelings of, 246–247; psychological and religious aspects of, 386; repressed, as a source of anxiety, 218–219

Hair, growth, distribution and texture of, 47, 71, 72, 83

"Happiest day," experiences connected with, 187; as related to school, 328

Healthy aspects of being in love, 281 *ff.*

Height, changes in, 46 *ff.*; and heredity, 59–61

Heredity: 55 *ff.*; and later careers of delinquents, 321; and environment in background of delinquents, 312; and mental illness, 60; as related to mental ability, 122 *ff.*

Heteronomous moral judgments, 387

Heterosexual behavior, 272 *ff.*

High school, adolescent attitudes toward, 325 *ff.*

High school marriages, 284 *ff.*

High-school policies regarding early marriages, 286–287

History, as a source of self-knowledge, 345

Homesickness, 235–236

Homosexual activity, 89

Honesty, 388–389

Hope, 11; role of in fantasies, 151; reviewing of, as aspect of maturity, 404

Hormones, 73

Hostility, as related to: competitiveness, 265–266; prejudice, 301 *ff.*; religion, 377–378; underachievement, 138

Hostility, irrational, 397–398; displaced, 304; of delinquents toward those who wish to help them, 321; toward delinquents, 317 (*see also* Anger *and* Anxiety)

Humility, 385–386

Humor, and creativity, 141

Hypotheses, ability to think in terms of, 118

Id, 25–26

"Ideal self," 23, 30 *ff.*

"Idealized self," 221

Identity (*see* Self)

Illegitimacy, 294

Imagination, functions of, 151 *ff.*

Inadequacy, feelings of, 87

Individual differences in response to social class pressures, 295–296

Infatuation, 276–277

Inferiority feelings, as related to mental ability, 112

Inner restraints, 4

Insight, into adolescence, 5

Insight into self, 145 *ff.*, 401; in college seniors compared with freshmen, 338; role of in self-assessment, 32

Institute of Child Welfare, University of California, 65, 85

Intellectual ability, and self-evaluation, 111–112

Intellectual discipline, in college, 337 *ff.*

Intellectual maturity, 399–400

Intelligence, as related to: academic achievement, 139; leaving school, 334; factors and components of, 139, 140 *ff.*; growth of, 120 *ff.*; of delinquents, 310; and popularity, 102 *ff.*; role of in vocational development, 359 *ff.*; and self-insight, 144; and vocational choice, 366

Intercourse, incidence of, 91–92

Interests, 95, 268; vocational, 360 (*see also* School)

Interpersonal relationships and anxiety, 214 *ff.*

Interviews, as source of knowledge regarding self, 28

Intimacy: need for, 215; nature of, 215

I.Q. (*see* Mental Growth *and* Intelligence)

Irrational fears, 206 (*see also* Anxiety)

Irrational ideas regarding self, 24–25

Isolation, by peers, 256 *ff.*

Joy, 186–188

Jump and reach, age changes in, 98–99

Kindness: as a trait desired in teachers, 331–332; ranking of as moral virtue, 388; role of in religious instruction, 377

Knowledge of self, premises underlying promotion of, 347 *ff.*

Language: of the dream, 171 *ff.;* "tribal," 268–269
Lawlessness, prevalence of, 308
Laziness, as perceived cause of failure, 330
Leisure time, 186–187
Liberal education, aims of, 336
Likes and dislikes, regarding school, 329
Literature, as a source of self-knowledge, 345
Logical communication, changes in, 117–118
Loneliness, 216, 253–254
Love, 181 *ff.;* between the sexes, 276 *ff.;* effects of, 184; origins of in monkeys, 182–183; shift from parents as primary objects of, 234
Lust, 215

Manifest anxiety, 222
Manifest content of dreams, 165
Marriage, early, 283 *ff.;* as related to going steady, 275
Masculinity, acceptance of, 35–36; effect of peers in formulating standards of, 86–87; use of automobile as symbol of, 270
Masturbation, incidence of, 89, 90; as related to anxiety, 216; emotional effects of, 91
Maturation, as a factor in decline with age in delinquency, 320 (*see also* Growth)
Maturing, early and late, psychological effects of, 85 *ff.*
Maturity, meaning and aspects of, 97, 402 *ff.;* in love relationships, 283; moral, 387, 389–390
Meaning, of religion, inquiry into, 382; role of in scholarship, 346; search for, 9–10; significance of in education, 342 *ff.*
Memory, gaps in, 148–149; distortions of, 310; as factor in intelligence, 140; of dreams, 164
Memory span, 132–133
Menarche, 70 *ff.;* earlier onset of, 74 (*see also* Menstruation)
Menstruation, onset of, 73 *ff.;* as related to changes in height, 47; psychological impact of, 76–77

Mental ability, as related to physical, 101–102; as related to socioeconomic status, 292
Mental health, 225–226; as related to: competitiveness, 264 *ff.;* falling in love, 281 *ff.;* moral issues, 390; sense of intellectual achievement, 119–120; role of heredity in, 60
Mental illness, 226; role of heredity in, 60
Mental maturity, 6
Monkeys, origins of affection in, 182–183
Moral aspects of adolescent sex behavior, 94 *ff.*
Moral attitudes, as related to socioeconomic status, 292 *ff.*
Moral convictions, of college compared with non-college youth, 339
Moral development, 387–390
Moral judgment, as related to mental ability, 135
Moral maturity, 387–390, 400
Moral qualities, emphasis on in self-description, 33
Moral realism, 387–388
Moral relativism, 387–388
Moral "types," 389 *ff.*
Mothering, effects of, 183; as related to sexual responsiveness in mature monkeys, 183
Motor abilities, development of, 97–108
Motor performance, as related to: skeletal age, 102; height, 102; popularity, 102; "good looks," 102; intelligence, 102

"Neurotic anxiety," 208
Nicknames, 64
Nocturnal emissions, 80, 89, 93
Nutrition, 60

Obesity, psychological implications of, 54
Occupational advantage, as hoped-for outcome of college, 340
Occupations (*see* Vocational development)
Oedipus complex, 26, 234
Ossification, 51–52
"Outsider's" view, value of, 250

Parental acceptance, 239–240

Parent-adolescent relationships, 229–251; as related to early marriage, 285

Parental difficulties in "letting go," 236 *ff.*

Parental domination, methods of maintaining, 237–238

Parental satisfactions, 250–251

Parents, as objects of spite, 317; role of in arousal of anger, 190–191

Parents' attitudes toward dating, 273

Peers, relationships with, 251–307

Penis, growth of, 71, 72; variations in size of, 81–83; effects of fat deposits on apparent size of, 53

Perception, as component of emotion, 178

Perception of feeling, as related to compassion, 407

Perception, of parents, 233–234; changes in, 238–239; role of in ascribed parental rejection, 242; in anger, 198–199; modifications of, 233 *ff.*

Perceptions, differences between parents' and adolescents', 249

Personal concerns, as contrasted with academic demands at school, 340–341

Personal problems, as related to goals in education, 343; as related to delinquency, 314

Personality, 393 *ff.*; as related to vocational development, 361–362; as revealed through fantasies, 161–162; as related to: early marriage, 284 *ff.*; falling in love, 281 *ff.*; emphasis on in self-descriptions, 33

Personality adjustment, as related to physical ability, 106 *ff.*

Personality development, as affected by early and late physical maturing, 86 *ff.*; as related to socioeconomic status, 293 *ff.*

Personality factors in choice of athletic activities, 107

Personality maladjustments, 224 *ff.*

Personality problems, 397 *ff.*

Personality traits: associated with prejudice, 305; with delinquency, 309 *ff.*; of popular and unpopular adolescents, 258–260; social reinforcement of, 311

Persistence and change in delinquent tendencies, 319–320

Perspiration, 72

Petting, 91, 274

Phenomenal self (*see* Self)

Phenotypes, 56 *ff.*

Philosophy of life, influence of college on, 337 *ff.*; role of religion in, 374

Physical ability, as related to mental ability, 101

Physical activity, decline in interest in, 101

Physical characteristics, and self-evaluation, 66–67

Physical development, 45–108; psychological repercussions of, 53–55, 58, 66–67

Physical education, ramifications of, 107–108; as a source of self-knowledge, 346

Physical fitness, 104

Physical growth, as source of anxiety, 212

Physical maturity, 6, 400

"Physical self" (*see* Body image)

Play, 108

Playfulness, and creativity, 141

Pleasure, 186–188

Pleasures of the mind, 119–120

Popularity, adult judgments of, 262–263; as related to dating, 275; as related to ability, 101 *ff.* (*see also* Sociometric tests)

Postponement of gratification, 364

"Practical ability," 98–100

Preadolescence, influence of genetic factors during, 58

Preadolescent sex practices, 89 *ff.*

Pregnancy, among early marrying girls, 285; sex differences in interest in, 95; premarital, 285

Prejudice, 300 *ff.*

Prestige, as incentive for finishing college, 337; as related to athletic ability, 103 *ff.*; as source of security, 217

Pride, in relation to anger, 192

Problem solving, as related to delinquency, 314; through fantasy, 153 *ff.*; in dreams, 169–170

Problems, emotional, incidence of, 224 *ff.*

Projective methods, 155 *ff.;* findings from, 17, 156 *ff.*, 225, 327

Proportions, bodily, changes in, 51 *ff.*

Psychological effects of physical change, 76 *ff.;* of early and late maturing, 85 *ff.*

Psychological implications of physical ability, 104 *ff.*

"Psychological mother," 403

Psychological reactions, to genital development, 81 *ff.*

Psychosomatic illness, 201

Puberty, 70 *ff.;* onset of in boys, 78 *ff.*

Pubescent, 70

Pubic hair, 80; character of as indication of pubescence, 78–79

Public opinion, as related to delinquency, 317 *ff.*

Q-sort, 30

Rationalization, of defenses against anxiety, 220 *ff.* (*see also* Unconscious *and* Self-idealization)

Reading ability, as related to remaining or dropping out of school, 334–335

Reading disability, possibility of remedying, 334

Realism, as an aspect of: self-acceptance, 33–34; maturity, 404

Realism of vocational choice, 365

Reason, and religion, 383–384

Recessive genes, 56–57

Rejection: by parents, 240 *ff.;* by peers, 256 *ff.;* of delinquents by pupils and teachers, 316

Rejection, parents' feelings of, 246

Rejection of self, symptoms of, 35–36

Relatives, in dreams, 166

Religion, and adolescents, 373–386

Religious beliefs, prevalence of, 374 *ff.*

Religious commitments, sincerity of, 383

Repression, 178–179 (*see also* Unconscious)

Ridicule, fear of, 203, 205

Rigidity, as symptom of anxiety, 223

Running speed, changes in, 100

Scapegoats, delinquents as, 318

Schizophrenia, 60

School: as portrayed in adolescent fantasies, 161, 327; as source of fear, 204; of joy, 187; class differences in attitudes toward, 291; delinquents' attitudes toward, 316; grievances and anger connected with, 191; role of in adolescence, 325–350; role of in guiding vocational choice, 369, 372

School achievement, and popularity, 102 *ff.*

School subjects, attitudes toward, 326 *ff.*

Schooling, effects of on intelligence, 125–126

"Secondary gain," 211

Security, concern for among "upward mobile" adolescents, 298; desire for as incentive for going steady, 275; strivings for as related to anxiety, 217; desire for as related to "downward mobility," 298

Self: as "center" of personality, 393; anger directed against, 199 *ff.;* attitudes toward as related to sex conduct, 95–96; components of, 22 *ff.;* concept of as related to vocational choice, 354 *ff.;* definitions of, 7–8; "finding of," 8; insight into, 144 *ff.;* known dimensions and unperceived influences on, 23–40

Self-acceptance: 33 *ff.;* and acceptance of others, 305–306; and self-rejection, balance between, 37 *ff.;* as related to competitiveness, 264 *ff.;* as related to remaining in high school, 335; influence of early and late maturing on, 85–88

Self-assertion, via use of automobiles, 270

Self-assessment, major themes in, 30 *ff.;* age trends in, 38–39; limitations of instruments used for measurement of, 31–32, 33; mention of anger in connection with, 201

Self-consistency, striving for, 395–396

Self-deception, 24 (*see also* Anxiety)

Self-determination, as related to anxiety, 212 *ff.;* struggle for, 231 *ff.*

Self-discovery, through dreams, 173; through physical education, 107–108; through reciprocated love, 281

Self-effacement, as defense against anxiety, 220 *ff.*

Self-evaluation, as related to: body

image, 62 *ff.;* mental ability, 111–113 (*see also* Insight into self)

Self-examination, role of in studying adolescents, 5; significance of in relation to prejudice, 307

Self-fulfillment, psychology of, as related to religion, 385–386

Self-idealization, 24 (*see also* Anxiety)

Self-improvement, adolescents' interests in, 329; as source of joy, 187

Self-regard: bolstering of through falling in love, 281; threats to as a source of anger, 192–193

Self-rejection, 34–35, 87, 199–200; as related to obesity, 54–55

Self-scrutiny, in college seniors, 338

Self-understanding, as an announced goal by college students and instructors, 341, 344; as related to promoting self-knowledge in others, 348 *ff.;* role of school in advancement of, 344 *ff.;* dreams as a source of, 167 *ff.*

Sex: activity, deferral of, 296; anxiety regarding, example of, 210–211; as related to: anxiety, 215; attitudes toward self, 95–96; class differences in attitudes toward, 291; in adolescent fantasies, 156, 158–160; mention of in self-evaluation, 40–41 (*see also* Heterosexual)

Sex differences in: automobile accidents, 270; dating behavior, 274, 275; early marriage, 285; fantasies, 161; freedom granted by parents, 244; motor ability, 98 *ff.;* religious attitudes, 375; sex activity, 92–93; school achievement, 138; traits regarded as socially desirable, 259 *ff.;* vocational development, 358–359

Sex dreams, in boys compared with girls, 93

Sexual: aggressiveness, 95; attitudes, 89 *ff.;* behavior in connection with dating, 274; behavior as related to socioeconomic status, 293–296; desire as related to being in love, 279, 280; interests, 89 *ff.;* maturation, 70–96; practices, 89 *ff.;* responsiveness in motherless monkeys, 182–183

Sexual development, 70–96; behavioral aspects of, 88 *ff.*

Sexual intercourse, incidence of, 89

"Sexual unemployment," 15

Sickness, as reported cause of school failure, 330–331

Skeletal age, 52

Skeletal growth, 51–52

Sleep and dream patterns, 163 *ff.*

"Slum sex code," 94

Slums, 296–297

Social acceptance and rejection, 256 *ff.*

Social attitudes and relationships, emphasis on in self-description, 33

Social class, and delinquent "sub-culture," 312 *ff.;* ramifications of, 287 *ff.* (*see also* Socioeconomic status)

Social cleavages, age changes in, 302–303

"Social distance," 303

Social issues, connected with sex practices, 93–94

Social reinforcement of personality traits, 395

Social relations, anger in connection with, 191

Social studies, students' liking for, 329

Social world, of adolescents, 229–322

Socioeconomic status: ramifications of, 287 *ff.;* and school achievement, 137; as related to athletic ability and strength, 102, 105; influence of on vocational development, 363–364, 366; of intellectually gifted, 135; as related to: early marriage, 285; self-description, 33; and sex behavior, 293

Sociogram, 257

Sociological and psychological dimensions, similarities and differences between, 299–300

Sociometric tests, results of, 256 *ff.*

Special abilities, role of in vocational development, 359 *ff.*

Speed, as variable in mental tests, 131–132

Speeding, 270

Spermatozoa, 71

Stability of vocational choices, 366–367

Stereotype, feminine, 36

Stereotypes, in self-assessment, 40–41

"Stored-up" anger, 195

Storm and stress, 15–16

Strategies, in dealing with anxiety, 149, 219 *ff.*

Strength, as related to: popularity, 102; skeletal age, 102; height, 102; social status, 102; intelligence, 102; school achievement, 102
Strength, changes in, 97 *ff.*
Stresses, of adolescence, 16–17
Striving, 4
Studiousness, and popularity, 103–104
Subjective elements in "objective" observations, 349
Super-ego, 25–26
Superior youth, 134 *ff.*
Suppression of emotion, 178–179, 205–206
Sweat glands, 83
Symbolism, of dreams, 171 *ff.*
Sympathy, as aspect of compassion, 406

TAT, 222
Teachers' qualities liked and disliked by students, 331–332; dislike for as perceived cause of school failure, 330; views concerning, 327 *ff.*
Tenderness, 279; suppression of, 280
Testes, growth of, 71, 72
Thinking, development of, 111 *ff.*; convergent, 140 *ff.*; divergent, 140 *ff.*; fantasy as a form of, 153 *ff.*; influence of peers on, 253; interplay of feeling with, 144 *ff.*; through free association, 172–173
Throwing, age changes in, 98–99
Time, conception of, 115–116
Tolerance, effect of college on, 338
Trends in adolescent development compared with earlier generations, 12–14
Tumescence, 77

Unconscious aspects of personality, 26–27
Unconscious elements in anxiety, 208–210; in perception of parents, 231
Unconscious motivations, in vocational choice, 362
Underachievers, 135 *ff.*
Unemployment, ratio of among youth, 368
Unhealthy aspects of being in love, 281 *ff.*
Unknown dimensions underlying ideas and attitudes pertaining to self, 25 *ff.*
"Upward mobile" adolescents, 297–298

Values, moral, 388 *ff.;* as related to socio-economic status, 364; of college students, 337 *ff.*
Vandalism, 321
Variability, in physical growth, 46 *ff.*
Verbal ability, role of in performance on mental tests, 125
Vocabulary, foreign, learning of, 132; "tribal," 268–269
Vocational choice, delays in, 335
Vocational development, 351–371
Vocational interests, 360 *ff.*
Voice, changes, 72, 80, 83–84

Ways of knowing adolescent self, 28 *ff.*
"Wet dreams" (*see* Nocturnal emissions)
Wish-fulfillment, through fantasy, 152
Wishes, 113–114
Worries, 203–204

"Youthese," 268–269